Second E

Music Appreciation

Histories & Cultures

Kendall Hunt publishing company

JEREMY L. SMITH • JAY KEISTER

Kendall Hunt
publishing company

www.kendallhunt.com
Send all inquiries to:
4050 Westmark Drive
Dubuque, IA 52004-1840

ISBN 978-1-4652-5332-3

Printed in the United States of America

Contents

Section I

Fundamentals of Music

One way to define music is by identifying its components, or elements. The basic components usually listed are rhythm, melody, harmony, tone color, texture, and form. We could argue as to the validity of this list, and we will see that music does not always include each of these elements, but all music includes at least some of these elements. Let's discuss each of these elements so that we can better describe the music that we will experience in this course.

Rhythm of the seasons.

I. Rhythm

Rhythm is perhaps the most basic element of music. Indeed, there are numerous examples of rhythm all around us: in nature, the cosmos, art and design, and our own bodies. In all of these cases, *rhythm* refers to events that reoccur regularly over time; in our case, ***rhythm*** is the passage of time in music. *Rhythm* may also be used in a more specific way, referring to specific patterns of longer and shorter durations. *Short* and *long* are terms describing the duration or the relative length of time that a sound "endures."

Listen to the following music with prominent rhythm patterns. Determine which of the patterns shown below best describes the main rhythm pattern heard in the musical examples.

Rhythm in nature.

Listening: Rhythm Patterns

Rhapsody: We Will Rock You (opening)
Beethoven: Symphony No. 5 in C minor (1st movement—opening)
William Tell Overture—Finale (0:13)
Bourree in E minor—J. S. Bach (opening)
Carol of the Bells

Identify the dominant rhythm pattern of each piece:

1. short short short long . . . ________
2. short short long . . ________
3. long short short long ________ . . ________

Rhythm in architecture.

When we dance or tap our feet to music, we become aware of the music's beat. ***Beat*** refers to a pulse underlying music. Listen to the following excerpts and tap your foot to the beat.

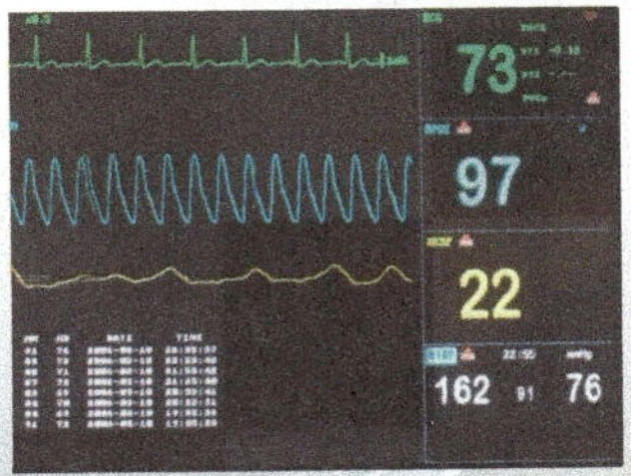

Rhythm in the body.

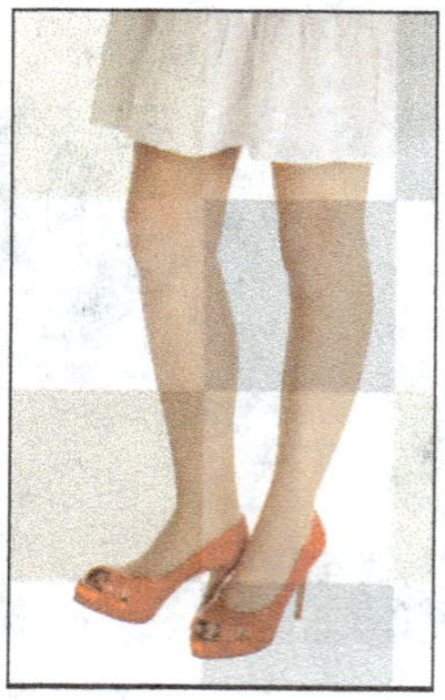

Tap your toe.

Listening: Prominent Beat Examples

Rhapsody: Stars and Stripes Forever - Boston Pops
We Got the Beat - The Go-Go's

In both of these examples, the beat is very prominent and easy to discern. You probably had no difficulty tapping your foot to it, but not all music has such a prominent beat. Listen to the following pieces and try to tap your foot to the beat. In both of these pieces, the beat is not prominent or easily discernable. In both cases, the beat is not the dominant element.

Listening: Less Prominent Beat Examples

Rhapsody: Bienningana: Eternal Sunrise - The Australian Aborigine
KYRIE - Gregorian Chants

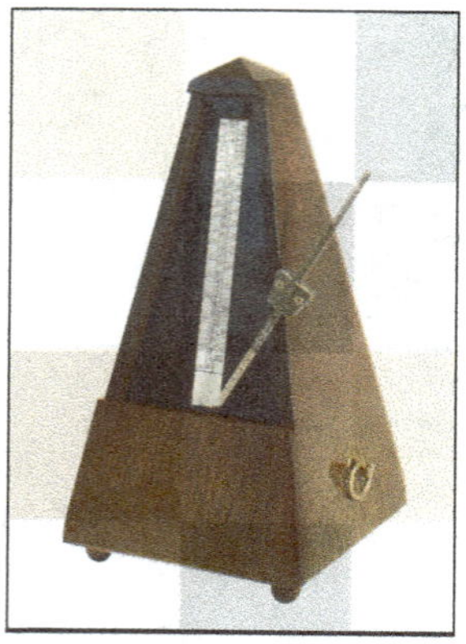

A metronome keeps a steady tempo.

Sometimes beats occur at a rapid rate, while at other times, beats occur at a slower rate. The speed at which the beats occur is called ***tempo***. There are also terms that indicate more gradual changes in tempo such as ***accelerando*** (a gradual speeding up of tempo) and ***ritardando*** (a gradual slowing down of the tempo).

If you've ever danced to traditional music, you know that there are specific beats within dance patterns that are emphasized with a strong step. The musicians play these beats louder or articulate them more firmly, creating an ***accent***. Furthermore, the accented beats set up a pattern of stronger and weaker beats for the dancer to follow. These patterns are called ***meter*** or ***time signature***. Most meters are essentially in two- or three-beat patterns; even music with four- and five-beat patterns can be understood as combinations of two and three beats.

Two-beat pattern:	**X** X **X** X **X** X **X** X
Three-beat pattern:	**X** X X **X** X X **X** X X
Four-beat pattern:	**X** X X X **X** X X X

Determining the meter of music is usually straightforward and simple.

- **Find the beat**, tapping your foot naturally.
- **Listen for clues** as to the accent/beat pattern. In most cases, the first beat or ***downbeat*** of the pattern is accented. There are exceptions, primarily in popular music. For instance, rock music drummers emphasize the 2nd and 4th beats, creating a basic element of the rock style known as the ***backbeat***. In disco music, every beat is emphasized equally by the drummer or drum machine's playing pattern, so you must find other ways to determine meter.
- **Listen for the bass line** as the next most obvious metric clue, whether played by the bass guitar, string bass, tuba or other instrument, the bass line often moves on the downbeat.
- **Listen to the chords** or harmony, as they generally change with the downbeat.
- **Listen for melodic clues** as well: accented syllables, melodic emphases, repetitive riffs.
- **Move to the music.** If marching to the beat works, then you've found a 2 or 4 beat pattern. If not, see if a 3 beat pattern works, either by moving or conducting.

TEMPO

Common Tempo Markings

- ***grave:*** 40–60 beats per minute
- ***lento:*** 40–60 bpm
- ***adagio:*** 66–76 bpm
- ***andante:*** 76–100 bpm
- ***moderato:*** 100–120 bpm
- ***allegro:*** 120–140 bpm
- ***vivace:*** 140–160 bpm
- ***presto:*** 160–200 bpm

Listening: Identifying Meter

Identify the meters in the music below.

Rhapsody: Stars and Stripes Forever - Boston Pops
My Country 'tis of Thee—The Mormon Tabernacle Choir
Open Arms - Journey
We Will Rock You - Queen
Take Five - Dave Brubeck

Just as an electric meter measures the flow of electricity, musical meters measure the flow of the passing beats, dividing them into manageable sets of beats called ***measures***. One measure is one unit of meter. In a four-beat meter, one measure contains four beats. In a three-beat meter, one measure contains three beats. We can say that a particular song is 16 measures (also known as ***bars***) long, or that a particular solo was only eight measures long.

Melody.

II. Melody

Melody is usually the most easily recognizable, most prominent part of a piece of music. It is the part that you might whistle or hum along with as you listen to your mp3 player on the way to classes today. It is the main theme of the music. Melodies consist of pitches in rhythm; ***pitch*** is the perceived highness or lowness of a musical sound. To explain "high" and "low" sounds to young children, teachers often use examples such as a bird's song for "high" or the growl of a big dog for "low."

"Melody is the essence of music."

—Wolfgang Amadeus Mozart (1756–1791), Austrian composer

Pitch is the way in which we perceive differences in the speed of sound wave vibrations. What we call "high" pitches are those whose sound waves are cycling at a faster rate. What we call "low" pitches are those whose sound waves are cycling at a slower rate. The usual term for "cycles per second" is ***hertz*** (Hz), so called after a 19th-century German scientist. Looking at a piano keyboard from the player's position, the lower pitches are to the left, and the higher pitches are to the right. The same arrangement is found in all of the keyboard instruments: organ, xylophone, orchestral bells, etc.

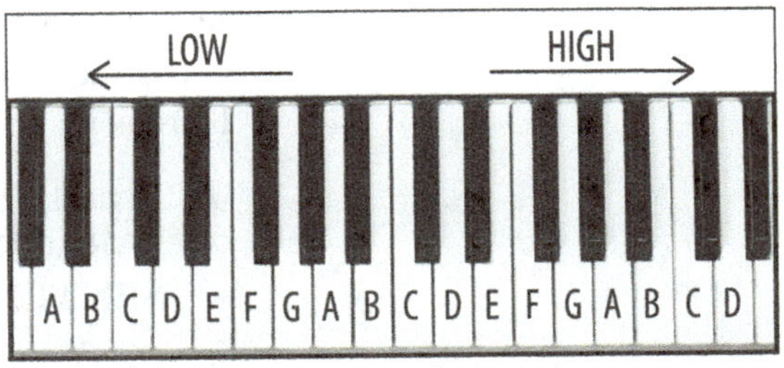

Low and high pitch on a piano keyboard.

Musicians don't usually use scientific terms such as *hertz* to refer to specific pitches; they use the ***musical alphabet*** of A B C D E F G. These seven letters are repeated several times on the piano keyboard. Sitting at a piano, play the lowermost white key and call it A. The next white key is B, and the next is C, and so on through the alphabet to G. After that, simply start with A again, repeating until you get to the uppermost white key, which is C. The black keys have names like F sharp (F#) and B flat (B♭), and sound halfway between the white keys on either side of each. The interval between each repetition of an alphabet letter is called an ***octave***, because there are eight notes. There are over seven octaves on a full-sized piano keyboard.

Musicians often describe a melody in terms of its movement or flow. For example, if a melody is smooth and moves mostly by stepping from one pitch to the next adjacent pitch, it is considered ***conjunct***. If the melody moves in a more erratic manner, skipping and leaping from one pitch to the next, it is considered ***disjunct***.

The listening examples that follow feature a melody that is disjunct and a melody that is conjunct. The piece with the conjunct melody will be easier for you to sing because it is smooth, while the piece with the disjunct melody will be more difficult for you to sing because of its erratic nature. Vocal melodies tend to be more conjunct than instrumental melodies, and particular instruments are more agile and can play disjunct melodies more easily than others. Listen to the following melodic examples and decide which is conjunct or disjunct.

Listening: Conjunct and Disjunct

Rhapsody: Ode to Joy - Wedding Music Experts
Somewhere Over the Rainbow - Tina Malia

Conjunct melody notated to show smooth, step-wise movement.

The graphics above are the musical notation of the melodies featured in the listening. Notice how the Ode to Joy melody is conjunct, moving smoothly up and down on the music staff.

A melody may also be called a **theme**, and it often consist of several parts, called phrases. A **phrase** can stand alone as a complete musical statement, like a sentence, but is only a portion of a complete theme or melody. If we wanted to, we could make a comparison of melody and phrase to a paragraph and a sentence. Here is an analogy illustrating this:

- In an ESSAY: In Music
- PARAGRAPH: Melody or Theme
- SENTENCE: Phrase

Each sentence in an essay has a certain "flow" to it, speeding up here, slowing down or pausing there, rising and falling in pitch and intensity according to the words and meaning. In music, we refer to this as the ***phrase shape***. Many musical phrases rise to a climactic point and then fall to a lower resolution, others rise or fall from the beginning to the end of the phrase, and some don't seem to come to rest at all, requiring additional phrases to come to a conclusion. The shape of each phrase is a function of the rise and fall of pitch and volume as well as the harmony that we assume in our minds. Look at the familiar melody below. Each line of music is a phrase. Note that the middle phrase is different than the others, and phrase shapes are shown by the shaped lines.

The melody of "Twinkle, Twinkle" to show phrase shape.

III. Harmony

Harmony among friends.

We often speak of interpersonal relationships in terms of harmony because of the similarities between people getting along and pitches "getting along." When two people get along well, we say they have a harmonious relationship; in much the same way, we can say that pitches "get along" or are harmonious.

In music, we speak of this relationship between simultaneous pitches as ***harmony***. When a pitch combination seems pleasing and stable, we say that the harmony is ***consonant***; when the pitch combination seems to clash and sound unstable, we say that the harmony is ***dissonant***. Of course, these are subjective terms: what one person accepts as consonant or harmonious may seem discordant or dissonant to another.

This perception is the result of experience and conditioning within a particular culture, or ***acculturation***. To novices, jazz may sound clashing or distasteful simply because of a lack of listening experience, but to a jazz musician who's heard many hours of jazz harmonies and has become comfortable with jazz, these dissonances are not only tolerable, but also "flavorful." This type of acculturation is similar to the way in which people acquired a taste for coffee, alcohol, spices *et al.*

Listening: Tonal vs. Atonal
Rhapsody: Threnody for the Victims of Hiroshima—Krzysztolf Penderecki
Beethoven: Symphony No.5 in C minor Op.67 - I Allegro con brio
Pierrot lunaire, Op. 21: Part I, Mondestrunken - Jan DeGaetani

Melody and harmony are both derived from a set of pitches in a pattern called a ***scale***. In a scale, the pitches progress in "alphabetical order," stepping from one to the next: A, B, C, D, etc. There are many different scales that have been used worldwide, but in traditional Western music, the two most commonly used over the past several centuries are the major and minor scales.

In an overly simplified way, we may describe music based upon major scales as "happy," and music based upon minor scales as "sad." The following Web site gives listening examples following its explanation of major and minor.

Video: Major vs. Minor
YouTube: Major and Minor
http://www.columbia.edu/itc/music/training/majmin/lesson6/index.html

Because these scales are so familiar to us, we have learned sound expectations, including a want for a specific ending pitch. When you heard the listening samples above, you were familiar enough with the major and minor scales being used that you expected the melodies to end on a specific pitch. This "home base" pitch around which the melody and harmony revolve is called the ***tonal center*** or ***key***. Listen to the piece shown below. **Does the piece sound consonant, stable? Can you tell when it is over? Does it sound final to you? Do you hear a tonal center in it?**

Listening: Tonal or Atonal?
Rhapsody: 5 Piano Pieces, Op. 23 - Anton Webern

Because there is no tonal center in *5 Piano Pieces* (above) by Anton Webern, you may have found the music aimless, wandering, and unsatisfying. Music without a tonal center, without a "home base" pitch, is called ***atonal*** music. The ending may not have sounded final, because the patterns you might expect did not end the piece. Listen to the final 40 seconds of the excerpt below, which is exceptionally tonal. Notice how Beethoven uses a well-known tonal pattern in the final moments of his *Symphony No. 5* below to set up our expectations for the final pitch. **Can you tell that Beethoven was finished with the piece? How does Beethoven let you know this?**

Listening: Tonal
Rhapsody: Beethoven : Symphony No.5 in C minor Op.67 - I Allegro con brio (final 40 seconds)

Most of the time, we perceive the harmony of a piece of music in terms of ***chords***, or combinations of pitches. The most obvious use of chords can be heard in songs that are accompanied by a single guitar player. Listen to the chords played in the examples below; notice the different effects produced by the different types of chords.

Listening: Chord Changes
Rhapsody: Are You Lonesome Tonight?—Elvis Presley
Greensleeves—Danny Darrow

The lowest pitches of a series of chords make up a separate musical line—not a melodic line, but a ***bass line***. In a pop/rock band, there is usually someone playing this line on the electric bass guitar. A series of chords used in a piece, called a ***chord progression*** or harmonic progression, often repeats many times within the work.

Listen to the 1960s popular songs below. Each uses a specific chord progression, called the ***blues*** progression, outlined clearly in its bass line. This progression should sound very familiar to you, as it has been used in quite a lot of jazz and rock music for decades.

Listening: The Blues Progression
Rhapsody: Lucille—The Everly Brothers
Wipe Out—The Surfaris
Batman—The TV Theme Players

The blues harmony has been used in popular songs from the 1870s throughout much of the 20th century. It was the basis of boogie-woogie, rock and roll, and most popular music through the 1980s and beyond. Listen to the pop music examples below. Each song is from a different decade of popular music, but each has the blues chord progression underneath the melodic line. Become familiar with the repetitive blues pattern of chords in these pieces.

The playlist features almost a century of blues-based music.

Listening: A Century of Blues
Rhapsody: Backwater Blues—Bessie Smith (1920s Blues)
In the Mood—Glen Miller (1940s Swing)
Good Golly Miss Molly—Little Richard (1950s Boogie Woogie)
Lucille—The Everly Brothers (1960s "Rockabilly")
The Blues Had a Baby—Muddy Waters (1970s R & B)
Pride and Joy—Stevie Ray Vaughan (1980s Rock)
Give Me One Reason—Tracy Chapman (1999 Country)
Crossroads—John Mayer (2008)

Because there is a limited set of chords within a particular key or scale, there are relatively few chord progressions that are commonly used. As a result, there are some chord progressions that have been used for much music across the centuries, as you will observe in the following humorous video.

Video: Pachelbel's Chords Today
YouTube: "Pachelbel Rant," Rob Paravonian
http://www.youtube.com/watch?v=JdxkVQy7QLM

IV. Timbre/Color

Timbre is to music what color is to art.

Surrounded by sounds at a party, we can often easily distinguish a friend's voice, even amid multiple voices and music. We can tell when that person is happy, sad, mad, or sick. We are also able to recognize the specific sound of a familiar recording in comparison to other recordings of the same piece. In each case, we are recognizing the *tone* or *timbre* of the sound.

When we attempt to describe a particular musical sound, we discuss the attributes of that sound as compared to other sounds. These distinguishing attributes make up what we call ***tone***, ***color***, or ***timbre***. Words commonly used to describe tone color include *bright, dark, warm, cold, harsh, gentle, fuzzy, clear, rich, thick, thin, focused, spread*, etc. Timbre for instruments is determined by a number of factors: the shape and size of the instrument, its construction, the materials used, how it is played, its range, its volume, etc. Every sound is produced by its own dis-

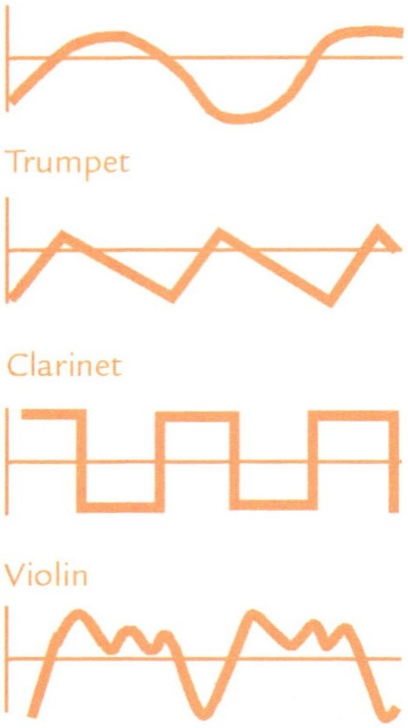

Graphic representation of various instrument tone wave forms.

tinct sound wave shape that is unique, much like the uniqueness of fingerprints or snowflakes.

SOUND

Sound can be fully described by defining the following parameters:

- **Volume:** perceived strength or loudness; wave amplitude
- **Pitch:** perceived high/low; frequency
- **Timbre:** perceived differentiating attributes
- **Duration:** perceived length; note value
- **Spatial location:** direction/position/proximity of sound source
- **Shape:** beginning/ending of sound; attack, decay, sound envelope

One of the ways we perceive timbre is related to our musical instrument families and the sounds that each makes. The orchestral instruments of Western classical music are generally divided into four families: strings, woodwinds, brass, and percussion. Each of these families has subcategories as well. To be able to identify the differing timbres takes practice as well as multiple exposures. It would be premature to expect yourself to be able to identify all of the different instruments at this point, without quite a bit of experience listening to each. In fact, even trained musicians sometimes have difficulty distinguishing between the subtle differences in timbre. The discussion that follows is designed to help you understand how the instruments are grouped and to introduce you to the different timbres of each. As you go through this course, review these sounds and attempt to identify the different instruments as they are found in each chapter's music.

Stringed Instruments

The stringed instrument family includes instruments with and without ***frets***, the markings that indicate pitches. The sound of a stringed instrument is produced by vibrating strings and is amplified by the hollow body of the instrument. Fretted stringed instruments include mostly folk instruments such as the ***guitar***, ***banjo***, and ***mandolin***. Traditional fretted instruments from other cultures include the Russian ***balalaika***, Indian ***sitar***, and Japanese ***koto***. For fretted instruments, the sound is made by plucking the strings.

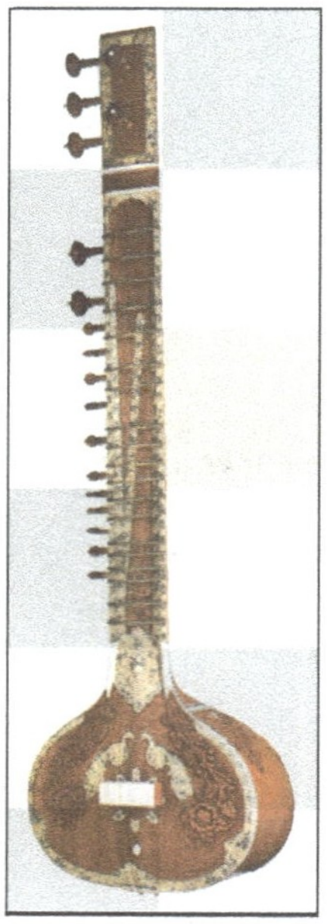

Indian sitar.

Classical guitar.

Russian balalaika.

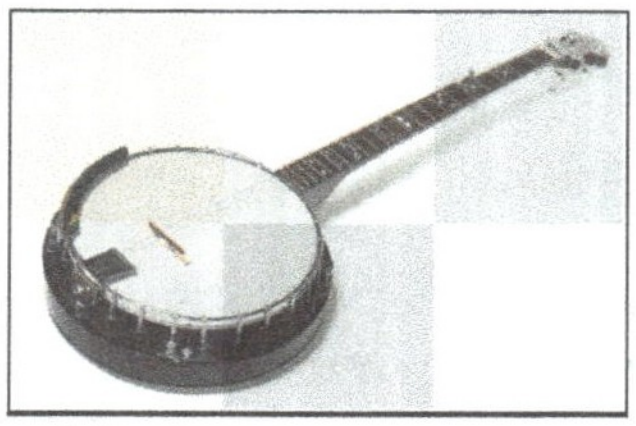

Folk banjo.

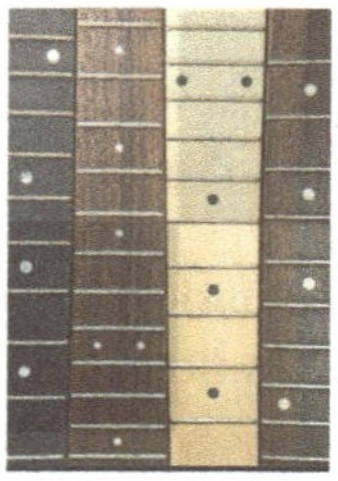

Fretted guitar necks.

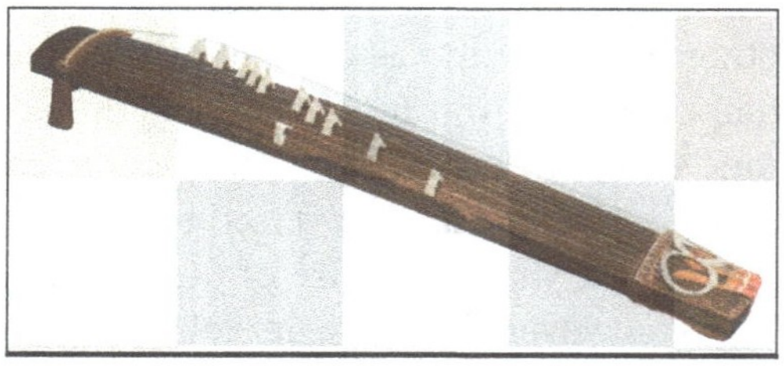

Japanese koto.

Listen to the musical examples for the fretted stringed instruments. What adjectives would you use to describe their tones? How can you tell apart their differing sounds?

Listening: Fretted String Instruments

Rhapsody: Guitar: Mediterranean Sundance—Al DiMeola
Balalaika: Tsiganka (Gypsy Girl) - Andreyev Balalaika Ensemble
Banjo: Dueling Banjos—Smokey River Boys
Lute: From the Dowland Lute Book: VI. Round Battle Galliard (39)
Sitar: Return from the Fair—Ravi Shankar
Koto: Geisha Girl - Chinese and Japanese Koto Harp

Western non-fretted stringed instruments are those of the violin family: violin, viola, cello, and bass. The traditional Chinese stringed instrument, the ***erhu***, is also without frets. On fretless instruments, the sound of the instrument is produced as a ***bow*** is drawn across the strings. The horsehair of the bow, coated with a sticky substance called ***rosin***, causes friction, which sets the strings into vibration. Because all of these are of similar construction, varying primarily in size, they sound very much alike, playing in their specific ranges. Together, they make a very ***homogeneous***, well-blended sound.

While the orchestral and traditional harps are stringed instruments without frets, their strings are plucked instead of bowed. Their sounds are more like the fretted instruments above; they are sometimes classified separately due to these differences. The Japanese koto shown above may also be considered a harp with frets.

Orchestral string instruments: violin, viola, cello, bass.

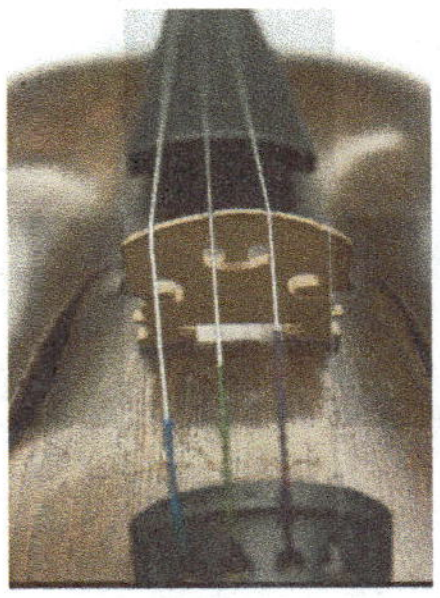

Detail of violin strings.

Students playing the Chinese erhu.

Harps.

Listen to the musical examples for the non-fretted stringed instruments. What words would you use to describe their tones? How can you tell their sounds apart?

Listening: Non-Fretted String Instruments

Rhapsody: Violin: Étude VI, "Die Letzte Rose"
Viola: 12 Studies for Solo Viola
Viola: Étude No. 12 in E Major, "Andante"
Cello: Yo-Yo Ma, "Prelude"
Double bass: Étude in C Sharp Minor, Op. 25, No. 1, Bl 98
Harp: Étude, Op. 25, No. 1
Erhu: "River Waters"

Recorders.
Courtesy of the author

Woodwind Instruments

At first glance, the woodwind instrument family may seem a little confusing. The family is so named since all of the original members of the family were made of wood. The saxophone was invented much later than the others (ca. 1835), but is included as a woodwind since it uses a single reed similar to the clarinet. The original woodwind instruments fall into three subcategories: flutes, single reeds, and double reeds. The ***flute*** family consists of two main types: end-blown flutes (***recorders***) and transverse flutes (found in school bands). In both cases, sound waves are created when air is blown across the lip of an opening in much the same way that you "play" a soda pop bottle. Both types of flutes come in a variety of sizes, the larger sizes having lower ranges, and the smaller ones having higher ranges. The difference in timbre between the two types is subtle, yet perceptible.

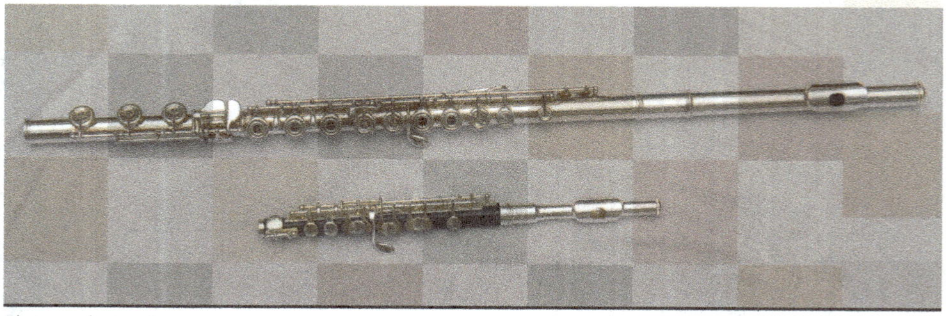

Flute and piccolo.
Courtesy of Jeff Montgomery

Listen to the flute recordings below. How would you describe the difference in tone color between the two types of flutes? What adjectives would you use to describe the tone to someone?

Listening: Flutes

Rhapsody: Recorder: Sonata in D Minor, HWV 367a: VII. "A Tempo di Menuet"
Piccolo: Piccolo Concerto in C Major, RV 444: III. "Allegro Molto"
Flute: Concerto for Five Flutes in A Minor, No. 2: III. "Allegro"

Soprano, alto, tenor, and baritone saxophones.
Courtesy of Jeff Montgomery

Detail of clarinet reed and mouthpiece.
Courtesy of Jeff Montgomery

B-flat soprano and bass clarinets.
Courtesy of Jeff Montgomery

The ***single-reed*** instruments are played by using a thin, specially shaped piece of cane or reed, which is set into vibration within the player's mouth by blowing air across it. This produces a particular timbre often aptly described as "reedy." The tone production is similar to blowing across a blade of grass to produce a whistling, buzzing sound. This subcategory includes ***clarinets*** and ***saxophones***, both of which come in a variety of sizes. The saxophone was invented in the mid-19th century, and although it is made of brass, it uses a reed like that of the clarinet, so it is considered a woodwind instrument.

Listen to the clarinet and saxophone sounds in the listening examples below. How would you describe the difference between the clarinet and saxophone tones? What terms would you use to describe their timbres?

Listening: Single-Reed Instruments
Rhapsody: Clarinet: "Invention for Clarinet and Bass Clarinet"
Saxophone: Histoire du Tango (arr. for saxophone quartet...)

The double-reed instruments use a reed consisting of two pieces of thin, specially shaped cane set into vibration within the player's mouth by air blowing between and across each. Their timbres are particularly "buzzy." Blowing into the flattened end of a drinking straw is a similar process. The instruments of this subcategory include the ***oboe***, the ***English horn***, and the ***bassoon***.

Listen to the sounds of these instruments in the listening examples below. How would you describe their tone colors? How can you tell them apart?

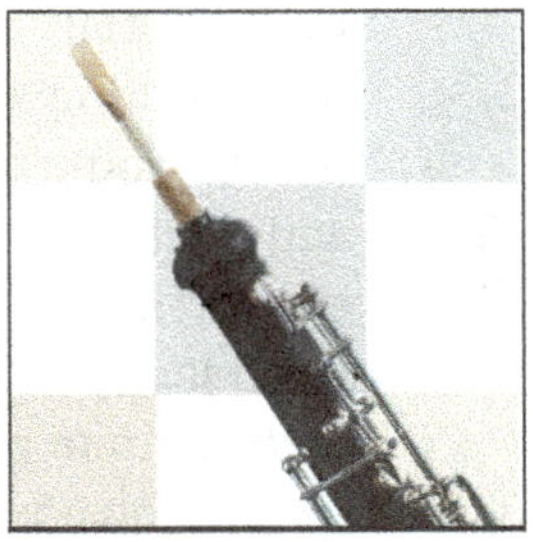

Oboe reed detail.
© 2012 by mkm3. Used under license of Shutterstock, Inc.

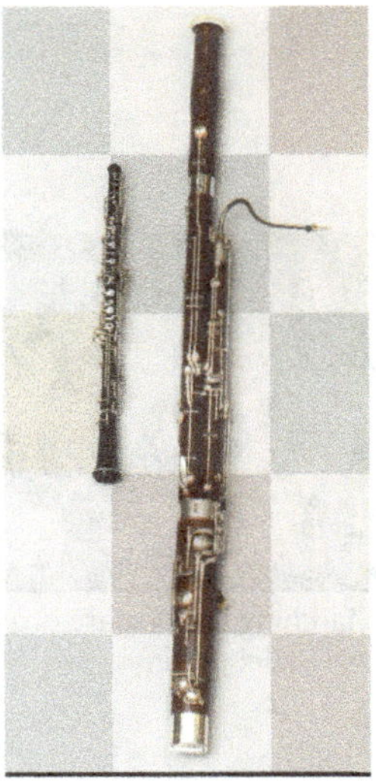

Oboe and Bassoon.
Courtesy of Jeff Montgomery

Listening: Double-Reed Instruments
Rhapsody: Oboe: "Vocalise-Etude en Forme de Habanera"
English horn: Concerto for English Horn and Orchestra: "Preamble and Amble"
Bassoon: Bassoon Sonata VI in C Major, Op. 24: I. Allegro Moderato

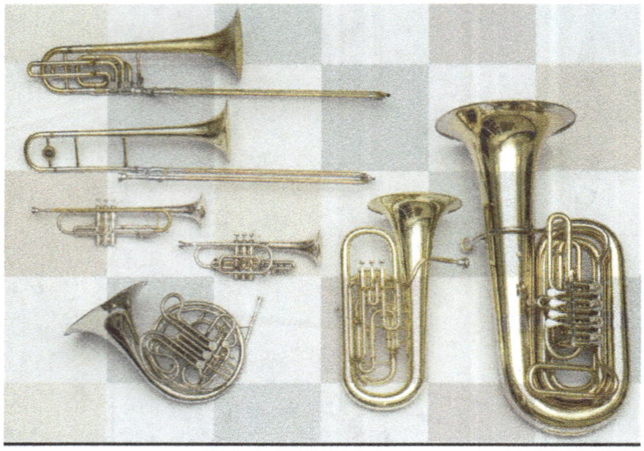

The brass family.
Courtesy of Jeff Montgomery

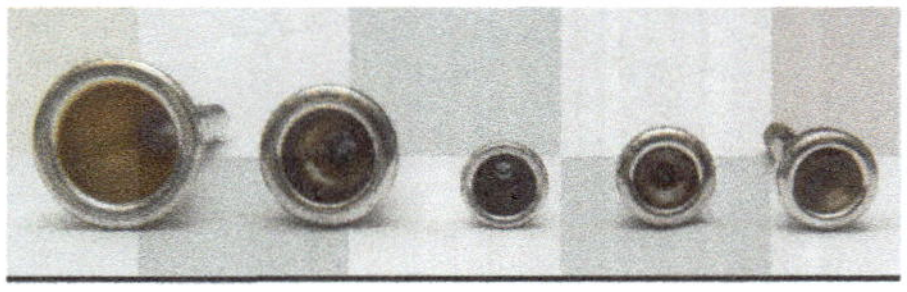

Brass mouthpieces.
Courtesy of Jeff Montgomery

Brass Instruments

Brass instruments are wind instruments that have two main points in common: all are made of metal, and all are played by buzzing the lips in a mouthpiece. The vibration of the lips, started by the air flowing between them, produces the sound for each. "Motorboat" sounds made by little kids in the bathtub are a rudimentary example of the same tone production process. This family includes ***bugles***, ***trumpets***, ***horns***, ***trombones***, and ***tubas***. The different timbres produced by these instruments are determined by the varying tube shapes and the different valve types. In addition, the trombone's slide gives it a sound distinct from the valved instruments.

Listen to the following brass sounds. How would you describe the individual timbres? Which instruments sound the most alike? Most different? How can you tell apart their tones?

Listening: Brass Instruments
Rhapsody: Trumpets: Symphonies de Fanfares: "Rondeau"
Horns: 4 Variations and Fughetta on a Russian Folksong
Trombones: Variations on Napoli (arranged for trombone ensemble)
Tuba: Serenade

Marching band snare drum line.
Courtesy of Jeff Montgomery

Percussion Instruments

In general, percussion instruments are struck to produce their sounds; the differing materials of which they are constructed and the sizes and shapes determine the resulting timbral differences. The family includes a wide variety of instruments. Some percussion instruments have ***definite pitch***, or pitch that can be exactly determined, while some do not. For instance, the keyboard percussion instruments such as the ***xylophone***, ***marimba***, and ***orchestra bells*** have definite pitch just like the piano keyboard, which they resemble, while most drums do not have definite pitch, although they may sound perceptibly higher or lower. The ***piano*** is considered a keyboard percussion instrument, since the strings are set into vibration by the striking of wooden hammers attached to the key mechanisms.

Listen to the following keyboard instruments. How would you describe the differences in tone colors between them? Can you hum the exact pitch of these?

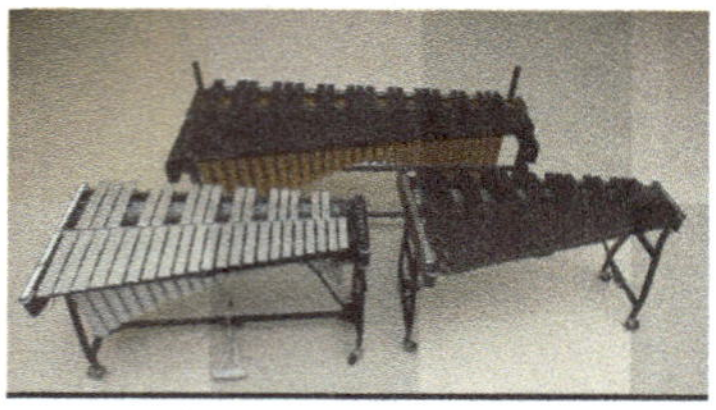

Keyboard percussion: marimba, xylophone, and vibraphone.
Courtesy of Jeff Montgomery

Listening: Keyboard Percussion
Rhapsody: Marimba: "White Squirrel"
Xylophone: Saint-Saens, The Carnival of the Animals: "Fossils"

Drums employ a membrane, either animal skin or synthetic, stretched across an opening that is struck to produce sound. Most drums do not have a definite pitch; however, the timpani is completely tunable, as it does have definite pitch.

Listen to the variety of drums in the following examples. How would you describe the tone color differences in each case?

Timpani, snare drum, bass drum, and tom-toms.
Courtesy of Jeff Montgomery

Listening: Drums
Rhapsody: Timpani: 2001: A Space Odyssey—, "Also Sprach Zarathustra"
Snare drum: "Downfall of Paris"
Rhythm instruments: "Bongos"
Djeimbe: "Djongdong/Wolosodong"

Gong, crash cymbals, suspended cymbal, bells.
Courtesy of Jeff Montgomery

Cymbals and ***gongs*** consist of metal plates or discs that are struck to produce sound. ***Triangles*** and ***chimes*** consist of metal rods or tubes that are struck to produce sound. The ***tambourine*** combines the qualities of a hand drum with metal jingles. Some of these metallic instruments have definite pitch, while others do not. Many of these instruments (including the timpani, cymbals, and tambourine) were introduced into Western classical music by knights returning from the Middle East after the Crusades of the Middle Ages (1100–1400).

Listen to the recordings of these instruments now. How would you describe the tone colors? Which of these have definite pitch?

A variety of small percussion instruments.
Courtesy of Jeff Montgomery

Listening: Metallic Percussion
Rhapsody: Gong: "Gong Lullaby"
Cymbals: The Sanguine Fan, "Cymbals Clashed Softly," "Cymbals Struck Singly"

Electronic Instruments

Yamaha DX7 synthesizer.
Courtesy of the author

The advent of electronics in the 20th century led to an expanded palette of sounds to be exploited by composers and performers. Electric and electronic pianos and organs were some of the first to be developed, but even electronic "wind" and percussion instruments became available during the final quarter of the century. Computers and synthesizers, widely available since the 1970s, allowed for the most significant, limitless tonal explorations. Their ability to synthesize traditional instrument sounds, sample and manipulate analog sounds, and create new sounds via computer opened up vast new territories of exploration for musicians. Many traditional musicians of the time feared that they would be replaced by electronic performers, computerized soundtracks, and synthesized recordings; although this happened to a degree, they have instead largely been augmented by these new sounds, while traditional music making continues to draw audiences. In the university setting, many young composers have composed with computers generating not only the sounds, but also the music itself, resulting in a totally distinct, new style. You may have experienced similar as science-fiction and horror movie soundtracks.

Below is music demonstrating the sound capabilities of the Moog (one of the earliest synthesizers) and other electronic instruments. If you are interested in exploring computer music further, search online using keywords such as *computer music, digital instruments*, and *noise*.

Listen to the modern music below. **How would you describe the timbres in this music? Have you ever before heard sounds like these used in music? When and where?**

Listening: Electronic Instruments

Rhapsody: "Analogies - Analog Computer Music" (The Moog)
Transmutations for Orchestra and Electronic Instruments Movements Two and Three
Uncle Weird's Fun House - Schaeffer
1984 for Electronic Instruments, Tape and Orchestra

Tenors and basses.
Courtesy of Jeff Montgomery

The Human Voice

There are as many different vocal timbres as there are people who sing; however, we tend to group vocalists into categories based upon singing range. Female voices are usually in the soprano or alto ranges, but there are also more specific range designations: soprano, mezzo soprano, alto, contralto, et al. Furthermore, some soprano timbres have a very light and agile quality, making them better suited for the performance of music by specific styles and composers; there are also soprano voices that are very dark and heavy, making them better suited to perform music of other eras and composers. Male voices are usually in either the tenor or bass ranges, but there are also countertenor, tenor, baritone, and bass ranges.

Just as with instruments, the timbre and range of the human voice depends upon the size and construction of the "instrument" or vocal apparatus. Vocal training also plays a role in the development of the range and timbre, although the singer is still partially defined by his or her anatomy. The untrained singer will usually have a range of an octave or so, while some trained singers have ranges of three, four, and five octaves.

Different singing styles feature different timbres as well. Listen to the music listed below. Compare the dark, velvety tone of jazz singer Ella Fitzgerald and the nasal tone of Edith Piaf with some of the popular stylists of current music to whom you listen. **What differences in tone do you hear? How would you compare/contrast their tones?**

Listening: Contrasting Vocal Timbres

Rhapsody: Misty—Ella Fitzgerald , "Misty"
Non, Je Ne Regrette Rien—Edith Piaf, "Non, Je Ne Regrette Rien"

Choir.
Courtesy of Jeff Montgomery

Marching band.
Courtesy of the author

Chamber orchestra.
Courtesy of the author

Tone Color In Ensembles

Composers manipulate tone color in much the same way that painters combine colors in their artwork. Sometimes the tone colors of a particular piece of music are homogeneous, as in the case of pieces for string orchestra. Sometimes tone colors used in a piece of music have quite a variety, showcasing the different sounds and possible combinations. Look online at the following sites for further samples of orchestral instrument sounds.

http://www.sfskids.org and http://www.playmusic.org

The variety of common performing ensembles is related to the tone colors produced by them. An ***orchestra*** is primarily made up of string instruments; the ***string orchestra*** consists entirely of string instruments, and the so-called ***symphony orchestra*** has strings plus two to four of each of the primary woodwind, brass, and percussion instruments. Wind and percussion instruments alone make up a ***band***, whether it is a marching band, concert band, jazz band, or brass band. Marching bands tend to be large, with potentially several hundred members, while a jazz band usually has only 20 members. For each of these groups, the relative proportions of the different instruments create varying timbres. Orchestras have a different timbre than concert bands, which sound different from brass bands mainly due to their different orchestration, or instrument usage.

Chamber ensembles are small performing groups, designed to perform in small places; these ensembles take advantage of their various instrumentations to make a variety of timbres. Duos, trios, quartets, etc., feature all sorts of instrument combinations, some of which defy traditional groupings. For instance, a ***woodwind quartet*** consists of four woodwinds (excluding saxophone), but a ***woodwind quintet*** adds a horn—a brass instrument. Perhaps the most common chamber ensemble is the ***string quartet***. Most composers since the Classical era have written for string quartets; Haydn, Mozart, and Beethoven are renowned for theirs. **Listen to the string quartet piece below. What are the similarities and differences in the instruments' tones? How well do they blend?**

String quartet.
© 2012 by Nicholas Sutcliffe. Used under license of Shutterstock, Inc.

Listening: String Quartet
Rhapsody: Beethoven, String Quartet, Op. 18, No. 1, in F Major,: I. Allegro con Brio—Beethoven

DYNAMICS: VOLUME

Musicians refer to the sound attribute known as volume (loudness) as ***dynamics***, and traditional Italian terms are used to address specific dynamic levels. When music gradually gets louder, the Italian term used is ***crescendo***. When music gradually gets softer, the Italian term ***diminuendo*** is used.

Here is a chart showing the usual terms in order of increasing volume:

ppp	very very soft
pp	pianissimo - very soft
p	piano - soft
mp	mezzo piano - medium soft
mf	mezzo forte - medium loud
f	forte - strong or loud
ff	fortissimo - very strong/loud
fff	very very strong/loud

The Piano Forte

If *piano* means "soft," why do we call the household keyboard instrument a piano? Anyone can observe that it can be played loud, soft, and everything in between. There's a story here! The predecessor of the piano, the harpsichord, was able to play at one set volume due to its construction—either piano or forte. When the piano was invented, its key feature was that it could play any dynamic level, dependent upon the performer's technique. For that reason it was originally called the ***pian' e forte***. In the centuries since, it has become known as simply the piano—and that's the rest of the story.

Courtesy of PhotoDisc

Learning to identify particular instrument timbres and combinations is something that takes experience and repetition, much the same way that learning to identify different coffees takes experience and repetition. You probably didn't immediately memorize the tone of your friends' voices, and you probably won't immediately memorize all the different instruments' tones either. The key here is to listen attentively, describing and comparing the different timbres. Close your eyes as you sample the different instrument tones. **How would you describe each? How would you compare them? Do you hear similarities within each family?**

V. Texture

If we were to describe a sweater or fabric, we could discuss the way in which the different threads are woven together, the resulting complexity of the surface design, and the way it feels to the touch. We could talk about how one color of yarn is most prominent, while others are in the background. All of this describes the texture and overall "feel" of the sweater.

In much the same way, we can describe the ***texture*** of a piece of music by comparing how the different musical lines interact with each other, and the resultant sound that is created. In order to discuss musical texture, we must understand rhythm, melody, and harmony; they are truly the elements of music, while texture describes their relationships.

On the simplest level, musical texture refers to how "thin" or "thick" a piece sounds. Music having a thick texture is often described as "lush," "full," or "heavy," while that with a thin texture is "light," "transparent," or "open." The texture is a product of the number of separate music parts, lines, or layers occurring at a given point. It also is impacted by the ranges of these parts, as well as how they interact.

In a rock song, there usually are several layers to the texture: bass guitar, drummer, rhythm guitar, keyboard, backup singers, lead guitar, other lead instruments, and lead singer. All of this together can create a variety of textures. The following examples are pieces with light textures from a variety of styles. Jack Johnson is accompanied by guitar alone, creating a very simple and light texture. The piano solo by Mozart is likewise, very simple and open sounding, and the concerto for lute is accompanied by a small string orchestra.

A dessert crepe has a light, thin texture.

Listening: Thin Texture Examples
Rhapsody: Better Together - Jack Johnson
Piano Sonata #11 in A, K 331 - 1. Andante Grazioso
Antonio Vivaldi (1678–1741) Concerto in D for Lute and Strings

A piece of cake with many layers and a thick, rich texture.

The examples below are pieces with thicker textures. The Chicago tune begins with only piano, then the rhythm section joins in, followed by the wind players, and finally by the vocalist to gradually build a thicker texture. The Brahms piece alternates moments of simpler, thinner texture with moments of thick texture made up of chorus with orchestra. The Rachmaninoff piano piece has several layers occurring simultaneously and over a wide range, with the pianist playing fistfuls of notes at a time to produce a thick and complex texture.

Listening: Thick Texture Examples
Rhapsody: Saturday in the Park - Chicago V
J. Brahms - A German Requiem - How Lovely Is Thy Dwelling Place
Rachmaninoff - Prelude in B-flat Major, Op. 23 No. 2

In each of the following examples, there is one melody part accompanied by harmony and rhythm lines. Each of the additional lines is there to add depth to and complement the melody, creating ***homophony***. *Homo* is used here to mean that all the parts sound together as one entity: all are tied to the single melody. Notice that although these examples are very different, they are all homophonic. Most music that we listen to is homophonic. Indeed, it is rare to hear anything except homophony in popular music.

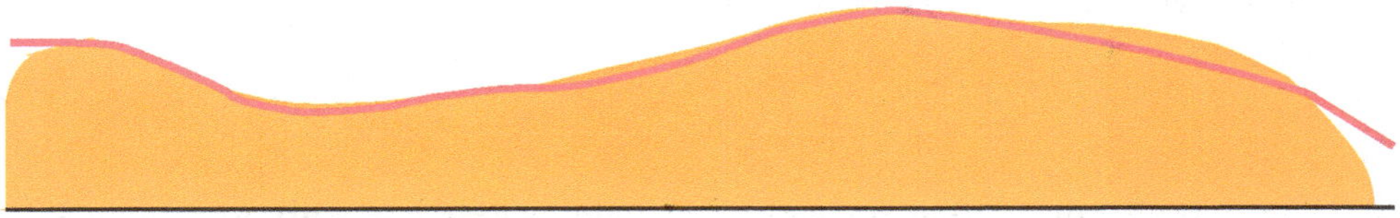

Homophony: A single melody plus accompanying lines of harmony and/or accompaniment.

Homophony: A single melodic line with harmony/accompaniment.

Listening: Homophony
Rhapsody: Love Story - Fearless
A Quiet Place—Take 6, "A Quiet Place"
Chopin - Prelude No. 20
Allegro - Wolfgang Amadeus Mozart

During the Renaissance and Baroque eras, however, a musical texture called ***polyphony*** was common. In polyphonic music, multiple melodic lines of (presumably) equal interest occur simultaneously, each vying for the listener's attention the way the rings of a three-ring circus compete with each other. This makes for a very busy, complex texture. Although each of the polyphonic examples below is very different-sounding, each features multiple simultaneous melodies.

The first is an organ fugue by Baroque composer, J.S. Bach. Note how it begins with a single voice, then a second, third, and fourth are added, each playing the original melody, but beginning at different times. In *The Chain* and *If Only*,

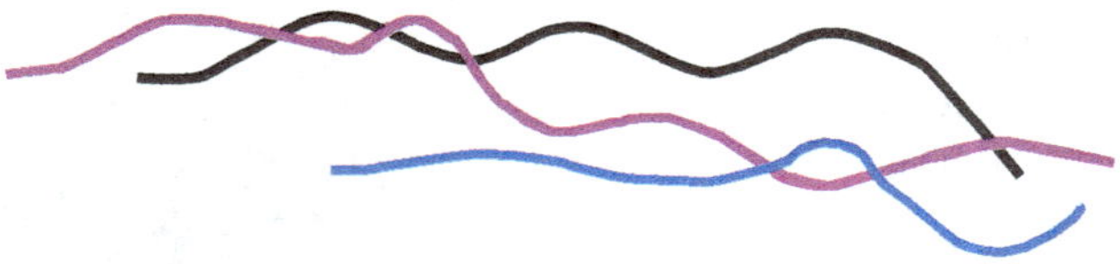

Polyphony: Multiple melodies occurring simultaneously.

Polyphony: Multiple equal melodic lines, each vying for attention.

Monophony: A single melodic line.

each singer has a different melody and all sing at the same time. (See timings.) In the "Tonight" quintet, each group of singers enters at a different point, each singing its own melody. Dixieland classic, *When the Saints Go Marching In* begins with solo improvisation by the trumpet, clarinet, and trombone making a polyphonic texture.

Listening: Polyphony

Rhapsody: Fugue in G Minor "Little"
The Chain - Ingrid Michaelson (from 1:45 on)
The Book Report - Company (beginning)
If Only (Quartet) (Broadway Cast Recording) at 3:30
Tonight (Quintet)
When the Saints Go Marching In

There is also music that consists of a single melody line with no accompaniment. This texture is called ***monophony***, with "mono" meaning one. Anyone singing or playing a melody with no harmony or accompaniment is performing monophonic music. Any group that sings or plays a melody in unison, with no harmony or accompaniment, is also performing monophonic music. Listen to the following monophonic example: it is from the Middle Ages, an era when much music was written in a monophonic texture. Monophony has not been common in "art" music since that time, although we may hear brief instances of it in even music of today.

Monophony: A single melody alone.

Listening: Monophony

Rhapsody: Gregorian Chant, "Antiphonae"—Gregorian Chant

Both classical and popular music is mostly homophonic, but sections of monophonic and polyphonic texture may be used as contrast or variety. Listen to the following well-known musical examples. In *The Stars and Stripes Forever* march, there is polyphonic texture starting at 2:58 when the piccolo solo is added on top of the original melody. In Handel's Messiah, the texture changes from monophonic to homophonic to polyphonic throughout the work. **Can you identify the textures as they occur?**

Listening: Mixed Textures
Rhapsody: "The Stars and Stripes Forever"
"Hallelujah"

Listening Guide: Texture in The Stars and Stripes Forever

0:00	homophonic: 1 melody + harmony/accompaniment
1:39	monophonic: trombones and trumpets alternate, playing in unison
2:03	polyphonic: 1 previous melody + 1 new piccolo melody
2:34	monophonic: trombones and trumpets alternate, playing in unison
2:58	polyphonic: 2 melodies from 2:03 + 1 additional trombone melody

Texture can sometimes be difficult to determine. Like learning to identify the different instrument timbres, it takes experience and repetition. Texture and timbre are concepts that we will work on throughout this course.

To determine the texture of a piece of music, first identify the melody. Then evaluate what else is going on. Is there a bass line instrument playing? Is there a chord instrument playing? (piano, guitar, etc.) Are there back-up singers? If there are instruments or singers that simply "decorate" or "support" what the main melody or main singer is doing, that would be homophony. If there are multiple players or singers doing their own thing, and each is equally important, equally prominent, then that would be polyphony. As stated previously, most music that we listen to is homophonic, so that's a good guess; polyphony is pretty rare in popular music.

Let's compare the textures to some non-musical things that might help you to understand. If you have ever been to a circus, you might recognize that a single, star performer in a single ring would be like monophony. If that star performer had other performers assisting him/her, that would be like homophony. If there were different performers in each of the three rings, performing simultaneously, that would be like polyphony.

Dancers could also be used to illustrate the textures. For instance, a solo performer would be monophonic, but if the performer had a partner and one led while the other followed as in a couples dance, that would be homophonic. If we were at a high school dance with lots of people doing their own thing, that would be polyphony.

VI. Form

When we look at the architectural plans for a house, we can see the different rooms, and we can compare their shapes, sizes, and locations. We can also see that the architect used certain design elements throughout the house. If we discuss

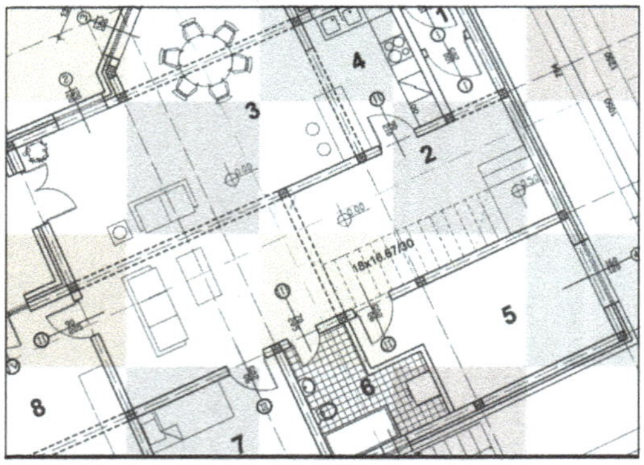

Form in architecture.

music in the same way, comparing the different sections of the music and how they relate, we are talking about *form* or format. In order to understand form, we must first understand rhythm, melody, harmony, and texture; form consists of all the elements in a larger sense.

In popular music, form is easy to identify; pop songs usually have a form consisting of a verse, a chorus, and a "bridge." Some songs have only two main sections, plus an introduction. We know when we encounter a different section, because the melody and/or harmony changes. We must be able to recognize repetition versus contrasting material; we must also be able to recognize variations on the original melody. Understanding form requires more familiarity with the music.

Let's observe the form of a straightforward popular song. Use the Listening Guide to help you identify the sections of Jack Johnson's *Better Together*. Each verse has different words set to the same melody. A chorus usually has the same words and melody each time. The "bridge" is simply a new (contrasting) melody and words somewhere in the middle of the song. In the case of this song, the chorus does not come back as usual.

Listening: Form of a Pop Song

Rhapsody: Better Together - Jack Johnson

0:00	Introduction
0:09	Verse 1
0:43	Chorus
1:01	Instrumental Interlude
1:17	Verse 2
1:53	Chorus
2:11	Instrumental Interlude
2:28	Bridge: New material
3:03	Instrumental Coda

Listen again to Sousa's "The Stars and Stripes Forever" march. Listen for the different sections and the melodies that each section features. Follow the listening guide below to help understand the form.

Watching the marching band go by.

Listening: Form of The Stars and Stripes Forever

"The Stars and Stripes Forever"

0:00–0:05	introduction
0:05–0:20	A: first melody—homophonic
0:20–0:35	A: repeat—homophonic
0:35–0:51	B: second melody—homophonic
0:51–1:07	B: repeat—homophonic
1:07–1:38	C: third melody—homophonic
1:38–2:03	D: fourth melody—monophonic
2:03–2:35	C': third melody + piccolo melody—polyphonic
2:35–2:58	D: fourth melody—monophonic
2:58–end	C": third melody + piccolo melody + trombone melody—polyphonic

This march features all three principles of form: ***repetition***, ***contrast***, and ***variation***. Notice that the first melody (A) was repeated, and was then followed by a contrasting second melody (B) that also was repeated. Following, the contrasting third melody (C) and yet a fourth contrasting melody (D) alternate; the repetitions of (C) are varied through the addition of one, then two additional melodies. The form can be represented as follows:

A A B B C D C' D C''

All doors are made up of the same elements, but each emphasizes different elements and uses them in different ways, resulting in different styles.

VII. Style

We could probably name someone who has his or her own particular style of clothing. When we analyze their style, we see that there are certain pieces or elements that are common to the different outfits, and that there are certain colors, patterns, or combinations that are often repeated. These clothing elements combine to make that person's style in much the same way that the musical elements combine to create a particular style.

You already know a lot about musical style, although you may never have thought about it. You are probably able to distinguish between many different popular music artists and styles. You already have some understanding of rhythm, melody, harmony, color, texture, and form in order to talk about style, because **style** is a product of the ways in which each of these musical elements are handled.

Do you recognize disco, hip-hop, and country music when you hear it? How do you know the differences? Discuss the style differences between popular music of the 1970s, 1980s, 1990s, and 2000s, and give specific examples. How would you describe these differences in style?

A recent book explains style differences this way.

The difference between music and a random or disordered set of sounds has to do with the way the fundamental attributes (of sound) combine, and the relations that are formed between them. When these basic elements combine and form relationship with one another in a meaningful way, they give rise to high-order concepts such as meter, key, melody, harmony, etc.
—This Is Your Brain on Music

As we discuss the musical styles of different historical eras, different countries and cultures throughout this course, we will hear differences in the ways the musical elements have been used. The traditional eras of Western European art music are shown below. They roughly correspond to the eras of the other arts.

Medieval era: 450–1450
Renaissance: 1450–1600
Baroque era: 1600–1750
Classical era: 1750–1810
Romantic era: 1810–1900
Modern era: 1900–2000

VIII. Mood

In music, mood refers to the emotional content perceived in the music or the emotions produced by the performance of music. The composer can create musical mood by multiple means:

- repetition of specific rhythms,
- choice of tempo,
- shape of melodic lines,
- repetition of melodic or rhythmic motives,
- choice of tonality, dissonance/consonance,
- combinations of timbres,
- sounds of specific instruments, especially those with cultural connotations,
- manipulation of textures, and
- melodic and/or tonal references to memorable, cultural events

Look again at the list above and notice that all of our musical elements are represented. Like style, mood is produced by the composer's manipulation of the elements. Mood and style are not elements themselves, but they are the product of the way in which the composer handles the elements.

Section II

Music in the West

2 Medieval Music

Introduction: The Foundation of Chant

Chant is the primary music developed for worship rites in the Christian church. It emerged out of Jewish and Pagan practices, although the precise extent to which these contemporaneous religious traditions influenced chant is sometimes difficult to discern. As the Christian leaders developed a full rotation of prayers for the entire year (liturgy), they found a need for many musical settings; and after many years of expanding the number and then cutting it back again, we are now left with about 3,000 chants still in use, all of which may be traced back to the medieval era. Since Christianity was an illegal religion throughout the Roman Empire until the fourth century (313 AD), detailed records about chant practices have mostly been lost, if they were ever kept. Once things turned around and Christianity was enforced as *the* state religion, there may have been even less of an incentive for singers to codify their musical practices against the threat of destruction.

Up to about the year 900, chant was both preserved and developed in an **oral/aural tradition**, where singing the music over and over, for generations, served to keep melodies somewhat intact and recognizable over time, but also quite flexible and variable. By studying the tendencies and patterns of notated chant, historians are often able to theorize about what chant sounded like in its pre-notated past. One prominent chant scholar, Alejandro E. Planchart, has argued that melodies composed for prayers of the greatest religious significance were the ones that were most likely to survive over time and thus to retain traces of earlier musical styles. The chant "**Haec dies**," for example, is sung during Mass on Easter Sunday, and its mesmerizingly repetitive, highly ornamented style is of a distinctly different character than many others. No event in the Christian calendar is more important than Easter, as it celebrates Christ's resurrection (Christmas comes in second on this scale), and "Haec dies" is the prayer that many remember most as they recall their worship experience, as it is sung at the highest service of the day—the mass—and at the most reflective point in that service—just after the gospel. So "Haec dies" may be the most important chant of all; and there is good reason to suspect that it retains an Eastern flavor that was at one time more common in chant composition, but later gave way to a sound more recognizably "Western" (see listening guide below).

Score of Gregorian Song.

The Musical Style of Chant

What is most notably "Western" in the musical style of chant is the seemingly **goal-directed** nature of the melodies. Even the most elaborate chants often seem to be moving clearly either *toward* a specific pitch or *away* from one, while others seem to hover on a specific pitch to the point where it is clear that the goal is to make it feel stable, as a place of arrival and comfort. Theorists of the medieval era developed a system of **modes** to teach their students about the nature of chant melodies. These were meant mainly to classify chants, but it is easy to see how the system they developed—with its clear purpose to establish a hierarchy of pitches—would lead to music of a more goal-directed nature.

The most noticeably distinguishing feature of chant is its **monophonic** texture: all chants are comprised of a single melody, which may be sung by one singer or a group of singers (often described as a chorus). In terms of form, some chants were designed to be **responsorial**, in which case a single singer alternates with a chorus; others were meant to be **antiphonal**, where one group of singers answers another; and some, finally, were described as **direct**, where one singer or group of singers performs the work all the way through without any alternation. Today it is rare that singers follow any of these directions, and thus, by default, chant is most often performed by choirs these days, in the direct style.

In melodic terms, most chants move in step-wise motion (**conjunct motion**), although they do sometimes feature leaps (**disjunct motion**). Their melodic shapes are often arch-like, although many seem instead to reach a certain goal and hover there for a time before returning down the range to a point of repose. Many chants are noteworthy for the elegant nature of their overall shape, which has become a hallmark for melodic design in the West ever since.

As sung prayer, chants are comprised of basically two essential ingredients—melody and text—and the relationship of the two is what helps us immediately distinguish among them. In **syllabic** chant, each syllable receives a single pitch. When a number of syllables of the text receive three to six or so pitches, but no more than this, the chant is described as **neumatic**. Finally, when there are a number of syllables that receive seven or more pitches, the resulting chant is described as **melismatic**. Musically rich, melismatic chants were usually featured on festive occasions, as they are notably exuberant in nature. Both examples discussed below are melismatic chants.

Guided Listening

"Haec dies" (Gradual, Easter), a Responsorial and Melismatic Chant

http://app.rhapsody.com/search?query=haec+dies

Original text	*English translation*
Haec dies, quam fecit Dominus: *exsultemus, et laetemur in ea.*	*This is the day the Lord has made:* *we will rejoice and be glad in it.*
Confitemini Domino, quoniam bonus: *quoniam in saeculum misericordia ejus.*	*Praise the Lord, for he is good:* *his mercy endures for ever.*

0:00 First line is sung with melisma on the first two words *"haec dies"* and extended melisma on the last syllable *"-nus."*

0:27 Second line is sung with melisma on the syllable *"-mus"* and extended melisma on the last syllable *"-ea."*

1:12 Third line is sung with extended melisma on the "o" vowels.

1:54 Fourth line is sung with melisma on the "u" vowels.

The first pitch heard in this chant is the same pitch heard at the end of the second line ("ea"). This same pitch is then used to start the third line and the singers return to this pitch at the very end of the fourth line. Using this pitch at the beginning and end of each section gives a reference point to the singers (making it easier for them to sing the right notes) and to the listeners (making the piece sound more organized and cohesive as a whole).

Early Music Notation

Ex. 1 Manuscript missal with un-heightened cheironomic neumes.

If the two images directly above seem rather unremarkable visually (or even distractingly messy), they represent a major advance in music history that developed in the late ninth and early tenth centuries. Musical notation, of which two kinds appear above, developed out of a felt need to unify chant. There was a political as well as a religious impetus for the effort, as it stemmed from an alliance between the reigning pope and King Charlemagne the Great, both of whom had amassed great power in this era. Later, musicians developed heightened or **diastemmatic** neumes (groups of notes) that indicate pitches (but not rhythmic values). This type of notation represented an advance over so-called **cheironomic** neumes, which represented hand gestures, shown in Example 1 above. The latter gave the singers an idea of the melodic profile for a given chant with the purpose of jarring a singer's memory, and so this notation did not work if the singer had not already memorized the tune at hand.

Because the diastemmatic type served to clearly establish the identities of various pitches on the page, it led to new developments in music composition. First, as manuscripts could be used by groups but were normally meant to serve one person for individual study, notated music in manuscript helped relegate the task of composing new music to the work of a single person. Collaborative composition is rather common in popular fields and in some other cultures. Thanks to this notation, though, single-person-authored music became the norm in the West and has been ever since. Second, these same individuals soon found that, as they worked with these manuscripts, they could conveniently experiment with musical **texture**—by adding new melodies to the existing ones—and also experiment with **harmony** by exploring different sound combinations on the page, all before the crucial moment when the music would be realized in sound. Rhythm proved more difficult to notate, and even though considerable focus went into the problem of marking time in notation, there remained in the West a certain lack of development in rhythmic ideas.

For all these reasons, as far as technology goes, there was probably no single event more important in Western music history than the development of music notation, and the immediate consequence was a period of noticeable advancement in music for the church, as this was where all the notational developments took place.

The Development of Polyphony

After 900, one of the most notable developments in music history was the cultivation of music with multiple melodies. The result was a texture that many call "harmony" and that we tend to speak of as **polyphony**. This was a watershed moment in the history of Western music, as it marked a noticeable change in compositional expectations. Many still performed chant, but monophonic sacred music (i.e., chant) was composed much less frequently and received with much less fanfare. From this point on, music of the West was viewed as in some way multi-part. Intriguingly, chant, as it turns out, even though monophonic, was not yet to be set aside, even when the new forms were created. Rather, it was to serve as the foundation of all new music at this time. Composers found that if they preserved the pitches, but varied the rhythms, of their chant melodies, they could greatly expand the time involved in performing certain prayers and add much in the way of melodic diversity and harmonic depth. This new music based on chant they called **organum**, and it introduced two new music textures: 1) a note-against-note style, which is akin to homophonic texture, and 2) a sustain note style, which sets one note against many others and is thus a form of polyphony. After experimenting with various forms of improving and harmonizing chants, composers, especially those centered in France's great Cathedral of Notre Dame, used the new notation system developed in the tenth century to turn simple chants into expansive works of great musical richness.

School of Notre Dame

In the heyday of the great Gothic Cathedral of Notre Dame, the composers **Lèonin** (fl. c. 1150) and **Pérotin** (fl. c.1200) dominated the musical world. Their music, to many, is worthy of comparison to the great architectural achievement of the Parisian cathedral in which they worked. As noted above, both composers called their music **organum**. Together they composed a repertory of liturgical music for soloists (based closely on responsorial procedures, see below) so impressive that the book in which they copied it all down was known as the ***Magnus Liber***. Nearly all of it was based on chant. Thanks to the writings of a student at the time (whom we now refer to as "Anonymous 4"), we know that Lèonin was famous for writing long passages of sustain note organum in two voices and that Pérotin had substituted works in place of Lèonin's that extended to three and four parts.

Note in the following examples that pitches of the original chant are slowed considerably as a fast-moving melody above them moves through repeating and reiterating patterns, coming into harmonic tension at points of **dissonance**, and then to release and stability at points of consonance.

Notre Dame.

Guided Listening

Excerpt of Lèonin's "Viderunt omnes" for Two Voices, Notre Dame School Polyphony (Organum)

http://www.rhapsody.com/artist/antony-pitts/album/leonin--perotin-sacred-music-from-notre-dame-cathedral/track/viderunt-omnes-2-part-organum

Original text of plainchant	*English translation of plainchant*
Viderunt omnes fines terrae salutare Dei nostri: *jubilate Deo omnes terra.*	*All the ends of the earth have seen the salvation of our God:* *sing joyfully to God, all the earth.*
Notum fecit Dominus salutare suum: *ante conspectum gentium revelavit iustitiam suam.*	*The Lord has made known his salvation:* *He has revealed His justice in the sight of the nation.*

0:00–0:03	The soloist sings the first two notes. The lower part then enters, following the pitch established by the soloist. They didn't have pitch pipes or pianos around in the 1100s, so this is how they ensured that everybody would start on the right note.
0:32	Up to this point, the entire piece has been performed on a single syllable ("*vi*" of "*viderunt*"). At 0:32 all the voices move together to the second syllable ("*de*"). Because this is only an excerpt of the piece, you will only hear the words "*viderunt omnes*" in this track.
0:52	All voices move to the syllable "*runt.*" Notice how the lower part holds each pitch for a long time, moving much more slowly than the upper part. The lower part is actually a preexisting plainchant, the composer of which is unknown. The upper part was written by Lèonin to embellish the plainchant.

Guided Listening

Pérotin's "Viderunt omnes" for Four Voices, Notre Dame School Polyphony (Organum)

http://www.rhapsody.com/artist/antony-pitts/album/leonin--perotin-sacred-music-from-notre-dame-cathedral/track/viderunt-omnes-4-part-organum

Original text of plainchant	*English translation of plainchant*
Viderunt omnes fines terrae salutare Dei nostri: *jubilate Deo omnes terra.*	*All the ends of the earth have seen the salvation of our God:* *sing joyfully to God, all the earth.*
Notum fecit Dominus salutare suum: *ante conspectum gentium revelavit iustitiam suam.*	*The Lord has made known his salvation:* *He has revealed His justice in the sight of the nations.*

0:00–0:08	All voices enter on "*vi*" of "*viderunt,*" then the upper voices briefly drop out, leaving only the lowest part holding "*vi.*"
0:08	The upper voices reenter in triple meter, continuing with the syllable "*vi.*"
1:14	All change to "*de.*"
1:56	All change to "*runt.*"
3:24	End of "*viderunt,*" beginning of "*omnes.*" The only words heard in this excerpt are "*viderunt omnes.*"

Features to notice:

- This piece uses a preexisting plainchant in the lowest voice. The three upper voices were composed by Pérotin to add interest to the plainchant.
- All voices are singing the same text at the same time, even though some voices are moving more quickly than others.
- This piece is five minutes long, but the only text sung is *"Viderunt omnes,"* which is not repeated. This means that the voices remain on each syllable for a long time. When many notes are sung to a single held syllable, it is called a **melisma**.

Listen and view the score on **YouTube: http://youtube/bpgaEFmdFcM**

Rhythmic Notation and the Motet

In the sustain-note style of organum it would not be necessary to define rhythms precisely, as the singer of the faster part could devise some kind of cue to let the other singer know when to change the underlying, slow-moving drone note. Nor was it very difficult to sing the other kind of organum—note-against-note—without notation. In certain ways, this musical style of singing is akin to what we often see and hear when pop music musicians today "harmonize" a given melody. As long as they know the tune, those who sing "in harmony" do not normally need to use notation (but see the Spinal Tap scene at Elvis's grave, when this doesn't work out so well: http://www.youtube.com/watch?v=Fx9EDv_hgeM).

Thus it was not at the outset, but rather in the midst of writing music for the *Magnus Liber* that composers such as Lèonin and Pérotin first grappled with the problem of notating rhythms.

At first they tried to develop a notation system to set up a standard rhythmic pattern for large stretches of music. Once they understood the notation, then, everyone would know the pattern, such as long-short or short-short-short, etc. This type of rhythmic notation was called **modal notation** and it is interesting for the way it forced music into strong repetitive patterns (much as various dance music styles do today). But when this uniformity in pattern began to interfere with the way singers wanted to express their lines, a new system was developed, which became the basis for what has been used in Western notation ever since. In the new system, called **mensural notation**, the rhythmic value of a note was indicated by its shape and design. Specifically, the relative length of its rhythmic value would depend on a number of visual elements: for example, if it was a rectangle, square, or diamond; if it had a stem or not; if it included a dot or not; and if its body was left void or filled in with ink. All those elements could change the value. This gave the composers the chance to vary rhythms quite drastically for various individual lines of a multi-part piece. But the number of rhythmic values available (or that could be notated) were still limited by the number and types of shapes recognized by the system. This was one more reason why, in the West, so many musical rules had to be written down and studied. If the rhythmic limitations of the system did in fact impede certain kinds of rhythmic growth in music of the West, at the time it was greeted with enthusiasm. Musicians soon decided that they could study rhythm with as much intensity as they had studied harmony and melody. With such skills mastered, they found they could specialize more deeply in and experiment more with the elements of what they came to regard as a full-fledged art form of far-reaching capacities. And even if all this originated in the confines of the cloister and church, once the system was developed, there was the potential to easily expand their musical orbit into the world outside, to what we tend to call **secular music**.

Medieval Secular Song: Music of Mischief-Makers and Kings

At the same time that the composers of the Notre Dame School and their successors were developing polyphonic styles and a new notational system for rhythm, a number of musical traditions were forming outside the church. It was in this secular realm that music became associated with certain poetic topics that remain important to this day, including the protest, the satirical, and, especially, the love

Musicians playing a tabor and pipe for dancing, c. 1340.

song. Secular music itself of the 1100–1300 era was almost exclusively monophonic while these first traditions were at the height. It was not until several of them had actually died out that the kinds of poems they wrote would be set to polyphony. So, the secular songwriters were not as advanced, it would seem, as their contemporaries in the church. But in their tunes, some of them quite beautiful indeed, we hear the last great flowering of the medieval monophonic tradition.

According to their own jocular pose, which surely fit some of them to a tee, **Goliards** (1100–1300) were university and church dropouts who lived and espoused a *carpe diem* (seize the day) lifestyle of heavy drinking, unfunded travel, and general social mischief. (If this might seem to make them endearing rather than obscure, many have been turned off to them or just confused about them thanks to a mid-twentieth-century musical tribute by Carl Orff. His famous *Carmina Burana* hardly seems to portray a group of merry pranksters, but rather a violent battle or some thunderous parade.)

Goliard songs were composed with Latin texts, as befitting the educational achievements of their practitioners and audiences. Goliards often treated the church and political establishments as their subjects of satire, opening a mode of protest that would reemerge strongly at the end of the medieval era (see below). But they did not always act as social commentators. They also sang about things that have apparently always mattered to the college-aged: love, partying, and money (requests for money are the most common element found in all correspondences among medieval students and their parents).

The French **troubadour**, **trouvère**, and **trobairitz** of the twelfth and thirteenth centuries composed songs in their native Occitan (troubadours of the southern areas) and Old French (trouvères of the north). Trobairitz were female singer-composers. The term we use for their main subject, **courtly love**, was not in general use until the nineteenth century. At the time *fin'amour* (high or refined love) was discussed much more often, and this is what helps us understand what was meant at the time, as long as we take the word "refined" to suggest something rare and strange. Troubadour love was neither platonic nor familial—marital love was never mentioned, for example. Instead, it was illicit—based on adultery and jealousy—and also unrequited. In the language of **feudalism**, lovers cast themselves as vassals to express with humility and frustration their love for another who had summarily rejected them. Troubadours assigned themselves legendary biographies in *vidas* that were often copied with their songs; they appeared before each other and others as chivalrous knights in the style of contemporary Arthurian romances. Singers from all classes could rise to the status of troubadour, but it is noteworthy that Richard the Lionhearted and a number of other nobles were typical representatives of this tradition. It will be rare to find nobles as composers in the rest of Western music history. The origins of troubadour ideas are very likely Islamic and Andalusian, as there were similar Arab poet-musicians in the ninth century. But by the twelfth century, this was the music and poetry of castle life. As idealized song, it rightly evokes the kind of setting most often evoked in movies and stories of today. Whether they actually lived such lives or not, the typical troubadours presented themselves as rarified, knightly subjects and used refined language to exalt others—"putting them on a pedestal." As much as it was all very idealistic, a strong civilizing force was behind this movement in a time that used to be known as the "dark ages."

Philippe de Vitry, Guillaume de Machaut, and the Ars Nova

Many who study the music of the medieval period, as we have been busy studying it here, sense that the pace of things picks up dramatically after the invention of rhythmic notation. This perception is probably shaped by certain twentieth-century ideas about musical evolution, as many in the last century rather automatically equated certain forms of musical complexity with ideas about progress. It is a debatable formula, of course. But there can be no question that by the end of the medieval era, things had become thoroughly intricate. Books discussing new advances in rhythmic notation were commonplace throughout the thirteenth and fourteenth centuries, and there were many innovations to discuss. When adding shapes and filling in notes to alter the rhythmic value were not sufficient, composers at the time resorted even to red and blue ink to indicate various different values. At the time, they proudly said it was all part of a "New Art" in music; and the term *Ars Nova* is now accepted as the name for the whole 1300–1400 period. By the end of the medieval era, all the advances in measuring rhythms and representing them in notation had taken things well beyond the system we treat as standard today.

Thanks to their preoccupation with rhythmic ideas, Ars Nova composers also began to explore various ways to control larger and larger units of musical time, coming up, in the end, with complicated musical **forms** based—as is all musical form—on repetition, variation, and contrast. The most advanced of these forms was the most common, and it was termed **isorhythm** (the term itself was introduced in the early twentieth century). In this formal method, a composer treated the pitches and rhythms of a line of music as if they were two completely separate units, both of which could be divided into cycles and repeated over and over throughout a piece. Described in this way, it doesn't seem apt to make things particularly complex. But, as it turns out, our brains are built so that if you change the expected rhythm of a melody when you repeat it, it sounds almost unrecognizable. Ars Nova composers paid no attention to this issue of our limits of perception. They seemed instead to revel in the task of making pitch and rhythm cycles that would not coincide.

(Try singing "Happy Birthday" over and over in different rhythms; see http://legacy.earlham.edu/~tobeyfo/musictheory/Book2/Assignment Page2011/A1_2011.html.)

At the same time, it was common for a group of performers to sing (or play music based on) two different texts simultaneously. However unusual this practice, it can be traced back to Lèonin and Pérotin's *Magnus Liber* (Big Book) of organum, where we find Latin religious-inspired texts added to a part that was once meant to sing all the notes on a single syllable. Adding words to Notre Dame organum actually became the basis for a whole new musical type, or genre, which we call the **motet** (after the French word for "word," *mot*). At first, composers of motets kept to the Latin language and religious subjects of the original music when they added words to melodies that were sung to a single syllable most of the time. Eventually, motet composers began to put newly composed love songs in the upper parts, and these were typically in French (as they came essentially from the waning troubadour tradition). Thus, when we come to the period of isorhythmic motets, audiences were doubly challenged: in addition to comprehending all those repeating cycles in melody and rhythm, they had to grapple with the words of two (or three) songs being sung at them at the same time, sometimes in two different languages.

One of the reasons why audiences may have liked this complex music was that it often dealt with controversial subjects. This was a time of great strife in both the political and religious realms, which were then so interrelated as sometimes to be nearly indistinguishable. The Papal Schism of 1378–1417 in many ways epitomized the political instability of the time; there were as many as three elected popes serving in Rome and Avignon, two of whom had been elected by the same council. Eventually they all retired and a new pope was elected. But to many, this seemed not only confusing and very distracting, but also indicative of the corruption and fraud they saw too often shaping the behavior of their leaders.

Following the satirical songs of the Goliards, musicians of the Ars Nova often set similarly satirical texts, well before the time of the Schism. The most famous of these was an allegorical poem, ***Roman de Fauvel*** (1310–1314), about a "curry-colored" horse who ends up taking over the house of his former owner, and rises to great power and prominence after he meets Dame Fortune and marries Dame Vainglory. (The English expression "curry favor" derives from this work.) The horse's name, Fauvel, suggests falsity as well as his strange color, and is also an acrostic for six vices: each letter of his name stands for a different one (*F*lattery, *A*varice, etc.). As an allegorical figure, Fauvel represents the woeful lack of ethics that artists at the time perceived in their rulers.

Included in the *Roman de Fauvel* are a number of isorhythmic motets, including five by the noted composer and music theorist **Philippe de Vitry** (1291–1361). Vitry may have been the author of the treatise on rhythmic notation called the *Ars Nova*, and was widely regarded as the leading figure in the musical world of his time. In his "Fauvel" motets, Vitry displayed an intricacy and complexity that he and his musician and poet friends must have felt fit the satirical topics they all relished.

Guided Listening

"O canenda vulgo per compita; Rex quem metrorum depingit prima figura; Rex regum," Motet by Philippe de Vitry from *Roman de Fauvel*

http://youtube/4td8ldYiwp4

Roman de Fauvel is an epic poem that uses satire and allegory to condemn corruption in the political and religious institutions of late medieval Europe. The story follows the exploits of Fauvel, an ambitious donkey- or horse-like creature, as he moves from the stable to a prominent position at the French court. The name Fauvel is an acronym of the French words for several vices: *flatérie* (flattery), *avarice* (greed), *vilanie* (depravity; note that "u" and "v" were interchangeable), *variété* (fickleness), *envie* (envy), and *lascheté* (cowardice).

The three voices sing the three different texts below simultaneously, making the piece sound very complex. Although it may seem disjointed, each part was carefully composed to work together with the others. The amount of text assigned to each part reflects their relative speeds. Focusing your listening on the low, slow part may help you to feel oriented.

Consider the three texts below. How do they compare to each other? How do they function within the plot of *Roman de Fauvel*? Notice that the first letters of each line in the *motetus* form an acrostic of the name Robertus, which refers to Robert of Anjou, King of Sicily (or King of Naples), who ruled from 1309 to 1343. Who is Robert of Anjou, and why is he portrayed as a model of justice, courage, and virtue?

*Original text**	*English translation**
Triplum (top voice)	
O canenda vulgo per compita	*O unspeakable madness of our age,*
ab eterno belial dedita	*the very delirium of rabid dogs*
seculorum nephanda rabies	*(it should be openly exposed at every crossroad*
et delira canum insanies	*how you have been from time immemorial*
quem cum nequis carpere dentibus	*in collusion with the devil),*
criminaris neque lactrattibus	*why do you, inviting damnation, proceed against that just man*
damnum colens tu quid persequeris	*whom you cannot tear with your teeth,*
virum iustum et tuo deseris	*nor indict with your barking?*
rege regi quem decor actuum	*Why do you forsake your king,*
illuminat quem genus strenuum	*honoured by the grace of his royal deeds,*
et sanctorum multa affinitas	*whom an illustrious family of close affinity with the saints,*
sibi facta lux splendor claritas	*and the radiance, splendor, and brilliance given to him*
corruscantem reddit pre ceteris	*place shining above all others,*
quemadmodum nocturnis syderis	*just as gleaming Phoebus on arising*
iubar Phebus perventus abtulit	*seems actually to remove the light from the night stars:*
dei proth dolor lapsum pertulit	*you ally yourself to the very sin against God,*
iherusalem dominum proprium	*miserable to say, that Jerusalem committed*
ihesum spernens habes in socium.	*in spurning her rightful Lord, Jesus.*
Motetus (middle voice)	
Rex quem metrorum depingit prima figura	*The king whom the first letters of these lines depict,*
Omne tenens in se quod dat natura beatis	*contains within himself all things that nature gives to the blessed,*
Basis iusticie troianus iulius ausu	*is the base of justice, a Trojan Julius in courage,*
Ecclesie tuctor machabeus hector in arma	*a Maccabean protector of the Church,*
Rura colens legum scrutator theologie	*and a Hector in arms, honouring his country*
Temperie superans augustum iulius hemo	*and yet remaining a scholar of the covenants of theology;*
Virtutes cuius mores genus actaque nati	*he surpasses Julius Augustus as a man of moderation.*
Scribere non possem possint tuper ethera scribi.	*Since I cannot describe in words the virtues,*
	character, family, and deeds of a man so endowed,
	may these things be celebrated above in the heavens.
Tenor (lowest voice)	
Rex regum.	*O King of Kings.*

Outside of the *Fauvel,* this could well serve as a straightforward work of royal flattery. But all the claims about virtue would come off as ironic in the context of the allegorical Fauvel tale about a horse (king) that embodies all the vices.

Guillaume de Machaut (1300–1377)

Machaut, the greatest composer of the second generation of the *Ars Nova*, was also one of Europe's most venerated poets. He wrote isorhythmic motets of great complexity, for which he is duly famous. But he also was better known for his French-texted poems and songs on the subject of courtly love. In his *chansons* (songs), all settings of his own poems, Machaut followed set patterns in line lengths, rhyme schemes, formal repetitions, and refrains so consistently that his forms are known now as *forme fixes* (fixed forms). Machaut, who survived the Black Death and gained great fame as a high-ranking courtier and church officer as well as a poet and musician, was also famous for inserting himself into his poems, suggesting they might convey some kind of quasi-biographical reality. To this day people argue, for example, about whether the love he expressed for a nineteen-year-old poetess in the poems of his sixth decade was based on truth or fantasy, or just an artistic friendship. Even if unrequited love remains the order of the day, the sentiments expressed in Machaut's chansons are some of the most beautiful of the Western tradition.

One of the most famous pieces of music that Machaut composed was also, for the time, one of the most unusual: a setting of all the **Ordinary** items of a **mass**, his "Messe de Nostre Dame." During medieval times the entire mass was usually sung as chant. The Ordinary items were those prayers that were the same every day, and they included the Kyrie, Gloria, Credo, Sanctus, and Agnus Dei (in Machaut's day they also sang a dismissal formula, "Ite missa est," which future composers did not include in their settings). Masses had **Proper** items too. These were the prayers that changed according to the feast day and season. The Ordinary chants were sometimes fine melodies, but the most elaborate melodies of chant were Proper items, such as the two Graduals, for Christmas and Easter, discussed above. Machaut's was one of the first ever complete **polyphonic settings** of the Ordinary items by a single composer, and it has long been regarded as a masterpiece. In three movements of the mass, Machaut used isorhythm, and thus to listen to them is to hear Machaut in his typical mode of complexity. Yet the other two—Gloria and Credo—were composed in a more direct way, foretelling a style that would preoccupy composers after the medieval period, when a return to "naturalism" and immediacy in expression replaced the former fixation on complexity.

Instruments of the Medieval and Renaissance Eras

There is a notable lack of historical treatments of instruments in standard texts of the medieval and Renaissance eras. This would seem a gross historical distortion. All indications, in diaries, chronicles, etc., suggest instrumental music was then as much a part of everyday life as it is today, and perhaps more so a part of life if we restrict things to the realm of live performance. Some of the most admired musicians of the medieval and Renaissance eras were instrumentalists as well as singers. The instruments they played, if arguably inferior in strength and reliability to those of today, were by no means less ingeniously constructed or less versatile. Early Music fans today truly love the sound of their "early instruments." Some even find that they have developed distaste or even disdain for the modern equivalents, such as the piano or the trombone.

Before turning to some of the individual instruments that were popular in the medieval and Renaissance eras, it is worth making a few general points, which may help explain their undeserved neglect. First, we can blame the medieval and Renaissance musicians themselves. Unlike the music designed for church usage, instrumental music was still being taught in the one-on-one/teacher-student method. Professional musicians, furthermore, wanted to keep their skills a trade secret and actually formed guilds to shield themselves from any others who might rise up in competition.

Secondly, very few works were expressly written for instruments, at least in any way that helps us determine how they would be performed. It is true that one way the professionals kept things secret was by teaching improvisation rather than note-reading skills, although many instrumentalists probably did know the way notation worked. But it was still the custom for the scribes who copied music into manuscripts hardly ever to mention what instruments, if any at all, should be used in performance. Even when music was printed rather than copied in manuscripts, the tendency was not to provide any instructions about instrumental performance. Some today assume, probably correctly, that the scribes and printers left out these seemingly crucial instructions so as not to restrict anyone from playing the works with any instrument they wanted to use. But for whatever reason, when these scribes left out this information, it just helped keep historians in the dark.

Thirdly, most of the instruments used at the time were not of Western origin. While this would hardly seem a good reason to exclude them from discussion, it does make special demands on the historian, who must suddenly deal with a global situation. In earlier times the non-Western origin (mainly Arabic) of so many instruments was tossed off as irrelevant, but this is no longer a viable stand we can take today. Rather, the history of instruments helps us understand special currents of Eastern influence on Western culture.

One further general point of note: there was a change in what we call the aesthetic approach to instruments, and this also tends to cloud our understanding of their use in performance. In the medieval period, it was very much "anything goes." They did have a sense that certain instruments were loud and suited for the out-of-doors (**haut**) and others were better suited for the indoors (**bas**) (see below). But otherwise they seemed happy to combine one kind of sound with any other, enjoying the diversity that instruments of different types created in the performance. In the Renaissance, however, musicians and their audiences preferred a much more homogenized sound, one that could be created by a family of instruments. Instrument families, cultivated in the Renaissance, were built around the basic human range types (soprano, alto, tenor, bass). It is wonderful to see these families today, as it is no longer fashionable to use bass recorders or treble sackbuts (the direct ancestor of the trombone). But with families of all sorts in place, there was even less reason to specify anything about instrumental performance, as instrumental groups could perform virtually anything that had been composed for singers.

All the trends mentioned above began to break down with a rise in amateur music-making in the late sixteenth century. The change is easy to attribute to the advent of print and a concurrent change in social views about musical performance. Music printers soon developed business savvy and discovered not only that they had vast new markets to satisfy with their products, but also that they could enlarge their customer base by printing instruction manuals to explain and demystify music notation. This was the advent of a truly widespread musical literacy, which grew and grew in the West until the advent of recording.

We still see this today. Have you ever encountered an ad with the enticing claim that you can learn "how to play guitar in two weeks"? It stems from the early days of print (and you can see this too in the history of chant). To ease the process, those who devised these manuals ended up recreating musical notation systems in ways that made it all seem easier to manage. Professional musicians may have worried that this infringed on their ability to control the field, but, as often happens with an infusion of amateur interest, it only widened their opportunities to perform, as now they faced an audience much more aware and appreciative of their efforts.

Finally, by happy coincidence, Renaissance social behavior manuals, such as *The Courtier* by Baldassare Castiglione, were at the same time encouraging both men and women to become proficient in instrumental music as well as in singing. Altogether, by the end of the sixteenth century, two rather important changes had developed: 1) women were among the most famous and important performers, and 2) instrumental music was now poised to rise quickly to the levels once reserved only for singers.

Medieval and Renaissance Instruments

CATEGORY	INSTRUMENT	RELATED MODERN INSTRUMENT	HISTORY AND ORIGIN	DESCRIPTION
haut (loud, suitable for outdoor use)	sackbut	trombone	15th century, probably invented in Burgundy	brass; thicker walls, narrower bell, and softer timbre than modern trombone
	shawm	oboe	Middle Eastern origin, introduced to Europe during the Crusades	woodwind; double reed, cone-shaped bore, nasal timbre, powerful sound
	cornett	most similar to modern trumpet, but not directly related	originally created by carving holes in animal horns; examples survive in Sweden from the 10th century	sound made with lip vibrations (like a brass instrument), but made of wood and having finger-holes, making it look like a woodwind instrument
	pipe	penny whistle	origins obscure, commonly used in Middle Ages and Renaissance; pipe and tabor performed together by a single musician, often to accompany dancing	duct flute with three or four holes, played with one hand
	tabor	snare drum		side drum with one or more snares (strings of gut that rattle against the drum head as it vibrates)
bas (quiet, suitable for indoor use)	recorder	modern recorder	invented (or imported to Europe) during the Middle Ages; in common use into the Baroque period	wooden duct flute with a thumb-hole and (typically) seven finger-holes; made in different sizes, with ranges corresponding to vocal ranges (soprano, alto, tenor, bass)
	fiddle	most similar to modern violin	origins obscure; Medieval bowed fiddle used by troubadours in 11th century, replaced in the Renaissance by the viol	stringed instrument played with a bow; sometimes with frets on the fingerboard (like a modern guitar)
	viol	"cousin" of modern violin family	developed in late 15th century, supplanted by violin family in the Baroque period	fretted, bowed string instrument with a wooden body; made in various sizes, all of which were played on the lap or resting on the legs (not on the shoulder like a modern violin or on the floor like a modern cello)
	lute	most similar to modern guitar	Arab ancestor of the lute was introduced into Europe by the Moors during their occupation of Spain; European lute established by 1350; lute held in high regard during the Renaissance; large repertoire of pieces; often used as accompaniment for voice	plucked, fretted string instrument with a wooden body; usually with 6–8 pairs of strings, tuned in unison (each pair is called a "course")
	harp	modern harp	Frame harps appeared in Europe by the 9th century	plucked string instrument whose resonating soundbox is roughly perpendicular to the strings; strung with wire or gut

3

The Renaissance

Introduction to the Renaissance

Some time ago it was fairly typical to view the medieval period as a Dark Age (in the West), with headlines about the Crusades and Black Death only sensationalizing the kind of problems people endured as they stood immersed in economic, social, and political upheaval, much of it attributable to the pernicious effects of power struggles involving church and state. But a closer look shows a number of bright spots at this time, such as during the ninth century (when notation was invented) and the great twelfth-century Gothic movement that gave us the expansive organum of the Notre Dame School. Overall, so much ingenuity was demonstrated in the arts throughout this era that some feel medieval accomplishments in music have rarely been surpassed. Nonetheless, there *were* problems at the time that weighed things down, including massive crop failures, plagues, and the Papal Schism (1378–1417). When they all finally passed, it may well have left many with a sense of energetic "rebirth." If they stopped to question why they felt this way, they may have sensed that they lived at the outset of an era some call Early Modern and others call the **Renaissance** (Fr. rebirth). In music, we set the dates for the Renaissance at 1450 to 1600, but even by 1400 many of the characteristic traits were in place.

Melozzo da Forli, "Angel playing music."

In the fields of painting, sculpture, literature, and political theory, the Renaissance has always been treated as a period of great rediscovery, a time when all the glories of the ancient world were proudly marched back into the mainstream, infusing everyone with a new secular spirit, at least at the higher class levels of society. At the time, an industrious group of scholars who translated the Greek works of Socrates, Aristotle, and many others into their own Latin founded an educational movement of far-reaching impact known as **humanism**. Putting their focus on the capacities of man, the humanists pushed intellectual inquiry away from the mystical and symbolic ideas that had been espoused by their "scholastic" forbears, who were often closely affiliated with the church. Amazing works of art by the likes of Leonardo da Vinci, Raphael, and Michelangelo are among the best fruits of the time. But it did not all move forward. The post-Renaissance execution of Galileo Galilei, founder of modern science, has been seen by many to represent the last gasp of an Age of Faith before an Age of Reason. Some point to this as revealing the strength of religion

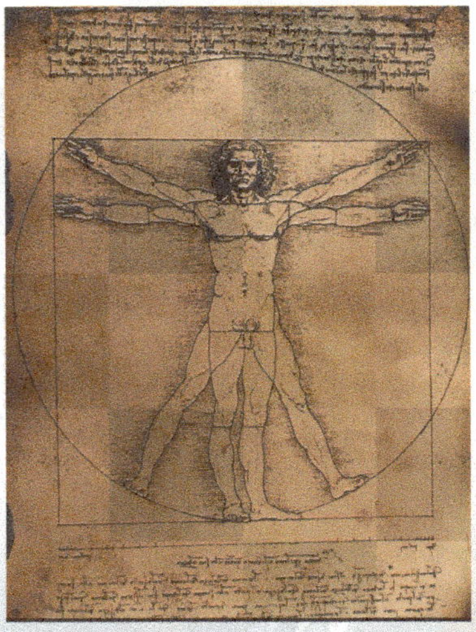

"The Vitruvian Man" by Leonardo da Vinci.

Michelangelo's "David."

in the Renaissance, a view which music history tends to support. Others see this as reflecting just how deeply the Renaissance movements had challenged the tenets of sacred medieval thought, and there are elements in music that reflect this as well. But this is to look rather far ahead.

Turning back now to the start of the new era, we begin with an interesting problem. Thanks to the issues surrounding music notation—and a somewhat determined effort to eradicate pagan music for prayer in the development of chant—in music there was no way to have a rebirth of ancient works on the scale of other arts. There was a rather cryptic music notation in place from ancient Greece, but no one could decipher it. So, as much as Renaissance musicians might have wished to recapture the music of the ancient world, none of them knew precisely, or even roughly, what it all sounded like. Musicians discovered that they were left out of the whole classical revival party just when it was all getting started.

The humanistic spirit, however, was something that the era's musicians certainly possessed. Indeed, since they were freed from the confines of an ancient system, Renaissance composers might be seen to have enjoyed clear advantages over their colleagues in other arts in expressing their new, spirited approach. The great age of musical complexity had not ended yet for them, though. They treasured too much their recent advances in rhythmic notation and other ideas to just let it all go, especially when it came off as somehow impressive. Throughout the Renaissance, composers were highly aware that their fellow composers would be judging their music, and so they felt the need to impress a very discerning audience. But at the same time, Renaissance composers were becoming more and more inspired by the idea that a general auditor could be moved by their sounds.

To this day we rely on music to alert our emotions to what lies behind the words of a song or a scene in a film. Renaissance composers were among the first to explore how music could work in tandem with other forms of expression, such as the word or the visual image. (Setting the proper emotional stage for prayer could be seen as one of the primary functions of chant. But from a Renaissance perspective, this was limited, as so many chants, with only subtle differences in the way they projected the text, could be seen to accomplish the same, undifferentiated, heightened state.) It is striking that from the start of the musical Renaissance, composers could be seen to devise more and more ways to draw the listener in. Eventually, composers attempted to react to every discernible emotional reaction that could be called for by the associated text. Thus it is possible to see something truly "early modern" developing in the Renaissance, in the sense that it puts music in the role we tend to see it in today—underlying and expressing emotions behind an idea.

As musicians developed ways to communicate with this idea about expressive immediacy, they cultivated the use of **chords** built on the **harmonic interval of the third**. This was meant, at first, to draw in the listener in the same way that perspective—the simulation of three-dimensional space on a two-dimensional surface—served painters of the era. For reasons that are somewhat difficult to justify by math alone (as the reckoning of a third as a consonant interval doesn't really "add up"), chords based on thirds seem to us as natural as a Raphael depiction of a courtyard with all its carefully developed perspective. From this time forward, or at least until some tried to destroy the system (in the early twentieth century), chords built on thirds would function as the basic building blocks of harmony in the West.

Even for Renaissance composers, though, the luxuriant sound of the third was not enough to fully serve their purposes. To coordinate things so that music could complement and enhance the ideas expressed in texts or dramatic scenes, they relied on all the musical elements—including rhythm, melody, harmony, and form—but gave special attention to **texture**. By alternating moments of dense polyphony with other moments of clear homophony, or adding or reducing voices at key places, or devising new schemes that mixed things up further, Renaissance composers turned their music into a kind of heightened speech. In the poetry, drama, and prose of the Renaissance, the humanist movement promoted a new emphasis on **rhetoric**, the art of persuasion. Today we tend to dislike certain aspects of rhetoric, which get cast as indulgent, superfluous, and most often redundant, but we still admire art, speech, and music that we believe can move us. The foundations for using music in this way were laid in the Renaissance.

In the 1500s, the West confronted two related events of major importance: the invention of **printing** and the **Reformation**. The effects of both can be clearly seen in the musical world. As far as printing is concerned, its main effect was to bring notated music to the ears of many, where before it had been the province of just a few. By their nature, **manuscripts** had kept matters confined to closed circles, although there were still ways to distribute things more widely. But with the advent of printing, mass production became the norm. Now people who had never met a certain composer could still hear his or her music. But music was still notated in the same way, and by now, of course, it took considerable training to be able to perform music from this rather advanced notation. So, in some ways, music was still confined to those who could bring musicians before them, and the idea of a mass, popular style was still a ways away. Yet it is telling that certain popular forms, such as the English ballad, did get their start at this time.

Soon after 1517, when Martin Luther voiced his complaints against what he saw as the abuses of the church, his followers took an irreversible step. They broke with the church to form a new denomination, now known as Lutheranism, under the banner of "protest." From this point forward, Christian Europe would be divided between those that held to the old faith, now designated as Catholic, and those who joined one of the new Protestant ones. Geneva, England, and other areas in northern Europe got swept into the new movements, while most of southern Europe, especially Spain and Italy, remained staunchly Catholic. Since music was so closely linked to prayer, it was thought to be a crucially important issue at this time, although views on music could be widely divergent. Catholics saw music as part of their venerable tradition, although they soon took steps to keep it under control. Protestants had widely differing views about music, depending on their denomination. The most radical suggested it might be good to drive music out of the church altogether, although no one actually went that far. Luther was a composer himself, and had very strong views about the role music might play. Many at the time viewed developments in music that made it more rhetorical as very important; music became a means to persuade others to remain in one faith, or to join a new one.

Statue of Martin Luther in front of the Frauenkirche in Dresden, Germany.

The Mass

Music historians see the development of the polyphonic **mass** in the early Renaissance as one of the most important accomplishments of Western culture and the main achievement of the fifteenth century. Certainly, in these pieces, musicians grappled with musical problems on an unprecedented scale. Masses were comprised of a whole series of movements (or units), and at this time composers were making audible links among them all. Composers of song cycles, opera cycles, progressive rock concept albums, and modern film scores owe a debt to the development of the **cyclic mass** in the Renaissance. As discussed in the last section, Guillaume de Machaut had already tackled all the Ordinary texts of the mass: the Kyrie, Gloria, Credo, Sanctus, and Agnus Dei. But Machaut did not try to unify them in any overt musical sense. Renaissance composers used specific musical devices to make their settings of all five movements so interrelated that they stood as one large whole.

Portrait of Guillaume du Fay and Gilles Binchois.

Intriguingly, the scope of musical time involved in performing a typical mass cycle, about 20 minutes, is almost exactly the same as that of Bach's cantatas, the most famous cycles of the late Baroque, as well as the great progressive rock albums of the 1970s, such as Pink Floyd's *Dark Side of the Moon.* Furthermore, just as Pink Floyd ventured into an even larger cyclic canvas with *The Wall*, some in the Renaissance got more ambitious than others (or "over the heads," as some critics of both maintain). The most massive work in the Renaissance was a cycle comprised of six full masses (and thus twenty interrelated movements). This complex, known as the Six Anonymous Naples *L'Homme Armé* Masses of the 1470s, was named after a single tavern tune ("The Armed Man") that runs through all twenty movements. It was never published in print and was left unattributed in the sole manuscript in which it was preserved, so we don't know who wrote it. It may have been composed by a group of musicians in collaboration. To this day, music historians study it carefully in the hopes of discovering its author(s), so he, she, or they can get their belated congratulations in the form of historical recognition.

In the masses of this time, we find some of the era's most ingenious musical techniques as well as some of its most compelling music. But, after its invention in the early Renaissance and the explosion of works in the mid-century, the mass as a cutting-edge genre took a backseat to the motet, where composers found a better means to develop their abiding interest in expressing texts. Many of the techniques, such as parody (see below) and "pervasive imitation," would appear in the mass and motet (and in other musical types too). Masses, especially in the hands of a master such as Pierluigi Palestrina, would represent some of the most important, and political, music ideas of the day. These techniques, terms, and representative efforts, such as Palestrina's, will be discussed below in the context of the motet.

Guided Listening

Agnus Dei from *L'homme Armé* Mass by Guillaume du Fay (1397–1474)

This mass uses a preexisting secular melody, "L'homme Armé" ("The Armed Man"), in the tenor voice. A mass that borrows from a secular source in this way is called an **imitation mass**. In the sixteenth century, it was common for favorite melodies to be borrowed and reused many times by many different composers. Although it may seem like stealing to us, the attitude toward intellectual property was different at that time. There were no copyright laws as we know them, and it was usually considered an honor to be quoted or imitated by other composers.

The "L'homme Armé" melody is difficult to hear in the context of the mass because it is used as an internal, structural voice instead of the dominant melody. If you wish, you can hear the original "L'homme Armé" melody here: http://www.rhapsody.com/artist/jeremy-summerly/album/dufay-missa-l-homme-arme/track/lhomme-arme.

The Agnus Dei, which is the final movement of the mass, contains three sections. The third section is a **canon**, meaning that it contains imitative sections that follow strict rules (think of "Row, Row, Row Your Boat"). In this case, the rule for the canon is stated as a riddle. The solution to the puzzle provides the formula that will produce the correct notes and rhythms for the singers to perform. The riddle reads, "Cancer eat plenus sed redeat medius" or "The Crab goes out full but comes back half." Part of the answer to the riddle is to sing the notes at half their original duration for the second part of the section. The notes must also be sung in reverse order at one point, which is implied by the backwards or sideways walk of the crab.

http://www.rhapsody.com/artist/jeremy-summerly/album/dufay-missa-l-homme-arme/track/agnus-dei

		Original text	*English translation*
0:00	Top two voices enter.	*Agnus Dei, qui tolis peccata mundi, miserere nobis.*	*Lamb of God, who takes away the sins of world, have mercy on us.*
0:14	Bottom two voices enter. "L'homme Armé" melody is sung in the tenor part, but is difficult to follow.		
2:32	Second section begins with a duet.	*Agnus Dei, qui tolis peccata mundi, miserere nobis.*	*Lamb of God, who takes away the sins of world, have mercy on us.*
3:38	After a brief duet with a different combination of voices, a third voice enters and it becomes a trio.		
4:45	Final section (including the "crab canon") begins.	*Agnus Dei, qui tolis peccata mundi, dona nobis pacem.*	*Lamb of God, who takes away the sins of world, grant us peace.*

The Motet

From the start of the Renaissance era, the **motet** was known simply as a musical setting of any Latin text. Most motets were on sacred subjects. Some served specific church functions, but many also were designed as showpieces for specific one-time events, such as the consecration of a new cathedral or to mourn the death of a notable individual. At the very start of the Renaissance, some composers were still writing complex isorhythmic motets in the medieval style, although even in these the sound was decidedly more "modern" in the sense of including the sound of the third in smoother rhythms and textures. The more cutting-edge composers, especially in England, were now experimenting with new ways to communicate with immediacy. There was even a term coined for the new musical style: **contenance angloise** (English face or manner), and it was represented very well in the music of **John Dunstable** (Dunstaple) (c. 1390–1453), an Englishman whose "Qualm tu pulchra es" epitomized the new style and the early Renaissance motet generally. When listening to the following example, note how clearly the words are enunciated and how the simple style, featuring thirds in smooth rhythms, brings an almost sensual feeling to the musical surface, mainly through the use of successive chords that feature the interval of the third. The luxurious sensual approach was fitting for the Song of Songs biblical source (see text below), but it also sounds natural and direct, which were the traits so admired in the new style. The top line is much more tuneful than many of the medieval motets and at times more tuneful than many medieval songs. Even if the Latin is unfamiliar to many of us today, most listeners can sense that this composer is trying to reach out to us and draw us in.

Guided Listening

"Quam pulchra es" by John Dunstable (c. 1390–1453)

Dunstable was an important figure in the popularization of the ***contenance angloise*** (English manner), which was a style of composing counterpoint that used very careful control of dissonance and featured harmonic thirds and sixths. Our modern system of harmony is based on thirds, so the sonorities in "Quam pulchra es" are more pleasing and familiar to our ears than earlier music that emphasized fourths and fifths and handled dissonance more loosely.

The text comes from Song of Songs (also known as Song of Solomon or Canticles), one of the shortest books of the Old Testament of the Bible. Although it is sometimes understood as a picture of God's love for Israel or Christ's love for the church, on the surface it is a poem about earthly love and erotic pleasure. Dunstable portrays the meaning of the text with rich harmonies and subtle word painting, while also providing a setting for the text that allows it to be easily understood.

http://www.rhapsody.com/artist/ensemble-amadis/album/music-and-chants-from-the-time-of-joan-of-arc/track/quam-pulchra-es-john-dunstable

		Original text	*English translation*
0:00	The male speaker begins, praising the beauty of his beloved.	*Quam pulchra es et quam decora carissima in deliciis.*	*How beautiful and fair you are, my beloved, most in your delights.*
		Statura tua assimilata est palmæ, et ubera tua botris.	*Your stature is like a palm-tree, and your breasts are like fruit.*
		Caput tuum ut Carmelus, collum tuum sicut turris eburnea.	*Your head is like Mount Carmel, and your neck is like a tower of ivory.*
1:19	After a brief pause, the female speaker responds to her lover by inviting him to go to the fields with her for an erotic encounter.	*Veni, dilecte mi, egrediamur in agrum.*	*Come, my beloved, let us go into the fields.*
		Et videamus si fructus parturiunt, si floruerunt mala punica.	*And we will see if the blossoms have born fruit, and if the pomegranates have flowered.*
		Ibi dabo tibi ubera mea.	*There will I give my breasts to you.*
		Alleluja.	*Alleluia.*

Drawing of Josquin des Prez.

By mid-century, 1450, composers of motets had fully assimilated the new English style and were now pushing it toward new expressive purposes. One of the most revered composers of this time was **Josquin des Prez** (c. 1450–1521). His music and career were so well admired that he, like a number of popular music stars in recent times, is usually referred to by only his given name, "Josquin." (One other example of his popularity: music sellers often ascribed music to him that he never composed, in the hope that consumers would buy music if they thought it was by Josquin.) Pushing further some of the naturalism of his predecessors, Josquin and those of his generation basically established the standard **"SATB"** (soprano, alto, tenor, bass) choir, allowing most singers to sing more naturally, within their own range. Josquin also explored and perfected a kind of texture that we call **pervasive imitation**. In this texture, the composer created musical lines melodies that various singers (those assigned to one part) would sing at different times. In musical circles it was important to note that the imitation of most Josquin motets was not fully continuous, but rather would break off at some point. Only occasionally did composers of this time write **canons** where the voices followed each other strictly and exactly. Whether it was a canon, or the more frequently used "pervasive imitative," the result was a texture that seemed natural, and even playful, in its homogeneity, as it was all based on the rather democratic idea that every part had an equal role to play in the texture. Although this was the most famous of the developments in texture at this time, it was by no means the only one. By shifting from one texture to another, Josquin found he could focus in on certain texts, bringing out their special importance for his listeners.

Guided Listening

"Ave Maria . . . virgo serena" by Josquin des Prez (c. 1450–1521), Motet

http://www.rhapsody.com/artist/the-tallis-scholars/album/the-tallis-scholars-sing-josquin/track/josquin-ave-maria-for-four-voices

		Original text	*English translation*
0:00	The four voices enter, one by one, in imitation of one another.	*Ave Maria, gratia plena.* *Dominus tecum, virgo serena.*	*Hail Mary, full of grace.* *The Lord be with you, serene virgin.*
1:01	Duet between soprano and alto is then imitated by the tenor and bass voices (paired imitation). Then, all voices singing together build to a peak on "laetitia" ("joy").	*Ave cujus conceptio,* *Solemni plena gaudio,* *Coelestia, terrestria,* *Nova replet laetitia.*	*Hail to you whose conception,* *With solemn rejoicing,* *Fills heaven and earth* *With new joy.*
1:48	Another point of paired imitation begins.	*Ave cujus nativitas* *Nostra fuit solemnitas,* *Ut lucifer lux oriens,* *Verum solem praeveniens.*	*Hail to you whose birth* *Was to be our solemnity,* *As the rising morning star* *Anticipates the true sun.*
2:34	Yet another point of paired imitation begins.	*Ave pia humilitas,* *Sine viro foecunditas,* *Cujus annuntiatio,* *Nostra fuit salvatio.*	*Hail pious humility* *Fruitful without man,* *Whose annunciation* *Was to be our salvation.*
3:08	Instead of counterpoint, this section uses chordal writing in which all the voices sing the same words at the same time (mostly). Meter changes from duple to triple.	*Ave vera virginitas,* *Immaculata castitas,* *Cujus purificatio* *Nostra fuit purgatio.*	*Hail true virginity,* *Immaculate chastity,* *Whose purification* *Was to be our purgation.*
3:38	Return to duple meter; paired imitation once again.	*Ave praeclara omnibus* *Angelicis virtutibus,* *Cujus fuit assumptio* *Nostra glorificatio.*	*Hail shining example* *Of all angelic virtues,* *Whose assumption* *Was to be our glorification.*
4:42	Chordal writing returns to allow for clear presentation of the final words.	*O Mater Dei,* *Memento mei. Amen.*	*O Mother of God,* *Remember me. Amen.*

Things seem to have stagnated a bit after the great advances of Josquin. If in his hands the motet was most often a vehicle for powerful and even dramatic forms of expression, many of his followers found themselves entranced solely by the technicalities associated with pervasive imitation, finding in the texture the fertile means to explore their musical ingenuity and their interest in musical richness and naturalism, but often at the expense of expression. Those today who admire the sheer sonic beauty of the music of the "post-Josquin generation" exclaim with admiration that they could "make the phone book sound great." But those who prefer to see a close connection between ideas and musical expression criticize them for writing music that seems oblivious to the text (and so they say that these composers "made everything sound like the phone book"). Things might have remained in this controversial state of non-expressiveness, were it not for the advent of print culture and the Reformation. These were the two events that brought about the most significant changes in compositional perspectives about the motet and its production.

Music in Print

When, in the mid-1450s, Johannes Gutenberg and partners invented the Western printing press with movable type and brought out their magnificent Bible, they did not concern themselves with music. But as the custom at the time was to include musical notes with the Psalter (the complete psalms of the Old Testament), it was not long before printers after them began to explore ways to incorporate music into their printed books. The craftsman and inventor who put music printing on the map was Ottavio Petrucci, whose work of 1501, if exacting and inefficient in some ways, set a new standard in elegance. Petrucci set special standards with the musical repertory he chose to print. Featuring the music of Josquin and also many motets, as well as lighter fare, he reflected the field in the way composers found most helpful for their professional growth. Soon thereafter, however, Renaissance craftsmen and women (and there were important women printers at this time) developed a way to print music as efficiently as any other kind of text, and for some time music would be produced on a scale that could be compared to its relative place in today's media.

One of the most obvious effects of print on music composition was its encouragement of modeling practices. As in the field of visual arts, where printed versions of famous paintings had a similar influence, the main effect of printing was to set standards for others to learn from and to try to outdo. The result in music was a new generic type called the **parody motet** (or **chanson** or **mass**, see below), based on the technique they referred to as parody or, more often, **imitation**. For these works, composers usually made a clear reference to the music of someone else, often works they discovered in printed collections. Through this practice composers raised the standards of their art, as they also spread new ideas about music's capacity for expression to the furthest reaches of the West.

Reformation(s)

When Martin Luther posted his ninety-five theses, or arguments with the church, in 1517, he seemed to expect that he'd be engaged in a fairly contained debate soon thereafter. Scholars now tend to agree that that would indeed have been the case were it not for the effects of print. As the means to foment rebellion, nothing could have been more effective than the mass production of propaganda for a specific cause. If printed music was hardly as incendiary as the typical political tract, print proved in the end to render music a rather powerful tool for protest in the Reformation era, when Protestants and Catholics more often than not saw each other as archenemies.

In territories where Catholicism remained strong, such as Italy and Spain, the uses of motets as political tools could be rather subtle, as the threats seemed remote enough that composers there could bask in the glory of their creations. But the very fact that composers such as the great Pierluigi Palestrina and Victoria composed more motets than many of their predecessors could be seen as an important consequence of religious politics. In the areas of Europe, such as the Netherlands, where religious wars were at their hottest, music could be used as a propaganda weapon, a means of spreading provocative ideas far and wide.

Page from a 1545 Protestant songbook.

Most difficult, but also most powerful, were the works of composers who worked in countries founded on a different religion. Such was the case for William Byrd (1540–1623), a professed Catholic Englishman who served as a court musician for Queen Elizabeth. Reacting to the religious turmoil left her by her sibling royals, the very Protestant Edward VI and the *very* Catholic Queen Mary Tudor (later known un-affectionately as "Bloody Mary"), Elizabeth quickly established herself as something of a moderate when she came to the throne. But during her long reign, she felt sufficient threat from Catholic forces to take up some of her sister's vicious means of religious and self-preservation, including hideously brutal public executions featuring hanging and quartering. For the consolation of friends and coreligionists, Byrd wrote motets that celebrated the lives and mourned the deaths of some whom Elizabeth had executed. But some of the most powerfully political music he wrote was directed to the Protestant establishment and to the queen herself. Even in print, Byrd included motets that seemed to make a pointed case for the English Catholic minority. In 1575, after extolling the queen as a musical judge *par excellence* in his preface, Byrd placed a motet that essentially told her that she was on the wrong side. In Byrd's motet *Emendemus in melius*, his semi-hidden message was that if the queen remained a Protestant, she would suffer eternal damnation; Byrd ended with a sentiment, "Let our people go," that would resonate for many years thereafter with all who felt persecuted by the powers that be.

Guided Listening

"Emendemus in melius" by William Byrd (c. 1540–1623), Motet

http://www.rhapsody.com/artist/william-byrd/album/motets-and-anthems-of-william-byrd/track/emendemus-in-melius

		Original text	*English translation*
0:00	All five voices sing the same words at the same time (with few exceptions), making it very easy to understand the text.	*Emendemus in melius* *Quae ignoranter peccavimus;* *Ne subito praeoccupati die mortis,* *Quaeramus spatium poenitentiae,* *Et invenire non possimus.*	*Let us amend* *The sins that we have committed through ignorance;* *Lest the day of death should come upon us suddenly,* *And we seek a place for repentance,* *But cannot find it.*

(continued)

		Original text	English translation
1:42	Top voice sings a high G (the highest note in this piece) on "mi-" of "miserere"	Attende, Domine, et miserere, Quia peccavimus tibi.	Hear, O Lord, and have mercy, For we have sinned against you.
3:05	Another high G in the top voice ("-no-" of "honorem")	Adjuva nos, Deus salutaris noster, Et propter honorem nominis tui Libera nos.	Help us, O God of our salvation, And, for the glory of your name, Deliver us.
3:52	A third and final high G in the top voice ("li-" of "libera")		

"Susanna at the Bath."

Secular Vocal Music in the Renaissance: Chanson and Madrigal

As they moved toward expressionism in their motets and masses of the early fifteenth century, composers seemed to revel in medieval styles when composing secular songs, which, as a genre, consequently hit something of a rut. Specifically, the courtly love theme and the *forme fixes* that had been so vital to the medieval genre were still running strong by the middle of the fifteenth century. One reason for this was probably the abiding love for romantic chivalry or neo-feudalism that the songs seemed to convey so well.

The chanson really changed, however, with the advent of print. One of the first casualties was the *forme fixes*; these complicated forms were no longer favored at all in the sixteenth century, when the chanson suddenly diversified considerably. If print opened music up to wide markets, booksellers wanted wares that would sell to their local clientele: this tension between potential international outreach and national consolidation tendencies shaped the chanson "product," so to speak. In Northern, Franco-Flemish areas, composers specialized in a style that related rather closely to the sixteenth-century motet. The **Franco-Flemish chanson** was less obviously "popular" than some other types. But some of them were distributed widely and attracted many compositional imitations. In one of the greatest imitation "complexes" of the sixteenth century, some 50 or so Catholic and Protestant composers set the same poem, one based on the biblical character Susanna, and even kept one of the parts basically intact, as they sought to outdo each other in a musical version of the ongoing religious war that had been spurred by the Reformation.

Guided Listening

Lasso, "Susanne un jour" ("Susanna Fair")

http://www.rhapsody.com/artist/various-artists/album/franco-flemish-masterworks/track/susanne-un-jour

The text of "Susanne un jour" comes from the Book of Daniel in the Old Testament in the Bible. This section is considered apocryphal by Protestants and Jews, but remains part of the Roman Catholic and Eastern Orthodox Bibles. In the story, two older men come across Susanna while she is bathing and begin to lust after her. They approach Susanna and tell her that they will accuse her of promiscuity unless she has sex with them. Susanna refuses to be blackmailed, is arrested, and is condemned to death. Daniel intervenes, the truth is discovered, and the old men are then executed for making the false accusation. In Reformation and Counter-Reformation art and writing, Susanna was used as a symbol of moral purity in the face of perversion and persecution.

		Original text	*English translation*
0:00	Brief paired imitation (top two voices followed quickly by bottom two voices).	*Susanne un jour d'amour solicitée* *Par deux viellardz, convoitans sa beauté,*	*Susanne, in a day of love, approached by* *Two old men lusting after her beauty,*
0:24	Notice how the top voices all cadence together, but the lowest voice moves on to the next phrase, "par deux viellardz . . ." When a cadence overlaps or becomes the beginning of the next phrase in this way, it is called an **elision** or an **elided cadence**. This continues throughout the piece, giving a sense of perpetual motion until . . .	*Fust en son coeur triste et desconfortée* *Voyant l'effort fait à sa chasteté.* *Elle leur dict, Si par desloyauté* *De ce corps mien vous avez jouissance,*	*Became sad and displeased in her heart* *Seeing their pursuit of her chastity.* *She said to them, "If through disloyalty* *You take pleasure from my body,*
1:30	All cadence together on "fait de moy" ("my responsibility"). This is the first cadence that is not elided. Following the cadence, all voices sing the next phrase "si ie fay résistance" ("if I resist") with the same rhythms and syllables of text at the same time. Both of these features are designed to emphasize these phrases and the fundamental moral message of the text.	*C'est fait de moy. Si ie fay résistance,* *Vous me ferez mourir en deshonneur.* *Mais j'aime mieux périr en innocence,*	*It is my responsibility. If I resist,* *You would make me die in disgrace.* *But I prefer to perish innocent,*
2:21	Even though B-flat has been used throughout the piece, the final cadence uses a B-natural instead. In modern music theory, we would say that this makes the final chord major instead of minor, which is surprising in the context of a piece that is minor overall. This is called a **Picardy third**, and was common in the Renaissance.	*Que d'offenser par peché le Seigneur.*	*Than to offend the Lord with a sin."*

To hear the piece performed on organ, click here: **http://www.rhapsody.com/artist/various-artists/album/susanne-un-jour/track/lassus-canzona-susanne-un-jour-libro-quinto-1605**

In Paris, things developed much differently; two **Parisian chanson** types emerged that had little to do with the motet or with politics per se. One was a lyric, melody-rich setting of the *carpe diem* (seize the day) theme and requited love. The other, called the narrative chanson, although not as frequently composed, was much more memorable, with its depictions of street fairs and battles, featuring the ingenious manipulation of musical notes to bring all the vivacious scenes alive.

Overall, nothing perhaps better demonstrates the effect of print on music than the history of the Renaissance chanson. Once an international style with regressive tendencies, by the end of the Renaissance it had splintered off into distinct styles, all with entertainment for identifiable market groups as the goal.

If the chanson was the genre that could boast the greatest shift, it was the **Italian madrigal** that became the true touchstone for secular music in the sixteenth century. Given that it began in about 1520 and reached a height by the end of the century, it could be said to be the first musical child of print, and, given its immense popularity that has lasted to this day, it could also be seen as reflecting the power of the new media.

In the early madrigal, composers experimented with the setting of refined Italian poetic types, such as the sonnets of Petrarch and his followers. But, as had the chanson, the madrigal gave way to lighter forms, such as the **ballatte**, where nonsense syllables such as "fa-la-la" became mainstays (and for those trying to identify madrigal types, "giveaways"). Most importantly, in all madrigal types, there was a cultivation of one idea: **word painting**. This was the process where ideas suggested by the text were portrayed somehow in the musical notes. In the light madrigal, the composers usually gravitated toward words with rather obvious musical potential, such as the directional words "up" or "down" or "high" or "low," which they could easily express with melodies that went up in range, or moved downward, etc.

Guided Listening

"My Bonny Lass (She Smileth)" by Thomas Morley (1557/8–1602)

The ballett (also *balletto* [Italian] or *ballet* [French]) is a sixteenth- or seventeenth-century dance that includes a **refrain** (returning section, like a chorus) of nonsense words, usually "fa-la-la." In "My Bonny Lass," there are actually two distinct refrains that recur. Like many balletts, this piece is in **strophic form**, which means that the same music is repeated for every stanza of text. The combination of the strophic form and the use of two refrains means that this piece contains quite a bit of repetition, which is a common feature of music for social dancing in any time period (including the present day).

http://www.rhapsody.com/artist/pro-cantione-antiqua/album/traditional-glees-and-madrigals/track/my-bonny-lass-she-smileth

		Original text
0:00	First stanza sung homophonically (all sing same words and rhythms at same time).	*My bonny lass she smileth,* *when she my heart beguileth.*
0:06	Fa-la-la refrain (characteristic of balletts) is sung contrapuntally (interlocking and contrasting melodies in the different parts).	*Fa la la la . . .*
0:18	First stanza is repeated at lower dynamic level.	
0:23	Refrain returns.	
0:35	Second stanza sung to same music as first stanza.	*Smile less, dear love, therefore,* *and you shall love me more.*
0:40	Second refrain (also contrapuntal).	*Fa la la la . . .*
0:47	Second stanza repeated at lower dynamic level.	
0:52	Second refrain returns.	
1:01	Third stanza.	*When she her sweet eye turneth,* *O, how my heart it burneth!*
1:06	First refrain returns.	*Fa la la la . . .*
1:18	Third stanza repeated at lower dynamic level.	
1:23	First refrain returns.	
1:35	Fourth stanza.	*Dear love, call in their light,* *or else you burn me quite!*
1:39	Second refrain returns.	*Fa la la la . . .*
1:47	Fourth stanza repeated at lower dynamic level.	
1:51	Second refrain returns.	

Guided Listening

"As Vesta Was (from Latmos Hill Descending)" by Thomas Weelkes (1601), English Madrigal

The Renaissance was a time of many religio-political wars throughout Europe. In England, the Protestants supported Queen Elizabeth I, but the Catholics hoped that Anna of Denmark (who was Catholic), the wife of James VI of Scotland, would become the ruler of England. Voicing support of Anna could be considered treason against Elizabeth, so messages of that kind were expressed in more subtle ways. In this case, the allegorical figures of Vesta and Oriana are used to obfuscate an anti-Elizabeth, pro-Anna message. On the surface, it seems that the "maiden queen," Oriana, represents Elizabeth. But Vesta, the Roman virgin goddess of family, hearth, and home, is a more appropriate metaphor for Elizabeth, who never married and was known as the "virgin queen." An interpretation of the song that casts Elizabeth as Vesta and Mary as Oriana would be supporting Elizabeth's descent from the crown and celebrating Anna's coronation and long life.

Musically, "As Vesta Was" is an excellent example of **word painting**, in which the musical setting of the words was used to demonstrate and exemplify the meaning of the text. For example, when the word "ascending" appears in the text, the music also ascends. See further examples in the guide below:

http://www.rhapsody.com/artist/the-cambridge-singers/album/flora-gave-me-fairest-flowers/track/as-vesta-was-from-latmos-hill-descending

		Original text
0:00	The first three words are sung homophonically, then the voices split into independent melodies (polyphony). On "descending" the voices sing descending patterns of pitches.	*As Vesta was from Latmos Hill descending,*
0:20	Rising figures on "ascending."	*She spied a maiden Queen the same ascending,*
0:37	Simple melody with repeated notes suggests simple country swains.	*Attended on by all the shepherds' swain;*
1:00	More falling figures on "running down amain."	*To whom Diana's darlings came running down amain,*
1:19	Two voices sing "two by two," then three sing "three by three," then all voices sing "together."	*First two by two, then three by three together,*
1:34	Solo voice exemplifies "all alone."	*Leaving their goddess all alone, hasted thither;*
1:45	Light imitative section suggests "mingling," "mirth," and "entertain."	*And mingling with the shepherds of her train,* *With mirthful tunes her presence did entertain,*
2:04	Homophonic chords used to set apart the final phrase that follows them.	*Then sang the shepherds and nymphs of Diana:*
2:15	Extended repetitions of "long live fair Oriana" exemplify the meaning of the phrase (with decidedly "long" held notes, and ending with the sound "Aaaaa Naah" (Anna), the true heroine of the set.	*Long live fair Oriana.*

Even in the **serious madrigal**, poetic refinement soon gave way to the rather obvious presentation of *risqué* topics, although you needed to be in on the joke to grasp this aspect. Some of the in-jokes were fairly well known. "Death," in the late Renaissance madrigal, for example, was almost always treated as an innuendo for sexual fulfillment, and thus all the dying that went on, even if it was portrayed gloomily as a kind of word painting, was not really so bad a thing to experience, no matter what it sounded like.

Guided Listening

"Moro, lasso, al mio duolo" by Carlo Gesualdo (1613), Madrigal

Carlo Gesualdo was an Italian nobleman, the Prince of Venosa and Count of Conza. Gesualdo is a colorful character in the history of music because of the strangeness of his composition style and the scandal in his personal life. Four years after he married his first wife, he ordered her assassination and that of her lover. He remarried a few years later, but the marriage was not a success, and he seems to have suffered from depression, mental instability, and a tendency toward self-harm.

Gesualdo's compositions mirror the strangeness of his personal life. His madrigals use chromatic harmony, striking dissonances, and sudden changes of mood and texture. He often chose erotic, dark, or sorrowful texts, and his settings seem designed to convey the language with the greatest possible intensity. Although some of his contemporaries were experimenting with these same materials and techniques, none took them to such extremes.

http://www.rhapsody.com/artist/maurice-bourbon-ensemble-metamorphoses/album/gesualdo--madrigaux-livre-vi/track/moro-lasso-al-moi-duolo

		Original text	*English translation*
0:00	Descending opening phrase establishes melancholic mood. Surprising harmonies introduce the listener to Gesualdo's chromatic language.	*Moro, lasso, al mio duolo,* *E chi può darmi vita,* *Ahi, che m'ancide e non vuol darmi aita!*	*I die, alas, in my suffering,* *And she who could give me life,* *Alas, slays me and does not want to help me.*
0:17	Word painting enlivens "vita" ("life"). Listen for recurrences of this figure.		
0:56	Words of first three lines repeat. Music is similar, but varied from the first iteration.		
1:48	Single line of text used to transition to final section	*O dolorosa sorte,*	*O sorrowful fate,*
2:08	Final section of the piece is dominated by the phrase "mi dà morte" ("gives me death"). Notice the frequent use of dissonance in this section.	*Chi dar vita mi può,* *Ahi, mi dà morte!*	*She who could give me life,* *Alas, gives me death.*
2:48	Final section is repeated		

The Baroque Era

4

Introduction: The Foundation of a Common Practice

© Rufous, 2013. Used under license from Shutterstock, Inc.

The Baroque era (1600–1750) in Western music history began in the nicely round and easy to memorize year of 1600, and with a great triumph, namely the **invention of opera**. This innovation ranks, along with the invention of music notation (c. 900), music printing (c. 1500), and phonographic recordings (c. 1900), as one of the most important in the whole Western tradition. It was a watershed moment, meaning that it marked a division point in history. Certainly, from this point on, music would never be the same. But opera's invention was also the result of much consistent thought and practice throughout the previous Renaissance era. It was mostly from a Renaissance perspective that the invention seemed like such a triumph, at least if the goal was to make music as expressive and powerful as Greek theater. Musicians of the time, we should note, only knew about Greek music through reading rather glowing accounts of it (they never understood the ancient music notation, as we've noted above). For those working on the expressive issue, the problem, as they saw it, was to find a musical texture that allowed individual singers to be as flexible and emotive as possible: in other words, to give soloists—singers who were articulating the words of a play—every opportunity to move audiences and draw them into the drama. To realize this ideal, a group of musicians and theorists decided, after some trial and error, that instrumentalists should now be required to read a new kind of music notation (called "figured bass," see below), one that allowed them to follow a singer's possibly impromptu rhythmic and dynamic shifts. The immediate result for the instrumentalist/singer relationship was something very close, in certain ways, to the way we set up singers with a "backup band" today. The backup band consists of instrumentalists that appear on stage with a singer as he or she performs in the spotlight, producing the main, or only, melody of a musical composition.

Baroque performers responded fairly quickly to the new demands of operatic music, suggesting that instrumentalists at the time had already developed some of the skills they needed to accompany singers in the new style. But there is no surviving evidence that they had ever bothered before to codify the practice in notation systems. Furthermore, and most importantly, it was only *after* the new instrumentalists' duties were put down in music notation—in figured bass—that the real changes in music history started to come about. Since the whole point was to highlight the activities of singers, it is somewhat ironic that it was the instrumentalists who ultimately gained the most by the new arrangement, at least in terms of long-term historical significance. Yet just as opera was developing as a great forum for the vocal arts, instrumentalists found that they too had a much stronger footing in the music world, as new opportunities to join orchestras and even to study music at newly instituted conservatories emerged for them for the first time in music history.

Let's pause for a moment to consider the human voice as a music-making device. The human body has always seemed rather strange and enigmatic, and there has always been something a little mysterious (if indubitably "natural"—see below) about how our voices make music. Instruments, however, were easy to study, and—thanks to the great work of Renaissance instrument makers such as the Stradivarius family—they could readily be improved upon and developed into complex but rationally organized machines, especially in the post-opera invention era when the instrument makers were working in ways that seem almost magically successful when looking back at all this. Soon the typical instrument, once treated as a substitute for the voice, would be admired for its own special qualities and championed for its unique contribution to the musical work. It was at this time, in fact, that instruments were first treated **idiomatically** (cultivated for their distinctive capacities). To this day composers are often evaluated on how well they "write for individual instruments," and they tend to be criticized if their music does not exploit the capabilities of the instruments they designate for performance. But it's really today's musical performers who like to judge composers on this basis.

At the time of the Baroque, all the new emphasis on instruments fit the spirit of this **Enlightenment Age**, when man's ability to understand the world was championed as an outgrowth of reasoned thinking and the application of scientific methods. Without making too much of it, Baroque musicians, inspired by the capabilities of instruments, made a huge contribution to the "science of music," as it were, by discovering (or inventing, again, perhaps) what we today call **tonality**. Tonality is a system based on three particular musical elements—melody, harmony, and form. Added, however, were a few principles—mainly that scales contained the material for building harmonies and that a hierarchical system should be followed involving harmonic progressions.

What was not really novel at all was the way in which tonality put limits on the number of pitches that could be used in a work of music. It was in the medieval era, and perhaps long before, that the infinitely large palette of possible intervals between notes became limited to two: namely the **half step** and the **whole step**. Musicians in the West also understood the idea of **octave equivalence** well before the Baroque, and had developed various **scales** (or modes) based on the idea that a select number of pitches (usually seven) could serve as the basis for a composition. But it was in the Baroque period that a further, decisive, limitation came about. After that time musicians dealt almost exclusively with just two scales: **major** and **minor**. The pattern of half and whole steps within an octave of a scale was severely limited, but creative people can respond to limitations by developing impressively elaborate structures (think of the way perspective was developed in painting, or how the special requirements of so many architectural works led to masterpieces of engineering and art).

Similarly, the **triad**, a chord built up of the intervals of a third—another essential element of tonality—was not a novelty of the Baroque. A triad likely resulted the first time three different people sang a piece of music together "in harmony." Renaissance musicians championed the sound of triadic music, as we've discussed above. But it was in the Baroque period that a hierarchy of triads was set up based on intervallic principles. Now and forever after, the **dominant** chord, one built on the pitch a fifth above the **tonic**, was determined to have special force—second only to the **tonic**—and all the triads of a scale fell under it as **predominant** chords (chords that would lead us to the dominant) of various importance.

With this hierarchical tonal system came a whole array of possible chord progressions, although they were always based on the idea that things moved **toward a harmonic goal**. The ultimate goal, or stopping point, was an arrival at the tonic chord, after a notable appearance of the dominant, and this was when (and how) a section or the whole piece ended. However, by means of **modulation**—moving from a tonality built on one scale to a tonality built on another—composers found they could delay the move to that predestined tonic as long as they wanted to and in various elaborate ways. Through the studied use of permissible chord progressions and modulation schemes, composers created musical **forms** of a special type (which we will discuss in more detail in our treatment of the Classical era) and found that they could treat musical elements like words of a literal language, although they did not yet decide upon a syntax, leaving that for composers of the next epoch, known as the Classical.

As we will soon discover, composers such as Johann Sebastian Bach, Antonio Vivaldi, and Georg Friedrich Handel did many amazing things with the tonal system. But even after they did, tonality, as a limiting system *per se*, was by no means exhausted. Rather, it was developed even further in the Classical era. From there, things eventually coalesced into a "problem" for composers of the late nineteenth century. With the belief that it was possible to communicate musically solely through the means of relations among the musical elements, led by instruments, the full expressive idea of opera was re-championed in the works of Richard Wagner and tonality itself was all but destroyed, at least to some and for some time.

So, in the end, a parable of sorts can be seen in the developments of the Baroque era. It was for the sake of vocal expression that the capabilities of instrumental music were first explored. But by the end of the nineteenth century, those very capabilities would be exploited to a point that ultimately challenged the validity of the tonal system that had been developed soon after opera itself had been invented.

The Invention of Opera

The roots of opera were deeply enmeshed in Italy's great Renaissance city of Florence, where humanism truly flourished. Under the banner of improving various art forms, a number of groups were formed there that became known as "cameratas" (named after the typical meeting place, which was someone's "room" or "chamber"). The point was to discuss interesting intellectual ideas in a convenient, convivial, and inspiring social setting. It was in the rooms of one Count Bardi that a group including some of the foremost experts on Greek theater and several musical composers and singers started to meet in the 1570s. This intellectual social group, known as the **Florentine Camerata**, has been rightly credited with the creation of a whole new music genre. Their goal was simply to recreate Greek theater of the past, but in researching the past and putting their findings into practice, they made a significant impact on music. It was a retro movement of sorts, but many at the time, including their own members, would soon describe what they came up with as something distinctly "new" (*Le nuove musichi*).

Although they never successfully deciphered Greek music notation, the Camerata made two key discoveries about the theater that related to musical developments. First, they discovered that Greek plays were sung throughout; second, they discovered, probably to their delight, that Greek music was known at the time to be a very powerful force that filled audiences with such strong feelings that it could influence their behavior. Both of these findings—the technical issue and the expressive nature—led to the formation of a new musical style that they called **monody**.

The technical issue—the need for constant singing throughout a play—presented a special problem. Everyone knew how to set poetry to music, but that kind of literature was only used sparingly in a dramatic work. And, unless one counts the liturgical setting of Latin texts (which no one did), no one in the Renaissance, or probably at any time after the Romans and Greeks, had worked out how music could be used to set the essential prose material of a play. But this kind of text was, at least as far as they saw it then, the main stuff of the dramatic work: it included all lines that were needed to advance the plot, which would include most of the words involved in any theater production. What they came up with they titled *stile recitativo*, and it remains an important part of opera to this day, although it's now called **recitative**. As the word suggests, the idea was to make what was sung sound as close as possible to the spoken word, or at least similar enough to serve the same purpose. For parts of the play that needed to be in verse, they didn't need to invent anything, as they already had the madrigal and related genres that served the kind of text that fit poetic forms. But they did give this "formal" kind of music a name—**aria**—that would be crucial for the future. This is yet another term that remains in use to this day.

Especially for recitative, but soon for arias as well, it was found best to use instruments with a single singer (or a pair of singers) rather than to include other voices in the texture. (Monophonic singing, such as in chant, may well have been the most authentic choice, but they didn't want to go back to that style.) To make this music as speech-like as possible and still retain the harmonic aspect, they devised a system known as **figured bass** (or ***basso continuo***), where a single line, composed only for the bass, was notated, and numbers were used to indicate the kinds of harmonies that were to be played above it. Especially at the time of opera's invention, but also for many years afterward, composers did not specify exactly what instruments would be used for the bass parts or for the chords, although they probably did have instruments in mind. From paintings of operatic performances and some descriptions and stage directions, we get the sense that various instruments could be used for the bass part—such as string bass, cello, and/or bassoon—and another set would be used to play the chords—in this case, various kinds of keyboards, lutes, guitars, and the like.

In solving the problem of how to make the sung music sound like speech—with the development of recitative—the Camerata also solved the problem of making the music more expressive of the emotions that the theatrical works were meant to evoke. Interest in the emotional aspects of music was not restricted to the Florentine Camerata, although they were among the first to emphasize how much it meant to them. For the remainder of the Baroque period, composers cultivated specific, single emotions, such as deep sadness, great joy, etc., in their works following the **Doctrine of Affections**. They criticized certain polyphony of the time—the madrigal and motet—for its complex tangle, when a group of singers performed texts, articulating words at different times. It turned out that all the flexibility afforded by the new instrument-based music texture gave performers the opportunity to slow down, or get louder or softer, etc., without having to worry if other singers would follow their lead. Instrumentalists, it seems, found it fairly easy to follow the whims of a single leader, and so the new texture was just what was needed to make music more expressive. Once this was combined with their skills in histrionics on stage, singers found they had the means to "milk" the texts they were singing, just as many singers do today, to get across a strong emotional feeling in their performances.

By the turn of the seventeenth century (c. 1600), the earliest operas were being performed. They included some wonderful music, but tend to be seen today as rather experimental, and are usually relegated to museum-like performances. But within a decade opera was to find one of its great composers, **Claudio Monteverdi (1567–1643)**, who stepped in a few years later—in 1607—with a version of the Orpheus myth that remains one of the most popular in the genre.

Claudio Monteverdi, at about age 30.

Statue of Orpheus holding a lyre in an ancient Greek style on top of a building in Vienna.

Guided Listening

Recitative, "At the bitter news" and Arioso, "Thou art dead" from Act II of *Orfeo*, Music by Claudio Monteverdi, Libretto (Story and Lyrics) by Alessandro Striggio (1607), Opera

Orfeo tells the story of Orpheus and Eurydice, which comes from Greek mythology. The story has been retold many times, and we have accounts of it from Virgil, Ovid, and Plato. On the day that Orpheus and Eurydice are married, she is fatally bitten by a snake and taken into the underworld, the dominion of the god Hades. Orpheus vows to travel to the underworld and retrieve Eurydice. He succeeds in charming Hades (and the other figures that he encounters) with his singing and playing, and Hades agrees to let Eurydice return to Earth with him. However, Orpheus must walk in front of her and not look back until both have left the underworld. Orpheus looks back a moment too soon and Eurydice vanishes again, this time forever.

The scene covered in this guide shows Orpheus receiving the news that Eurydice has died and making the decision to travel to the underworld to get her back.

Recitative, "At the bitter news"

http://www.rhapsody.com/artist/various-artists/album/monteverdi-lorfeo-emi-classics/track/orfeo-atto-secondo-in-un-fiorito-prato-messagiera
(listening guide begins at 2:46)

		Original text	*English translation*
		Shepherd I	
2:46	Simple recitative (accompanied by *basso continuo* only). The shepherds comment on Orpheus's reaction to the news that his new bride, Eurydice, has died.	*A l'amara novella* *Rassembra l'infelice un muto sasso* *Che per troppo dolor non può dolersi.*	*At the bitter news* *the unhappy man seems like a speechless rock* *and through too much grief cannot grieve.*
		Shepherd II	
		Ahi, ben avrebbe un cor di tigre o d'orsa *Chi non sentisse del tuo mal pietade* *Privo d'ogni tuo ben, misero amante.*	*Ah, he would have the heart of a tiger or bear* *that did not feel pity at your misfortune,* *deprived of every happiness, wretched lover.*

(continued)

Arioso, "Thou art dead"

http://www.rhapsody.com/artist/various-artists/album/monteverdi-lorfeo-emi-classics/track/orfeo-atto-secondo-tu-se-morta-orfeo

		Original text	English translation
		Orpheus	
0:00	Orpheus overcomes his shocked silence and laments her loss. An organ holds long notes in the background.	*Tu se' morta, mia vita, ed io respiro?* *Tu se' da me partita* *Per mai più non tornare, ed io rimango?*	*You are dead, my life, and do I breathe?* *You are gone from me* *never to return, and do I remain?*
0:52	When Orpheus mentions going down into the underworld to retrieve Eurydice, the vocal line descends as if to demonstrate the idea.	*No, che se i versi alcuna cosa ponno,* *N'andrò sicuro a' più profondi abissi,* *E, intenerito il cor del re de l'ombre,*	*No, for if my verses can do anything,* *I will go surely to the deepest abysses,* *and having softened the heart of the King of Shades,*
1:15	The image of bringing Eurydice back up to Earth is illustrated with a flourish in the high register on the word *stelle* (stars).	*Meco trarrotti a riveder le stelle:* *O, se ciò negherammi empio destino,* *Rimarrò teco, in compagnia di morte.*	*I will bring her back to see again the stars:* *Oh, if wicked destiny refuses me this,* *I will stay with you in the company of death.*
1:40	Orpheus's growing determination is depicted by a rising vocal line.	*Addio, terra, addio cielo e sole, addio.*	*Farewell earth, farewell heaven and sun, farewell.*

Guided Listening

Aria, "Powerful spirit" from Act III of *Orfeo* (*Orpheus*), Music by Claudio Monteverdi, Libretto by Alessandro Striggio (1607), Opera

http://www.rhapsody.com/artist/various-artists/album/monteverdi-lorfeo-emi-classics/track/orfeo-atto-terzo-possente-spirito-e-formidabil-nume-orfeo

		Original text	English translation
Aria		*Orpheus*	
0:00	Orpheus addresses Charon, the ferryman of the river Styx. He must convince Charon to grant him passage into the underworld. To impress and charm the ferryman, Orpheus sings in a florid style. Notice the violin flourishes above the *basso continuo.*	*Possente spirto, e formidabil nume,* *Senza cui far passaggio a l'altra riva* *Alma da corpo sciolta in van presume,*	*Powerful spirit and fear-inspiring god,* *without whom to take passage to the other bank* *a soul, freed from the body, presumes in vain,*

http://www.rhapsody.com/artist/various-artists/album/monteverdi-lorfeo-emi-classics/track/orfeo-atto-terzo-ritornello-violino-i-e-ii

0:00 Instrumental interlude (*ritornello*) performed by *basso continuo* and two solo violins.

http://www.rhapsody.com/artist/various-artists/album/monteverdi-lorfeo-emi-classics/track/orfeo-atto-terzo-non-vivio-no-che-poi-di-vita-e-priva-orfeo

0:00	Orpheus's aria continues, this time joined by cornettos above the *basso continuo.*	*Non viv' io, no, che poi di vita è priva* *Mia cara sposa, il cor non è più meco* *E senza cor com' esser può ch'io viva?*	*I do not live, no, since when, deprived of life,* *was my dear bride, my heart was no longer with me,* *and without a heart how can it be that I live?*

http://www.rhapsody.com/artist/various-artists/album/monteverdi-lorfeo-emi-classics/track/orfeo-atto-terzo-ritornello-cornetto-i-e-ii

0:00 The *ritornello* returns, this time performed by two solo cornettos and *basso continuo.*

Orpheus's aria continues for several more verses, which are not included in this listening guide. If you would like to hear them, follow these links:

- Next verse: **http://www.rhapsody.com/artist/various-artists/album/monteverdi-lorfeo-emi-classics/track/orfeo-atto-terzo-a-lei-voltho-il-camin-per-laer-cieco-orfeo**
- Ritornello, featuring harp: **http://www.rhapsody.com/artist/various-artists/album/monteverdi-lorfeo-emi-classics/track/orfeo-atto-terzo-ritornello-arpa**
- Next verse: **http://www.rhapsody.com/artist/various-artists/album/monteverdi-lorfeo-emi-classics/track/orfeo-atto-terzo-orfeo-son-io-che-deuridice-i-passi-orfeo**
- Final verse: **http://www.rhapsody.com/artist/various-artists/album/monteverdi-lorfeo-emi-classics/track/orfeo-atto-terzo-sol-tu-nobile-deo-puoi-darmi-aita-orfeo**

After Monteverdi's great achievement, the Italian style of opera, with its distinctive recitative and aria elements, became an international standard, spreading to France and England. The English composer Henry Purcell wrote several *masques* as well as an opera, *Dido and Aeneas*. In the example below, note how repetitions of the "basso ostinato" (a constantly repeating pattern in the bass) bring out the pathos of the drama at the point when Dido announces her wish to end her own life.

Guided Listening

Recitative, "Thy hand Belinda" and Aria, "When I am laid in earth" from Act III of *Dido and Aeneas*, Music by Henry Purcell, Libretto by Nahum Tate (1689)

The plot of *Dido and Aeneas* is taken from Virgil's *Aeneid*, an epic poem. The story follows Dido, Queen of Carthage, who falls in love with the Trojan hero Aeneas. When Aeneas abandons her to pursue the destiny that the gods have foretold for him, Dido dies of a broken heart.

http://www.rhapsody.com/artist/various-artists/album/purcell-dido-and-aeneas-decca-international/track/thy-hand-belindawhen-i-am-laid-in-earth

Recitative		**Dido**
0:00	Abandoned by her lover, Aeneas, and sensing that her death is near, Queen Dido asks for comfort from her servant, Belinda.	*Thy hand, Belinda, darkness shades me,* *On thy bosom let me rest,* *More I would, but Death invades me;* *Death is now a welcome guest.*
Aria		
1:10	*Basso ostinato* alone in cellos and double bases	*When I am laid in earth,* *May my wrongs create* *No trouble in thy breast;*
1:31	Dido begins to sing her farewell. Under her, we hear the *basso ostinato* with strings.	
1:54	*Basso ostinato* repeats as the singing continues.	
2:17	*Basso ostinato* repeats.	
2:40	*Basso ostinato* repeats.	
3:04	*Basso ostinato* repeats.	*Remember me, but ah! forget my fate.*
3:25	*Basso ostinato* repeats.	
3:47	*Basso ostinato* repeats.	
4:08	*Basso ostinato* repeats.	
4:34	The voices drop out and the *basso ostinato* repeats with strings only.	
4:52	*Basso ostinato* repeats with the strings a final time.	

Instrumental and Concerted Music of the Early to Mid-Baroque

People who bought their music in the 1500s would have expected to find it scored for voice alone, although there were exceptions (and of course what they did with this vocal music was their own business; they could well have played it all on instruments). From 1600 onward, though, they would have to look carefully to find music that excluded instruments on the page. Changes are never quite as abrupt as they seem from a distance, but it is clear that music composition and consumption shifted rather dramatically after the first operas were produced. It happened quickly enough that the printers had not fully developed the means to print the new styles, and some composers actually went back to manuscripts for promulgating their art. Nonetheless, thanks to engraving techniques, music for any number of instruments could soon be produced, and music exclusively for voices soon became the exception rather than the rule.

Opera was not the only form of music to feature instrumentalists and vocalists together. In the church and outside the church, many musicians adopted the new style featuring recitatives and arias in works that were never staged (unlike opera). These operatic-styled works we now call **cantatas** or **oratorios**, although at the time they didn't feel the need to be so specific, and sometimes just called them "music." In some cases it is almost impossible to tell cantatas and oratorios apart from opera, at least without knowing whether or not they were actually staged. One feature that did begin to distinguish them early on was the featured use of chorus, which was not as common in opera. By the end of the Baroque period, we will see that Bach and Handel had clear ideas about these works and how they were different from the operas of the time, especially their choruses.

Thanks to all the new activity, singers were getting used to sharing the stage with the *basso continuo* group and other instrumentalists. But this era also witnessed the first great influx of music composed exclusively for instrumentalists. Some composers, many of them instrumentalists themselves, wrote for individual instruments, such as keyboards or guitars (more often lutes). We call these **solo** works, and they featured improvisatory writing of a "show-off" variety as well as music associated with dance, some of which were called **sonatas** (a term that would remain in use long after the associations with dance forms had passed). In these dance works we find one of the signal moves toward tonality, in that the basic harmonic movement became predictable and usually involved a decisive move toward the dominant harmony in one section, and then a move back to the tonic in another. Today we call this **binary** form, and it was the standard for the dance style of music at this time (and for many years afterward). It is worth noting here that only some of these pieces actually served the needs of dancers. Many others were what we call "stylized dances," in that the music, as much as it fit the dance style, was intended for purely musical consumption.

Not all composers wrote for soloists. Some provided music for small groups of performers, and others still wrote for larger groups of instrumentalists. Because musicians at the time thought of them quite differently, today we make a clear distinction between pieces written for these small and large ensembles. The former we tend to call **chamber** music and the latter we call **orchestral** or **symphonic**. At the time, it is probably worth noting that smaller groups would likely perform in a room, or chamber. Later, it becomes more important to note that when writing for chamber ensembles, composers specifically designed their music for one person per part. Conversely, even though orchestras then were smaller then than they are now, composers soon began to treat orchestral music as music where multiple instrumentalists would read a single musical line together, acting as a chorus of sorts.

One of the great chamber types was the **trio sonata**. It was scored for two violins—treated as soloists—and an accompaniment group (the *basso continuo*) who performed the figured bass, just as they would in operas, cantatas, and oratorios. The word "trio" applies to the lines of music, of which there were three. It doesn't account for the "chording" instrument, or fourth player, who read the numbers. So, if you are ever asked, "How many performers does it take to play a trio sonata?" be sure to say, "Four or more!" Just as in the **sonata** for keyboards and lutes, the tonal system can be seen to emerge in these chamber pieces. In fact, one of the main kinds of trio sonata, the **chamber sonata**, was really nothing more than a set of dances for the four-person "trio" lineup, and so it too followed the binary form. The other type, which they called a **church sonata** (as some were featured in church), relied less on the dance and more on what we call "abstract" forms (meaning "purely" musical). It is not obvious that one type of trio sonata was valued over the other, but it is nonetheless clear that as the Baroque period moved forward, composers became more and more comfortable writing for instruments without having to resort to models in dance music and music for voice.

replaced by quartet -Haydn

Guided Listening

Trio Sonata in C major, Op. 4, No. 1 by Arcangelo Corelli (1694)

http://youtube/irqPhfCPRvQ

Arcangelo Corelli (1653–1713) was one of the first composers to earn his fame through instrumental composition alone. His body of work is small and he composed primarily in only three genres (solo sonata, trio sonata, and concerto), but his pieces were very influential.

Although this trio sonata has four movements, the entire piece only takes about six minutes to perform.

0:00 First movement, **Prelude**, begins. A "walking" bass line can be heard in the cello.
0:35 The bass line is now moving twice as fast.
0:46 The bass returns to its original pace.

1:19 Second movement, **Corrente**, begins. A corrente is a lively, triple-meter dance. In this case, the first violin and cello have the important parts.
1:32 Section A is repeated.
1:46 B section begins.
2:04 Syncopation is used to embellish the movement toward the final cadence.
2:11 B section is repeated.

2:40 Third movement, **Adagio**, begins with slow, sustained notes.
2:57 A strong **dissonance** (clash between notes) is resolved into a more **consonant** (restful, pleasant) harmony. This happens several times in sequence, and the sequence itself will return several times.
4:14 After a brief pause, cadential chords signal the end of the movement.

4:33 Fourth and final movement, **Allemanda**, begins. The two violins move against each other while the cello moves quickly underneath them.
4:54 Repeat of the A section, followed by a pause.
5:15 Beginning of B section.
5:28 A sudden (and brief) shift from major to minor.
5:36 B section is repeated.

It is probably fair to say that the most durable of the Baroque instrumental forms was the **concerto**; composers still write these quite frequently today. In the Guided Listening below, note the discussion of **Vivaldi** and **ritornello** form, as the latter idea—with its pitting of a small group of soloists against a larger group—has been a hallmark of orchestral concertos ever since. Vivaldi's *Four Seasons* stands as one of the most treasured of concerti, and also, as it tells a story, is an early example of orchestral **program** music (music based on a story or idea).

Guided Listening

First Movement (*Allegro*) of the Violin Concerto in E major, Op. 8, No. 1, "Spring" by Antonio Vivaldi (early 1700s)

Antonio Vivaldi (1678–1741) composed over 500 concertos in his lifetime. Many of these pieces were intended for performance at the Ospedale della Pietà, an all-female orphanage where Vivaldi taught and gave recitals. Although he was a priest by profession and is now known primarily as a composer, his contemporaries knew him as a violinist. His virtuosity is reflected in the way he wrote for the violin, and is especially apparent in his violin concertos.

The standard form for the first movements of Baroque concertos is called **ritornello** form. In this form, a section returns over and over again, in whole or in part, and is always played by the full orchestra. This repeated section is called the ritornello. Sections that feature the soloist alternate with statements of the ritornello.

Published with the "Spring" concerto is the following sonnet:

Original text	*English translation*
Giunt' è la Primavera e festosetti	*Spring has arrived and merrily*
La Salutan gl' Augei con lieto canto,	*The birds hail her with happy song*
E i fonti allo Spirar de' Zeffiretti	*And, meanwhile, at the breath of the Zephyrs,*
Con dolce mormorio Scorrono intanto:	*The streams flow with a sweet murmur:*
Vengon' coprendo l' aer di nero amanto	*The thunder and lightning, chosen to proclaim her,*
E Lampi, e tuoni ad annuntiarla eletti	*Come covering the sky with a black mantle,*
Indi tacendo questi, gl' Augelletti;	*And then, when these fall silent, the little birds*
Tornan' di nuovo al lor canoro incanto:	*Return once more to their melodious incantation:*
E quindi sul fiorito ameno prato	*And so, on the pleasant, flowery meadow,*
Al caro mormorio di fronde e piante	*To the welcome murmuring of fronds and trees,*
Dorme 'l Caprar col fido can' à lato.	*The goatherd sleeps with his trusty dog beside him.*
Di pastoral Zampogna al suon festante	*To the festive sound of a shepherd's bagpipe,*
Danzan Ninfe e Pastor nel tetto amato	*Nymphs and shepherds dance beneath the beloved roof*
Di primavera all' apparir brillante.	*At the joyful appearance of spring.*

Many of the images evoked in the poem can be heard in the music. In fact, Vivaldi wrote some lines of the sonnet into the score to make it clear that particular musical moments pertained to specific imagery. The first eight lines correspond with the first movement of the concerto.

http://www.rhapsody.com/artist/various-artists/album/vivaldi-the-four-seasons-bach-air-pachelbel-canon-mend/track/le-quattro-stagioni-the-four-seasons-op-8-concerto-no-1-in-e

0:00 Ritornello part 1.

0:07 Ritornello part 1 returns, this time ***pianissimo*** (very quietly).

0:14 Ritornello part 2.

0:23 Ritornello part 2 returns, *pianissimo*.

0:30 "Spring has arrived and merrily / The birds hail her with happy song." Solo violin and two additional violins perform high figures that resemble birds chirping.

1:04 Ritornello part 2 returns.

1:12 "And, meanwhile, at the breath of the Zephyrs, / The streams flow with a sweet murmur." Flowing figures begin quietly, then grow louder. This gesture is repeated.

1:35	Ritornello part 2 returns.
1:42	**Tremolos** (trembling sound created by quick repetitions of a single note) in the orchestra, fast rising scales in violins. The mood shifts from cheerful to somewhat ominous. "The thunder and lightning, chosen to proclaim her, / Come covering the sky with a black mantle."
1:49	Solo violin performs agitated figures, continuing the feeling of unrest.
2:09	Ritornello part 2 returns, this time in minor.
2:17	"And then, when these fall silent, the little birds / Return once more to their melodious incantation." Solo violin again evokes the birds' song.
2:35	Ritornello part 1 returns, this time with slight variations.
2:46	Final solo violin section.
3:01	Ritornello part 2 returns.
3:09	Ritornello part 2 returns, *pianissimo* at first, then growing louder approaching the final cadence.

Bach, Handel, and the Late Baroque

Johann Sebastian Bach (1685–1750)

If there ever was a composer who had music in his blood, it was the German composer Johann Sebastian Bach (1685–1750). Not only could he trace his musical ancestry back well into the early Renaissance period and perhaps earlier, he would also father a number of composers and performers of great stature and fame. Bach's music continues to be revered above almost any other composer's in Western tradition, and for good reason, but this was not fully recognized at the time he was composing it. In his own lifetime, Bach was known more for his performance skills, as an organist and also, rather late in his career, as a conductor and music director of the great Lutheran church in Leipzig, *Thomaskirche*, where he ran a church music establishment and served as a teacher. Bach apparently never set foot outside Germany—in notable contrast to his great musical cosmopolitan colleague Friedrich Handel (see below). But Bach did move around a lot *within* Germany, holding a number of different positions at various musical establishments of various sizes that made various demands on him. Bach's employment history is worth noting for (at least) two reasons.

First, with Bach we find someone who really embodied the idea that music was a profession as well as an art, if only because in so much of his music one can find a special job-related reason why it was composed. The instances when Bach composed music just for the sake of doing so stand out; he wrote a justly famous "B minor Mass," for example, in that "art for art's sake" spirit. Bach's "purposeful" works ranged widely. He composed quite a bit of music simply with the intention of teaching others. Because he wrote so much music of this kind—a type we call now **didactic music**—specifically to teach members of his own family, much of it is decidedly difficult to perform and difficult to comprehend or analyze. Obviously, the target audience, Bach's offspring, included some outstanding musicians in their own right, and Bach needed to challenge and inspire them with musical works of a notable complexity.

Thomaskirche in Leipzig, Germany, where Bach served as cantor.

Bach also wrote works for himself. All accounts suggest he was an extraordinarily talented improviser as well as a composer; many of his most exciting musical works were never written down, and we will never experience them (sadly!). But on some occasions, such as when he was asked to test out the capabilities of a new organ (a job he seemed very much to enjoy), Bach wrote out the notes that he would play for those attending the church where the organ was located. Some of Bach's solo organ works are incredibly rich in musical display—they are real showpieces—and most rank among the best and most important works ever written for that instrument.

Twice in his career, Bach worked for patrons (we'll discuss this term at more length when we get to Haydn) who expected him to write a lot of music for entertainment purposes. For these assignments, Bach produced concertos, works for chamber ensembles and solo instruments following the forms that had been developed in the early and mid-Baroque period, such as the binary dance form and the solo-ritornello concerto forms we discussed above. Bach wrote no operas, but his Passions (settings of the gospels of St. John and St. Matthew) alone show that he was an extraordinarily powerful musical dramatist.

Bach did most of his compositional work for religious establishments, and the sheer amount of church music he produced is staggering. Because he viewed himself as a professional composer and not as an artist in the way we define the term, with implications of high status and "genius," Bach was more than willing to work often and steadily as a composer—he didn't wait for "inspiration." So, Bach was extraordinarily **prolific**, which means simply that he wrote a lot of musical works. (It is amusing, in this light, to note that he also apparently sired nineteen or more children; he did a lot of . . . well, everything.) Every Sunday, and sometimes more than once a week, Bach was asked to produce a full-scale **cantata**, and by this time the cantata had grown into a composite work of about twenty minutes including seven or so movements of intricate music. Many of Bach's cantatas opened with a grand chorus that was fully orchestrated, then ran through various arias and recitative sections (like an opera), ending with a hymn-like setting featuring a chorus again. Revealing his Lutheran roots, as well as his position as a music director at Lutheran establishments, Bach made many references to the monophonic chorales (tunes for religious texts) that had been established at the time of the Reformation when Martin Luther wrote a few himself. In his many cantatas—of which we believe there may have been 500 or more (about half of them have been lost)—chorales often function in the same way that chant functioned in medieval and Renaissance church music before the Reformation.

Lutherans rightly take pride in Bach's extraordinary musical accomplishments, and he was by all accounts a sincerely devout and rather intellectually stimulated theologian. This is reflected in the way he cast ideas of profound insight into some of his major works, such as the St. Matthew and St. John Passions, which he composed in a grand cantata-based style. But what Bach is perhaps most known for, across the genres and styles of music he composed, are his demonstrations of awe-inspiring counterpoint.

Guided Listening

First Movement of *Wachet auf, ruft uns die Stimme* by Johann Sebastian Bach (1731), Cantata

This cantata contains seven movements, the first of which is based on a sixteenth-century Lutheran **chorale** (hymn or religious folk song of the Lutheran church) entitled *Wachet auf, ruft uns die Stimme*, which is also the name of the entire cantata. The chorale tune is structured in AAB form. There are seven musical phrases within this form: A(1, 2, 3) A(1, 2, 3) B(4–7, 3). As you can see, phrase 3 occurs at the end of both A sections and the B section, so the same melody is sung (with different words) at the end of every section.

The texture is very complex, but the returns of the three parts of the ritornello help the piece sound organized and coherent. Throughout the piece, statements of the ritornello overlap and alternate with phrases from the chorale, so you may hear part of a ritornello section during a chorale phrase.

http://www.rhapsody.com/artist/various-artists/album/bach-js-johannes-passion-wachet-auf-ruft-uns-die-stimme/track/chor-wachet-auf-ruft-uns-die-stimme

Section A

0:00	Ritornello part 1, first statement		
0:09	Ritornello part 2, first statement		
0:17	Ritornello part 3, first statement		
		Original text	*English translation*
0:33	Chorale phrase 1	*Wachet auf, ruft uns die Stimme*	*Awake, a voice is calling*
0:51	Ritornello 1		
0:59	Chorale phrase 2	*Der Wächter sehr hoch auf der Zinne*	*From the watchmen high in the tower*
1:18	Ritornello 2		
1:29	Chorale phrase 3	*Wach auf, du Stadt Jerusalem*	*Awake, Jerusalem*
Section A is repeated, with new words			
1:50	Ritornello 1, 2, 3		
2:23	Chorale phrase 1	*Mitternacht heißt diese Stunde*	*Midnight is the hour*
2:41	Ritornello 1		
2:49	Chorale phrase 2	*Sie rufen uns mit hellem Munde*	*They call us with clear voices*
3:09	Ritornello 2		
3:19	Chorale phrase 3	*Wo seid ihr klugen Jungfrauen?*	*Where are the Wise Virgins?*
Section B			
3:41	Variation of ritornello parts 1, 2, and 3; modulation to a new key		
4:05	Chorale phrase 4	*Wohl auf, der Bräutgam kömmt*	*Get up, the Bridegroom comes*
4:20	Ritornello 1		
4:25	Chorale phrase 5	*Steht auf, die Lampen nehmt*	*Rise up and take your lanterns*
4:44	Extended free imitation by altos, tenors, and basses, followed by chorale phrase 6	*Alleluja*	*Alleluia*
5:29	Ritornello 1		
5:39	Chorale phrase 7	*Macht euch bereit* *Zu der Hochzeit*	*Prepare yourselves* *For the wedding*
6:17	Chorale phrase 3	*Ihr müsset ihm entgegen gehn*	*You must arise and meet him*
6:40	Ritornello 1, 2, 3		

In this class we've been discussing various textures, such as the imitative texture that was used quite frequently in the Renaissance, especially in sacred works. With Bach we find the same kinds of ideas, but combined now with a new approach to form and harmony, as was encouraged by the new opportunities to work in a music governed by ideas. With the rules of tonality setting the boundaries he needed to control his actions, Bach created **canons**, where one line of melody was set against itself (which we've discussed with Palestrina, Josquin, and others), and **fugues**, which alternated imitative passages and "free" counterpoint. In "free" passages the melodies placed in counterpoint were not directly related to one another. Like some of his Renaissance forebears, Bach experimented with various ways to turn a single melodic line into different things by either: 1) slowing it down proportionally (**augmentation**), 2) speeding it up proportionally (**diminution**), 3) making it move from its last note back to its first note (**retrograde**), or 4) making all the intervals reverse direction so that what had originally gone up a certain interval would now go down (**inversion**).

In some ways, it's easier to show how all this was done through the notation itself. But even if it looks, and perhaps sounds, easy, it turns out that it is very difficult to make music of this kind that pleases audiences. One of the reasons why Bach is considered such a musical genius is that he seemed to have a Midas touch when it came to composition. Everything he tried turned to musical gold. By exploring and mastering so many contrapuntal techniques, Bach set a standard for compositional excellence that is still regarded with awe to this day.

Guided Listening

"Little" Fugue in G minor by Johann Sebastian Bach

http://www.rhapsody.com/artist/various-artists/album/sony-classical---great-performances-1903-1998-sony-classical/track/fugue-in-g-minor-bwv-578-instrumental

A fugue is a contrapuntal composition for two to five parts. Every fugue begins with an **exposition** in which the subject (the main theme) is presented in each part. After the exposition, sections of free counterpoint (called **episodes**) alternate with returns of the subject.

In this fugue, there are four parts. A single instrument, an organ, plays all of the parts. The chart below shows the pattern of episodes and statements of the subject in this piece. Voice 1 is the highest and voice 4 is the lowest. See if you can follow the high and low statements of the subject as you listen.

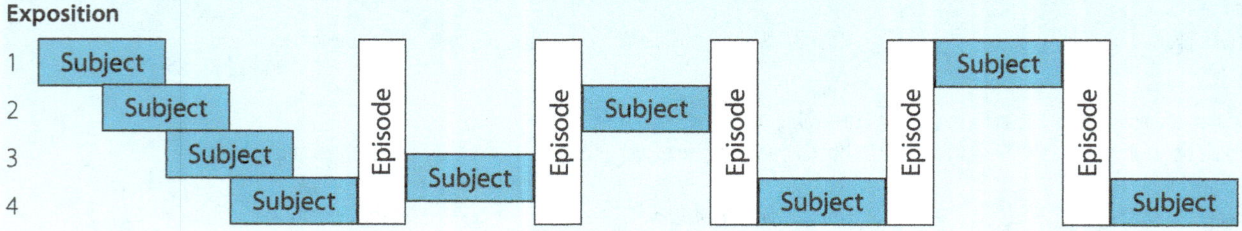

Listen and follow a visualization on **YouTube: http://youtube/p1XD1MSES_8**

Georg Friedrich Handel (1685–1759)

As you might note from their birth and death dates, Handel was born in the same year as Bach and outlived him by nine years. They were almost exact contemporaries, and as the two most prominent composers of the late Baroque, they were using many of the same forms and writing music often for the same or similar forces. Yet there are many points of divergence in their careers and in the way their music was treated. If Bach could count over a hundred musicians in his family tree, Georg Friedrich was the first and apparently only Handel to compose music. Like many before and after him, Handel was drawn to music despite his family, who saw it as a dead-end job. Handel proved them wrong, though, as he—

unlike Bach—became a figure of great international fame, moving from Germany to Italy and then England, where he became a British citizen and worked directly for the king. As noted above, Bach had twenty-odd children. Conversely, Handel never married and may have been gay, although it is difficult to establish sexual preferences with certainty from this historical distance.

The differences between Bach and Handel continue. Whereas Bach never wrote any operas, Handel composed some forty of them. Operas were his mainstay from the time of his first compositions to the point—rather dramatically in his career—when he turned to oratorios (discussed at length below). It is important to note that Handel's operas were loved during the composer's lifetime and that, because of them, he died a rich and famous man. After his death, however, the operas disappeared from the repertory and were only recovered in the mid-twentieth century. This "up and down" pattern of reception stands in sharp contrast to that of Bach's music, which was rediscovered in the nineteenth century and has been thoroughly revered ever since. Handel's *Messiah,* however, never had to be "revived," and may be the most continuously well-known and well-loved work in the whole Western tradition. For that reason, it is rather gratifying to learn that Handel wrote it to benefit a charitable institution in Dublin and later arranged a performance at London's "Foundling Hospital," which continues to show its appreciation for this generous act to this day.

The **oratorio** was a genre that had its roots in the late Renaissance era. Oratories were buildings—essentially lecture halls—that were put next to churches and cathedrals at the time, and the musical oratorio grew out of church leaders' need to educate their flock about the Bible and religious customs. By the time of Handel, the idea of treating biblical stories as the basis for musical dramas was common for all Christian faiths. In particular, the English had for many years identified with the great stories of the Old Testament, as they saw themselves as a chosen people comparable to the ancient Jews. Even Handel's *Messiah,* if obviously celebrating Jesus Christ, is told mainly from an Old Testament perspective. During Lent operas were banned, but because oratorios were religious and did not feature sets and costumes (generally), they were not, and the English oratorio could ride on the success of opera, which was very popular at this time. Oratorios, in fact, may have surpassed operas in public attendance, although they were not as frequently composed, and therefore more of a rarity. It is worth noting, in any case, that Handel stopped composing operas after his *Messiah* was performed in London.

Musically, Handel, like Bach, was a great contrapuntalist, although he never took things to the extremes that Bach did in composing his great canons and fugues. What stands out instead in Handel's music is the dramatic force that he brought not only to his operas, but also to oratorios such as *Messiah.* In the oratorio, the chorus—often voicing the views of the chosen people—was where Handel showed his considerable genius as a musical dramatic. In the famous "Hallelujah Chorus," for example, Handel moved within a very short time from a monophonic texture to one decidedly more polyphonic and then to the powerful homophonic texture for the word "hallelujah" itself. To this day, audiences not only love to hear this work, they love to sing it too; throughout the nineteenth and twentieth centuries (and hopefully the twenty-first), "sing-along" *Messiahs* have brought as many as thousands together to perform Handel's explosive choruses within a dramatic religious story.

Guided Listening

"Hallelujah" Chorus from *Messiah* by Georg Friedrich Handel (1741), Oratorio

An **oratorio** is literally "something sung in an oratory," which is a hall or chapel used for prayer. Oratorios resemble operas in some ways, but they are religious in subject matter and rarely staged (the action is described or suggested rather than played out). The role of the chorus is generally more varied in oratorios as well. Sometimes the chorus participates in the drama or contemplates events, and sometimes the chorus narrates the story.

Messiah tells the story of the life of Christ, which is split into three parts. The famous "Hallelujah" chorus concludes the second part, and is a celebration of the resurrection and triumph of the gospel.

http://www.rhapsody.com/artist/his-majesties-clerkes--anne-heider/album/hallelujah-great-choruses-from-handels-messiah/track/hallelujah

0:00	Brief instrumental introduction with strings and harpsichord.	
0:08	Chorus enters with two "Hallelujah" motives that will recur throughout the piece. Listen for them echoed in the strings.	*Hallelujah!*
0:18	"Hallelujah" motives are repeated at a higher pitch level.	
0:29	Chorus sings a new theme in unison.	*For the Lord God omnipotent reigneth.*
0:56	Starting with the sopranos, all the parts enter with different figures, some on "Hallelujah," others on "for the Lord . . ."	
1:28	Quietly at first, then louder, all sing together.	*The kingdom of this world* *Is become the kingdom of our Lord,* *And of His Christ, and of His Christ;*
1:50	Imitative section begins with bass voices. Tenors, then altos, then sopranos follow.	*And He shall reign for ever and ever,*
2:18	Sopranos begin a long ascent on long notes, alternating with "for ever and ever, Hallelujah," from the other voice parts.	*King of kings, and Lord of lords,*
3:00	Sopranos reach the summit of their rising line.	
3:08	A brief imitative section, starting with basses and sopranos.	*And He shall reign forever and ever,*
3:22	Tenors and basses now sing, "King of kings . . ." while sopranos and altos respond with "for ever and ever, Hallelujah."	*King of kings, and Lord of lords,*
4:12	Extended "Hallelujah" for the final cadence.	*Hallelujah!*

The Classical Era

5

Introduction: From the Baroque to the Classical Style: The Rococo

© Sergey Nivens, 2013. Used under license from Shutterstock, Inc.

In Western music history, the so-called Classical era is considered the most important period of them all, which is why so many (confusingly) call the whole tradition we've been tracing "classical music." For all its greatness, this era was heralded by perhaps the humblest move in stylistic history: a shift from the contrapuntal heights of geniuses of the Late Baroque like Bach to the disarmingly simple style championed by the new composers of the Rococo, which featured **animated homophony** (a style that features a kind of pseudo-counterpoint, as it features rhythmic motion but with no real counterpoint). Given the starkness of the overall change in styles, it is intriguing to discover that some of Bach's sons, such as Johann Christian Bach (note the different middle name) were the best composers of the new style.

Now let's unpack the above contention a bit. Before the Rococo, Bach *père* ("dad," Johann Sebastian Bach), along with Handel and many of their contemporaries, seemed unable to resist any chance to put musical melodies against each other, to the point where every part had a crucial part to play in a robustly complex texture. The typical composer of the Rococo generation, by contrast, would rather have one melody stand out and let the rest of the parts simply work to support it. Under a main melody, in the new style, the other parts performed a succession of chords, usually broken up so they sounded like they were doing something more interesting (but they really weren't doing much!). The most famous technique of "animating" chords was called **Alberti bass**, named after the keyboard composer Domenico Alberti (1710–1740). It was used extremely often by composers, and would last well past the Classical era: a humble invention, perhaps, but one with staying power and one that helped create a style. Perhaps this reminds us of the invention of figured bass?

From a distance, the move to animated homophony may sound a lot like the development of opera at the opening of the Baroque period. In some ways there were similar ideas behind both, giving the Baroque period a nicely rounded form as a historical epoch. Opera was invented with the purpose of bringing out a melody, for the sake of emphasizing certain words and making the drama more expressive. In the Rococo, animated homophony was also developed for the purpose of making one voice stand out, but now instruments were involved as much as singers. Furthermore, Rococo composers were more interested in the nature of the melody than the effectiveness of the drama, and they were less concerned with expressivity than with making pleasant and natural-sounding works for light entertainment, such as dances and other relaxed forms of after-dinner pleasantry.

Were Rococo composers just trying to relax a bit after all the vastness and seriousness of the great achievements of the late Baroque? Just a look at the succession of kings in France suggests that the urge to "lighten up" was a force that stretched beyond the confines of musical style. In France, Louis XIV (1638–1715) reigned for seventy-two years, the longest in French history, and he was responsible for what became known as "absolute monarchy," thanks to his extraordinary control over almost everything conceivably controllable in his dominions. On his passing Louis was succeeded by his five-year-old great-grandson, Louis XV, who was himself succeeded by a grandson, Louis XVI. Historians debate what XV and XVI did, but most concede that during their reigns, royal power was weakened to the extent that they led things down the path to the French Revolution of 1789, when the absolute monarchy collapsed and the great democratic-inspired "rights of man" were established.

It is tempting to see a parallel between the demise of the absolute monarchy and the demise of Late Baroque contrapuntal majesty. But there was something hiding in the new Rococo style that, once discovered, proved extremely important to the future of Western music. It was something we call **period** or **periodic phrasing**. In 1976, John D. White described a period as "a structure of two consecutive phrases, often built of similar or parallel melodic material, in which the first phrase gives the impression of asking a question which is answered by the second phrase." What is particularly valuable in this definition is the mention of the **question** and the **answer**; we tend to call periods constructions where one part is the **antecedent** and the other a **consequent** to reflect this linguistic parallel. For composers, one of the easiest ways to build antecedent-consequent periods is to end the "question" on the dominant chord, as it leads so clearly to the tonic in the tonal system. The consequent could then end quite affirmatively on the tonic itself, as the expected answer. Harmony, then, was quite useful for those creating periods of antecedent-consequent phrases, but melody, rhythm, and form were important too. These were the elements that composers manipulated to ensure that things were balanced, mainly by having it seem that the same amount of time and melodic and rhythmic interest was spent on the question as would be spent and bestowed on the answer. **Balance**, as we might gather from this, was an aesthetic goal at this time. The musical result was a sonic equivalent of the aristocratic conversation at Versailles—the carefully modulated and clever, but never too serious or pompous, discourse of those "in the know," asking charmingly conventional questions and getting charmingly expected responses. To various degrees, all of the great Classical composers (especially Mozart, Haydn, and Beethoven) realized the way their music, when balanced in this way, could be charming and appealing. Yet each would also find the means to push this system to the point where the idea of achieving balance drew the listener into rather challenging and awe-inspiring feats of dramatic development. In the following discussion of these great composers of the Classical era, aware that each had something of the Rococo in their style, we will consider the ways in which they left that era behind to build musical edifices of grand proportions and to serve rather grandiose goals.

Wolfgang Amadeus Mozart (1756–1791)

In awarding him the extended name Johannes Chrysostomus Wolfgangus Theophilus, Mozart's parents apparently noted his exceptional nature right from the start. Mozart would soon emerge as Europe's most bewilderingly talented child prodigy of all time; with his father at his side, he toured many of Europe's great cities, such as Vienna, Paris, London, Munich, Prague, and The Hague. Everywhere he went he was treated as a phenomenon, if of a kind he would later deride as something akin to a circus performer. When he grew older, Mozart and his father nearly parted ways when Mozart, a typical upstart teenager, declared himself unwilling to settle for a position once held by his "dear old" father. (We've added scare quotes on "dear" here because the elder Mozart, if an obviously gifted teacher and assiduous manager, still emerges as one of the main villains of the history and legend surrounding his son.) Mozart's father wanted his son to settle down in Salzburg. Mozart wanted to work instead at the Viennese court of Joseph II (Joseph Benedikt Anton Michael Adam), the Enlightened Holy Roman Emperor and brother of the notorious Marie Antoinette. Mozart did find *a* position and *some* work for this ruler, although, importantly, not the *top* position and not *enough* work. In mid-career, he saw himself embodying the role of the misunderstood genius. Hardly into his middle age, Mozart died at 35, underemployed, and in somewhat mysterious circumstances—murdered by a jealous colleague, as some imaginatively thought then, or struck down by a terrible case of strep throat caused by a lack of sunlight, as we now believe. Yet he had produced by then such a stream of masterpieces that his contribution to the Western tradition is almost always spoken of in deeply glowing terms.

Mozart performing with his father and sister.

Save for Beethoven, perhaps, no one in Western music has captured the historical imagination more than Mozart. Yet we have only begun to gather just how colorful a field of individuals are history's musicians. It's not surprising that Mozart was the most Rococo of the three giants of the Classical style (Haydn, Mozart, and Beethoven). What could be more suited to a performing child prodigy than a style that championed charm and elegance over the pomp and circumstance of the late Baroque? At the age of five, Mozart was already composing works that thoroughly delighted the kings and queens of Europe, while making a deep impression at the same time.

Mozart, who was so often observed, was himself a keen observer. Throughout his career, Mozart demonstrated an acute understanding of people and personalities, finding the most endearing or telling traits to bring out in the most unlikely of subjects—both musical and personal. In planning his concertos, for example, Mozart first determined who would be playing them; sometimes it was himself, sometimes his perhaps equally musically gifted sister—nicknamed Nannerl by his Wolgangerl—and sometimes friends or promising students. Rarely did he compose for strangers, it seems. Then he geared his musical ideas to suit, represent, and probably ultimately amuse the relevant character.

Mozart was perhaps at his most musically autobiographical in his piano concertos (although this might be said about his piano sonatas and operas as well), which number among the most admired in the repertory. We call them autobiographical, but of course this was not the kind of self-assessing product we tend to expect from written work, where tangible facts and readily understandable opin-

Johann Christian Bach.

ions are revealed in basically expected ways. Rather, the concertos were self-revealing vignettes of a sometimes mischievous, sometimes caustic, sometimes caring, but always astute, observer of character. Most impressively, Mozart brought out so many of these ideas in a purely instrumental musical form, one that he had inherited from the Baroque, but more particularly from the great Rococo example of Johann Christian (J. C.) Bach (the stylish son of Johann Sebastian).

The **Classical solo concerto**, as our eighteenth-century "J. C." designed it to be, was a showcase vehicle for a virtuoso. It can also be seen as an instructive means to demonstrate the principles of **tonality**. Retained from the Baroque was the idea that the *tutti* (orchestra) and *solo* (the soloist) would alternate. Onto this basic formula was grafted one of the most sophisticated forms in Western music history, the **double-exposition sonata**. To understand the characterization aspect of this musical genre, we must first discuss the idea that music possesses **themes** and **motifs (motives)**. Of these two terms, the motif is the more basic: a motif is the smallest unit of music that communicates a recognizable idea. Motifs are usually defined by a noticeable and thus memorable rhythmic gesture, although they often possess an inkling of a distinct melodic shape as well (such as a featured interval, say a third, fourth, second, etc., and perhaps a distinct move up or down). Motifs may suggest certain harmonies, but the whole point of keeping them concise is so they can be introduced and reintroduced in all sorts of harmonic situations (as in the tonic key, dominant, or any other harmonic area). The musical **theme** shares many traits with the musical motif, and usually contains a motif within it. A theme, however, is a section of melody usually defined as a full phrase (or half a period—see discussion of this in the prior section), and so it forms a more definable unit. A theme is usually stated clearly at some point near the opening of a work, or, if there are several themes, at a structurally significant point thereafter. After being introduced, a theme is reintroduced only once or twice, usually to signify the entrance of a new character or the arrival "home" after a long musical adventure.

At the opening of a Classical concerto, the orchestra exposes, as it were, all the motifs and the main themes of the concerto by stating them in turn. This is the business of the **first exposition**. One of its most important traits is harmonic, as it stays in what we call the **tonic** throughout. When the first exposition comes to a close, as you might expect, we open the curtain to reveal the soloist, who leads us through a **second exposition** of the same material, re-exposing all the themes with all their motifs in place. Why do we need to hear all (or many at least) of the themes again? It turns out there were probably two reasons. One is that we need to understand that the soloist is the leading character in the musical play. The other—less imaginative but no less important—reason is that the soloist will lead the music for the first time away from the stable tonic key in this second run-through. In the second exposition, specifically, we begin with a statement of the **first theme** group (sometimes just one, sometimes a little set of them). After this there is a short unstable section called a **modulation**, where we undergo a decisive move from one harmonic area to another. This modulatory music is led by the soloist. Usually the modulation takes us to the dominant harmony, where we now hear the **second theme** group, more noticeably contrasting with the first because of the shift in harmony. Once we have thus sorted out the harmonies and presented all the themes, at the end of the second exposition things come to another noticeable pause and the **development** section begins. Both the orchestra and the soloist are featured in the development section, whose essential trait is harmonic instability. The point here, in fact, is to elude any sense that there is an underlying key governing things. Themes, as such, are no longer present. Rather, it is here where motifs ring through the texture unattached to their themes and modulation becomes nearly a "way of life." Then, we reach the climax of the story—a defined place near the end of the development. At this point, all the instability and modulation stop as we start to move decisively toward a specific harmony, namely the dominant. Many call this section a **re-transition**, as it so obviously leaves us anticipating something stable and thematic (because, of course, we've been so long deprived of hearing both). After the re-transition, we arrive at the **recapitulation**. Here all the themes are presented (or represented) in the same positions where they first appeared, and all the harmonic instability comes to a stop, as we remain throughout in the tonic harmonic area. In the Classical solo concerto, the recapitulation section differs from the second exposition in that it remains in the tonic. It differs from the first exposition in that both the soloist and orchestra perform together.

Guided Listening

First Movement, *Allegro* of Piano Concerto in A major K. 488 by Wolfgang Amadeus Mozart

As in all first movements of Mozart's concertos, this piece is written in **sonata form**. However, in order to accommodate the back-and-forth between the orchestra and the soloist, the form has been expanded to **double exposition form**. In this variation of sonata form, the orchestra plays the first exposition alone, after which the soloist joins for a second statement of the same themes. Other than the change in performance forces, the most important difference between the two expositions is that the first remains in the tonic key, while the second modulates to the dominant.

http://www.rhapsody.com/artist/christian-tetzlaff/album/mozart---piano-concertos/track/piano-concerto-no-23-in-a-major-k488-cadenza-by-mozart-i----

Exposition 1

0:00	Strings introduce the first theme.
0:16	First theme repeated by woodwinds.
0:32	Strings introduce the second theme, part 1.
1:08	Woodwinds repeat second theme, part 1.
1:22	Strings introduce the second theme, part 2.
1:27	Strings introduce the closing theme, part 1.
1:51	Woodwinds introduce the closing theme, part 2.

Exposition 2

1:59	Piano plays first theme.
2:27	Orchestra plays first theme, part 2.
2:56	Piano plays second theme, part 1.
3:11	Woodwinds repeat second theme, part 1.
3:25	Piano plays second theme, part 2.
3:34	All play closing theme, part 1.
4:03	Piano trill leads into return of the first theme, part 2.
4:15	After a brief pause, a new theme is introduced by the strings.

Development

4:39	Woodwinds perform variations of the new theme. Piano and orchestra briefly interject.
5:03	Woodwinds play in imitative counterpoint. Under them, the piano plays running scales.
5:17	Sustained dominant note in the low strings signals the beginning of the **retransition** (transition back to the main themes, to the recapitulation).
5:37	Piano flourishes lead into the recapitulation.

Recapitulation

5:54	Themes from the exposition are heard in the piano, woodwinds, and full orchestra.
7:47	Piano plays the new theme.
8:53	Piano **cadenza** (unaccompanied free section for the soloist; although sometimes improvised or composed by a performer, this particular cadenza was composed by Mozart).
10:03	Trill, then higher trill signal the end of the cadenza.
10:17	Orchestra plays the closing theme.

Mozart's concertos, as noted above, were based on the procedures devised mainly by J. C. Bach. In his operas, Mozart struck out on paths also paved to a certain extent by others, but the results were so original that it is difficult to view some of his works as less than "without model" (*sui generis*); they are certainly of a standard no one at that time had ever heard before. Historians have often noted that Mozart composed in all the standard operatic types of the era, including the comic and serious kinds with Italian texts and the German-texted *singspiel,* which featured spoken dialogue as well as singing. If rivaled by his own *Magic Flute* and *Marriage of Figaro,* his finest opera (to many, including one of this text's authors, the best opera ever written) was his *Don Giovanni.* Resembling very much a *drama giocoso* (jocular drama) but listed by Mozart as a thoroughly comic opera (*opera buffa*), this is a retelling of the famous Don Juan tale. It can send shivers up the spines of all but the most unreceptive listeners, especially when Don Giovanni (Juan), after making so many sexual conquests, is greeted at dinner by the ghost of the father of one of his victims, who then drags him into Hell. Throughout the opera, characters of serious and comic natures and purposes follow Don Giovanni through his exploits to complain about him, fall victim to his tricks and designs, and finally chase him down and bring him to grim justice. We've emphasized Mozart's approach to comedy, but he had a serious side as well, as he revealed very poignantly and profoundly in his famous *Requiem,* composed near the end of his life. Something of the social libertine seemed to dwell in Mozart's character as well. It is, in any case, remarkable how Mozart portrays the Don Juan character as somehow noble while facing such a terrible end, however justified it might have been.

Guided Listening

Don Giovanni by Wolfgang Amadeus Mozart, Opera

Don Giovanni tells the familiar story of Don Juan, seducer of women, whose salacious deeds ultimately lead to his downfall. In this retelling, Don Giovanni has killed the Commandant, the father of one of his conquests, in the first scene. Seeing a statue of the Commandant later in the street, Don Giovanni is unrepentant and, in his boasting, invites the statue to dinner. In the scene below, the statue, possessed by the ghost of the Commandant, appears at Don Giovanni's door.

http://www.rhapsody.com/artist/various-artists/album/mozart-don-giovanni-dg/track/don-giovanni-a-cenar-teco-minvitasti

0:00 Two tense and ominous chords signal the arrival of the Statue of the Commandant.

		Original text	*English translation*
		Statue of the Commandant	
0:10	The Statue of the Commandant arrives.	*Don Giovanni, a cenar teco m'invitasti, e son venuto.*	*Don Giovanni, you invited me to dinner and I have come!*
		Don Giovanni	
0:33	Don Giovanni remains arrogant and proud, not realizing the danger he is facing. Sighing gestures from the high strings seem to signal Don Giovanni's precarious situation.	*Non l'avrei giammai creduto. Ma farò quel che potrò!*	*I never would have believed it, but I will do what I can.*
		Leporello, un'altra cena fa' che subito si porti!	*Leporello, see to it that another dinner is served at once!*
		Leporello (Don Giovanni's servant)	
0:48	Leporello, on the other hand, is frightened and tries to warn Don Giovanni.	*Ah, padron, siam tutti morti!*	*Ah, master, we all dead!*
		Don Giovanni	
		Vanne, dico . . .	*Go, I said!*

		Original text	*English translation*
		Statue of the Commandant	
0:56	The bass voice of the Commandant sounds firm and serious compared to the higher voices of Don Giovanni and Leporello.	*Ferma un po'.* *Non si pasce di cibo mortale* *chi si pasce di cibo celeste.*	*Wait a moment!* *He who dines on Heavenly food* *has no need for the food of the mortals!*
1:30	The Commandant reveals that he has come for a more serious reason. Strings and woodwinds play ascending and descending scales in the background.	*Altre cure più gravi di queste,* *altra brama quaggiù mi guidò!*	*Other more serious considerations* *have caused me to come here!*
		Leporello	
1:56	Leporello sings in quick rhythms, again stating his fear. At the same time, Don Giovanni remains calm, singing in slower rhythms. The Commandant sings even more slowly and regularly, showing his control over the situation.	*La terzana d'avere mi sembra, e le membra fermar più non so.*	*I feel as if I have a fever, for I cannot control my limbs.*
		Don Giovanni	
		Parla dunque: che chiedi, che vuoi?	*Speak then! What do you ask? What do you wish?*
		Statue of the Commandant	
		Parlo, ascolta, più tempo non ho.	*I will speak, listen, my time is short.*
		Don Giovanni	
		Parla, parla, ascoltando ti sto.	Speak then, for I am listening.
		Statue of the Commandant	
2:49	The Commandant uses Don Giovanni's pride to trick him into striking a deal that will condemn him.	*Tu m'invitasti a cena, il tuo dover or sai.* *Rispondimi: verrai tu a cenar meco?*	*You invited me to dinner, now you know your duty.* *Answer me: will you come to dine with me?*
		Leporello (tremando)	
3:34	Leporello tries to protect Don Giovanni by declining the invitation.	*Oibò, oibò, tempo non ha, scusate.*	*Oh my! Excuse him, but he doesn't have time.*
		Don Giovanni	
3:42	Don Giovanni refuses to be intimidated. The high string sighs return.	*A torto di viltade tacciato mai sarò!*	*No one will say of me that I have ever been afraid.*
		Statue of the Commandant	
3:52	The Commandant urges him to make a decision.	*Risolvi!*	*Make up your mind!*
		Don Giovanni	
		Ho già risolto.	*I have done so already!*
		Statue of the Commandant	
		Verrai?	*You will come?*
		Leporello	
4:06	Leporello tries one more time to stop Don Giovanni.	*Dite di no, dite di no!*	*Tell him no, tell him no!*
		Don Giovanni	
4:09	Don Giovanni agrees to come.	*Ho fermo il core in petto: non ho timor, verrò!*	*My heart beats firmly. I'm not afraid: I'll come!*
		Statue of the Commandant	
4:20	The Commandant asks for Don Giovanni to shake his hand on the agreement.	*Dammi la mano in pegno!*	*Give me your hand upon it!*
		Don Giovanni	
4:31	Upon shaking hands with the Commandant, Don Giovanni is startled by a deadly chill. Tremolos in the orchestra reflect the change in Don Giovanni's demeanor.	*Eccolo! ohimè!*	*Here it is! Oh me!*
		Statue of the Commandant	
		Cos'hai?	*What is wrong?*
		Don Giovanni	
		Che gelo è questo mai!	*What is this deadly chill?*
		Statue of the Commandant	
4:37	The Commandant reveals that Don Giovanni will soon die and tells him to repent if he wishes to avoid damnation.	*Pentiti, cangia vita! È l'ultimo momento!*	*Repent! Change your ways, for this is your last hour!*

(continued)

		Original text	English translation
		Don Giovanni (vuol sciogliersi, ma invano.)	
4:44	Despite urgings from the Commandant and Leporello, Don Giovanni refuses to repent.	*No, no, ch'io non mi pento! Vanne lontan da me!*	*No, no, I will not repent! Get away from me!*
		Statue of the Commandant	
		Pentiti, scellerato!	*Repent, scoundrel!*
		Don Giovanni	
		No, vecchio infatuato!	*No, you old fool!*
		Statue of the Commandant	
		Pentiti!	*Repent!*
		Don Giovanni	
		No!	*No!*
		Statue of the Commandant	
		Sì!	*Yes!*
		Don Giovanni	
		No!	*No!*
		Leporello	
		Sì, sì!	*Yes, yes!*
		Don Giovanni	
		No, no!	*No, no!*
		Statue of the Commandant	
5:21	After a brief pause, the Commandant announces that Don Giovanni has run out of time and then disappears. Flames appear and the ground under Don Giovanni begins to tremble.	*Ah, tempo più non v'è!*	*Ah, your time is up!*
		Don Giovanni	
		Da qual tremore insolito sento assalir gli spiriti! *Donde escono quei vortici di fuoco pien d'orror?*	*What strange fear now assails my soul!* *Where do those flames of horror come from?*
		Chorus of Demons	
5:40	From off stage, a chorus of demons taunts Don Giovanni.	*Tutto a tue colpe è poco!* *Vieni! c'è un mal peggior!*	*No horror is too dreadful for you!* *Come, there is worse in store!*
		Don Giovanni	
5:48	The chorus of demons, Don Giovanni, and Leporello sing in alternation and simultaneously, reflecting the confusion and panic of the scene.	*Chi l'anima mi lacera!* *Chi m'agita le viscere!* *Che strazio, ohimè! che smania!* *Che inferno! che terror!*	*Who lacerates my soul?* *Who torments my body?* *What torment, oh me, what agony!* *What a Hell! What a terror!*
		Leporello	
		Che ceffo disperato! *Che gesti da dannato!* *Che gridi! che lamenti!* *Come mi fa terror!*	*What a look of desperation!* *The gestures of the damned!* *What cries, what laments!* *How he makes me afraid!*
		Don Giovanni and Leporello	
6:17	Don Giovanni screams as the flames and earth engulf him. Leporello screams in horror.	*Ah!*	*Ah!*
6:25	Although the majority of this piece is in minor, the final chord is major, implying that everything is resolved and that justice has been served.		

Franz Joseph Haydn (1732–1809)

Joseph Haydn was not a child prodigy on the unprecedented scale of his friend and admired colleague Mozart, but he was likely an extremely talented youth. Haydn was the child of parents of humble means who, as far as Haydn himself was concerned, set him up well for a lifelong career in music. After standing out for his musicianship in church choirs near his hometown of Rohrau, Austria, a young Haydn auditioned for and won a position in the prestigious choir of St. Stephen's Cathedral in Vienna. That Haydn was poor is well suggested in his autobiographical comments; looking back on these days, he often mentioned his hunger (as well as his dirty clothes) and how he strategically put his talent to use in the search for nourishment. After an interlude of freelance teaching, mainly for a pittance, Haydn got his real break when he came to the notice of **Prince Paul Anton Esterházy** (d. 1762), one of the wealthiest aristocrats in Europe. From 1761, on and off (and mostly "on") until his death, Haydn worked for this family, at an immense castle and other family residences—the main one rivaling Louis XIV's Versailles! Haydn was in some ways simply a servant, although a well regarded one. Late in his life, the reigning prince granted him permission to tour England and other centers where his music had been deeply appreciated through printed editions and performances by others, as well as the accounts of those lucky enough to see it performed at Esterházy residences. One failing of Haydn's was that he had an unhappy marriage, and thus perhaps it suited him to pour extra effort into his work. It is nonetheless astonishing to note how much music Haydn wrote at the behest of the prince. Haydn's main patron, Prince Nikolaus, was very musically inclined and even played a strange and unwieldy instrument called a **baryton**. However unpromising and inelegant the instrument, Haydn wrote over a hundred works for it (which are hardly ever played today, even though some contain rather fine music). As the prince also loved Italian comic opera, Haydn wrote dozens of works of this kind and conducted one a week, whether one of his own or one by someone else. It was through this enforced study of light, Rococo-styled Italian operas that Haydn came to develop a fluid style with a lot of the charm, wit, and elegance that we also hear in Mozart's music.

Later in life Haydn wrote some outstanding oratorios, *The Creation* and *The Seasons,* to coincide with a trip to London, where the German-born Handel had set a high standard for works of this type. Haydn also wrote a number of works for solo piano, a number of concerti (or concertos)—including an especially wonderful work for trumpet and orchestra—and an number of **string quartets**. With two violins (known as the first and second), a viola, and a violoncello, the string quartet ensemble gave Haydn the perfect opportunity to cover all the triads and extended harmonies for tonal adventures; he was the one who truly brought the genre to the fore. Haydn was known at the time as "Papa Haydn" and is still

The Esterháza castle in Fertod, Hungary.

called by some the "father of the string quartet." In his hands and those of Mozart (with whom Haydn performed a number of them), the string quartet became the true standard for chamber music composition, replacing the trio sonata of the Baroque. Each one is an individual gem, but as with nearly all of his works for chamber, solo, and orchestra, Haydn's mature string quartets were all multi-movement works that included at least one in **sonata form**.

For all his other accomplishments, Haydn's main focus throughout his career was on the **symphony**, of which he wrote some 112, mainly for the orchestras stationed at Esterháza. Not surprisingly, Haydn has also been dubbed the "father of the symphony," a fitting tribute to the quantity and extraordinarily high quality of these works.

Just as the string quartet was a sonata cycle for four specific instruments, the symphony was a sonata cycle for orchestra. Before turning to some of the characteristic features of Haydn's symphonic writing, it is useful now to describe the typical four movements of the **sonata cycle**, which was the basis for nearly all the symphonies, string quartets, solo sonatas, and various other works of the era.

The **first movement** of a sonata cycle might feature a **slow introduction** as a sort of prelude. But some begin right away with a quick, **Allegro** tempo and immediately follow the **sonata form** (many dub the form "sonata-allegro" for this reason). As noted above, the sonata features three main sections: the **exposition**, **development**, and **recapitulation**. The themes and motifs are laid out in the exposition, with the first theme performed in the tonic, and then, after a **modulation** to the new key (usually the dominant, but in the case of minor-keyed sonatas, the median key), the second theme group presented in the newly established harmonic area. The development section remains harmonically unstable nearly throughout and features motifs rather than themes. By the development section's end, however, there is a decisive move to the dominant harmony to set things up for the recapitulation. In the recapitulation, the first and second themes are both presented in the same tonic harmonic area. Some composers add a theme- and tonic-affirming **coda** after the recapitulation as something of a postlude, to bring things to an even more resounding close.

In most cases, the **second movement** of a sonata cycle contrasts notably with the first. Here the tempo is usually at a walking pace (**Andante**) or even slower (**Largo**) and the point is to have a melody "singing" throughout, with the other musical lines playing a subsidiary, accompanying role. Sometimes these so-called **slow movements** follow an abbreviated sonata form (sometimes called **sonatina**), where specific, contrasting themes do appear, but with less development. In many cases, though, the sonata form is hardly present at all in these movements, and a simple **ABA** (**song form**) is used instead. One further possibility of note is the **theme and variations** form. In virtually all theme and variation works, the piece begins with a simple or direct statement of the theme. After that, the composer uses his or her ingenuity to vary the music in ways that retain some aspect of the opening music (usually keeping the harmonic movement intact throughout) while changing other aspects—such as adding ornamentation or even substituting what sounds like a wholly new melody over the same harmonies. Jazz musicians, as we will note again later, understand the theme and variations as the formal basis for most of the music they perform. The theme and variations often ends with another A, because works return in the end to a simple statement of the theme. It is usually sketched out as follows: **A A1 A2 A3 . . . A**.

The dance-music origins of the Classical sonata are revealed in the inclusion in the sonata cycle of a paired dance, the **minuet and trio**, as the **third movement**. This movement simply presents a series of binary forms, although it has enough complexity to warrant some explanation. What happens in the minuet and trio can be sketched out as follows: **AA BB CC DD AB**. The A and B are the two parts of the minuet, and the C and D are the two parts of the trio. The tempo is understood to be moderate or **Moderato**.

The **fourth movement** of a sonata cycle is the fastest in terms of tempo, often **Allegro** or even **Presto** (very fast). For the most part, it is meant to be more lighthearted than any of the other movements, and the typical form is the **Rondo.** The principle behind the rondo is to keep bringing certain material back into the foreground (the first A section), in various amusing ways. Various forms of the rondo were common at the time, but the one that eventually became the norm was **A B A C A B coda**. Some composers, like Haydn and especially Beethoven, combined the rondo form with the sonata to create a **sonata-rondo**, using the B section for the second theme and the C section for the development.

Just to follow all these formal procedures would seem to be challenge enough for any composer. But as with all conventions, they actually could help a composer, as they gave him or her useful limitations and prevented the all-too-easily-disabling idea of freedom of choice, which has crushed many a creative artist. Through these conventions, Haydn also explored various special entertainment techniques, many of which revolved around musical humor. It was not only in his famous "Surprise Symphony" that Haydn seemed to tease and challenge his audiences. Throughout his symphonic works, and in his string quartets and other works as well, Haydn set up expectations, foiled them, and then revealed the value of an alternative, all the while maintaining the sense of balance that Mozart also achieved and that both had learned from the deceptively simple offerings of their Rococo forebears.

Guided Listening

Second Movement of String Quartet, Op. 76, No. 3 (*Emperor*) by Joseph Haydn

This string quartet is called the *Emperor* because the second movement (covered in this listening guide) is a theme and variations based on a hymn that Haydn wrote for Franz Joseph, Emperor of Austria, which later became Austria's national anthem. It remained the anthem until after World War II, when it was changed due to associations with Nazi propaganda. Today Germany uses the hymn as its national song, singing only the third stanza.

http://www.rhapsody.com/artist/royal-philharmonic-chamber-ensemble/album/haydn-string-quartets---emperor-lark-hunt/track/string-quartet-no-3-in-c-major-op-76---emperor-ii-poco-adagi

0:00 **Theme**—First violin plays theme, others play simple chordal accompaniment.

1:20 **Variation 1**—Second violin plays theme while first violin plays decorative figures.

2:32 **Variation 2**—Cello plays theme, others play harmonies and counter melodies.

3:57 **Variation 3**—Viola plays theme, others play syncopated accompaniment, more dissonance and chromaticism than previous variations.

5:19 **Variation 4**—First violin plays theme, polyphonic texture, pitch level seems to rise throughout this variation.

6:45 **Coda**—Sustained note in cello, fading away to nothing.

Ludwig van Beethoven (1770–1827)

© Gang Liu, 2013. Used under license from Shutterstock, Inc.

Beethoven stands before us as a veritable giant: by far the most colossal figure of Western music. Under his shadow several generations of composers struggled, finding it both exhilarating and challenging to express the level of profundity and creativity that characterized so much of his work. Many have wrestled simply to gain an understanding of what he did to their field of musical composition. The string quartets and piano sonatas he wrote at the end of his life, for example, left many at the time completely baffled, and it is generally agreed that it took about a century for them to be appreciated fully. At his most characteristic, Beethoven was a pattern-breaker, but it helps to know that he modeled both his career and his music on the achievements of Mozart and Haydn.

© EugenZ, 2013. Used under license from Shutterstock, Inc.

With Mozart in mind, Beethoven's father and friends in the German town of Bonn (where Beethoven was born) groomed the young Ludwig to be the next great child prodigy, even to the point of falsely advertising his age as six (Mozart's age when he began his tours). After this plan failed, Beethoven honed his musical skills and gathered support in a well-directed effort to make a proper move to Vienna, one that did set him on the path to recognition on a nearly unprecedented scale. No less than 20,000 citizens attended Beethoven's funeral. So it may be fair to say that Beethoven failed where Mozart succeeded, as a child prodigy, and yet succeeded just where Mozart failed, in his Viennese career. If this would seem to give Beethoven some kind of advantage over his great compositional forebear, a closer look at Beethoven's life and career presents little that could be seen as smooth or pleasant. Beethoven was as tragic a figure as he was colossal.

Beethoven's last resting place.
© Bertl123, 2013. Used under license from Shutterstock, Inc.

Historians are no longer as sure as they once were about the nature of Beethoven's youth and upbringing. One of the things obscuring our understanding was Beethoven's own effort to shape his public persona once he established himself in Vienna. But it seems clear that Beethoven's childhood was disturbing in many ways. His father, Johann, who was employed as a singer and music director, emerges as a stern, abusive figure. After the death of Beethoven's mother Maria, Johann succumbed to alcoholism, and it was probably an act of desperation for Ludwig to go to the town magistrate and get a court order. Beethoven used this legal instrument to assume his father's position and used the earnings to properly raise his two younger brothers. Such responsibilities are not usually suited to teenagers, so it must have been a relief for Beethoven to leave Bonn for the great promise of self-fulfillment in Vienna; and the support Beethoven received at this time from friends and sponsors emerges as one of the story's few bright lights. Beethoven set out with the idea that he would study composition with Mozart. But the two never met, as Beethoven arrived in Vienna the year Mozart died. Beethoven did get the chance to study with Haydn, however, which his supporters viewed as nearly as exciting a prospect (Beethoven found Haydn—who was stretching out on *his* own late in life—somewhat neglectful, however).

Beethoven's arrival in Vienna must have seemed freeing on a personal level. The composer never overcame the idea, however, that his younger brothers were irresponsible people and that it was his responsibility to take care of them, even when he became as overbearing and destructive as his father had been. Well before his personality began to deteriorate, Beethoven had to face yet another devastating fact: he discovered that his hearing loss was progressive and would surely lead to deafness. It is, of course, easy to appreciate why a composer and musical performer would find hearing loss so devastating, but as he came to terms with his disease, Beethoven saw the disablement as a social as well as a professional tragedy.

Schonbrunn Palace Garden, Vienna, Austria.

When he arrived in Vienna, Beethoven was in his mid-twenties, handsome, talented, free at last, and looking to enjoy himself in a grand manner he probably saw as fitting for someone in his circumstances—probably in the same way as do today's young music and movie stars. Letters attest that he took dancing lessons, bought stylish clothes, and dined out extravagantly. He also had affairs with some of the rich and famous, women who apparently fell for him despite his common birth. This was an age when social class mattered much more than it does today, although it was also the age when democratic ideals were inspiring momentous social changes such as the French and American Revolutions, all of which Beethoven understood and felt deeply. Ultimately, Beethoven made an important statement about social class. No matter how much he depended on them, Beethoven declared himself the equal of his patrons, whether directly or indirectly, and this assertion forms a major part of his legacy.

When he learned of his deafness, Beethoven nearly abandoned life altogether, mentioning suicide in his famous **Heiligenstadt Testament** of 1802, which he addressed to his brothers. Here, again—if this time for the best—Beethoven put his responsibilities to others before his own needs and desires: thankfully, he decided not to end his life. Instead he went on to pen one of his most life-affirming works, his Second Symphony. With the knowledge of his oncoming deafness, however, Beethoven turned from that well-mannered, stylish youth to the irascible, even terrifying adult we've come to see portrayed most vigorously today. After dedicating himself to assisting one of his brothers, Carl, who was struck with tuberculosis, Beethoven sued for parental rights over his nephew Karl and took the child away from his mother. Beethoven's approach to raising the child may have been as stern and rough as his own father's approach (if more well-meaning, one gathers). In any case, when Karl attempted suicide, Beethoven was devastated. Hopefully, the fact that his path-breaking music was reaching more and more appreciative audiences helped mitigate these tragic circumstances.

As nebulous as such things must be seen to be, Beethoven's personal traits stand close to the surface of his musical compositions. In some works we hear a youthful smoothness combined with ambition. In other works we hear the characteristic roughness, rebellion, and irascibility of the young, frustrated adult. With some it is a sense of *striving* that stands out above all else, or the sense that a *struggle* has been overcome. In the Ninth Symphony, where all of these qualities seem to coexist, Beethoven describes for us something no less profound than the true meaning of happiness and brotherhood.

If his father had any lasting psychological effect on his music, it was probably manifest in the rebellious and ambitious element of so many of his works. (Note: scholars have long decided that Beethoven had clearly defined "**early**," "**middle**," and "**late**" periods.) When Beethoven dedicated some of his earliest works to Haydn, it could have been simply a gesture of respect, but these works are so massive and complex that they seem intended to show that he planned to outdo his famous teacher from the start. When Beethoven turned to the symphony and string quartet, as well as the piano sonata and piano concerto, he kept the same basic formulas in place, but he soon found the minuet and trio too tame for his needs. More to Beethoven's taste was the raucous and exhilarating **scherzo and trio**, which was patterned in the same way as the minuet, AA BB CC DD AB, but with a much brisker tempo (often **Presto**) and a much less genial spirit. It was in Beethoven's famous **middle** or "Revolutionary" period that the composer made one of his most impressive stamps on composition by linking all the movements of a work through musical means. Usually by repetition of musical material throughout the movements, and in the most famous case, through the repetition of a motif, in the Fifth Symphony, Beethoven extended his musical arguments beyond the level of a single movement to encompass as much as a hour of purely instrumental music. Characteristically, the arguments that Beethoven chose to develop over such an extended musical canvas tended to be profound and problematic. We've mentioned already the lofty program of the great Ninth Symphony, one of the masterpieces of Beethoven's **late** period. As Beethoven left no clue about his ideas surrounding the middle-period Fifth Symphony, what he was trying to represent remains a mystery, and it is entirely possible that the "idea" itself is something he never pinned down in words or in anything other than musical images. But there is no doubt that whatever he meant to represent in the Fifth Symphony, it possessed and conveyed such a musical depth that it would inspire composers for many years thereafter.

Guided Listening

Symphony No. 5 in C minor, Op. 67 by Ludwig van Beethoven (1807–1808)

Beethoven's Fifth Symphony is perhaps the most well-known symphony in the Western canon of music.

The first movement was described by Beethoven as "fate knocking on the door" and features a short-short-short-long motive that recurs incessantly throughout the movement. The same motive appears in the other three movements as well.

First Movement, *Allegro con brio* (sonata form)

http://www.rhapsody.com/artist/berliner-philharmoniker/album/beethoven-symphonies-nos5-and-6-pastorale/track/1-allegro-con-brio---symphony-no5-in-c-minor-op67---1-allegr

0:00 **Exposition** begins; theme 1, based on the four-note short-short-short-long motive.
0:45 Horns modulate to key of second theme.
0:47 Theme 2, a more lyrical melody, heard against the four-note motive in the bass.
1:06 Closing theme, a descending passage of **staccato** (short, separated) notes followed by the four-note motive.
1:25 Exposition repeats.
2:49 **Development** begins; incessant repetition of the four-note theme, many modulations.
4:09 **Recapitulation** begins, followed by a brief oboe cadenza.
5:46 **Coda** begins.

Second Movement, *Andante con moto* (theme and variations form)

http://www.rhapsody.com/artist/berliner-philharmoniker/album/beethoven-symphonies-nos5-and-6-pastorale/track/2-andante-con-moto---symphony-no5-in-c-minor-op67---2-andant

0:00 Low strings introduce the first theme.
0:56 Four-note motive appears in second theme (two quick notes lead into short-short-short-long).

Third Movement, *Allegro* (scherzo and trio form)

http://www.rhapsody.com/artist/berliner-philharmoniker/album/beethoven-symphonies-nos5-and-6-pastorale/track/3-allegro---symphony-no5-in-c-minor-op67---3-allegro

0:00 Low strings quietly play the rising scherzo theme.
0:19 Four-note motive played ***fortissimo*** (very loud) by horns.
4:19 Timpani play the four-note motive, under a slow *crescendo* leading into the final movement (no break).

Fourth Movement, *Allegro* (sonata form)

http://www.rhapsody.com/artist/berliner-philharmoniker/album/beethoven-symphonies-nos5-and-6-pastorale/track/4-allegro---symphony-no5-in-c-minor-op67---4-allegro

0:00 **Exposition** begins; theme 1.
1:05 Theme 2.
1:33 Closing theme, featuring clarinet and violas.
1:52 **Development** begins, four-note motive returns.
3:44 Brief return of material from the scherzo (third movement).
4:16 **Recapitulation** begins.
7:31 **Coda** begins; tension builds and is resolved over and over again until the final cadence.

The Romantic Era

6

Part 1: The Lyrical Urge

Especially in his Fifth Symphony, but also in many other works, Beethoven erected compositions that are perhaps best understood as musical monuments. As we discussed above, the **motif**, the smallest definable unit of music, was what Beethoven treated as the essential building block to create these edifices. Part of the exhilarating challenge, as Beethoven surely saw it, was to see how long a musical argument he could sustain with such basic material. In certain ways, then, Beethoven represented the new democratic ideal, reigning over musical kingdoms by the sheer force of his creativity, needing no independent wealth or ancestral precedent to establish his claim. By the time he died, in 1827, the European world was well into a post-revolutionary phase, and along with hard-won advances and losses in the areas of "liberty, equality, and fraternity," the next generation of composers had to confront all the colossal forms—the giant symphony, opera, and mass—that the era's great "revolutionary composer" had left for them in his wake.

Concert offered to the Pope Pio IX in Palazzo Vecchio, Florence.

Composers after Beethoven did much more than simply recognize the achievement: they also grappled with the composer's legacy to the point where it seemed almost counterproductive. Yet, for all the attention they gave to the work of one composer, they were not simply followers, either. Indeed, one of the greatest accomplishments of the **Romantic era** (1820–1910), often described as nineteenth-century music, was its **rediscovery of melody**, the element that many—unlike Beethoven—thought should be the most prominent feature in a musical design.

It is instructive to consider what melody was in Beethoven's hands and what it was to be in the hands of the next generation. Beethoven wrote many successful works for singers, and his slow movements for instrumental forces are as moving as any aria on any profoundly sad topic. Yet, for all that, relatively few of Beethoven's melodies are truly **lyrical**: they seem not to be designed with melodic beauty as their main goal, and often sound awkward when sung on their own. Because a great melody demands its own space, it doesn't easily parse into motifs. Consequently, lyrical composers often found it difficult to chop up their melodies into motifs and delve too deeply into the unstable world of musical development. Conversely, and not surprisingly, the development section (and musical development generally) was where they could most easily fail, and this was precisely the place where Beethoven excelled.

Romantic composers gravitated to the lyrical mode of expression for a number of reasons. First, it fit their interests, which were becoming more and more particularized and subjective. What more than song could more deeply express the ideas of a particular subject? Second, the lyrical approach created a more intimate atmosphere, opening a protected space that many composers wished to inhabit in the face of the new mass publics brought on by new democratic urges. Students of the Romantic era, in fact, like to point out that the nineteenth century was **an era of extremes**, where some composers looked to fill the largest halls with music that would last longer than it had ever lasted before, while others looked for ways to miniaturize music so that it was confined to a discerning few (players and their close friends and lovers, presumably). And there were composers who liked to wear both hats, producing music to serve the masses, ideally, as well as the elite of the intimate chamber.

Further attracting composers to lyric ideas was a burgeoning interest in literature. Composers at this time were looking for ways to express their deepened interest in and understanding of poetry in musical terms. Among poets, musicians, and other artists of the era, there was a common interest in profound, subjective expression, but also in nationalism. As with the writers of the era, composers of this time started to focus attention on the interior spaces of thought in their subjects, on the one hand, and the generalized and idealized, broader ways of life of their countrymen, on the other. **Nationalism** was a strong force throughout this era, and **folk music** and poetry were thought to be art forms that went to the heart of a nation. Writers and composers of this era embraced more and more what they believed to be the simple and direct expressions of their countrymen. (That nationalism could become so blinding and dark as to inspire Nazism was probably not fathomed at the time, although historians see the seeds for those horrors as having been firmly planted by these early Romantics.) Finally, among the attractions of lyricism, on a more practical level, were the instruments that were being invented and redesigned in something of a whirl of industrial energy. Whereas in the past it was understood that certain instruments would serve various purposes, now nearly all were designed so that they could "sing" with greater ease and effectiveness. The piano underwent perhaps the most intense development along these lines. Along with the voice itself, among solo instruments it best served the expressive needs of what one writer has termed the "Romantic Generation."

Settings of German poetic texts did not originate with Romantic composers. Beethoven wrote songs that fully qualify as ***lieder*** (the word in German and Dutch for "songs"). But the genre really began to flourish when it fell into the hands of a younger group of composers, especially **Franz Schubert (1797–1828)**, **Robert Schumann (1810–1856)**, and **Clara Wieck Schumann (1819–1896)**.

Franz Schubert.

Schubert's short life presents many mysteries to us today, especially when it comes to the matter of his sexual orientation: at least one prominent musicologist has argued he was attracted to men, and another of equal prominence insists he was only attracted to women. The orientation issue means so much to scholars because Schubert's social life was deeply important to him and difficult to disentangle from his music. For friends and presumably lovers, Schubert wrote *lieder* and other works continually and seemingly impulsively. In 1815 alone he apparently composed upwards of 400 songs. By his early thirties, Schubert was part of a distinguished circle, an intimate group of supporters that encouraged him in his extraordinarily lyrical approach to musical composition.

Some of Schubert's *lieder* followed the patterns of folk music, with a **strophic** design, something familiar to all who listen to folk songs to this day. In settings of this kind the composer furnished music for one stanza and allowed the singer to repeat that music for all the further stanzas of the poem. Because the poetic tendency was to ensure that stanzas contained the same number of lines and syllables with the same pattern of accents, this was considered a basic, and often the best, way to set multi-stanza poems to music. But composers were aware that some words had a special significance, and thus they modified their settings sometimes to paint them in a different way. When composers basically kept the strophic form recognizable but made changes for the sake of expression, we call the form **modified strophic**. Finally, there were occasions when the composer decided to abandon the strophic idea altogether and follow a design that had little to do with the poetic form (with no large scale, but some small-scale musical repetitions), which we call **through composed**. Among some of Schubert's greatest masterpieces were through-composed *lieder*, where he followed the dramatic curve of a poem with his music rather than adhering closely to its formal properties.

Guided Listening

Erlkönig by Franz Schubert, Lied (1815)

Erlkönig is a ***lied***, or German art song of the nineteenth century. Like most *lieder* (plural of *lied*), this song is for a solo voice and piano. This song is **through-composed**, meaning that Schubert wrote new material for every part of the song instead of using repeated sections. The text of *Erlkönig (Elfking)* was written by Johann Wolfgang von Goethe and tells the story of a boy and his father who are riding a horse through the woods at night when the boy begins to see visions of the Elfking.

http://www.rhapsody.com/artist/runi-brattaberghans-otto-ehrstrom/album/brotid/track/erlkonig

0:00 The piano plays an introduction. The rapid triplets evoke the rhythm of the horse's hooves on the ground. The minor key establishes the darkness of the setting and foreshadows the fearful events that will unfold.

(continued)

	Original text	*English translation*
	Narrator—middle range	
0:24	*Wer reitet so spät durch Nacht und Wind?* *Es ist der Vater mit seinem Kind;* *Er hat den Knaben wohl in dem Arm,* *Er faßt ihn sicher, er hält ihn warm.*	*Who rides so late through the night and wind?* *It's the father with his child;* *He has the boy safe in his arm,* *He holds him secure, he holds him warm.*
	Father—low range	
1:00	*"Mein Sohn, was birgst du so bang dein Gesicht?"*	*"My son, what makes you hide your face in fear?"*
	Son—high range	
1:09	*"Siehst, Vater, du den Erlkönig nicht?* *Den Erlenkönig mit Kron und Schweif?"*	*"Father, don't you see the Elfking?* *The Elfking with crown and flowing robe?"*
	Father—low range, reassuring	
1:26	*"Mein Sohn, es ist ein Nebelstreif."*	*"My son, it's a wisp of fog."*
	Elfking—major mode, playful and embellished	
1:36	*"Du liebes Kind, komm, geh mit mir!* *Gar schöne Spiele spiel' ich mit dir;* *Manch bunte Blumen sind an dem Strand,* *Meine Mutter hat manch gülden Gewand."*	*"You dear child, come along with me!* *Such lovely games I'll play with you;* *Many colorful flowers are at the shore,* *My mother has many a golden garment."*
	Son—high range, frightened	
2:00	*"Mein Vater, mein Vater, und hörest du nicht,* *Was Erlenkönig mir leise verspricht?"*	*"My father, my father, and do you not hear* *What the Elfking promises me so softly?"*
	Father—low range, calm	
2:14	*"Sei ruhig, bleibe ruhig, mein Kind;* *In dürren Blättern säuselt der Wind."*	*"Be quiet, stay quiet, my child;* *In the dry leaves the wind is rustling."*
	Elfking—major mode, dance-like accompaniment	
2:24	*"Willst, feiner Knabe, du mit mir gehn?* *Meine Töchter sollen dich warten schön;* *Meine Töchter führen den nächtlichen Reihn,* *Und wiegen und tanzen und singen dich ein."*	*"Won't you come along with me, my fine boy?* *My daughters shall attend to you so nicely.* *My daughters do their nightly dance,* *And they'll rock you and dance you and sing you to sleep."*
	Son—high range, growing fear, dissonance	
2:43	*"Mein Vater, mein Vater, und siehst du nicht dort* *Erlkönigs Töchter am düstern Ort?"*	*"My father, my father, and do you not see over there* *Elfking's daughters in that dark place?"*
	Father—low range, ever calm and reassuring	
2:56	*"Mein Sohn, mein Sohn, ich seh es genau:* *Es scheinen die alten Weiden so grau."*	*"My son, my son, I see it most definitely:* *It's the willow trees looking so grey."*
	Elfking—affectionate, then insistent	
3:15	*"Ich liebe dich, mich reizt deine schöne Gestalt;* *Und bist du nicht willig, so brauch ich Gewalt."*	*"I love you; I'm charmed by your beautiful form;* *And if you're not willing, then I'll use force."*
	Son—high range, terrified	
3:27	*"Mein Vater, mein Vater, jetzt faßt er mich an!* *Erlkönig hat mir ein Leids getan!"*	*"My father, my father, now he's grabbing hold of me!* *Elfking has done me harm!"*
	Narrator—middle range, more speechlike than the characters	
3:42	*Dem Vater grausets, er reitet geschwind,* *Er hält in Armen das ächzende Kind,* *Erreicht den Hof mit Mühe und Not;* *In seinen Armen das Kind war tot.*	*The father shudders, he rides swiftly,* *He holds in his arms the moaning child.* *He reaches the farmhouse with effort and urgency.* *In his arms the child was dead.*

Younger than Schubert, but strongly influenced by his achievement, were Robert and Clara Schumann, who married in 1840. Before their marriage Clara had been a child prodigy on a truly Mozartian scale. Fitting for the new era, Clara's musical prowess was demonstrated almost exclusively on the piano, even to the point where her father, as he planned her tours, collaborated with piano makers to encourage sales and serve new marketing purposes. Clara did compose music as well; and some of her finest works are *lieder*, which were also composed by Robert, her husband. Robert actually wounded himself in an attempt to stretch his fingers to perform on the piano with greater dexterity. He decided to abandon piano performance as a career option and began to write music that he knew would be played by his profoundly admired and adored wife.

Clara and Robert Schumann, after a daguerreotype, c. 1850.

Clara was the daughter of Friedrich Wieck, Robert's composition teacher. When the two met, Wieck seemed to encourage their musical relationship. But when the relationship went in other directions, Wieck turned against his prized composition students. Some suspect that Wieck knew Robert had contracted syphilis on his trips abroad. In any case, he opposed the marriage and introduced a fair dose of antagonism into what had been an intimate world of music and love; and, when Robert went insane later, things turned to real tragedy. But many of the Schumanns' songs were written in the happiest times of their lives, capturing feelings shared between two immensely sensitive and talented musicians. Their *lieder* may be the most intimate of all Romantic works, treasures of an age that prized the subjective realm perhaps more than any other.

Guided Listening

"Liebst du um Schönheit" by Clara Schumann (1841), Lied

Clara Schumann's father, Friedrich, directed her musical education meticulously and sometimes tyrannically, but his role as her mentor and manager was critical to her success, as she herself regularly acknowledged. Clara was a child prodigy and made her formal solo début as a pianist at age 11. She quickly gained international acclaim as a piano virtuoso, and had opportunities to meet and befriend many important composers of the era, including Felix Mendelssohn, Berlioz, Chopin, and Liszt.

Clara married Robert Schumann in 1840, after a long legal battle with her father over the matter. Robert had failed as a performer after an injury to his hand, and was virtually unknown as a composer. After a brief productive period of composing in the early years of their marriage, Clara put aside her own composing to care for her eight children and to promote and perform Robert's works. Robert struggled with mental instability all his life, and in 1854 he was confined to an asylum at his own request, where he died two years later. To support her family, Clara resumed her career as a touring piano virtuoso, playing across Europe into her seventies.

"Liebst du um Schönheit" is a love poem set by Clara Schumann in 1841, a year after her marriage to Robert. The piece is in **modified strophic form**, meaning that the same melody and accompaniment are heard in each section, but with slight variations. This method of organization allows for both familiarity and freshness in each strophe.

http://www.rhapsody.com/artist/barbara-bonney/album/robert-and-clara-schumann-lieder---frauenliebe-und--leben/track/2-liebst-du-um-schonheit

0:00 Brief piano introduction

Strophe 1

0:07	A	*Liebst du um Schönheit, o nicht mich liebe!* *Liebe die Sonne, sie trägt ein gold'nes Haar!*	*If you love for beauty, don't love me!* *Love the sun, with her golden hair!*

(continued)

		Strophe 2	
0:34	A¹	*Liebst du um Jugend, o nicht mich liebe!* *Liebe den Frühling, der jung ist jedes Jahr!*	*If you love for youth, don't love me!* *Love the spring, which is young each year!*
		Strophe 3	
1:00	A²	*Liebst du um Schätze, o nicht mich liebe!* *Liebe die Meerfrau, sie hat viel Perlen klar!*	*If you love for money, don't love me!* *Love the mermaid, she has many pearls!*
		Strophe 4	
1:28	A³	*Liebst du um Liebe, o ja—mich liebe!* *Liebe mich immer, dich lieb' ich immerdar!*	*If you love for love, oh yes—love me!* *Love me for ever, and I will love you eternally.*
2:02	Brief piano coda		

Guided Listening

"Du ring an meinen finger" from *Frauenliebe und -leben* by Robert Schumann (1840), Lied

Schumann set this song cycle in 1840, the same year that he married Clara Wieck, the daughter of his piano teacher. Clara's father did not approve of the match, so there had been an ugly legal battle over the matter from April 1839 to August 1840. When it became clear in July 1840 that Clara's father was unable to corroborate his accusations against Schumann and a victory for the couple was expected, the composer had a surge of productivity that included *Frauenliebe und -leben*. When *Frauenliebe und -leben* was published in 1843, it was Clara, a piano virtuoso, former child prodigy, and composer herself, who edited the collection.

Frauenliebe und -leben (A Woman's Love and Life) is a song-cycle that follows the life of a woman with the man she loves, from her perspective. "Du ring an meinen finger" ("You ring on my finger") is the fourth song of the cycle. At this point in the story, the woman has become engaged to her beloved. She considers her ring as a symbol of her love and devotion to her future husband and she looks forward to their life together.

http://www.rhapsody.com/artist/leon-fleisher/album/schumann-song-cycles-op-24-42-and-48/track/frauenliebe-und-leben-op-42-iv-du-ring-an-meinem-finger

		Original text	*English translation*
0:00	The melody used for this section returns, but is slightly different each time.	*Du Ring an meinem Finger,* *Mein goldenes Ringelein,* *Ich drücke dich fromm an die Lippen,* *Dich fromm an das Herze mein.*	*You ring on my finger,* *My little golden ring,* *I press you devoutly to my lips* *And piously to my heart.*
0:23		*Ich hatt ihn ausgeträumet,* *Der Kindheit friedlich schönen Traum,* *Ich fand allein mich, verloren* *Im öden, unendlichen Raum.*	*I had dreamt it,* *The lovely, tranquil dream of childhood,* *I found myself alone, lost* *In bleak, infinite space.*
0:46	Return of the first melody, slightly varied.	*Du Ring an meinem Finger* *Da hast du mich erst belehrt,* *Hast meinem Blick erschlossen* *Des Lebens unendlichen, tiefen Wert.*	*You ring on my finger,* *You have taught me for the first time,* *And I have opened my eyes unto* *A life of endless and profound worth.*
1:10	This section builds to a climax on "ganz" ("completely") with higher notes in the voice and fast, full chords in the piano.	*Ich werd' ihm dienen, ihm leben,* *Ihm angehören ganz,* *Hin selber mich geben und finden* *Verklärt mich in seinem Glanz.*	*I will serve him, live for him,* *Belong to him completely,* *Give myself and find myself* *Transfigured in his radiance.*
1:36	Another return of the first melody, slightly different from the previous iterations.	*Du Ring an meinem Finger,* *Mein goldenes Ringelein,* *Ich drücke dich fromm an die Lippen* *Dich fromm an das Herze mein.*	*You ring on my finger,* *My little golden ring,* *I press you devoutly to my lips* *And piously to my heart.*
2:04	Short piano interlude concludes the piece.		

When we listen to the songs (*lieder*) of Schubert and Schumann, we immediately notice the **prominence of the piano**. All three valued the piano highly and were noted performers on the instrument. The piano's role is essential, as followers of Schubert and the Schumanns well recognized. In the future some composers would take things to the point where the voice could be seen as the simple conveyer of words, while all the expression was captured in the hands of the pianist. If the lyrical urge was too prominent for the early nineteenth-century composer to surrender so much to the piano, it does point to the fact that at this time the piano reigned as an up-and-coming force in compositional circles and even in fashion.

The great classical piano sonatas of Beethoven and Mozart remained in the repertory throughout the nineteenth century and beyond, and many played the harpsichord works of J. S. Bach on the piano, even though they were designed for a different instrument. The cutting edge of new composition emphasized the lyrical possibilities of the instrument, along with a heavy dose of "show-off" virtuosity that naturally came with so much intense interest in the instrument. As he wrote a number of great cycles of **character pieces** of great ingenuity and expression, Robert Schumann's piano works number among the finest of the time. Clara Schumann was considered by many to be the finest piano performer of her time.

Because they were so often seen performing or associated with the instrument even more frequently, **Frédéric Chopin (1810–1849)** and **Franz Liszt (1811–1886)** left for us perhaps the most seminal works for piano of this era, and arguably of all time. Both approached the sonata in various ways, but mainly explored new and different forms, looking always for compositional vehicles that would allow them the room they desired to explore the depths of lyrical virtuosity. Both wrote works they named études (studies) that took the idea of "study" to its very highest level. These **études** were works that demanded more of the pianist than ever before. Designed not simply to challenge and teach, they were meant to stand as permanent examples of an intensely expressive art.

Frédéric Chopin (1810–1849).

Franz Liszt (1811–1886).

Guided Listening

Mazurka No. 5 in B-flat major, Op. 7-1 by Frédéric Chopin (1832)

Chopin was born near Warsaw, Poland, to a Polish mother and a French father. Although he spent the majority of his life and career in France, he had strong emotional ties to Poland and evoked Polish folk melodies and idioms often in his compositions. The **mazurka** is a traditional Polish dance in a fast triple meter with an accent on the second beat of each measure. The melody of Chopin's "Mazurka No. 5" was inspired by native folk tunes, and the harmonies suggest the drone of a village bagpipe. In a Parisian salon, this composition was treated as a concert piece, whereas in Poland, it could have been used to accompany actual dancing.

http://www.rhapsody.com/artist/various-artists/album/chopin-the-complete-piano-works-mazurkas-1/track/chopin-mazurka-no5-in-b-flat-major-op7-1

0:00	A section—quick triple-meter dance with second beat accented
0:13	Repeat of A
0:26	B section—lyrical interlude
0:37	Repeat of A
0:51	Repeat of B, then A
1:16	C section—exotic-sounding melody with accompanying drone in bass
1:27	Repeat of A
1:41	Repeat of C, then A

Guided Listening

Étude No. 3 (*La campanella*) of *Six Grandes Etudes de Paganini* by Franz Liszt

http://www.rhapsody.com/artist/thomas-otten/album/liszt-tristan-und-isolde---piano-transcriptions/track/franz-liszt-grandes-etudes-de-paganini-no-3---la-campanella-

Franz Liszt wrote six **études** (studies) based on themes by Nicolò Paganini, a famous violin **virtuoso** (performer with a very high level of technical skill). Liszt himself was a virtuoso pianist, so he reworked Paganini's violin themes for piano. As you might have guessed, the techniques demanded in these pieces are very challenging and demand a virtuoso performer. *La campanella* (the little bell) is in theme and variations form with two themes and a coda at the end.

0:10 Introduction of the first theme. Notice the high repeated notes, reminiscent of a little bell.

0:26 Large leaps are the major technical challenge through this section.

0:44 Introduction of the second theme.

1:36 Quick repetition of individual notes (difficult to produce quickly, evenly, and clearly).

2:22 High, fast scales and figuration in the right hand.

2:45 A **trill** (quick alternation between two pitches) begins in the first two fingers, then is executed with the ring and pinky finger of the right hand so that the first two fingers will be available to play other pitches.

4:07 The final boisterous statement of the first theme includes quickly repeated chords, which demand that the performer use quick arm movements in addition to quick finger movements.

4:22 Coda brings closure to the piece.

Watch an amazing performance of *La campanella* by Valentina Lisitsa on **YouTube: http://youtube/vwc-nmyPm4I**

Part 2: Orchestral Music

When music historians make the claim that Beethoven straddled the Classical and Romantic periods of music history, they often have in mind his Fifth and Sixth Symphonies, and how these two gigantic works contrast with one another. Nicknamed the "**Pastoral**," **Beethoven's Sixth** is noteworthy for its **program**. Programmatic works were purely instrumental works—often (but by no means exclusively) composed for orchestra—based on a story, painting, idea, etc., that we call **extra-musical** (as it originates outside of the musical notes of the score). Although many have claimed Beethoven's Fifth has a program, it actually does not—or, at least, it has no program authorized by the composer. For all its suggestiveness of something profound and story-like, the Fifth Symphony stands as the paradigm of **absolute music**: a work put together through the manipulation of motifs and themes, with the idea of statement, development, and resolution (based on sonata form) as its underlying principle.

Franz Liszt conducting in Budapest.

The program for Beethoven's "Pastoral" is, by striking contrast, a series of countryside scenes. As had Vivaldi (in his "Four Seasons") along with a number of other composers, Beethoven published descriptive words to evoke the images he meant to describe musically, such as "scene at a brook" (second movement) and "thunderstorm" (fourth movement). The point of describing these scenes was to give audiences the information they needed to relate to them in the way the composer had envisioned them, enriching the audience's experience as they listened to purely instrumental musical depictions. As far back as the Renaissance (and even the medieval era), composers had experimented with the idea that music could conjure up images such as battle scenes, storms, bustling street fairs, etc. But when Beethoven penned and published his "Pastoral" Sixth after his Fifth, he drew special attention to the way a "purely" musical structure (instead of a program) and an extra-musical program could serve as the basis for further large-scale composition.

Given his tumultuous character, Beethoven's musical storm is particularly satisfying (and it is fun to compare it to Vivaldi's "Enlightenment" storm of a former era), but perhaps the most important idea that Beethoven explored in his Sixth Symphony was how a scene could replace a harmonic progression as the means to build a large-scale musical edifice. In the first movement of the "Pastoral," in order to set the countryside scene, Beethoven spun out what was for him a rather a long melody, and then, rather than reduce it down to its motifs, he simply moved the whole melodic structure up into a new harmonic area, specifically to one we call the **mediant**. His choice of this "new" harmony is intriguing, as the mediant, as its name suggests, is not as functional a harmony in the tonal system as the **dominant**, nor is it obviously one of the **pre-dominant** harmonies that would lead to the dominant and then, ultimately, to the **tonic**. Composers at the time greeted Beethoven's interesting harmonic move as a welcome way of prolonging things; to evade the dominant like this was to open up a potentially infinite amount of musical space. But it also denied the whole tonal system its purpose of directing musical progress, and so it was in some ways the seed for a destructive idea that eventually came to dominate musical thought in the West.

Hector Berlioz (1803–1869).

One of the first and most important composers to embrace the programmatic ideal after Beethoven was the admittedly "Beethoven-obsessed" French composer **Hector Berlioz (1803–69)**. Berlioz was also obsessed with Shakespeare and one particular British Shakespearean actress, Harriet Smithson, so it is probably fair to say that obsession was a motivating force for him and we shouldn't dwell too much on his Beethoven issues.

His unrequited love obsession with Smithson is in fact the subject of Berlioz's first programmatic masterpiece, *Symphonie fantastique (Fantastic Symphony)* of 1830. In this strange and tragic story, the protagonist finds that he cannot get a melody representing the "beloved" out of his mind—Berlioz called this melody an ***idée fixe*** (fixed idea) and it appears, in various transformations, throughout the symphony. At one truly desperate point, the protagonist takes opium in an attempt to divert his attention from his obsession. But rather than take his mind off his troubles, the drug causes him to hallucinate about his own execution and hellish future, which is full of goblins tauntingly singing the melody in grotesque transformations in front of him for all eternity. Berlioz liked to encourage his audiences to think of him as a "passionate" creature not unlike this protagonist, but this did not keep him from developing special skills as a composer—nor, as it turns out, from marrying Smithson, although their marriage ultimately failed.

Not only was Berlioz a **gifted melodist**, he was one of the finest **orchestrators** in the Western tradition. His treatise on the use of instruments—describing what they do best, how they can be best combined, etc.—remains one of the seminal works in the field, and should be read by anyone composing for the orchestra. Indeed, Berlioz's *Symphonie* was written for the largest known orchestra ever to perform at the time, and it is through his brilliant use of instruments that the story comes to life in this programmatic masterpiece.

Guided Listening

Symphonie fantastique by Hector Berlioz (1830), Program Symphony

Berlioz wrote *Symphonie fantastique* when he was in his late twenties, drawing the story from his own infatuation with actress Harriet Smithson. The narrative concerns a lovesick artist who attempts to poison himself with opium, but instead experiences drug-induced visions in which his beloved becomes a melody, "a recurrent theme that haunts him everywhere." This theme, the ***idée fixe*** (fixed idea), can be heard prominently in all five movements of the symphony but is slightly altered each time, reflecting the changing perspective of the artist and his feelings toward the woman.

In the last movement, *Dream of a Witches' Sabbath*, the artist has killed his beloved, has been executed for the crime, and now sees a vision of his tormented afterlife, surrounded by witches and ghouls. The *idée fixe* returns again, but it is now deformed and grotesque as his beloved joins in the "devilish orgy."

In addition to the *idée fixe*, another melody appears several times throughout this movement. The melody is drawn from a plainchant, ***Dies irae*** *(Day of Wrath)*, that has played a prominent role in the **Requiem Mass** or **Mass for the Dead** of the Catholic Church since the fourteenth century. The text of *Dies irae* speaks of the wrath of God on the final judgment day, and its melody is used here to portray impending doom and evoke death and damnation.

Movements of the *Symphonie fantastique*:

I. *Reveries, Passions:* Largo, Allegro agitato e appassionato assai (lively, agitated, and impassioned)
II. *A Ball:* Valse, Allegro non troppo (waltz, not too fast)
III. *Scene in the Fields:* Adagio
IV. *March to the Scaffold:* Allegretto non troppo
V. *Dream of a Witches' Sabbath:* Larghetto, Allegro assai

http://www.rhapsody.com/artist/royal-philharmonic-orchestra/album/berlioz-le-carnaval-romain-symphonie-fantastique/track/symphonie-fantastique-the-fantastic-symphony-v-songe-dune-nu

0:00	Tremolo in the high strings sets an eerie mood.
1:22	*Idée fixe* is heard in the high E-flat clarinet, transformed into a grotesque and witch-like version of the original theme.
1:41	The deformed *idée fixe* returns, this time joined by other instruments representing the hellish creatures that surround the artist.
2:49	Tubular bells evoke church bells.
3:17	*Dies irae* is heard in the low voices as the bells continue to chime, then the theme is taken up by other groups of instruments and accompanied in a variety of ways.
4:57	Repetition of the *Dies irae* gives way to an imitative section that evokes the chaos of the scene.
6:44	A melody in the bassoon is interrupted many times by other instruments.
6:59	*Dies irae* returns in fragments, mixing with the chaotic dancing music, and building to a climax.
7:45	Repetition of a single chord at the peak of the phrase evokes obsession and desperation.
8:02	Yet another statement of the *Dies irae* is heard over a dance-like melody.
8:31	*Col legno* (with the wood) technique, in which the violins and violas strike their strings with the wooden part of the bow, is used to evoke witches' laughter.
9:08	Overlapping partial restatements of the *Dies irae* build toward the final conclusion.

Franz Liszt, the phenomenal pianist, was a Berlioz follower, and historians often neglect Liszt's seminal contributions to symphonic literature. But Liszt was an innovator in his own right, developing Berlioz's means of **thematic transformation** to the point where he could avoid closure altogether as he subjected a recognizable melody to different contexts as a surefire way to tell a story in music. Berlioz, like Beethoven, had cut his programmatic work into movements, but Liszt told the whole story in a single long movement. Liszt was followed by a group of composers known for expressing nationalistic ideals in their music by using the same or similar programmatic techniques, such as **Modest Mussorgsky** of Russia and **Bedřich Smetana** of the Czech Republic, among others. Many have credited advances in programmatic ideas as the inspiration for **Pyotr Ilyich Tchaikovsky's** enchanting ballets, including his well-loved *Nutcracker*.

Resisting the programmatic urge were a number of composers who looked to the past as a means of musical advancement; they were headed up by the great German master **Johannes Brahms (1833–1897)**. Brahms championed an approach to composition that drew deeply from the contrapuntal achievements of J. S. Bach, Haydn, Mozart, and Beethoven, all of whom he saw as setting the path to musical progress by their manipulation of tonal and thus "purely musical" ideals. Brahms was in fact one of the worst afflicted by Beethoven's intimidating shadow. Unlike Berlioz, Brahms really *did* have Beethoven "issues." Brahms withdrew works, put others through numerous revisions, and agonized over the results of others, all in an effort to live up to the standards set by his colossal musical predecessor. In Brahms's music many hear a return to ideals of balance and classical concision, but from early on in the reception of his music, many noted that his approach to motifs and development was in its own way pointing to the demise of tonality on which so many of the Classical structures were based. We will return to Brahms in the next section as we end the story of Romantic music with a work of his, *A German Requiem*, which critics claimed fulfilled the composer's self-imposed lofty goal of meeting Beethoven's compositional standard.

Guided Listening

First Movement, Symphony No. 4 in E minor, Op. 98 by Johannes Brahms (1885)

Fearing that his orchestral work would never equal the standards established by Beethoven, Brahms once exclaimed, "I shall never compose a symphony!" Despite his insecurities, and with encouragement and support from Robert and Clara Schumann, Brahms became the leading German composer of his time in every genre except opera. Brahms labored on his first symphony for over twenty years, finally completing it in 1876 when he was in his forties. When he began his fourth symphony in 1884, Brahms had established himself as a worthy symphonist, sensitive to the Beethovenian legacy but not intimidated by it. Brahms was creatively self-possessed and financially secure, free to compose as he wished without concern for the requirements of a patron or the demands of the general public. Given this freedom, he undertook his Symphony No. 4 with the goal of writing a timeless masterpiece, drawing on the past to create a work for the ages.

http://www.rhapsody.com/artist/royal-philharmonic-orchestra/album/brahms--symphonies-1-4/track/symphony-no-4-in-e-minor-op-98---i-allegro-non-troppo

Exposition

0:00 Theme 1—listen for variations of this theme returning throughout the symphony; notice also that this theme appears at the beginning of both the development and the coda.

2:27 Theme 2—major mode.

3:03 Closing.

Development

4:08 Development begins with theme 1.

Recapitulation

7:07 Theme 1, subtle at first, then more clearly at 7:32.

9:31 Theme 2.

10:06 Closing.

Coda

11:14 Coda begins with theme 1, boldly stated.

Part 3: Opera and Choral Works

As noted above, the Romantic era was an age of extremes. At one pole were the small forms of piano music and *lieder*; at the other were the nineteenth-century works for chorus, orchestra, and opera. It was again Beethoven who set the stage for some of this activity, although his one opera, *Fidelio*—if well known and well studied—was not as influential as his choral works such as the *Missa solemnis* and Ninth Symphony. In the area of choral works, the Late Baroque may have had an equally prominent influence.

One of the most important contributors to the **choral repertory** of the early Romantic era was **Felix Mendelssohn (1809–1847)**, the grandson of the great Jewish philosopher Moses Mendelssohn. One of the most treasured composers of the entire era, Mendelssohn produced some of the finest Romantic orchestral, chamber, and piano music. He was also the one most responsible for the "rediscovery" of the great choral music of J. S. Bach. His father had converted to Lutheranism before his birth, and Mendelssohn would take up a position at the same *Thomaskirke* where Bach had worked, conducting many of Bach's choral works for the first time since Bach's death. In Mendelssohn's *St. Paul* and *Elijah* oratorios, one can detect the influence of both Bach and Handel.

Brahms also looked to his musical past for inspiration, although in some cases there were personal motives as well. It is often noted that Brahms lost his mother in 1865 and that he was still mourning the death of his close friend Robert Schumann (d. 1853) when he composed his momentous ***German Requiem***. But Brahms went to considerable lengths to make the work as broad-reaching as possible, purposely choosing texts that all the faithful would embrace and even declaring that he thought of the work as a "human" requiem. Brahms's work focuses on the mourners, following a dramatic arc that leads the listener through many of the so-called "stages of grief" discussed today. Just before we come to the "acceptance" stage, with a depiction of heaven in "Wie lieblich sind deine Wohnungen" ("How lovely are thy dwellings"), Brahms takes us through a period of "anger and bargaining" with a great contrapuntal device of a complex **fugue** that he cast over a single sounding **D pedal**—a single low note held and performed by the basses and timpani drums. The contrast between the frenetic and complex musical movement in the upper voices—as an expression of anger and maybe denial—and the constancy of the lowest note—confirming the fact of death—makes for one of the most gripping moments in all of Western music. Such passages confirm that Brahms's understanding of the music of Bach and Beethoven had given him the tools to produce music of great power, but also the capacity to comfort those who needed it most of all.

Guided Listening

A German Requiem by Johannes Brahms (1868)

The **Requiem Mass**, or **Mass for the Dead**, is a Catholic service designated for funerals or remembrance of the dead. Unlike the Catholic Requiem, which uses a fixed Latin text, Brahms's Protestant Requiem is in German, with texts drawn from the Lutheran Bible. Brahms himself selected the texts, choosing passages that comfort mourners and emphasize the peace and joy of the departed.

After a poor performance at the premiere in Vienna, Brahms conducted the second performance of *A German Requiem* in Bremen in 1868. This performance was met with both critical acclaim and enthusiasm from audiences. Robert Schumann described Brahms as a genius very early in his career, and this work was seen as the fulfillment of Schumann's prophecy and marked a turning point in Brahms's career.

III. Herr, lehre doch mich

http://www.rhapsody.com/artist/johannes-brahms/album/a-german-requiem/track/ein-deutsches-requiem-op-45---ein-deutsches-requiem-op-45-ei-3 (at 6:53)

6:53 Fugue over pedal point builds tension through the conclusion of the third movement, leading into the fourth movement.

IV. Wie lieblich sind deine Wohnungen (text from Psalm 84)

http://www.rhapsody.com/artist/johannes-brahms/album/a-german-requiem/track/ein-deutsches-requiem-op-45---ein-deutsches-requiem-op-45-ei-4

	Rondo form	*Original text*	*English translation*
0:08	A	*Wie lieblich sind deine Wohnungen, Herr Zebaoth!*	*How lovely is Thy dwelling place, O Lord of Hosts!*
1:26	B	*Meine Seele verlanget und sehnet sich nach den Vorhöfen des Herrn; mein Leib und Seele freuen sich in dem lebendigen Gott.*	*My soul longs and even faints for the courts of the Lord; my flesh and soul rejoice in the living God.*
2:20	A^1	*Wie lieblich . . .* *Wohl denen, die in deinem Hause wohnen,*	*How lovely . . .* *Blessed are they that live in thy house,*
3:41	C	*die loben dich immerdar!*	*that praise Thee evermore!*
4:31	A^1	*Wie lieblich . . .*	*How lovely . . .*

Opera at this time ranged from small-scale comedies to truly mammoth affairs—volcanic eruptions were featured in some, and in others, stage elephants were known to walk under the same lights as the singers. In much the way we treat films today, operas of the nineteenth century were anticipated, loved, and hyped when they worked, or hated and panned when they disappointed. Theaters at the time wanted to be able to predict what composers would present to their publics, and composers were usually happy to do their part and follow basic conventions, producing works that were in many ways predictable. So, even if there was a lot of cross-fertilization, national traditions are fairly easy to detect in the nineteenth century. In **France**, for example, small-scale comedy was developed in some theaters, while the **Grand Opera** encouraged the most spectacular effects of the entire era. In **Italy**, the **voice** was cultivated as the prime dramatic instrument, while in **Germany**, composers turned to the **orchestra** to move the drama forward. By the end of the century, a new kind of **realism** was on the cutting edge everywhere. In this movement—often called **versimo**—gritty stories were the norm. Such operas featured those on the lower rungs of society, or those shunned by "good" society, and audiences then were captivated by cruel beauties of the criminal class, such as Georges Bizet's Carmen character.

Guided Listening

"L'amour est un oiseau rebelle" (Habanera) from *Carmen* by Georges Bizet (1875)

Although *Carmen* was only moderately successful when it first opened, it has since become one of the most popular and successful operas of all time. Set in nineteenth-century Spain, the story of *Carmen* centers on the title character, an alluring and self-possessed young woman whose sensuality captivates everyone around her. A naïve army corporal, Don José, becomes infatuated with Carmen and devotes himself entirely to her, but she soon turns her attentions to a new suitor, the bullfighter Escamillo. In a fit of rage and jealousy, Don José stabs Carmen to death in the final scene while crowds cheer the bullfighting nearby.

Carmen is one of the earliest and most important **realistic operas.** Far from the stories about kings, queens, gods, and goddesses of the Baroque period, the story of *Carmen* concerns working-class characters and those who live on the outskirts of society (gypsies, bandits, prostitutes). On-stage behavior includes smoking, drinking, and fighting, and the chorus includes a group of working women who have made themselves comfortable on a hot day by loosening and removing items of clothing. The morality of the principal characters is questionable at best and reprehensible at worst. The story was shocking to a nineteenth-century audience, but it demonstrates a shift in opera toward plots that treat issues of everyday life, even when they are dark or unpleasant.

In order to evoke the Spanish setting, Bizet incorporated Spanish popular songs, folk songs, and flamenco melodies throughout *Carmen*. The **habanera** rhythm was drawn from a sensual dance that originated in Spanish-controlled Cuba (*habanera* literally means "thing from Havana") and eventually gave rise to the tango.

http://www.rhapsody.com/artist/georges-bizet/album/bizet-carmen-highlights-rca/track/carmen---act-i-lamour-est-un-oiseau-rebelle-1997-remastered

		Original text	English translation
0:00	Habanera rhythm used as an ostinato in the bass; minor mode.		
		Carmen	
0:06	Carmen enters with a descending chromatic melody.	*L'amour est un oiseau rebelle Que nul ne peut apprivoiser; Et c'est bien en vain qu'on l'appelle, S'il lui convient de refuser. Rien n'y fait, menace ou prière, L'un parle bien, l'autre se tait; Et c'est l'autre que je préfère, Il n'a rien dit, mais il me plaît.*	*Love is a rebellious bird That no one can tame; And you call him in vain, If it suits him to refuse. Nothing works, neither threat nor prayer, One man speaks well, the other is silent; And it's the latter that I prefer, He says nothing but he pleases me.*
0:40	Change to major mode; chorus repeats Carmen's melody while Carmen sings "l'amour" ("love") above.		
0:57	First statement of the refrain (melody is drawn from Carmen's original melody, but this section of text returns several times).	*L'amour est enfant de Bohème, Il n'a jamais connu de loi, Si tu ne m'aimes pas, je t'aime; Si je t'aime, prends garde à toi!'*	*Love is like a gypsy child, Who has never known constraint, If you don't love me, then I love you; If I love you, you'd best beware!*
1:13	Chorus shouts, "Prends garde à toi!" ("You'd best beware!")		
1:36	Chorus sings refrain, in alternation with Carmen.		
2:21	New text sung to Carmen's original melody.	*L'oiseau que tu croyais surprendre Battit de l'aile et s'envola; L'amour est loin, tu peux l'attendre; Tu ne l'attends pas, il est là! Tout atour de toi, vite, Il vient, s'en va, puis il revient; Tu crois le tenir, il t'evite; Tu crois l'eviter, il te tient!*	*The bird you thought that you had caught Beat its wings and flew away; Love is far away, but you wait and wait; When least expected, there it is! All around you, swiftly, It comes, it goes, and then returns; You think you've trapped it, but it escapes; You think you're free, but you are trapped!*
2:55	Again, change to major mode; chorus repeats Carmen's melody while Carmen sings "l'amour" ("love") above.		
3:11	Three returns of the refrain (Carmen, chorus, then Carmen) bring the piece to a close.		

The composer who dominated the **Italian opera** scene throughout the first three decades of the nineteenth century was **Gioachino Rossini (1792–1868)**. Rossini was called the "Italian Mozart" at the time, and the name still fits him well, as he combined a comic genius with a full understanding of tragedy. But what Rossini and the whole Italian school really specialized in, more than anything else—and in ways very different from Mozart—was the dramatic capabilities of the voice. If any music in the nineteenth century was truly "melody-led," it was Italian opera. This did not mean that Rossini neglected the instruments of his orchestra. In fact, many know him best for his fully instrumental operatic overtures (introductions to the opera), such as the famous overture to *William Tell* (also known to many as the theme of *The Lone Ranger*). But the dramatic success of a Rossini opera depends on the singer and the way his or her melody makes a listener captive to the dramatic situation. For all his success and prowess, Rossini is one of very few known composers who retired from music in mid-career, and his reason for doing so—to become a world-famous chef—is rather charming and unexpected (some restaurants still serve "pasta a la Rossini").

Members of the Dnepropetrovsk State Opera and Ballet Theatre perform Rossini's *The Barber of Seville* on June 25, 2011 in Dnepropetrovsk, Ukraine.

It was thanks in part to his understanding and emulation of Rossini's focus on the voice that **Giuseppe Verdi (1813–1901)** would become the next leader in Italian opera. Verdi demonstrated his comic skills in his last opera, the Shakespearean *Falstaff.* But throughout his career he more often explored serious topics that led toward the realism of the next generation, including a famous depiction of a noble courtesan (kept woman) in *La traviata*.

Giuseppe Verdi (1813–1901).

Guided Listening

Recitative, "Follie!" and Aria, "Sempre libera" from *La traviata* by Giuseppe Verdi, Opera

La traviata (The Fallen Woman) is the story of Violetta, a courtesan, who sacrifices her own happiness to protect the man she loves. In this scene, Violetta is trying to convince herself not to fall in love with Alfredo, a man of good standing, because their love would ruin Violetta's free lifestyle and Alfredo's reputation. The aria covered below is a **cabaletta**, a special type of fast aria designed to conclude a scene with energy and drama.

http://www.rhapsody.com/artist/various-artists/album/verdi-la-traviata-deutsche-grammophon-dg/track/follie-delirio-vano-e-questo---sempre-libera

		Original text	*English translation*
Recitative			*Violetta*
0:00	Orchestral accompaniment.	*Follie! Follie! Delirio vano è questo!* *Povera donna, sola,* *abbandonata in questo* *popoloso deserto che* *appellano Parigi.* *Che spero or più?* *Che far degg'io?*	*Madness! Madness! All this is vain delirium!* *Poor woman, alone,* *abandoned in this* *crowded desert that* *they call Paris.* *What hope remains?* *What can I do?*
0:25	Vocal flourishes with minimal accompaniment.	*Gioir!* *Di voluttà ne' vortici perir!* *Gioir!*	*Pleasure!* *Perish in a vortex of indulgence!* *Pleasure!*
0:50	Introduction to cabaletta.		

(continued)

		Original text	English translation
Aria (Cabaletta)			
1:11	Simple dance-like accompaniment from the orchestra gives the focus to the singer.	*Sempre libera degg'io* *folleggiare di gioia in gioia,* *vo'che scorra il viver mio* *pei sentieri del piacer.* *Nasca il giorno, o il giorno muoia,* *sempre lieta ne' ritrovi,* *a diletti sempre nuovi* *dee volare il mio pensier*	*Always free I must remain* *Frolicking from joy to joy,* *Flowing along the surface* *of life's path as I please.* *From dawn to dusk,* *Happily I turn to* *Ever new delights* *That make my spirit soar.*
		Alfredo (offstage, an echo in Violetta's memory)	
1:59	Echoes from an earlier aria in which Alfredo declares his love for Violetta.	*Amor è palpito dell'universo intero,* *misterioso, altero,* *croce e delizia al cor.*	*Love is the heartbeat of the entire universe,* *mysterious, proud,* *the torment and delight of the heart.*
		Violetta	
2:38	More extravagant vocal flourishes with little accompaniment.	*Follie! Gioir!*	*Madness! Pleasure!*
2:10	The cabaletta returns.	*Sempre libera . . .*	*Always free . . .*
		Alfredo (echo)	
3:59	Alfredo's echo returns, this time adorned with scales and other flourishes from Violetta.	*Amor è palpito. . .*	*Love is the heartbeat. . .*

Verdi also depicted a failed interracial marriage that led to murder in *Otello*, a work that many consider to rival in dramatic power the Shakespeare play on which it was based. Significantly, in his *Otello* Verdi was guided by a younger composer named Arrigo Boito (who adapted the text as the librettist) and explored new ways to use the orchestra for dramatic development, showing his awareness of the work of the great German operatic master **Richard Wagner (1813–1883)**.

Usually we find that musicians turn to theater after they have mastered musical composition. Wagner, however, is noteworthy for coming to music composition after he had already decided he wanted to work in the theater. Yet it is very difficult now to imagine that Wagner was ever new to music composition. His work is always strongly and recognizably innovative, but also grounded firmly in the musical ideas propounded from the time of the Late Baroque. Indeed, no composer was more aware than Wagner of how music had been put on an evolutionary path by Bach and Beethoven. Whether Wagner or Brahms was Beethoven's true musical heir was a point of debate at the time—and Wagner's propensity to win over fans was hampered by his petty jealousies, debts, and prejudices (he was overtly anti-Semitic). But everyone involved knew well that Wagner had taken musical dramatization to new and virtually unprecedented heights.

Unsatisfied with the word *opera*, Wagner preferred to call his works **music dramas**. Something of a "control freak," he wrote all the words that were sung in these theatrical works as well as all the notes, and he was also closely involved in the staging. In fact, he would end up supervising the building of a whole complex, in Bayreuth, so he could control performances of his works as much as possible. Wagner described his ideal as ***Gesamtkunstwerk*** (total art work), where every aspect was under his creative control—and even if he could never take complete control over the situation, he did get far in this, and the results were impressive.

The Wagnerian opera theater in Bayreuth, Germany.

Despite his all-encompassing approach, Wagner is especially known for the way he linked stories and evoked characters and ideas through music alone. His main device was something he called the ***leitmotif*** (leading motif). As had Beethoven, Wagner used small musical units as a means of developing ideas, but he took the process further. Using many leitmotifs at once, Wagner created a dense web of musical signifiers, all of which encourage us to make mental note of complex dramatic ideas that could be attributed to something as seemingly simple as the appearance of a character onstage. Like Beethoven, Wagner was also inspired by the cyclic urge—the idea of linking works together to make something new and altogether grand. And with these *leitmotifs* in operation, Wagner realized a powerful cyclic vision. In his *Ring* cycle, he told a single continuous story over the span of four full-length operas (or, to use his terminology, music dramas). As he developed the leitmotif idea as a dramatic structural device, Wagner discovered, finally, that he could take music beyond the limits of tonality itself. Once that bridge was crossed, it would be very hard for Wagner's followers (and even his detractors) to go back to the tonal system; and so, because of him, musical composition in the West would never be the same.

Guided Listening

"Leb' wohl" from *Die Walküre* by Richard Wagner (1856, First Performed in 1870)

Die Walküre (*The Valkyrie*) is the second opera in a cycle of four, collectively called *The Ring of the Nibelung* or simply the *Ring* cycle. The story of the cycle concerns a treasure of gold hidden in the Rhine River and guarded by three Rhine Maidens. Alberich the Nibelung steals the gold and makes it into a ring that grants unlimited power to its owner. Wotan, father of the gods, tricks Alberich to obtain the ring for himself, so Alberich curses the ring so that it will torment its wearer and bring them misfortune and death.

In *Die Walküre*, Siegmund and Sieglinde, twin children of Wotan, have engaged in an incestuous and adulterous affair, and Wotan decides that they must be punished. Another of Wotan's children, his favorite daughter Brünnhilde, is one of the warrior-maidens known as Valkyries. Brünnhilde tries to protect Siegmund and Sieglinde from Wotan's punishment, but despite her efforts Siegmund is killed by Sieglinde's husband, Hunding. Sieglinde survives to bear their child, Siegfried, who will be the hero of the remaining two operas.

(continued)

In the final scene of *Die Walküre,* Wotan plans to punish Brünnhilde for her betrayal by removing her godhood (taking away her powers and making her mortal) and placing her in a magical sleep so that she will be at the mercy of the first mortal who finds her. She begs her father to soften her punishment by surrounding her with flames so that only a brave hero will be able to cross the fire and discover her. Wotan agrees to her request, tenderly bids her farewell, casts his spell, and then summons the god of fire, Loge, to create a magical ring of fire around her.

Throughout the *Ring* cycle, Wagner uses **leitmotifs**, short instrumental motives that are associated with a particular character, object, emotion, or event. These motives reappear many times, evoking their narrative associations and adding a new level of meaning to the on-stage action. The same technique is used by John Williams in his score for *Star Wars*, for example, when we hear the Imperial March while watching a scene featuring Anakin Skywalker. The march subtly foreshadows Anakin's fate to serve the evil Emperor as Darth Vader. The final words of *Die Walküre* are also used to foreshadow later events. Wotan sings, "Whosoever fears the tip of my spear shall never pass through the fire!" as the orchestra announces the theme of Siegfried, the hero that will awaken Brünnhilde with a kiss in the next opera.

A few leitmotifs heard in the listening guide below:

Magic Fire

Siegfried

Love

http://www.rhapsody.com/artist/valery-gergiev/album/wagner-die-walkure/track/wagner-die-walkure-act-iii-x-leb-wohl-du-kuhnes-herrliches-k

0:00 Hints of the famous *Ride of the Valkyries* can be heard in the transition from Brünnhilde's request to Wotan's farewell to her.

		Original text	*English translation*
		Wotan	
0:21	Wotan begins to say farewell to his favorite daughter, and in doing so he agrees to her request to be surrounded by a magic fire as protection from unworthy mortals.	*Leb' wohl, du kühnes,* *herrliches Kind!* *Du meines Herzens* *heiligster Stolz!* *Leb' wohl! Leb' wohl! Leb' wohl!*	*Farewell, you bold,* *wonderful child!* *You, my heart's* *holiest pride.* *Farewell, farewell, farewell!*

		Original text	English translation
		Wotan	
1:06	Wotan continues even more tenderly with a low melody doubled first by the clarinet, then by the French horn.	*Muss ich dich meiden,* *und darf nicht minnig* *mein Gruss dich mehr grüssen;* *sollst du nun nicht mehr* *neben mir reiten,* *noch Met beim Mahl mir reichen;* *muss ich verlieren* *dich, die ich liebe,* *du lachende Lust meines Auges:*	*If I must reject you* *and may not lovingly* *welcome you again with my greeting,* *if you may no longer* *ride beside me,* *or bring me mead at table;* *if I must lose* *you whom I loved* *you, laughing joy of my eyes:*
1:57	As Wotan sings of the fire that will surround Brünnhilde, the accompaniment changes to the "magic fire" leitmotif.	*ein bräutliches Feuer* *soll dir nun brennen,* *wie nie einer Braut es gebrannt!* *Flammende Glut* *umglühe den Fels;* *mit zehrenden Schrecken* *scheuch' es den Zagen;* *der Feige fliehe* *Brünnhildes Fels! -*	*then a bridal fire* *shall burn for you,* *as it never burned for any bride!* *A blaze of flame* *shall burn around the rock;* *with devouring terror* *let it scare the fainthearted;* *let cowards run away* *from Brünnhilde's rock! -*
2:29	As Wotan sings the final words of the opera, Siegfried's leitmotif is prominent in the brass instruments of the orchestra.	*Denn einer nur freie die Braut,* *der freier als ich, der Gott!*	*For only one shall win the bride,* *one freer than I, the God!*
3:04	One of many leitmotifs associated with love can be heard first in the high woodwinds, then throughout the orchestra, continuing through the end of the track. This evokes Wotan's love for his daughter and foreshadows the love between Brünnhilde and Siegfried.		

7

Twentieth Century, 1900–1999

Style and Characteristics

There was no one overriding style or set of characteristics that defined the concert music of the twentieth century. Instead there were several significant styles that were adopted by composers that found varying degrees of acceptance with concert audiences. The end of the Romantic period, as exemplified by composers like the impressionist Claude Debussy and the German operatic composer Richard Wagner, found composers questioning the basic tenets of musical composition that composers had accepted for 900 years. Central to the evolution of Western art music had been the concept that a musical composition was based on a tonal center, a pitch upon which a scale and resultant harmonies were derived. The term that came to define that concept was the word "**key**." Compositions were often named with the key of the piece being a prominent part of the name, such as *Symphony #5 in C minor* by Beethoven. Perhaps the most significant aspect of twentieth-century music was the realization by composers that a tonal center was not essential to a musical composition.

A New Musical Language—Re-Evaluating Common Practices

Composers in the latter part of the nineteenth century and in the early years of the twentieth century began questioning all of the assumptions about music that composers had accepted for centuries. It was the general tenor of the times. In all areas of intellectual endeavor, the ideas that had been central to every discipline were being reevaluated. In biology the theories of how living things came to be in their present form had been questioned by Charles Darwin and Alfred Russel Wallace. In physics the concept of quantum mechanics explained how particles behaved on the sub-atomic level, while Albert Einstein's General and Special Theories of Relativity revealed nothing less than a completely new view of the entire universe. Based as it was on the idea that space and time were inextricably connected in a new concept called space-time, Einstein's unique insight set the long-accepted Newtonian views of the universe on their heads. Pablo Picasso and other artists created entirely new ways to visually represent the world. Picasso's "**cubist**" style of the early twentieth century allowed three-dimensional objects to be represented in their entirety on a two-dimensional surface. He did this by deconstructing the subjects he painted and presented all of their parts on the two-dimensional plane of a canvas, even if their shape no longer resembled the object as one would see it in the "real" world. All of these ideas represented radically new ways of explaining the world in which we live. Composers sought nothing less for their art, a completely new musical language.

Twentieth Century

Some Prominent Composers	Genres
Richard Strauss, 1864–1949	Tone Poem, Opera
Arnold Schoenberg, 1874–1951	Chamber Symphony, Concerto, Chamber Music
Maurice Ravel, 1875–1937	Ballet, Opera, Chamber Music
Béla Bartok, 1881–1945	Concerto, Chamber Music, Orchestral Works
Igor Stravinsky, 1882–1971	Ballet, Symphony, Chamber Music
Anton Webern, 1883–1945	Chamber Music, Orchestral Works
William Grant Still, 1895–1978	Symphony, Chamber Music, Movies
George Gershwin, 1898–1937	Tone Poem, Rhapsody, Opera, Concerto
Aaron Copland, 1900–1990	Ballet, Symphony, Chamber Music
Dmitri Shostakovich, 1906–1975	Symphony, Opera, Chamber Music
Alan Hovhannes, 1911–2000	Symphony, Chamber Music
John Cage, 1912–1992	Chamber Music
Pierre Boulez, b. 1925	Chamber Music, Orchestral Works
Terry Riley, b. 1935	Chamber Music, Orchestral Works
Philip Glass, b. 1937	Symphony, Concerto, Opera, Chamber Music
Ellen Taaffe Zwilich, b. 1939	Symphony, Concerto, Chamber Music, Orchestral works

Serialism

The most significantly different concept to arise from this attempt to reinvent the musical language of the time was the adoption of **atonality** as the basis of musical composition. Atonality means that there is no recognizable tonal center in a piece, no home key around which everything else revolves. Since scales and harmonies had always been based on the tonal center of a piece, new concepts regarding melody and harmony were necessary if **atonal music** were to be realized. The resultant melodic and harmonic traits of atonal music were dissonant, harsh, and unpredictable. Composers found that writing in this style was difficult because there were no patterns or conventions, such as scales and chord progressions, on which to base their music. So they created some. In order not to emphasize any one pitch, which would have resulted in an implied tonal center, composers ordered pitches in random sounding rows or series that they then manipulated as if they were traditional scales, creating melodies and harmonies based on those **tone rows**. This type of music was alternately known as **serialism**, being based on a "series" of pitches, or **twelve-tone music**, since it was based on the twelve pitches that were put in a tone row. The Austrian composer **Arnold Schoenberg** (1874–1951) is acknowledged as the composer who brought atonal music to the forefront of the musical world. He subsequently created the serial techniques by which atonal musical materials could be organized, which were the basis of twelve-tone music. Other composers, most notably, **Anton Webern** (1883–1945) and **Pierre Boulez** (b. 1925), built on Schoenberg's ideas with even more radical extensions of serial technique.

Expressionism

Most twelve-tone music was extremely dissonant and consequently unsettling in its effect on the listener. This type of music fit well with a general artistic trend prominent in Germany during the late nineteenth and early twentieth centuries called **expressionism**, which sought to explore the dark side of human experience and the unconscious mind. These ideas were in vogue at the time due in no small part to the influential ideas of the Austrian psychoanalyst, Sigmund Freud. Artists of all types created works of an unsettling nature, the most famous example being the painting *The Scream,* 1893, by the Norwegian painter Edvard Munch. This painting, depicting the unexplained anguish of an androgynous "everyman," whose pain is ignored by the seemingly unmoved couple in the background, has become synonymous with expressionism.

As you listen to the following two movements from a solo piano work by Schoenberg, look at the painting by Munch. Does the music reflect what you are seeing in the painting? What sort of emotional reaction do you have to this music? Is it enjoyable? Do you think the composer intended for it to be enjoyable? Or is there another reason for this music?

Five Piano Pieces, two movements—
Arnold Schoenberg
Langsam (Slowly)
Sehr rasch (Very quickly)

As was mentioned above in regard to the piano sonata by Beethoven, a solo piano composition such as this would most likely be heard in a **recital** hall, or some other smaller venue, rather than in a large concert hall. What makes a certain type of performance more appropriate for one venue or another; the size of the performing ensemble, the emotional content of the music, the time period during which the music was written?

Primitivism

Many composers in the early years of the twentieth century incorporated dissonance into their music as a common harmonic quality. Some added irregular rhythmic patterns, unpredictable meter changes, and short motivic melodies along with a primal quality that earned it the stylistic name **primitivism**. This type of music made extensive use of percussion instruments and strong, irregular rhythms that conjured up images of primitive societies in Europeans' minds. The Russian composer, **Igor Stravinsky** (1882–1971), wrote the definitive work in this style, the revolutionary ballet *Le Sacre du Printemps* (*The Rite of Spring*). With its enormous orchestra, relentlessly driving rhythms, and **unresolved dissonances**, *The Rite of Spring* was the epitome of the primitivistic style.

The Rite of Spring, excerpt "Adoration of the Earth"—
Igor Stravinsky

Neoclassicism

Europe was devastated after World War I, 1914–1918, with many orchestras disbanded and concert halls and opera houses in ruins. Taking into account the financial difficulties in mounting performances of large works, many composers took to writing smaller-scale works, chamber music, rather than compositions for large orchestras. The emotional angst so thoroughly explored by expressionism before the war found little favor among audiences on the war-torn continent. A less emotional style was desired and the result was **neoclassicism**, music that was smaller in scope, more restrained in its emotional demands, and reminiscent of earlier eras. During this period between the two World Wars, composers looked to the Renaissance, Baroque, and Classical periods and adapted genres and styles from those eras for modern sensibilities. While a composer might write a symphony, based on the Classical period model, it would incorporate twentieth-century characteristics such as mildly dissonant harmonies and irregular rhythms. **Igor Stravinsky**, one of the most influential composers of the time, was again a leader, this time in the development of the neoclassical style.

Pulcinella

Shortly after the end of World War I, the Russian impresario **Serge Diaghilev** asked Igor Stravinsky to re-interpret several musical pieces written by the eighteenth-century Italian composer Giovanni Battista Pergolesi. This re-orchestration of Pergolesi's work was to be the basis of a new ballet for the Ballet Russes. Diaghilev and Stravinsky had previously collaborated on several ballet projects, including *The Rite of Spring,* but this commission would energize the neoclassical direction in which music was heading at the time. The story was based on the traditional characters of the "**Commedia dell'arte**," the Italian theatrical style prominent from the fourteenth through the eighteenth centuries. The Commedia dell'arte was known for its improvisational acting style in which the story, scenes, acts, and conclusion were worked out beforehand, but the specific words of the actors were improvised while the action unfolded. Over time, recurring characters developed who were represented in these productions through costumes and masks. Pulcinella was one of these characters, a rough sort of hunchbacked clown.

Basing the ballet on eighteenth-century theatrical traditions as well as eighteenth-century music firmly places this composition in the realm of the neoclassical. Stravinsky orchestrated the melodies with a sense of great restraint, retaining the clarity and elegant style of the original while imbuing the music with rhythmic quirks and dashes of harmonic flavor, clearly marking it as a twentieth-century creation.

Pulcinella, Overture and Allegro—
Igor Stravinsky

What Baroque or Classical period characteristics can you hear in this music? What twentieth-century characteristics are apparent?

Avant-garde: Experiments in Modern Music

From the 1930s until the end of the century, many composers looked for ever-more unique ways to compose and perform music. The advent of electronic means with which to both record and recreate sounds led to composers like **Edgard Varése** (1883–1965) creating compositions of recorded sounds manipulated in studios and presented "in concert" by playing a recording of the final version in a concert hall. This "**musique concrete**," or concrete music, never found much of an audience outside of a small circle of composers and within schools of music but stands as an interesting early attempt to use a new tool with which to create music, much as the computer has been used in recent decades. American composer **John Cage** (1912–1992) experimented with incorporating chance happenings into his compositions. His infamous composition *4' 33"* consists of a silent piano whose lid over the keyboard is opened for the first movement, closed for the second, and opened again for the third. The "composition" is made up of the chance sounds that happen to occur during the length of the piece. This extreme example of **aleatoric music**, music that incorporates chance happenings, belies a serious idea that Cage had. He believed that our definition of music shouldn't just be notes played on instruments in concert halls but should include all of the sounds in nature and the world that we tune out every day. Other composers, such as **Pierre Boulez** (b. 1925), pushed the serial ideas of Schoenberg to the limit, serializing all aspects of the music. This **total serialism** created music that was intellectually challenging in the extreme.

A prominent avant-garde American composer, **Henry Cowell** (1897–1965), experimented with novel approaches to tonality and rhythm and advocated unusual performance techniques on traditional instruments. His composition *The Banshee,* written in 1925, for solo piano makes use of some of these techniques including playing directly on the strings inside the piano. By striking the strings and sliding the nails of the fingers lengthwise on the strings, he created tone clusters of numerous adjacent pitches and an eerie "wailing" sound otherwise unobtainable through traditional performance techniques. In traditional Scottish and Irish folklore, the mythological banshee either heralded a forthcoming death or lamented a recent one.

The Banshee—
Henry Cowell

Traditionalism

Throughout the twentieth century, while many composers experimented with novel concepts and unique approaches to musical composition, there was an unbroken line of composers who wrote in a more or less straightforward extension of the tonal music of the Romantic period. These composers did not completely eschew the innovations of the twentieth century but rather incorporated them in a discriminating fashion, creating more audience friendly music. Rather than adopt the new concepts that often intimidated audiences, these composers extended the tradition of tonality-based music and evolutionary changes in Western art music. We have heard the music of some of the most prominent composers in this vein already, **Leonard Bernstein** (*West Side Story*), **Aaron Copland** (*Rodeo* and *the Fanfare for the Common Man*), **Samuel Barber** (*Adagio for Strings*), and

Richard Strauss (*Til Eulenspiegel's Merry Pranks*). **George Gershwin** (1898–1937), who blended traditional classical genres with the emerging jazz style of the time, created one of the most vibrant and popular musical styles of the twentieth century. **William Grant Still** (1895–1978) was the first prominent African-American composer who infused his work with African-American influences. Still broke through racial barriers both as a composer and conductor and became a successful composer and arranger for both radio broadcasts and Hollywood movies. Another composer whose works are very tonal but who explored exotic concepts from non-Western styles of music in his works was **Alan Hovhannes** (1911–2000).

A recent extension of the tonal line of traditional music can be found in the **minimalism** of late twentieth-century composers like **Terry Riley** (b. 1935) and **Philip Glass** (b. 1937). Minimalism is characterized by having a traditional tonal center and much repetition with layering of melodic or motivic elements. Terry Riley's composition, *In C,* is often considered the seminal composition in this style. Other composers in the late twentieth century have made extensive use of "quotations" of themes from earlier composers' works. This gives their compositions a dual character, acknowledging the early influences that are the basis of our current music while exploring the possibilities inherent in modern compositional techniques. **Ellen Taaffe Zwilich** (b. 1939), sometimes referred to as a neoromantic composer, is a prominent American composer in this vein. The early twentieth-century practices of blending traditional compositions with popular styles has also been a prevalent theme in late twentieth and early twenty-first century compositions. Folk, rock, blues, and jazz influences can be seen in the work of a number of late twentieth-century composers, including the American composer **Conni Ellisor**.

Twentieth-Century Tonality-Based Compositions

Rhapsody in Blue

George Gershwin wrote the *Rhapsody in Blue* in 1924 for Paul Whiteman's jazz band/orchestra, and it intrigued both reviewers and audience alike due to its treatment of jazz and classical styles as equals in one composition. Whiteman was an influential figure in New York's musical circles, and his presentation of "An Experiment in Modern Music" concert included the *Rhapsody in Blue.* The term **rhapsody** is used to describe a free-form musical composition of an effusive nature. The work is for solo piano and "orchestra." The original Whiteman band had only 18 instrumentalists, and the version commonly heard today is for solo piano and full symphony orchestra. The jazzy sounds that give the work its unique appeal had not been incorporated into large-scale classically based compositions prior to this. Gershwin was sufficiently encouraged by the response to the Rhapsody that the blending of the two styles became the hallmark of his compositional style. Other composers such as Leonard Bernstein and Duke Ellington have followed Gershwin's lead in writing music that blends the classical and jazz styles.

Rhapsody in Blue—
George Gershwin

Can you identify the "jazzy" sounds in this piece? How are they different from "classical" sounds? What elements of music can be considered jazzy?

Afro-American Symphony

William Grant Still was the first African-American composer of significance, and his work reached far beyond the concert hall through his work in radio and in Hollywood. Still grew up in Little Rock, Arkansas, and after dabbling with the more dissonant compositional styles receiving much attention early in the twentieth century, found his unique musical voice in the African-American-influenced compositions exemplified by the *Afro-American Symphony* written in 1931. The third movement of this symphony, Animato (Animated), uses bluesy, folk music-like tunes reminiscent of spirituals, a banjo, and vibrant rhythms.

Afro-American Symphony, 3rd movement "Animato"—
William Grant Still

Symphony #2, Mysterious Mountain

Alan Hovhannes (1911–2000) was an American of Armenian heritage. Hovhannes's music did not fit any of the prevailing twentieth-century styles, including the Romantic era extensions of Strauss, et al., but found a wider degree of acceptance after the premiere of his *Symphony #2, Mysterious Mountain* in 1955. The work presented a fresh alternative to both the serial composers and the Romantic traditionalists. Hovhannes's writing is very tonal but not in the line of Bach, Beethoven, and Brahms. It is usually based on a mode (scale) other than the major/minor tonalities of traditional Western art music. Often the modal basis of his compositions can be found in music of non-Western cultures. This gives his music an exotic, intriguing sound. The following example from the *Symphony #2, Mysterious Mountain,* is a double fugue, two separate themes treated fugally (imitative polyphony). This combination of exotic, modal writing within a traditional compositional technique such as the fugue makes Hovhannes's music difficult to categorize but eminently listenable.

Symphony #2, Mysterious Mountain, double fugue excerpt—
Alan Hovhannes

In C

Tonal music in the twentieth century found its most unusual outlet in the style developed in the 1960s called **minimalism**. Minimalist music emphasizes repetition, tone color, and rhythmic patterns. Some of the innovators in this style of music were **La Monte Young, Terry Riley, Steve Reich**, and **Philip Glass**. Minimalist music is relatively simple sounding and has gained wide acceptance among composers and the public alike because of its adaptability to almost all musical genres. There have been operas, chamber music works, as well as large orchestral compositions written in this style. Early minimalist works tended to be extreme in their exploration of the minimalist concepts. The example below by

Terry Riley, *In C*, is perhaps the most extreme minimalist composition of all time. The work consists of the repeated playing of high-register octave "Cs" on the piano while eleven instruments take turns playing short melodic motives, fifty-three in all, in overlapping rhythms and textures. After all eleven instruments have played one of the motives, they move on to the next one. This creates a subtle, ever-changing mass of sound that shifts the textural shape of the music much as clouds in the sky morph from one "shape" into another, slowly, almost unnoticeably. The effect is mesmerizing, hypnotizing, and, to some people, very annoying. While a composition such as *In C* may not be everyone's idea of great music, the idea behind it is very powerful. Compositions have now been written in all genres based on minimalist concepts.

In C–
Terry Riley

How does this music affect you? Do you like it? Dislike it? Does it make you relax? Does it make you want to pull your hair out? Listening to *In C* is a challenge in some ways. We expect music to *do* something. Have a beginning, go through some changes, and then come to a final sounding conclusion. We want to hear a balance of repetition and variety. Too much of one or the other and we shut down our ears and brains. We often cease to process what we hear when it doesn't meet our expectations. Minimalist music challenges the very expectations we bring when listening to music. In order to have an enjoyable and rewarding experience with minimalist music, we must change our expectations of what music is and does. The best way to experience any unfamiliar style of music is to approach it with an open mind. There is no question that this music is tonal, we hear the tonal center almost continually throughout the piece. There is no dissonance that requires resolving so there really isn't anything unpleasant, in the traditional harmonic sense, to make it difficult to listen to. What is difficult is what the music does, or doesn't do, to satisfy our expectations of what music should be.

Terry Riley and other minimalist composers have been influenced significantly by their knowledge of music from non-Western cultures, especially Indonesian gamelan music, western African drumming, and the music of India. Indian music can seem to go on for an extremely long time without much "happening." Is it simply a cultural expectation that can be learned and thereby make the music enjoyable? Possibly, but the time and effort necessary may be more than most people are willing to invest to find out. *In C* may be a bit taxing for a first exposure to minimalist music. Try listening to other minimalist works, such as the 4th movement from Philip Glass's *Symphony #3*, for example, to hear how the minimalist approach might be more appealing. Philip Glass has been the most successful minimalist composer, writing film scores, operas, and minimalist compositions in virtually all genres.

Symphony #3, 4th movement–
Philip Glass

Is this music more agreeable to you? Does it sound more like what you expect music to sound like? Does it sound like it is doing something, going somewhere?

Crossover Music

The term "crossover music" commonly refers to one style of popular music that has gained popularity among an audience of another style. It can also mean what composers such as George Gershwin and William Grant Still did earlier in the twentieth century, that is, unite other styles of music, like folk and popular styles, with traditional composition. American composer **Conni Ellisor** (b. 1957) has combined folk idioms with traditional classical methods in several works to create a style that is easily accessible to the listener while exploring new possibilities within the classical parameters of composition. In her 1996 work *Blackberry Winter,* Ellisor uses one of the simplest folk instruments, the mountain dulcimer, as a featured solo instrument with chamber orchestra. In this work she creates a nostalgic yet vibrant atmosphere, bridging the worlds of traditional folk music and twentieth-century composition. The challenge of creating new musical styles through a merging of pre-existing approaches is summed up by Ellisor in the following statement:

> ". . . much of the momentum of classical composition is related to modulations [i.e., changing from one key or tonality to another to create a sense of musical journey], and I never realized how true this was until I began working within the limitation of the dulcimer's anchored tonality. My solution was to create orchestral interludes that moved into new tonalities and allowed the dulcimer soloist time to retune the instrument for the next melodic statement. In writing this piece, I wanted to be respectful of the rich heritage of both the dulcimer and the classical chamber orchestra, but I felt a certain liberty in combining these traditions."

In the following example the distinctive sound of the mountain dulcimer opens the movement with a vigorous rhythmic pattern and melodic motive. The dulcimer is then joined by the orchestra, and the movement moves through several mood and tonality changes before ending in a final climactic rush of energy. As the composer's comments above indicate, this work pays homage to classical traditions through the movement through different tonal centers giving the work a sense of direction. The mountain dulcimer's presence provides the timbre of the folk music tradition while the simple melodic structure and rhythmic vitality idiomatic to the instrument reinforce the folk heritage the piece summons to the listener's mind.

Blackberry Winter, 3rd movement—
Conni Ellisor

The term "crossover music" can also be thought of as rock, jazz, R&B, etc., styles that make use of traditional classical music ideas and techniques. Early rock groups such as The Moody Blues (1960s), Deep Purple (1960s), and the Electric Light Orchestra (1970s) used orchestral arrangements and synthesized sounds to create music that bridged the pop and classical worlds. More recently rock artists like **Yngwie Malmsteen** and **Trey Anastasio** have created works for electric guitar and orchestra modeled on the concerto and suite genres of the classical music tradition. Anastasio's *Time Turns Elastic,* written in a collaborative effort with Don Hart and premiered in 2008, explores the lyrical character of the electric guitar similar to how a composer might write for a bowed string instrument such as the

Listening Chart

What is performing the music?	Cue	Description	Historical Period	Genre or Type of Piece	Composer	Keywords
Organ		Imitative polyphony with episodes	Baroque	Fugue	J.S. Bach	
Orchestra with soloist(s)	Electric guitar		20th Century	Concerto/Suite	Yngwie Malmsteen	
Orchestra with soloist(s)	Lute solo	Ornamentation on repeats	Baroque	Concerto	Antonio Vivaldi	
Orchestra with soloist(s)	Trumpet solo	Orchestral introduction	Classical	Concerto	Franz Joseph Haydn	
Orchestra with soloist(s)	Violin, oboe, recorder, trumpet	Sectional	Baroque	Concerto Grosso	J.S. Bach	
Small string group	Two violins with basso continuo	Lively	Baroque	Trio Sonata	Arcangelo Corelli	
Small string group	String quartet	Minor sound, variations	Class./Roman.	String Quartet	Franz Schubert	
Solo piano		Mostly a lyrical melody with accompaniment	Classical	Sonata	Ludwig Beethoven	
Solo piano		Rhythmically free, episodic, changes moods	Romantic	Ballade	Frederic Chopin	
Solo piano		Dissonant, atonal, unpredictable	20th Century	Solo Piano Work	Arnold Schoenberg	
Solo piano		Non-traditional playing techniques	20th Century	Solo Piano Work	Henry Cowell	
Orchestra	Dit-dit-dit-dah motive	Extensive thematic development	Classical	Symphony	Ludwig Beethoven	
Orchestra	Violins starts	Playful main theme in clarinet and horn	Post-Romantic	Tone Poem	Richard Strauss	
Orchestra		"Minor" sound, ominous, brass main theme, "major" ending	Romantic	Tone Poem	Modest Mussorgsky	
Orchestra	Flute starts	Dreamlike setting, rhythmically nebulous	Post-Romantic	Tone Poem	Claude Debussy	
Orchestra	Driving rhythm	Dissonant, unpredictable, short motives	20th Century	Ballet	Igor Stravinsky	
Orchestra	Strings and woodwinds	Light, neoclassical sound	20th Century	Ballet	Igor Stravinsky	
Orchestra	Clarinet starts	Bluesy, jazz inflections, piano prominent	20th Century	Rhapsody	George Gershwin	
Orchestra	Spiritual sounding melodies, upbeat	Banjo backbeats	20th Century	Symphony	William Grant Still	
Orchestra		Fugal, expansive sound, harmonically and melodically modal	20th Century	Symphony	Alan Hovhannes	
Orchestra	String orchestra	Minimalist, rhythmically energetic	20th Century	Symphony	Philip Glass	
Orchestra	Mountain dulcimer with orchestra	Energetic and lyrical	20th Century	Orchestral Work	Conni Ellisor	
Orchestra	Introduction before melody	Folk-like tunes, contrasting sections	Romantic	Symphony	Antonin Dvořák	
Various instruments	Piano prominent	Minimalist, motivic, repetitive	20th Century	Instrumental Work	Terry Riley	

In the "Keywords" column, write down words, musical or non-musical, that will help you remember the specific pieces you are hearing.

violin. Malmsteen's *Concerto Suite for Electric Guitar and Orchestra*, another collaborative work, written with David Rosenthal, highlights the composer's legendary lightning-fast guitar technique in a piece that is reminiscent of the virtuosic showpieces of the nineteenth century, with a decidedly modern twist.

"Vivace" from *Concerto Suite for Electric Guitar and Orchestra*
Yngwie Malmsteen with David Rosenthal

Summary

There are few if any classical musical traditions in the world that encompass the breadth and depth of the music of Western culture intended for concert hall performance. In non-Western cultures that have a significant classical music heritage of their own, such as in India or in Japan, there are certain similarities to the Western tradition of concert performances, but they are limited in their scope and diminishing in their position of prominence within those cultures in favor of concerts from the Western art music tradition. The classical music styles of Japan, Gagaku, and Nohgaku were important in the courts and theatres of Japan for centuries but never made the transition from aristocratic patronage to popular support through concert presentations. In India, which also has a very long history of "classical" music, concert presentations have been limited to recitals of small ensembles, and the type of music on those programs has remained fairly unchanged over the course of many centuries. In fact, in both of these societies the rise in prominence of Western classical music has rivalled the traditional classical music presentations of each culture in concert performances.

In looking back over the material presented in this chapter, one can see an extraordinary variety of musical styles and genres. Each historical period had certain characteristics or trends that composers worked within. Genres sometimes went out of favor in different periods while other genres retained their popularity across the centuries. The musical basis of the changes seen from one historical period to another is the evolution of the harmonic system that is the bedrock of tonality in Western music. The societal basis for the changes across the historical eras is centered on who was paying for the music to be composed and the intended audience. Before the Baroque era, and the establishment of a concert tradition, most musical activity was supported by the church. The Baroque period supported an approximately even division of patronage between the courts and the churches of Europe. The Classical period saw an increase in music supported by the courts and the aristocracy and a corresponding increase in music geared toward that sensibility. The Romantic period composer, no longer able or willing to depend on such aristocratic patronage, wrote for the general public in a purposefully attractive style in order to garner the support of a paying public. The early twentieth-century search for a new musical language and the subsequent adoption by many composers of an intentionally dissonant style turned many classical music patrons toward the emerging popular styles of jazz, Tin Pan Alley songs, and the Broadway musical, leaving classical music in an increasingly tenuous position. Without church or aristocratic patronage and a public increasingly unwilling to pay to attend concerts of dissonant music, composers turned to a new avenue of support for their composing, the university. A position on a university faculty allowed a composer to receive a comfortable income while pursuing the compositional style of their choice, often without regard for whether it was commercially viable or not. Through this means did the dissonant compositional style remain in vogue for most of the twentieth century. While many composers adopted the dissonant styles, others maintained a fairly traditional, tonal, musical outlook throughout the twentieth century. In the later years of the era the general consensus was reached that dissonant music did not provide what listeners wanted. The overall approach in the last twenty years or so has been one of tempering the more dissonant qualities with more easily accessible characteristics, principally through a return to tonality-based composition.

Suggested Further Listening

Adagio in G minor—Tomaso Giovanni Albinoni

Jesu, Joy of Man's Desiring—Johann Sebastian Bach

Symphony # 41 in C major, 4th movement—Wolfgang Amadeus Mozart

Ave Verum Corpus—Wolfgang Amadeus Mozart

Concerto for Trumpet and Orchestra in E-flat major, 3rd movement—Franz Joseph Haydn

The Creation—Franz Joseph Haydn

Symphony #7 in A major, 1st movement—Ludwig van Beethoven

Symphony #9 in D minor, 4th movement—Ludwig van Beethoven

Scenes from Childhood—Robert Schumann

Les Preludes—Franz Liszt

Variations on a Theme by Franz Joseph Haydn—Johannes Brahms

Overture to *Ruslan and Ludmilla*—Mikhail Glinka

Prelude to *Tristan und Isolde*—Richard Wagner

The Planets—Gustav Holst

"Four Sea Interludes" from Peter Grimes—Benjamin Britten

Ionisation—Edgard Varése

La Mer—Claude Debussy

Concerto for Orchestra, 2nd movement—Bela Bartok

Les Bandar-Log—Arnold Koechlin

A Survivor from Warsaw—Arnold Schoenberg

Final Alice—David del Tredici

Symphony #3—Henryk Górecki

Section III

The World of Music

Introduction: A Diversity of Sounds (and more)

In this book, we have seen how music in Western civilization began from an oral/aural tradition and developed into a highly literate tradition in which notation became an important tool to generate increasingly sophisticated forms of music. But this is just one story out of a multitude of stories of music that exist in the world. Although we do not have space in this book to tell all the stories of the world's music, we can travel across the globe to sample a variety of approaches to music-making that give us a fuller picture of how people have used music to express what it means to be human.

When we look beyond the Western tradition, we encounter a diversity of traditions across the globe that developed in various ways. In many countries of the world, there are kinds of music still maintained in a purely oral tradition of learning by ear, in which music is passed on to the next generation without a single sheet of paper indicating what musicians should play. Although a given style may lack notation, the oral/aural approach to music should never be thought of as "primitive." Not only is it possible to develop highly sophisticated musical structures in this way, but many societies that are highly literate actually maintain musical traditions that eschew all manner of musical notation. Furthermore, where notation does exist in many traditions of the world, it is often just a skeletal form outlining the basic structure of the music to be played, lacking any indication of the details that make music sound so exciting to our ears. This reminds us that music does not live in the silence of a sheet of paper, but in the activation of sound in the world.

As we begin this section, now is a good time to return briefly to the fundamentals of music and introduce a theoretical approach that will give us more to think about when we study music. **Ethnomusicology**, the study of music in (or as) culture, has been the discipline most concerned with understanding the music of the entire world and reminds us that music always exists within a particular cultural context. Thus, ethnomusicologists have shown us that music is more than just the sounds made by musicians and our understanding must go beyond the sonic features. Ethnomusicologist Alan P. Merriam created a simple three-part model for studying music that can be reduced to just three words: **sound**, **behavior**, and **concepts**. Merriam's model is based on the fact that music is not just sound by itself, but has a context that is an integral part of the whole that we call "music." The three elements of music are conceptualized as follows:

Sound (what we can hear): the sonic aspects of music that we learned in Chapter One, beginning with duration, frequency, amplitude and timbre that expand out into rhythm, pitch, melody, texture and so forth.

Behavior (what we can see): the ways people make music; who makes music (young/old; men/women; professional/amateur); where people make music (home, church, outdoors, etc.), when people make music (weddings, funerals, etc.) and how people make music (training, imitating); what people do when they make music (dance, celebrate, mourn, etc.).

Concepts (what people think and say): the ways people conceptualize music; the way music is valued (good or bad); classification systems ("strings," "horns," etc.); musical terms and descriptions ("key," "tune," "hot," "cool," etc.); musical meaning and beliefs about music (healing, magic, etc.); and why people make music (to "entertain" an audience, to make "art," to worship God, etc.).

When we listen to a piece of music, naturally it is the sound that strikes us first and often causes us to make immediate judgments about whether it is "good" or "bad" music. Thus, before we can even begin to analyze a piece of music as an integrated whole of Sound-Behavior-Concepts, our own conceptualizations about music emerge and can get in the way of our understanding. But this easy-to-remember three-part model of Sound-Behavior-Concepts is a reminder to not rush to such judgments when we first hear a piece of unfamiliar music. Better instead to withhold judgment, step back a moment, and ask the questions suggested by the model in order to understand what people are doing when they make music and why they are doing it.

This model will be important to keep in mind as we go through this section, exploring many different kinds of music around the world that often differs from the kinds of music we learned about in the West, not only in terms of what it sounds like, but the ways in which it is made and conceptualized as well. In learning to appreciate music, remember to keep your ears, your eyes, and your mind open.

In this unit we will also expand our understanding of musical instruments. Because of the extreme diversity of instrumental types in the world, the categories of string, brass, woodwinds, and percussion that we used in our study of Western music can be replaced in this unit with a more useful system of categorization. In 1914 German musicologists Erich Moritz von Hornbostel and Curt Sachs developed a system for classifying musical instruments that has become the standard in ethnomusicology, commonly referred to as **Hornbostel-Sachs**. Drawing on a model of instrument classification from ancient India, the basis of their system is simple: instruments are classified according to the nature of the sound-producing material. They created four categories that encompass all the world's acoustic instruments:

Aerophones: instruments on which sound is produced primarily from the vibration of a column of air. Examples of aerophones include flutes, trumpets, reeds and just about any instrument that we might think of as a "wind" instrument.

Chordophones: instruments on which sound is produced primarily from the vibration of strings. Examples include anything we think of as a "string" instrument: lutes (strings stretched across an instrument body with a neck extension, such as violin, guitar, banjo, etc.), zithers (strings stretched across an instrument body), harps (a frame with strings perpendicular to the instrument body) and lyres (a frame with strings parallel to the instrument body).

Membranophones: instruments on which sound is produced primarily from the vibration of a membrane or skin. Examples of membranophones include all manner of drums and are further subdivided according to the basic shape of the drum.

Idiophones: instruments on which sound is produced primarily from the vibration of the body of the instrument itself. This category includes all kinds of shakers, rattles, sticks, bells, and gongs. Essentially, any percussion instrument that does not use a skin or membrane fits in this category, which Hornbostel and Sachs found to be the largest category in the world of instruments.

This system has proven very effective for classifying any instrument of the world and was even expanded later in the 20th century (instruments that use an electronic sound source instead of an acoustic one are classified as electrophones or electronophones). As you listen to the examples in this unit, keep in mind the sound source of each instrument and you might find it a lot easier to understand the rich textures of music in our world.

Music of Indigenous Peoples

8

In this section we consider the music of indigenous peoples: ethnic minorities who trace their origins to a particular region located within the boundaries of a larger nation. While indigenous ethnic groups represent early strata of culture and maintain ancient cultural practices in their places of origin, they are typically marginalized, subjected to exploitation, and oppressed by the majority population. As they exist today, indigenous peoples are bearers of an invaluable vanishing resource of ancient cultural practices that they maintain through ceremonial events in which music is a central feature, often telling stories of their history, customs, and mythology. But their marginalized status also drives them to use their musical traditions to bolster unity and ethnic identity among their ethnic group while protesting against oppression by the majority population. Thus we will consider indigenous peoples' music both in terms of their heritage—their origins on the land—and in terms of their future—their struggles to maintain their culture.

Natives of North America

Native Americans make up a population of people throughout North America that is as diverse as the land of the United States, with its vast plains, arid deserts, lush swamps, and frozen tundra. As connection to the land is of paramount importance to indigenous groups, the many ethnic groups of Native Americans are categorized according to the geographic regions in which they are based: Plains, Northwest Coast, Southwest, Great Basin and Plateau, Southeast, and Arctic. Not surprisingly, this cultural diversity is reflected in musical differences; the different musical styles found in all these areas constitute a kind of musical map of the United States. Nevertheless, in spite of all of the variety of sounds, there are some common features that we can focus on to understand Native American music as a whole.

The most common feature of traditional Native American music is that it is based on the voice. Vocals may contain words sung in the native language of that particular tribe—words that recount their history, tell of social customs, or tell stories—or they may feature **vocables**—words that are only considered as sound and not in terms of lexical meaning. Like the syllables "fa-la-la-la" in a Christmas song, vocables such as "yah," "heh," and "weh" appear in many Native American songs, but they should not be thought of as "nonsense" syllables. As many Native American songs are believed to have originated from spirits, not humans, vocables are best understood as untranslatable syllables that may have obscure origins.

Supporting the vocals is the percussive texture of Native American music, typically drums, rattles, and jingles, although some traditions include other types of instruments such as flutes and strings. Rhythmically many songs feature an insistent pulse that drives the music forward and is especially prominent in music for dance, an important feature of ceremonies in Native American culture. Our first two examples feature two dance songs that we can compare and contrast.

A large powwow drum with sticks, ready to be played. Each drummer in the circle around the drum holds one stick, and together the group plays the drum rhythm in unison. The result is a high-volume, unified sound.

Example
"Fast Cheyenne War Dance"

http://www.rhapsody.com/members/wgcve5/playlists/mp.172553351

This is an example of the traditional style of the Plains—an area that encompasses the Midwest of the United States—and is perhaps the easiest to identify of all Native American styles. This dynamic sound is marked by high, strident voices, sometimes in falsetto with a nasal timbre. The first sounds heard here are the insistent drum pulse and the voice that joins in right away at a relatively high pitch with a timbre that sounds somewhat strained. The male lead vocalist is joined soon after by a group of female singers. The song is entirely made up of vocables such as "hey," "yah," "ho," and "weh." The entire song is driven forward by the insistent pulse of the drum, which is not played by a single person, but by a group of musicians gathered around a single large drum, each one holding a single stick to pound out a unified beat to accompany the dance (see photo). This group drumming, along with the group singing, acts as an expression of a community unified in their shared heritage and connection to the land upon which the dancers step.

As you listen more closely, note the melodic contour of the song. It starts on a high note sung by the leader, and after the rest of the singers join in, the melody begins to gradually descend in a stepwise manner. We can describe this song as having a descending, terraced contour, like a staircase that the singers go down for each musical phrase. As soon as the bottom is reached, the process starts over, with the leader starting again on the high note, soon followed by the group.

Example
"Hopi Basket Dance"

http://www.rhapsody.com/members/wgcve5/playlists/mp.172553351

A completely different musical style can be heard if we move from the Great Plains region to the Southwest region. This "basket dance" comes from the Hopi people, who live in the northeastern part of the Arizona desert. The Hopi have lived in this arid part of the country for hundreds of years and even maintain the oldest known village in North America at Walpi—a multi-house dwelling atop a mesa with no electricity or running water that is still inhabited today. Claiming to be descendants of the ancient Anasazi, who lived nearby before vanishing in the fourteenth century, the Hopi have maintained their way of life in the harshest climate of the Southwestern desert. This song has the feeling of music with an everlasting quality.

Compared to the Plains example, the most obvious difference is in the voices, which sing in a more relaxed tone in a lower register. But as in the "Cheyenne War Dance," the singers are using the vocables "hey," "weh," "yah," and "yo" and sing to a steady percussive pulse provided by the drum and jingles. The drum accompaniment is slower and less intense than in the Plains example, but notice how the drums create accents by briefly stopping the pulse. These accents can be heard at 0:11 and 0:23 and 0:39 and 0:53 and 1:11 and 1:24 and 1:39 and 1:54. If you pay attention to the melodic contour, you can also hear how a similar descending pattern is repeated, in which the singers start at a high pitch and end the phrase at a low pitch. Notice how the drum accents occur during these low pitches at the end of each phrase, marking the end of it before it starts over again.

A dancer at the 24th Annual Red Mountain Eagle Powwow in Scottsdale, AZ, November 2010.

Example
Protest Song by Buffy Sainte-Marie, "My Country Tis of Thy People You're Dying"

http://www.rhapsody.com/members/wgcve5/playlists/mp.172553351

Beyond the ceremonial songs that maintain their traditions, Native Americans also participate in modern music making. With a long history of oppression against their people since first contact with immigrants from Europe, it is not surprising that some Native Americans have used music for the purpose of protest. This song by Canadian singer Buffy Sainte-Marie, who is of Cree heritage, is particularly scathing in its criticism, expressing harsh anger at Western civilization in both her words and vocal quality.

As you listen to this song, you might feel your own strong emotions well up, and this is intentional on the part of the singer. You might feel anger, as the singer does, at the many atrocities committed against Native Americans, such as bargaining for their lands with disease-infected blankets or forcing children away from their parents to be educated in schools to eradicate their native language and culture. On the other hand, you might feel offended by the singer's relentless criticism of American culture, feeling that it is unfair or just too harsh. Such emotional responses are what make protest music so powerful and very divisive of opinion.

Aside from your own opinion about the song, there is one feature Buffy Sainte-Marie used in writing this song that is useful in understanding how musical meaning operates. The refrain of this song is based on a famous American patriotic song, "My Country 'Tis of Thee," from which she takes the first five pitches and uses the first four words, but adds new notes and the words "thy people you're dying" to complete the phrase. The effect can come as a shock, especially to people who value such a patriotic song. This can be described by the term *code switching*; one "code," in this case a familiar patriotic song, is referenced, then suddenly substituted with another "code," a protest song that attacks what the familiar song represents. This borrowing of one "text" within another "text" is referred to as **intertextuality**, the shaping of one text's meaning by another text. This technique is not just limited to folk songs with a message, but can be found

Native American singer and songwriter Buffy Sainte-Marie in concert in Ottawa, Canada, June 2008.

in many kinds of music. It is of the utmost importance that the composer knows the audience, as the effect depends on recognizing the text being borrowed. In the case of Buffy Sainte-Marie's song, the effect works well because so many Americans are familiar with the patriotic song that she cleverly turns on its head.

Aborigines of Australia

Inhabiting the continent of Australia for at least 40,000 years, the diverse peoples who were grouped together under the official designation of "aboriginal Australians" by the colonial government of Australia in the eighteenth century make up one of the oldest indigenous populations on earth. For Australian aborigines, like Native Americans, music has been an indispensable part of their culture since ancient times. In fact, music is an essential component of the creation myth common among aborigines and thus plays a major role in the ancient ceremonies that many groups maintain today.

The creation story of Australian aboriginal people involves the Dreamtime, a mythological time before the features of the world came into existence. The Dreamtime (or "Dreaming") was a time when spirit beings roamed the land creating everything we know today: physical features of the land, plants, animals, humans, as well as laws and customs for people to follow. As these spirit beings traveled across the land creating the world as we know it, they left what are referred to as "songlines," pathways that marked their movements. In accordance with tradition, aboriginal people today recount the work of the ancient creators by singing songs handed down to them that describe the geographic features of the desert outback, the water holes, and other landmarks. This not only serves as a kind of mythological history of the aborigines, it is also practical, allowing people to find their way across the vast Australian interior simply by singing the songs—virtually a musical map of their homeland.

This painting by an aboriginal artist from Australia is a good example of the style of "dots and lines" that exemplifies aboriginal design. Literally a map of the land, the dots arranged into lines depict the pathways walked not only by humans, but by the spirit beings during the ancient "Dreamtime." Aboriginal musical performance also resembles these patterns: many short songs (like dots) are strung together in sequences (like lines) that span a certain length of time.

Example
"Traditional Didgeridoo," Tjapukai Dancers

http://www.rhapsody.com/members/wgcve5/playlists/mp.172553351

While the traditional songs of the aborigines are little known outside of Australia—which is actually a benefit for traditional-minded aborigines who place rigid restrictions on who is allowed to hear certain kinds of songs—one instrument of the aborigines has become internationally well known. The didgeridoo (or didjeridu or many alternate spellings) is a long natural trumpet that may be the oldest type of trumpet on earth, originally made from a long, thick branch of eucalyptus hollowed out by termites. The player blows on one end of the tube and out the other end emerges a highly resonant drone sound. The reason for this drone is that there are no holes carved into the body of the didgeridoo that would normally allow for changing pitch as you would find on most aerophones of the world. Although lacking this feature for pitch manipulation, skilled players of the didgeridoo create an endless variety of sounds simply by manipulating their lips, air stream, and voice.

The single drone pitch is easy to hear from the very beginning of this song as the player establishes a clear rhythm by adjusting his mouth while he plays. This rhythm sounds something like "doo-doo-wah, doo-doo-wah" repeated over and over. As the solo progresses, you can hear the player generate overtones—pitches that are higher than the fundamental of the drone pitch. This makes a kind of sweeping sound that begins with high overtones and sweeps down to lower ones. The player then begins to insert imitations of animal sounds by manipulating his lips, tongue, and breath. One can clearly hear dogs and perhaps birds in this imaginative use of the didgeridoo.

Guided Listening

"Traditional Didgeridoo"

0:00	Song starts with a repeating ostinato ("doo-doo-wah").
0:39	Rhythm breaks and the player makes an overtone sweep.
0:43	Rhythm resumes.
0:50	Rhythm breaks again with another overtone sweep.
0:54	Rhythm resumes.
0:59	Rhythm breaks again with an even longer overtone sweep.
1:07	Rhythm resumes.
1:13	Player imitates an animal, followed by overtone sweep.
1:21	Returns to rhythm and inserts a brief animal call.
1:27	More animal sounds, extended this time.
1:36	Rhythm resumes.
1:43	Another overtone sweep with animal sounds resembling dog barks.
2:00	Rhythm resumes.
2:05	Series of accents.
2:15	Animal sounds, bird cries.
2:28	Accents.
2:37	Rhythm breaks and player does a long overtone sweep to end the piece.

The simplicity of the structure of the didgeridoo, as well as its versatility for the kinds of sound effects one can hear in this example, have made it a popular instrument found throughout the world, widely used by street performers and recorded by popular musicians worldwide.

The didgeridoo can be heard in a more modern context in another example by this same group of performers, the Tjapukai Dancers, who originate from Kuranda, a small village on Cape York in the northern part of Australia. Since 1987 this performance troupe of aboriginal Australians has made a living entertaining tourists in their homeland; they eventually moved their theatre to the city of Cairns in 1996. Like other indigenous peoples, this group of performers uses their traditional music and dance not only for their economic survival, but also to express a message of unity.

Example
"Proud to Be," Tjapukai Dancers

http://www.rhapsody.com/members/wgcve5/playlists/mp.172553351

A much milder protest song than "My Country Tis of Thy People," this song expresses pride in belonging to a culture with a 50,000-year-old tradition that white civilization has threatened and abused. In addition to stealing land, there are numerous atrocities in recent history that the group could have referred to, such as the government-sponsored program of kidnapping aboriginal children to be "adopted" by white families, a holocaust that has scarred an entire generation. But this song keeps the message hopeful, urging that black and white unite to avoid another "blunder" in the "land down under." The group uses modern instruments to communicate its message broadly, but you can hear the drone of the didgeridoo at the very beginning of the example.

Vanishing Cultures and Endangered Sounds: The Kaluli of Papua New Guinea

The harsh reality of indigenous peoples around the world is that just as these ethnic groups are endangered, so are their cultural traditions and their music. Modern societies—unbounded societies in which individuals are free to determine their social, economic, and cultural destinies—are antithetical to traditional bounded societies in which individuals' social and economic roles are mostly predetermined. Although traditional societies try to coexist with modern societies, it is extremely difficult for them, as the balance of power favors the modern world, irrevocably damaging cultures that try to maintain their traditional life ways. The last section of this chapter looks at one small-scale sociocultural group to understand the ecological effects of modern society on indigenous music.

Papua New Guinea is one of the most diverse countries on planet Earth. Occupying the eastern half of the island of New Guinea, the nation of Papua New Guinea is home to hundreds of different ethnic groups that speak over 800 distinct languages. This is extremely impressive when you consider that with approximately 6,800 languages on earth, Papua New Guinea is home to about 12% of all known languages. Out of all these different ethnic groups, the Kaluli, a small tribe of about 2,000 people who live in the rain forest, are one of the most researched by anthropologists and ethnomusicologists. Following on the work of anthropologist Edward Schieffelin, ethnomusicologist Steven Feld began studying the music of the Kaluli in the 1970s and has documented their musical culture in great detail. After several decades of studying and documenting the music of the Kaluli, Feld has shown us not just how music is structured by the environment in which it is made, but how changes in the environment lead to changes in music and the lifestyle of the culture as a whole.

"A Men's Work Group Clears a New Garden," Field Recording of the Kaluli

http://www.rhapsody.com/members/wgcve5/playlists/mp.172553351

Listen to the first few minutes of this recording of a group of fifteen men clearing trees to make a banana garden. From the very beginning you can hear the steady, repeating shout of one man and the sound of an axe, both working together to make a steady rhythm. At 0:47 you can hear several men begin to shout "Watch out!" as a big tree comes down. Then other songs by other men working can be heard, and at 1:14 the remarkable voice of a tropical bird. Behind this thick texture of individual songs is the constant sound of cicadas buzzing in the trees. What might sound like random or chaotic singing while working is heard not as separate sounds by the Kaluli people, but a whole musical experience in which all the sounds are part of the music. The shouts and work commands, the fragments of songs, the beating of the axes and machetes, the calling of nearby birds, and the drone of cicadas are heard by the Kaluli as harmoniously overlapping with each other, described with the Kaluli words *dulugu ganalan* or "lift-up-over-sounding."

For the Kaluli, the appreciation of music originates in their natural environment. Music is not something that happens in a quiet room precisely because in the rain forest there are no quiet rooms. Unlike a performance of Western classical music in which musicians try to isolate the sound of their music in the quiet of an enclosed room, the Kaluli make music in harmony with the sounds of nature. If they want to sing a song, for example, they don't look for "a quiet place," but instead find a nearby waterfall to sing along with or a place frequented by a certain kind of bird or other natural sound that matches the song they want to sing.

"Ulahi Sings While Scraping Sago Pith from a Sago Palm," Field Recording of the Kaluli

http://www.rhapsody.com/members/wgcve5/playlists/mp.172553351

Listen to the first minute of this song and you can hear how the Kaluli compose their music according to their environment. In the same way we have songs that are structured by individual verses and repeated refrains, the Kaluli have something similar, but they conceive of it using tree terminology. For the Kaluli, the refrain is the "trunk" of a song while individual verses are "branches" that branch off from the "trunk" of the refrain. This recording features a woman named Ulahi who is singing songs while working at scraping pith from a sago palm, a staple of the Kaluli. You can also hear her recently born infant crying while she sings.

Ulahi begins with the refrain or "trunk" in which she sings about her grandmother. The words of the refrain are "*wo ni nuwo*" ("oh, grandmother"). In the first verse that "branches off" she sings, "Grandmother, where are you going to sleep?" In the second verse she sings, "I'm going to sleep at ____________" and "I'm hungry at ____________," each time inserting place names. She goes back to the refrain again and starts the cycle over again. As she continues this form, inserting new place names into each verse, the song creates a musical "map" of the territory.

Guided Listening

0:00	The excerpt begins with her talking before she begins scraping.
0:07	*"Wo ni nuwo"* ("oh, grandmother"); she sings this phrase three times.
0:13	"Where are you going to sleep?"
	"I'm going to sleep at ____________,"
	"I'm hungry at ____________."
0:28	*"Wo ni nuwo eh / wo ni nuwo / wo ni nuwo."*
0:35	"Where are you going to sleep?"
	"I'm going to sleep at ____________,"
	"I'm hungry at ____________."
0:53	*"Wo ni nuwo eh / wo ni nuwo / wo ni nuwo,"* etc.

"Fo:fo: and Miseme Sing at Their Sago Place," Field Recording of the Kaluli

http://www.rhapsody.com/members/wgcve5/playlists/mp.172553351

This recording of two women singing while taking a break from their work demonstrates the "trunk and branches" structure as well as the overlapping aesthetic of "lift-up-over-sounding." Listen how the two women's voices are not completely in sync with each other. This is not sloppiness on their part. This subtle overlap is an essential part of "lift-up-over-sounding," in which all the forest sounds happen independently but alongside each other. The song is about the *dolosk*, a tropical bird also known as Golden Whistler, and you can tell each refrain because the line always ends with the word "yuu," which is the sound of the bird's call. Each verse or "branch" that follows mentions a place where the bird is calling.

Guided Listening

0:00	They begin their song by singing the trunk twice, each time ending in "yuu."
0:07	They sing the first "branch."
0:14	A man nearby begins rhythmically scraping sago while they sing the trunk again.
0:21	They sing another branch.
0:28	They sing the trunk again and the man starts whistling an imitation of the dolosk bird.
0:34	They sing another branch.
0:40	Trunk again.
0:47	Another branch.
0:53	Trunk again, etc.

As you might have guessed by now, birds are extremely important for the Kaluli. Living in a rain forest environment rich with birds and their elaborate calls led to the incorporation of birds into Kaluli cosmology. When a person dies or goes away (migration away from the village and to the city to never return), their soul becomes a bird. In this way, the Kaluli are constantly hearing the cries of their ancestors coming from the rain forest canopy. Thus, the cries of birds and the cries of the ancestors are brought together in song that causes weeping in Kaluli listeners who then feel the loss of loved ones.

The ability to capture these kinds of powerful emotions in song and cause others to weep is the most valued aspect of Kaluli singing and is captured in our two final excerpts of Kaluli ceremonial music. These recordings are extremely rare; the *gisalo* ceremony recorded by Steven Feld in 1984 was the last time such a ceremony was ever performed. With the Kaluli population dwindling, it is unlikely that this traditional ceremony will ever be performed again.

The bird of paradise (Raggiana Bird-of-Paradise), one of the world's most beautiful tropical birds, is the national bird of Papua New Guinea (as seen depicted in the national flag).

Ceremonial *Gisalo* Performed by Halawa, Field Recording of the Kaluli

http://www.rhapsody.com/members/wgcve5/playlists/mp.172553351

This is an excerpt of the all-night *gisalo* ceremony recorded by Feld at about 3:00 a.m. one night in 1984. It was performed in a communal longhouse, and you can hear the jingles of dancers moving through the space as they sing *gisalo* songs with their usual "trunk and branches" structure. The excerpt here begins with a song by Halawa, who succeeds in evoking powerful emotions in his listeners. At about 0:42 you can hear an explosion of emotion caused by this song as men begin to chant and women begin to weep. Halawa himself begins singing in a very strident, weeping voice. The grief expressed in these ceremonies is real and is incorporated into the ritual. When a dancer causes listeners to experience sadness that is so painful, some listeners feel anger so intense that they grab one of the resin torches used to light the longhouse and literally burn the flesh of the dancer as punishment. This unique ritual behavior led the anthropologist Edward Schieffelin to title his book about the Kaluli *The Sorrow of the Lonely and the Burning of the Dancers*.

The *kundu* drum from Papua New Guinea has also taken on the status of national symbol, as seen in the postage stamp on the right that includes a warrior's shield alongside the *kundu* drum.

Group Ceremonial Drumming: Ilib Kuwo, Field Recording of the Kaluli

http://www.rhapsody.com/members/wgcve5/playlists/mp.172553351

This excerpt of ceremonial drumming was made by Feld in 1999 and demonstrates all the aspects of Kaluli music we have examined here. As the track fades in, you can hear the sound of rattles attached to the drummers' costumes as they shout and dance across the space, playing hand drums called *kundu* or *ilib*. All of these overlapping sounds blend together into the Kaluli aesthetic of "lift-up-over-sounding."

Like vocal music, drumming is very emotional for the Kaluli, who hear the *kundu* drum sound as the voice of the Papuan bellbird or *tibodai*; this voice can also cause people to weep. Kaluli hear the drum sound as "tibo tibo," which is the sound of the tibodai bird's call. Listen closely and you can hear how the repetitious drumming sounds like "tibo tibo." But as this sound is played over and over, sometimes for hours on end, some in the audience hear the voice of the drum speaking "dowo dowo," which means "father, father." This sound of a bird spirit communicating in a child's voice calling for "father" can be too emotional for some Kaluli listeners and may even cause an attack on the drummers like the burning in the *gisalo* ceremony.

A group of dancers in full ceremonial dress in Papua New Guinea. The man on the left is holding a *kundu* drum.

Conclusion

Studying the music of indigenous peoples around the world gives us insights into the strong connection between music and place. Just as indigenous people define themselves according to their place of origin, their music is inextricably linked to that place. The resulting sound is unique to that environment and, as such, the music becomes just as fragile as it is unique. The biggest concern of indigenous peoples of the world is the threat to their places of origin and ways of life from the conflict between traditional and modern society. When a place of origin is threatened and people are relocated, these tensions manifest in sorrow, anger, and other powerful emotions that only music can express.

Asian Music: Orchestras, Ensembles, and Improvisation

9

For people in the West, traditional Asian music may be the least familiar and the most foreign-sounding to their ears. This is partly due to a long history of cultural differences and geographic distance between Asia and the West that was once summed up in the saying, "East is East and West is West and never the twain shall meet." That opening line from Rudyard Kipling's 1889 poem "The Ballad of East and West" has often been interpreted as saying that the Orient and the Occident will never understand each other because of insurmountable cultural barriers. But most people ignore the rest of the poem, in which a British officer and an Afghan chieftain meet in battle and earn each other's respect because they display honor and bravery that overcomes cultural differences.

Something similar could be said of Eastern versus Western music. The different musical systems that developed on opposite sides of the world may sound completely foreign to either side, but there are fundamental aspects of music that are shared by East and West. This chapter looks at just a few examples of Asian traditions in terms of how they are organized into orchestras, ensembles, and systems of improvisation.

When one thinks of the word *orchestra*, the image that comes to mind might be a large group of strings, brass, woodwind musicians, and percussionists, all being directed by a single person standing before the ensemble who is not playing an instrument. The time-honored image of the Western symphony orchestra is known throughout the world, but there are Asian orchestras and ensembles with an even older legacy that continue to thrive today.

Gamelan Orchestras in Indonesia

Indonesia is home to one of the richest orchestral traditions in the world. But it is not a single tradition, even though we can encompass all of it under the single term *gamelan*—an Indonesian ensemble consisting of metallophones, gongs, and other instruments. The diversity of gamelan ensembles throughout Indonesia—the fourth most populated nation on Earth, with 238 million people spread across 17,000 islands—reflects the official motto of the modern nation of Indonesia: "unity in diversity." Just as Indonesian people speak their own local language in addition to the official national language of Indonesian,

gamelan musicians specialize in their local tradition, but have a basic understanding of the structure of gamelan music.

A gamelan orchestra typically includes instruments of many kinds—drums, flutes, strings—but the primary instruments are idiophones, most of which are tuned to determinate pitches. Among the tuned idiophones are metallophones (tuned metal bars capable of playing melodies) and gongs, some hanging vertically from stands and others set horizontally in racks. These tuned percussion instruments allow for a very complex system of polyphony referred to as **stratified polyphony**—layered variations of a single melody. This complex texture is actually based on a simple formula: high-pitched instruments play with the highest rhythmic density (the busiest-sounding instruments playing the most notes in a kind of ornamentation); medium-pitched instruments play less dense parts, including the main melody that musicians are following; and the lower-pitched instruments play the fewest notes, serving more as time markers underneath the melody.

The lower-pitched instruments, it turns out, may actually be the most important, even though they play the fewest notes, because these instruments have a function that helps hold all of the sounds together in a cohesive time structure. We call this time structure in gamelan music **colotomic**—rhythmic cycles that are marked by punctuating instruments. In the same way that a sentence contains commas, semicolons, periods, or other markings to indicate its structure, gamelan music also features punctuation that marks musical phrases. These two organizing principles—stratified polyphony and colotomic structure—are evident in a relatively simple gamelan piece from Java, one of the largest islands and the cultural heart and political center of Indonesia.

Example
Javanese Gamelan, "Bubaran: Nudan Mas"

http://www.rhapsody.com/members/wgcve5/playlists/mp.172579335

In this example, it is relatively easy to hear how these principles of stratified polyphony and colotomic structure operate if you follow along with the notation of the piece as you listen. The numbers in the chart refer to specific pitches in the tuning system being used. Gamelan pieces use one of two tuning systems: the five-note system called *slendro* or the seven-note system called *pelog*, which is used in this example. In Javanese gamelan a single piece might use both tuning systems, but our example uses only the seven-note *pelog*, represented by the numbers 1, 2, 3, 5, and 6 (4 and 7 are omitted).

The numbers are arranged to show the main melody that all the musicians are following, even if they don't play it exactly as rendered here. The loudest instruments are playing these numbers exactly as indicated, making it easier to follow. The pitches of the melody are arranged in groups of four that sound on every beat of the music and fit into a cycle of sixteen beats. This sixteen-beat cycle is marked by the colotomic or punctuating instruments, indicated by the markings underneath the numbers. The asterisks indicate a gong called *kempul* (an onomatopoeia for the sound that it makes: "pool") that marks off time within the cycle. The plus sign at the end of each line is for the large gong (also an onomatopoeia for the sound that it makes: "gong") that marks the end of each sixteen-beat cycle. All sixteen beats are accounted for by the straight lines under each note that simply represent the basic beat of the piece.

The lines are structured into three parts: Intro, A, and B. There are no punctuating marks in the Intro until the very last pitch of that line, thus marking the start of the cycle. A and B are each repeated, and when they have both been played, the musicians go back to the beginning and the piece cycles through again.

Intro	- 1 1 1	5 6 1 2	2 1 6 5	6 1 6 5	
A	6 5 3 2	6 5 3 2	2 3 5 3	6 5 3 2	(repeat)
	- - - -	- * - -	- * - -	- * - +	
B	1 5 6 1	5 6 1 2	2 1 6 5	6 1 6 5	(repeat)
	- - - -	- * - -	- * - -	- * - +	

This chart functions as a "map" of the piece, but it is a flexible one; no two performances will be the same in terms of individual musicians' melodic variations and the tempo of the piece, which is determined by the conductor. But unlike the Western conductor, who stands in full view of the musicians and signals with a baton, the conductor of a gamelan orchestra plays drums and uses these drums to aurally cue the tempo and accents without the musicians even needing to look at the conductor.

In this recording of "Bubaran: Nudan Mas," the Intro is played by a single musician who plays a horizontal rack of small tuned gongs called *bonang*. During the Intro the *bonang* player is joined by the drummer/conductor, who cues the rest of the ensemble to start at the sound of the large gong on the last beat of the Intro. The ensemble plays through A and B several times and ends on the final note of B. As you listen, take note of three things:

1. The drummer/conductor who cues the musicians to start, speed up, and slow down by playing certain drum patterns;
2. The colotomic structure of the punctuating instruments (sounding "pool" and "gong");

Guided Listening

"Nudan Mas"

0:00	Bonang player begins softly playing the Intro and is joined by drummer/conductor.
0:07	A begins with all musicians joining in.
0:17	A repeats; follow along with this line and listen for the punctuating instruments.
0:26	B begins; note the new pitches of the melody, but the punctuation remains the same.
0:36	B repeats.
0:45	A returns; listen behind the main melody for the higher-pitched gongs playing a denser, "busier" part.
0:55	A repeats.
1:03	B begins.
1:13	B repeats; note the tempo speeding up during this line.
1:20	A returns at a much faster tempo than before.
1:27	A repeats at fast tempo.
1:35	B returns, beginning at fast tempo, but starts to slow at the end of the line.
1:42	B repeats; note the tempo slowing down in this line, cued by the drums.
1:56	Nearing the end of B, there is a pause before the last note of the melody.
1:59	Final gong sounds, bringing the piece to a close.

3. The stratified polyphony, which is heard in the higher-pitched instruments playing "busy" parts over the melody, the medium-pitched instruments playing the main melody represented by the numbers, and the lowest-pitched instruments, such as the large gong, only playing at the end of each line.

Example
Balinese Gamelan Gong Kebjar, "Hudjan Mas"

http://www.rhapsody.com/members/wgcve5/playlists/mp.172579335

Out of the many islands of Indonesia, one of the most remarkable is the island of Bali, which stands out from the rest of the nation in many ways. This small, 2,200-square-mile island is the number one tourist destination in Indonesia because of its natural beauty and vibrant culture. Part of what makes Bali so distinctive is that the population is predominately Hindu—unlike the rest of Indonesia, where the majority of people are Muslim—and musical performance for the Balinese is an act of religious devotion. Economically, Bali differs from the rest of Indonesia in that 80% of its economy today is based on the tourist industry, which has boomed since the latter half of the twentieth century.

These cultural differences from neighboring Java are matched by extreme musical differences as well. Even though Balinese gamelan music follows the same principles that govern Javanese gamelan, the music sounds radically different. In the early twentieth century, the Balinese developed a new style of gamelan music called **gamelan gong kebyar** (or kebjar)—literally meaning to "flare up" or "flower"—and this flashy style of playing was not only incorporated into temple ceremonies, it became a hit with tourists as well.

This example of the *kebyar* style from Bali sounds startlingly different from the previous example from Java. While this style does follow the principles of stratified polyphony (you can hear the higher-pitched instruments playing faster) and colotomic structure (you can hear punctuating instruments marking a time cycle), there are five distinct aspects not heard in Javanese gamelan:

1. Higher rhythmic density; as a flashy, virtuosic style, some instruments in this ensemble play flurries of notes at incredibly fast speeds;
2. Less "even" rhythm; unlike the even tempo of the Javanese gamelan, this ensemble starts and stops, sometimes abruptly;
3. Sectional playing; unlike the Javanese ensemble in which most instruments play throughout the piece, this Balinese style features passages in which sections of just one kind of instrument play, then followed by a section of another kind of instrument;
4. Shimmer; this is an effect created by using pairs of instruments that are virtually identical, except that they are tuned just slightly different from each other. The acoustic phenomenon of this tuning is a shimmering pulse that adds a rich tone color to the ensemble.
5. Interlocking; this Balinese style features a technique called *kotekan* in which extremely fast parts are interlocking—that is, two or more instruments alternating notes in a melodic line.

"Hudjan Mas"

0:00 Begins with the *gender* section of instruments (metallophones struck with a spiked stick).

0:05 *Gender* section is joined by a small timekeeping gong that plays a fast pulse (sounds like "tuk-tuk-tuk-tuk") and lower-pitched metallophones playing with less density; gender section here uses interlocking (*kotekan*).

0:11 At the sound of the large gong (*ageng*), the instruments suddenly stop; during this brief pause you can hear the shimmering sound so characteristic of Balinese gamelan.

0:13 The music starts again with interlocking *kotekan* parts.

0:20 Another pause in which you can hear the shimmering sound.

0:23 A passage begins that features the metallophones playing an uneven start/stop tempo.

0:45 The timekeeper gong returns to play at fast tempo and the metallophones play interlocking parts; the music continues to alternate between steady rhythm and start/stop.

2:13 Full ensemble begins to play.

2:23 Large gong sounds and music pauses.

2:25 Passage begins featuring the *reyong* (small kettle gongs in a horizontal rack); these musicians are playing extremely fast interlocking parts that start and stop.

2:44 Large gong sounds and new passage begins in slower tempo; the full ensemble joins in; especially prominent here are the *ceng-ceng* (cymbals).

3:00 As you listen to the rest of the piece, note how the dynamic levels shift between louder and softer as cued by the drummer/conductor; also note how the low-pitched and medium-pitched gongs keep the colotomic structure.

Example

Ketjak: The Ramayana Monkey Chant

http://www.rhapsody.com/members/wgcve5/playlists/mp.172579335

A performance of *ketjak* in Bali, Indonesia.

This same fast-paced style is also found in the Balinese "monkey chant" known as *ketjak* (or *kecak*). In the monkey chant there are no instruments, only voices that create a dynamic, high-density, interlocking sound similar to gamelan, complete with a colotomic structure. In this example you can hear many voices, most of them chanting the word "chak" in a highly syncopated rhythm. There are also some voices singing with a lower rhythmic density, marking the colotomic structure. The voices that can be heard emerging out of the thick rhythmic texture are actors who are portraying a story from the Hindu epic, the Ramayana, in which Prince Rama employs the monkey king Vanara to go to battle against the evil king Ravana to save Princess Sita. The monkey chant is truly a creation of modern Bali, designed in the early twentieth century for entertaining tourists, yet the story and its performance have great religious significance for the Balinese.

Gagaku in Japan: The Oldest Orchestra in the World

http://www.rhapsody.com/members/wgcve5/playlists/mp.172579335

One of the most modern countries in the world, Japan is also home to some of the oldest music in the world. The oldest and most revered musical tradition is *gagaku* (literally "elegant music"), an orchestra of winds, strings, and percussion that has been maintained by the Emperor of Japan since the eighth century. Although changes in the music have most certainly occurred over 1,400 years, the instrumental structure of the orchestra has been consistently maintained. Considering that this ensemble is based on even older music that originated in the ancient Chinese Tang Dynasty capital of Changan, *gagaku* as it exists today is like a time capsule from the ancient world.

Like a Western orchestra, the *gagaku* orchestra is divided into different sections of instruments, each with its own musical function. But instead of the Western focus on melodic and harmonic development, Japanese *gagaku*, like Indonesian gamelan, focuses on the texture of instrumental relationships within a rhythmic cycle. Rhythmic cycles in *gagaku* are crucial for all the musicians to synchronize their parts, but it can be a challenge to follow because the tempo of the rhythm is slow and sometimes stretches out, almost like a rubber band; thus we can describe this as "elastic rhythm." What's even more perplexing is that unlike a Western orchestra or a gamelan orchestra, there is no conductor at all in *gagaku*. All musicians are playing this elastic, "breathing" rhythm together without the aid of a conductor. When listening to such music, one should not expect the music to "develop" as with a Western symphony or expect the dynamic accents of Balinese gamelan, but rather enjoy the slow, shifting fabric of the music as it exists in the moment—a moment that has lasted over a thousand years.

There are two musical functions in *gagaku*: melodic and time-marking (like the colotomic structure of gamelan). In the *kangen* (literally "winds" and "strings") ensemble in our listening example, the melodic instruments feature three kinds of wind instruments: flutes (*ryuteki*), oboes (*hichiriki*), and mouth organs (*sho*). Time-marking instruments include not only percussion instruments, but string instruments as well. The percussion section includes a single small barrel-shaped drum (*kakko*), a single hanging barrel-shaped drum (*taiko*), and a small hanging gong-chime (*shoko*). The string instruments, rather than playing melody, play decorative patterns that simply mark the places within the rhythmic cycle, much like the "pool" sounds heard in Indonesian gamelan. The plucked lute (*biwa*) and the long zither (*koto*) play simple, elegant patterns that help stabilize the rhythm of the piece and as such are crucial to holding the entire ensemble together.

This piece, "Etenraku" ("Music of Divinity"), is based on a sixteen-beat rhythmic cycle that can be heard most clearly by following the large and small drum. The beat is very slow in this recording and difficult to follow in the beginning, but the rhythm becomes more stable as the piece progresses. After an eight-beat introduction in which instruments enter one at a time, the sixteen-beat cycle begins when the large drum first sounds, marking beat one.

Guided Listening

"Etenraku"

(Kangen: Etenraku Nokorigaku Sanben from the album *Gagaku and Beyond*—Tokyo Gakuso/Tadaaki Ohno)

If you listen on headphones, you can hear each instrument appear in order, and the sound is coming from the group as positioned on stage.

0:00	Flute begins (left side of stage, left channel) Intro section.
0:08	Small drum (right side) strikes.
0:09	Small gong (left side).
0:10	Small drum speeds up.
0:13	Soft stroke on large *taiko* drum "tsun" (center).
0:17	Mouth organs (right side) enter
0:19	Loud stroke on large *taiko* drum "DON" (center) and oboes begin (center); the sixteen-beat time cycle begins here.
0:39	*Biwa* enters (right).
0:58	Loud stroke on large *taiko* drum "DON" marks the end of the sixteen-beat cycle.
1:00	*Koto* enters (left).
1:35	"DON" end of sixteen-beat cycle.
2:09	"DON."
2:27	Melody changes to B section here.

As you listen to the rest of this piece, pay attention to the interaction of the instruments, how they mark time in the cycle, and how the music seems to gradually get more rhythmically dense.

The Art of Improvisation in Asia

In the same way that American jazz is based on the art of improvising music "in the moment," there are other traditions in the world of music in which improvisation is the main focus. This section will look at two traditions: Indian classical music and Arabic music in the Middle East. While the sounds of these two traditions differ from each other and differ from jazz as well, what all these kinds of improvisation have in common are rules that musicians follow when creating their own individual improvisations. In this way the music serves as an expression of particular individual performers as well as an expression of the culture from which it originates. This chapter will demonstrate that while a musical system provides the foundation for improvisation, it is the individual performer that gives improvisation its shape and its life.

Raga Improvisation in Indian Classical Music

Although it is often referred to by the term "classical," the setting for a concert of North Indian classical (or Hindustani) music looks very different from a concert by a Western symphony orchestra. First of all, there are very few musicians on stage—often only three—and each one of these provides one of the three different musical functions of the music. The **melodic function** is provided by a featured soloist whose improvisation is the main focus of the performance. The featured

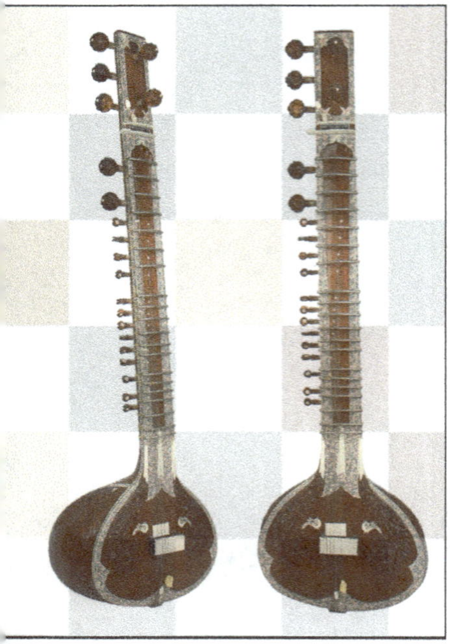

© M.E. Mulder, 2013. Used under license from Shutterstock, Inc.

soloist may play any number of traditional Indian instruments, such as the *sitar* (fretted plucked lute), *sarod* (fretless plucked lute), or *bansuri* (bamboo flute), or may be a vocalist. The **rhythmic function** is most often represented by a single player playing percussion, such as the *tabla*—a pair of drums played with bare hands. The **drone function** usually features a musician playing a drone—that is, a single, unchanging pitch—on a string instrument called *tambura*, especially designed to create a rich drone sound. Together these three musicians generate the three components of Indian music we will analyze here: **melody, rhythm,** and **drone.**

The melodic basis of Indian music is called *raga*—a framework for improvisation and composing. There are many distinct *raga* (literally "color") known to Indian musicians and performed today, each one having a name, a set of pitches used, and rules about how to play these pitches. Thus, when a musician plays a *raga*, such as our example, "Bhimpalasi," the performer of the melody should completely understand which pitches are to be used, which of those pitches receive special emphasis, what kinds of melodic movement there should be, and what kind of ornaments can be played. In addition to these technical details, each *raga* also has specific extra-musical associations with the time of day, the season of the year, and emotional moods. Only after understanding all of this information can a soloist truly improvise within a particular *raga* form.

The rhythmic basis is called *tala* (lit. "clap")—a system of rhythmic cycles. Like raga, there are many different *tala* rhythmic cycles in North Indian music, each with a name and a series of beats subdivided in different ways. For example, the most commonly used *tala* is called *tintal* and consists of sixteen beats, subdivided into 4 + 4 + 4 + 4. Also like *raga*, there are rules about how to play during the sixteen-beat cycle and beat 1 serves as the beginning and end of the cycle, acting almost like a magnet upon which the musicians synchronize the ends of their musical phrases during a performance. *Tala* is so important to the structure of a performance that not only must the musicians follow the cycle, but audience members familiar with Indian music also keep track of the *tala* during a performance by counting on their fingers. Knowing the *tala* enhances audience enjoyment as listeners can hear how the musicians are interacting in order to come together by landing perfectly on "beat one," which is called *sam*.

In a performance of Indian classical music, there are two main sections. The first is an introduction called *alap* in which the soloist explores the sound of the *raga*. This first section is in free meter, so there is no *tala* rhythmic cycle. As soon as the *alap* section comes to a close, the next section begins, called *gat*. The *gat* section opens with a specific melody played by the soloist, who is joined by the percussionist, who introduces the *tala* rhythmic cycle. This second section of the performance repeats the *tala* cycle over and over as the melodic instrumentalist and the rhythmic instrumentalist develop complex improvisations, leading to a climactic ending after an unspecified amount of time. Some *raga* performances can build and build for over an hour, depending on the musicians' choice.

Example
Ravi Shankar, "An Introduction to Indian Music"

http://www.rhapsody.com/members/wgcve5/playlists/mp.172579335

In this example, the most famous musician in modern North Indian classical music, Ravi Shankar (1920–2012), explains and demonstrates *raga* and *tala* in one very short lecture. Listening to this example before moving on to our example of an actual *raga* in performance will enhance your listening of the next example.

Example
Ravi Shankar, "Bhimpalasi"

http://www.rhapsody.com/members/wgcve5/playlists/mp.172579335

Guided Listening

"Bhimpalasi" Performed by Ravi Shankar

0:00	Ravi Shankar introduces the *raga* by playing the ascending scale and the descending scale. Note how there are seven notes in the ascending scale (the first and last notes are the same, an octave apart) while there are ten notes played in the descending scale (for the seventh and eighth notes he repeats the previous two notes before continuing to the bottom of the scale). He also demonstrates the *tala* of Ada Chautal, which is a cycle of fourteen beats (2 + 4 + 4 + 4).
0:40	The *raga* begins with a flourish played on the sympathetic strings of the *sitar.*

Listen carefully as he explores the notes of the *raga* in this short free meter introduction.

1:34	Beat 1 of the cycle starts and Shankar plays the main melody over the fourteen-beat cycle.
1:47	Beat 1 of the cycle returns; listen to how the melody ends exactly on this beat.
2:00	Beat 1; note how the melody again ends on beat 1.
2:14	Beat 1; note how Shankar does not accent beat 1 this time.
2:28	Beat 1; this time beat 1 is emphasized.
2:41	Beat 1; not emphasized.
2:55	Beat 1; not emphasized.
3:09	Beat 1; beat emphasized here.
3:22	Beat 1.
3:35	Beat 1.
3:49	Beat 1.
4:43	Beat 1 ends on the melody.
4:57	Beat 1 ends on the melody again.
5:00	He begins to explore the lower register of his *sitar.*
5:50	Beat 1.
6:03	Beat 1.
6:28	Beat 1.
6:41	Beat 1.
6:53	Beat 1.
7:31	Beat 1.
7:46	Listen to the pulsing strings underneath the melody.
8:28	Playing becomes more dense.
8:44	Beat 1.
8:47	More dense playing.
9:00	Begins long passage of dense playing.
9:20	Beat 1.
10:00	Notice the drumming playing long sequences of notes.
11:11	Flurry of notes on the *sitar* with strong pulse on drone strings.
11:50	Beat 1.
12:02	Beat 1 and end of piece.

"Bhimpalasi" is designated as an afternoon *raga* that is meant to have a mood of tenderness. Composer Alan Hovhaness describes it as having the "suppressed longing of a lover, but serene, with dignity, and yet throbbing with deep emotion." This is not just the personal interpretation of one person: it is the designated character of this particular *raga* itself. The goal of a great musician such as Ravi Shankar heard in this recording is to use his powers of improvisation within this set of rules to express the Indian aesthetic of *rasa* ("juice" or "flavor" or "essence"). Originating 2,000 years ago in the *Natyasastra*, an ancient Hindu treatise on dramatic arts, the *rasa* are emotional states, such as love, laughter, anger, compassion, horror, and wonder. The effectiveness of a performance of a *raga* is in how well the performer is able to capture these emotional states. Because of the spontaneous nature of improvisation, how the musician achieves this is different every time and unique to that moment.

Example
Maqam Improvisation in the Middle East

The system of melodic modes used for improvisation in Arabic music is called *maqam*. Like *raga*, *maqam* are named sets of pitches that have rules regarding the importance of certain notes, types of phrases, and melodic development within that *maqam*, as well as rules for modulation to other *maqam* (changing from one *maqam* to another in performance). Closely related to the Arabic tradition of *maqam* improvisation are the Turkish system, known as *makam*, and the Persian system, known as *dastgah*, which involves the use of more composed patterns of music. The basic concept in all three traditions is the same: improvisation is the focus of the music, but musicians must first know the rules.

Each *maqam* is based on a scale of seven notes and may be written out as A, B, C, D, E, F, G, but tonality radically differs from Western music. Whereas Western music divides an octave into twelve notes (A through G plus sharps and flats), Arabic music divides the octave into twenty-four notes (A through G with sharps, flats, half-sharps, and half-flats), so many *maqam* feature pitches that fall between the usual Western pitches. For example, *maqam bayati* consists of the notes D, E half-flat, F, G, A, B flat, and C. Thus, E half-flat would be only slightly lower in pitch than E and not as low as E flat. You could not possibly play E half-flat on a piano because the pitch lies "between" the two keys.

As you would expect then, Arabic music makes use of traditional instruments. An Arabic ensemble for playing *maqam* music, called *takht*, consists of several traditional instruments, such as the *qanun* (a plucked zither) and the *nay* (an end-blown flute). The most common string instrument in all Arabic music is the *'ud*, a plucked lute that is actually the ancient prototype for more common plucked lutes today such as the guitar. But whereas a guitar has frets (raised bars on the neck of the instrument) that help divide the pitches into sharps and flats as on a piano, the *'ud* is fretless, allowing the player to create the "in-between" notes common in Arabic music. But *takht* ensembles do include Western instruments that do not have frets, and the violin and cello are actually widely used in the Middle East.

Arabic improvisation can be done with any combination of instruments, from large ensembles to solo. Our example is by the Lebanese master musician and ethnomusicologist Ali Jihad Racy, performing on the *'ud*, accompanied on the *riqq* (a tambourine) by percussionist Souhail Kaspar. With only these two instruments to listen to, it is easy to get lost in the music, but if you follow along with the listening guide, you might be able to hear how the music changes from the free meter improvisation of the opening minutes to the composed section that makes up the majority of the recording. If you can follow the circuitous, snake-like melody on your own, you might be able to identify when the refrain comes in each time it returns.

Guided Listening

"Taqasim and Sama'i Bayyati Al-Aryan," Ali Jihad Racy with Souhail Kaspar

http://www.rhapsody.com/members/wgcve5/playlists/mp.172579335

0:00	Performance begins with an improvisation (*taqasim*) on the *'ud*; this section is in free meter.
0:33	After a brief pause, he begins to explore some of the higher-pitched notes on his instrument.
1:08	Note two instrumental "voices" here; while one "voice" stays on one note as a drone, the other "voice" rapidly explores several notes.
1:47	Another brief pause followed by another passage of higher-pitched notes.
2:52	Beginning of the composed song "Sama'i Bayyati" as percussionist enters; the piece begins with the first verse.
3:22	Refrain.
3:52	Verse; note how the *'ud* pauses slightly, but the percussionist plays through the pause.
4:20	Refrain.
4:46	Verse; the pause is more noticeable here as the percussionist pauses, too.
5:15	Refrain.
5:42	Verse; note the pause, followed by a change in rhythm.
6:40	Refrain.

Africa and Diaspora

10

© Tom Gowanlock, 2013. Used under license from Shutterstock, Inc.

The African continent looms large in the global imagination as a place of origins, largely because anthropologists trace the earliest evidence of the human species to the continent. If human civilization originated in Africa, it follows then that the earliest forms of music—essentially vocalizing and striking together objects such as stones—may have had their origins in Africa, too. Although considering Africa as the root of all music is speculative, when it comes to appreciating the world of music today, it turns out that Africa is ultimately the origin of much of the modern music we hear. Jazz, hip-hop, reggae, rock and roll, and blues all trace their origins back to Africa. It seems that everywhere we look in the world, we find music touched by African influence.

Regardless of origins, studying African music is obviously crucial to our understanding of music. Before we can summarize the diversity of its musical styles, it is necessary to define Africa in geographic terms to at least narrow down what we can consider in one short chapter. Africa is divided into two broad areas: the Maghrib, north of the Sahara desert, and the southern section, sub-Saharan Africa. While the northern part of Africa has much in common culturally with Western Asia and the Mediterranean, sub-Saharan Africa consists of a distinctive collection of cultures that share many common cultural and musical elements. In this chapter we will focus primarily on sub-Saharan Africa and identify key elements of music from those cultures that have put their distinct stamp on the music of the world.

Perhaps the most important cultural concepts underlying African music are **communality** and **functionality**, two concepts that are inextricably entwined and help produce the distinctive sounds of African music. Because traditional African societies strongly emphasize communal participation in almost all aspects of daily life, music must be functional and serve community needs. Rather than serving the needs of particular individuals, music is meant to serve society as a whole, and it does this by encouraging group participation. This function of social integration into the group results in the key elements of music that we will identify as we sample just a few of the diverse styles of African music.

Music of the Rain Forest

A good place to start examining the communal function of music in Africa is in one of the oldest societies in the world, the Pygmies of the rain forest areas of the Central African Republic, the Congo, and Cameroon. A generic term for several ethnic groups of forest dwellers, Pygmies attracted a great deal of attention from anthropologists in the twentieth century because many still lived a nomadic lifestyle based on hunting and food gathering, the oldest subsistence mode in human development. After anthropologist Colin Turnbull published his landmark study of the Efe or Mbuti ethnic group, *The Forest People*, in 1961, many people in the West became fascinated with Pygmy culture. What people found most compelling about Pygmies was their egalitarian lifestyle, in which individuals do not monopolize resources as they do in modern Western society, allowing the collective to live in harmony with each other and with their forest habitat. In Pygmy cosmology, the forest is like a parental spirit that provides them all with enough food to survive. Furthermore, they communicate to this forest spirit through song. Thus, the music of the Mbuti that Turnbull recorded in the forest revealed the sound of a peaceful, egalitarian society in which all the individual parts were integrated into a smoothly functioning whole.

This actually can be heard in our first example, labeled as "Elephant Song" by Turnbull from his historic recordings in 1961. While this music may be difficult to comprehend at first, there are a few things to listen for that can help in following along. The first sound that should stand out clearly to your ear is a pair of clapsticks that play a pattern that stays somewhat regular throughout the piece.

Clapstick pattern:

1	2	3	4	5	6	7	8
x	x	-	x	-	x	x	-

Notice that underneath this steady clapping sound are many voices that are hard to hear individually, but create a dense texture that is blended smoothly together. You can also hear one louder, male voice that rises above the others. Just beneath that male lead voice you can hear other voices that stand out, including a female voice. As you listen to this recording a few times, you will find that you will get better at picking out different voices amid the texture.

Guided Listening

Music of the Mbuti Pygmies: "Elephant Song"

http://www.rhapsody.com/members/wgcve5/playlists/mp.169886415

0:00	The recording starts right in the middle of the song and you can hear the prominent male lead voice from the start.
0:09	The male voice sings a phrase here, followed by
0:13	a female voice that "responds."
0:15	Listen here to how the texture of all the voices is made up of short repeating patterns.
0:26	Male voice returns.
0:46	Male lead switches to a kind of talking style.

1:04	The sound of rumbling of thunder reminds us that this is outside in the forest.
1:11	Male lead voice sings a phrase here, followed by
1:13	a female voice that "responds."
1:33	Male lead voice switches again to talking style.
2:03	Male voice sounds a long, extended tone; after this his tones get a bit longer.
2:31	The performance is interrupted by a sudden, loud crash of thunder, followed by group laughter.

What did we hear?

- Multiple pitches occurring simultaneously (polyphony).
- A variety of timbres: the thick textures created by the group of singers create one kind of tone color while the male vocalist stands out with a more strident vocal timbre.
- Singing that is conversational, not just singing that sounds like speech, but a kind of call and response between voices.
- Short repeating patterns (**ostinato**) that contribute to making a complex whole:
    - The clapsticks play a repeating pattern that acts as a time marker.
    - The voices sing in short repeating patterns that build up a dense musical texture.

These four features—polyphony, timbral variety, conversational singing, and ostinato—are the common elements in sub-Saharan African music that we will examine in this chapter. In our next example, we will add one more element that is widespread in African music: polyrhythm.

West African Drumming

Example
Fontomfrom

http://www.rhapsody.com/members/wgcve5/playlists/mp.169886415

The communal functionality of African music is most evident in drumming traditions found in West Africa. Listening to a drum ensemble, such as this Fontomfrom drum ensemble from Ghana in West Africa, gives us a sonic demonstration of how several individual parts are layered into a complex whole. While the individual parts can clearly be heard, no single part dominates the music, as in a typical contemporary popular song in which you often hear a lead singer or soloist supported by a group. Because of this communal sound as well as the absence of a melody for the ear to hold onto, many first-time listeners have trouble making sense of this music, thinking that it sounds chaotic. On the contrary, the overall sound is so ordered by each interdependent part that if one musician makes a mistake, it can affect other musicians in the group and cause the whole sound to fall apart. While this seldom happens in West Africa, such "train wrecks" can easily happen when students learn for the first time in university ensembles in North America. What better way to learn about the importance of community interdependence than that?

What seems to be the source of the confusion for novices is the phenomenon many describe as polyrhythm. While one rarely hears African people use the word—and it is somewhat controversial among African music specialists in ethnomusicology—polyrhythm is a concept we can use to make sense of this complex whole. We can begin to understand polyrhythm simply by going back to our study of rhythm in the fundamentals chapter of our book, when we demonstrated how rhythm is understood as either duple (using units of two) or triple (using units of three). But in music that we hear as polyrhythmic, duple and triple are not mutually exclusive—they are heard happening at the same time.

The simplest way to understand polyrhythm is to try and create this simultaneous duple and triple effect by yourself. First, sit up straight in your chair with both feet flat on the floor and place your hands flat on your legs just above the knees. With your right hand (if you're right-handed, otherwise you can reverse the hands), tap out a triple rhythm: 1-2-3. Make the first beat a bit stronger so you can keep track of where you are. Then, with your left hand, tap once in between the right-hand beats 2 and 3 so that the whole unit looks like this: 1-2&3. Once you have this much, add a left-hand tap on beat 1 so that the whole pattern looks like this:

A Simple Two-to-Three Polyrhythm:

Right hand	1	-	2	-	3	-
Left hand	1	-	-	&	-	-
Units of time	x	x	x	x	x	x

You can see how the right hand tapping 1-2-3 occupies two units of time for each tap, while the left hand tapping 1-& occupies three units of time for each tap. While you tap out this rhythm, you are probably hearing it as one phrase: 1-2&3. But after you get comfortable tapping this polyrhythm, try watching each hand one at a time and feel what each rhythm is like independently of the other. Listen what happens to the sound as you shift your attention back and forth between each hand. Not only can you start to hear the rhythm in units of two and three simultaneously, but you might be able to speed up your tempo and feel the rhythmic drive of this simple pattern.

After practicing this exercise in polyrhythm, you can listen to our first listening example with a deeper understanding of what is happening in this music. While there is more going on than just the simple two-to-three pattern we just learned, the entire performance can be conceptualized in units of twos and threes in various combinations that occur within a framework of twelve beats.

The first instrument to focus on is the *gongon*, the metal bell that can be clearly heard because it is the only instrument here that is not a drum. The pattern the bell plays provides a basic structure sometimes called a timeline. Here is what the timeline played by the bell looks like:

***Gongon* bell pattern:**

1	2	3	4	5	6	7	8	9	10	11	12
x	-	x	-	x	-	x	x	-	x	-	x

Keep in mind that when the bell player begins at :02, he does not play beat 1, so his first sound is the third beat of the pattern. If this is difficult to follow at first, just try to focus on the two "quick beats" of 7-8 and 12-1 to find your place in the pattern.

The rest of the ensemble consists of drums of various sizes. The largest drum with the lowest pitch is called *from*, a tall, barrel-shaped drum played with sticks, which gives the ensemble its name. The *from* is the first drum heard in this recording and is the leader of the group. The *gongon* bell begins at :02, and at :08 two other kinds of barrel-shaped drums join in: the *atumpan*, which is not quite as large as the *from*, and the *eguankoba*, which is smaller in size.

Although the music may sound a bit chaotic to your ears, listen carefully at the :27 mark. You can hear a slight pause in the drumming with the large *from* striking two very strong, emphatic beats at :27 and :28. From this point on, you can hear regular patterns played by each drum. Try following one drum sound and focus on its pattern, then shift your focus to another drum and follow its pattern. As you begin to discern the differences between the drums, listen how each pattern fits in with the timeline provided by the bell.

Ensemble drumming like the Fontomfrom has become so well known in world music that many people associate African music exclusively with drumming, but African music is much more than just drumming. In fact, in the remainder of this chapter we will no longer focus on drumming as we show how all five features we have discussed—polyphony, timbral variety, conversational singing, ostinato, and polyrhythm—appear in many kinds of African music.

Kora Music of Mali

One might think that the expression of community in African music would require a large ensemble of many players. But complex polyphony and polyrhythm can be played by a single player on a single instrument that can feature the rich variety of timbres, the layered ostinato, and the conversational style that distinguish music of sub-Saharan Africa.

In our listening example, "Kora Mali" by world-famous *kora* musician Mamadou Diabaté, we can hear the dense textures that are characteristic of this instrument. *Kora* music of Mali is built on multiple ostinato layering, which creates a smooth, flowing style called *kumbengo* that musicians often use as accompaniment to singing, but our example is only instrumental. In addition to this thick layered sound, musicians add dense flourishes of notes called *birimintingo* that add excitement and tension to the music. Renowned for his skill on the instrument, Mamadou Diabaté displays his *kora* prowess with many flourishes that are extremely ornate and executed at a rapid tempo.

The *kora* is an indigenous African string instrument that is unique in the world of music. Classified as a twenty-one-string bridge harp, the *kora* consists of a cowskin-covered calabash body with a wooden neck to which are attached two parallel planes of strings to be plucked by the fingers of each hand. In the photo you can see a *kora* player holding onto two wooden handles and plucking strings on the right side and left side accordingly with his thumb and forefingers.

Guided Listening

"Kora Mali" by Mamadou Diabaté

http://www.rhapsody.com/members/wgcve5/playlists/mp.169886415

0:00	Rapid, descending flourishes (*birimintingo*).
0:23	Flowing pattern (*kumbengo*) in which bass strings, medium-pitch strings, and high strings are interwoven.
0:40	Flourish.
0:47	Flourish.
1:08	Note high strings in a steady ostinato.
1:29	Flourish descending.
1:43	Flourish descending.
1:58	Listen to the highest string play an upward ascending melody and descending.
2:10	Flourish downward.
2:19	High hammer chords that become twice as fast.
2:42	Flourish downward.
2:49	Note high ascending and descending pattern.
2:56	Flourish downward.
3:29	Note high-note chords.
3:40	Flourishes downward.
3:58	Flourishes downward.
4:04	High hammer chords.
4:15	Song begins to fade on ascending and descending high notes.

Like many of the most famous *kora* players, Mamadou Diabaté comes from a musical family. The name Diabaté indicates that he comes from a family of griots, or *jeli* as they are known among the Manding in Mali. *Jeli* are professionals who preserve and transmit history and culture through their music. The son of another famous *kora* player, Sidiki Diabate, widely known as the "King of *Kora*," Mamadou was born into a family of *jeli* that has a very long history of this cultural preservation in Mali. So deep is this history that the Diabaté family has produced seventy-two generations of *kora* players.

While Mamadou's overall playing style is quite modern, incorporating jazz and pop, he nevertheless maintains the strong tradition of his family and his heritage as heard in this song "Kora Mali." Even with the elaborate flourishes that are Mamadou's own improvisations, the song itself is traditional and is commonly used at weddings in Mali. Even when African musicians such as Mamadou produce music for popular consumption, the music often reflects the communal functionality of African music.

Mbira Music of Zimbabwe

Another instrument that demonstrates these Africanisms in music is the ***mbira***. Classified as a *lamellaphone* (idiophone with metal keys that are plucked) that is found throughout Africa, the *mbira* is also known by many other names such as *mbila*, *likembe*, *sanza*, and an English name, thumb piano. The metal keys of different lengths are inserted into a board in such a way as to optimize the playing of certain melodies by the thumbs of both hands as they hold the instrument. Sometimes the instrument is inserted into a large resonator such as a calabash to enhance the sound. *Mbira* can be played solo or in groups and the instrument is often accompanied by rattles (*hosho*). *Mbira* music also typically accompanies vocals and often the singer is playing the *mbira*.

(Left) a simple *mbira*; (Right) *mbira* player Chartwell Dutiro plays for an audience in England in 2011. His *mbira* is not visible because it is inside a gourd resonator that sits on his lap as he plucks the keys with both hands.

Example
Mbira Dzavadzimu, "Nyamaropa"

http://www.rhapsody.com/members/wgcve5/playlists/mp.169886415

Our example features the *mbira dzavadzimu*, an ancient instrument that is sacred to the Shona people of Zimbabwe. The name literally means "voices of the ancestors" and as such, the instrument has a functional use of calling on the ancestors of the community. Try listening to this song a few times to see if you can hear how the different parts fit together.

We can start by listening for the layering of polyrhythm. The most noticeable sound as the track fades in is the *hosho* rattle that seems to have a triple rhythm that can be counted fast on your fingers in groups of three like this:

1-2-3/1-2-3/1-2-3 etc.

The *mbira* is playing a melodic pattern in a duple rhythm that lasts for 16-beats and can be counted on your fingers at a somewhat slower tempo in four groups of four:

1-2-3-4/1-2-3-4/1-2-3-4/1-2-3-4

One thing to note about the *mbira* melody is that it is actually played by two musicians playing interlocking patterns. In other words, each musician plays half the notes of the total melody, which can only be heard when the two musicians interlock their parts together. Malians have specific names for the two melodic parts: the higher tones that can be heard more clearly are called *kushaura*, while the lower tones that are a bit harder to hear are a second part called *kutsinhira*. Together these two musicians create a flowing, interlocking melodic accompaniment for the voice.

The singing voice provides a third layer of sound that is also complex. The singer is using three different vocal styles in this example: *mahonyera* (a low-pitched voice that is syllabic), *huro* (a high melodic style that includes special techniques such as yodeling), and *kudeketera* (an ancient form of poetic recitation). The song "Nyamaropa" is thought to be an ancient song type that is the basis for many of today's songs for the *mbira*.

Guided Listening

Mbira Dzavadzimu, "Nyamaropa"

http://www.rhapsody.com/members/wgcve5/playlists/mp.169886415

0:00	Example fades in with the sound of the *hosho* rattle that feels like a triple rhythm.
0:10	Voice begins; try counting 1-2-3-4 with your fingers right when the voice begins.
0:18	*Mbira* pattern repeats; the vocalist sings here in the high melodic style (*huro*).
0:27	*Mbira* pattern repeats; the vocalist switches to low style (*mahonyera*).
0:36	*Mbira* pattern repeats.
0:44	*Mbira* pattern repeats.
0:53	Vocalist goes back to the high melodic style (*huro*).
1:04	*Mbira* pattern repeats; listen for these repeats as you listen to the rest of the track.
1:23	Vocalist sings in the low style.
1:45	Vocalist goes back to high style.
2:11	Notice the yodeling the singer employs here, alternating head and chest voice.
2:35	The singer starts to sing **vocables**: "da didi da, da di da," etc.
3:20	Singer sings in high style; note how his singing approaches the sound of speech.
4:08	Singer returns to low style.
4:25	Singer sings in high style.
4:50	Low-style singing.
5:30	In this brief pause in the singing, note the interaction between the two *mbira* parts and the accents made by the players plucking the keys more forcefully.
5:43	Singer returns to high style.
6:04	Singer sings in low style as example fades out.

South African Vocal Music and the World

The lasting impact of African music on the rest of the world can be attributed to one of the great tragedies in the history of the world: the slave trade. From 1620 to 1865, nearly 600,000 Africans were brought to America by force and endured centuries of cruel and inhumane conditions. One of the few positives to emerge from this centuries-long holocaust was the spread of African culture, especially musical culture, to the New World. As we will see in Section IV on Popular Music, the elements common to music in sub-Saharan Africa made quite an impact on music outside of Africa. We will review some of those influences when we discuss African American music later.

To conclude this chapter, we will examine the migration of a single song that did not come by way of slavery, but through the mass media of the twentieth century, and has become iconic of Africa to the rest of the world.

With the industrialization of South Africa in the 1920s, young men left their families in the country and migrated to the Natal region to work in the coal mines. Music naturally fulfilled its communal function and these workers began to form choirs, usually grouped together according to the regions the men came from, thus creating an alternative community. These community choirs sparked a lively social scene and fierce competition among various groups singing in a distinctive style that soon spread to Johannesburg, one of the largest cities in Africa. This style of singing got its name from a song that was recorded in 1939 called "Mbube" ("The Lion"). You might recognize this song either by the lead singer's high, soaring falsetto vocal line or by the bass voices that chant "*uyimbube*" (Zulu for "You are a lion") throughout the duration of the song.

Guided Listening

"Mbube" ("The Lion"), Solomon Linda's Evening Birds, Rec. 1939

http://www.rhapsody.com/members/wgcve5/playlists/mp.169886415

00:00	Lead singer shouts a brief introduction in a song/speech-like manner.
00:05	Lead singer is joined by the rest of the group, who harmonize on a chord that ascends several steps and descends back again.
00:11	Bass voices begin to sing a phrase that becomes the foundation for the song; listen to how this phrase in the bass voices repeats through the entire song.
00:21	Lead singer sings a long, sustained note on a high pitch in falsetto "head" voice that falls down to mid-range voice.
00:30	Just as the bass voice pattern repeats, so does the lead singer's falsetto vocal phrase.
00:37	As the bass voice cycle repeats, the lead singer begins a different vocal phrase in mid-range voice.
00:46	Singer does a variation on the mid-range vocal phrase.
00:54	Falsetto vocal line returns and is sung twice.
1:10	Mid-range vocal phrase returns and is sung twice.
1:26	Falsetto line returns and is sung twice.
1:42	Lead singer begins to sing in a bass voice, blending with the others in the low register.
1:50	Mid-range vocal phrase returns and is sung twice.
2:07	The lead singer sings in the bass vocal range again.
2:22	Falsetto line returns and is sung twice.
2:40	The lead singer sings in the bass vocal range again as the song ends.

By 1948, this recording of "Mbube" had sold about 100,000 copies throughout Africa and inspired many similar vocal groups to sing in a style that became known as *mbube*. The trademark of this style is the extra emphasis on the bass voices. For example, Solomon Linda's group, the Evening Birds, expanded the usual vocal quartet by adding two extra bass singers.

Solomon Linda's song "Mbube" soon crossed the Atlantic Ocean and made an impact in America. In 1949, ethnomusicologist Alan Lomax played the song for folk musician Pete Seeger, who arranged and recorded the song for his group

The Weavers in 1951. Not knowing any of the words, Seeger misheard the bass voices singing "*uyimbube*" and instead taught his group to sing the nonsense syllables "wimoweh." Now renamed by The Weavers, the song "Wimoweh" became a Top Ten hit on the Billboard charts in the United States.

Example: "Wimoweh," The Weavers, 1951
http://www.rhapsody.com/members/wgcve5/playlists/mp.169886415

The song transformed yet again in 1961, when two producers with RCA Records and lyricist David Weiss made an arrangement with lyrics in English about a sleeping lion that was recorded by a doo-wop vocal group called The Tokens. Their version of the song, "The Lion Sleeps Tonight," became a number one hit on the Billboard pop chart and the version most familiar to Americans.

Example: "The Lion Sleeps Tonight," The Tokens, 1961
http://www.rhapsody.com/members/wgcve5/playlists/mp.169886415

The song resurfaced yet again when it was used in the 1994 Disney animated film *The Lion King*, making Solomon Linda's song the most well known African tune in history. Unfortunately, Solomon Linda never reaped the financial rewards for his song that others did. When he recorded the original in 1939, Gallo Records paid him a small fee, but it was the record company who collected royalties from the song's massive record sales. In the U.S., the Weavers' version of the song was actually copyrighted by a music publisher, Howard Richmond, under the fictitious name of Paul Campbell, allowing Richmond to collect massive royalties on the song for many years. It is estimated that Disney made up to $15 million on its version from *The Lion King*, prompting a lawsuit in 2004 from the estate of Solomon Linda, who had died poor back in 1962. As a result of the suit, ownership of the song reverted to the estate of Solomon Linda, and his descendants have only just begun the process of collecting millions of dollars in royalties due.

There is another legacy to "Mbube" that is not so corrupt and much more positive than the story of the financial exploitation of the song. The style of *mbube* singing that Linda had inspired throughout South Africa soon evolved into a new vocal style called *isicathamiya*, a term that contains Zulu words that translate as "walking softly (like a cat)." The idea of walking softly is a reference to the modification of Zulu dances by the singers, who step lightly rather than stamp heavily in the manner of traditional dances. But the term for softness also refers to the singing style that uses a softer tone of voice than the strident singing heard in *mbube* and focuses on smoothly blended singing. The most well known group of performers of the *isicathamiya* style is the South African group Ladysmith Black Mambazo.

Formed in the 1960s by singer Joseph Shabalala, the group Ladysmith Black Mambazo first became famous locally for the smoothly blended harmonies that Shabalala claimed to have heard while dreaming in his sleep and that enabled the group to win many singing competitions. The curious name of the group reflects the communal function of music that we have focused on in this chapter. Ladysmith is the name of Shabalala's hometown and his group, like most of these vocal groups in South Africa, was made up of fellow townsmen (initially, the first group consisted of Shabalala's relatives). The other parts of the name derive from the competitive function of these groups: "Black" refers to the black ox, the most powerful farm animal in South Africa, and "Mambazo" refers to an axe that allows the group to symbolically "cut down their opponent" in singing competitions. The group was so successful, in fact, that they were soon no longer allowed to compete and instead became regular entertainment presiding over the competitions. By the 1970s Ladysmith Black Mambazo had achieved stardom in Africa. They had a famous touring act, were making hit records in Africa, and were starting to gain international attention in Europe.

The international breakthrough for Ladysmith Black Mambazo came in the 1980s. After pop singer Paul Simon met Shabalala, he asked them to collaborate with him, and the result was the platinum-selling album *Graceland*, released in 1986. Unlike some of the music industry people who had ripped off Solomon Linda in the past, Simon credited Shabalala and Ladysmith for their work, making sure that they were financially compensated. Simon went further by promoting the group and producing their first album for release in North America. Today the group continues to make albums and tour the world.

While Paul Simon's album *Graceland* was an album of pop songs, Ladysmith helped give the album a distinct African sound. This song from *Graceland* provides a good example of how Simon and Shabalala's styles blended and also demonstrates many common features of the *isicathamiya* style that made the group famous.

Guided Listening

"Homeless," Paul Simon with Ladysmith Black Mambazo

http://www.rhapsody.com/members/wgcve5/playlists/mp.169886415

00:00	Vocalists begin singing in Zulu language; note the call-and-response interaction between the lead singer and the rest of the group.
00:23	Listen for the special effects that begin here; tongue trilling, ululation.
00:39	Singers switch to English language, singing "homeless, homeless" as a chorus that repeats several times.
1:02	Listen for the responses of the bass voices singing "homeless."
1:18	Note the tongue trilling effect.
1:35	Vocalists use vocables: "too-loo-loo."
2:22	Paul Simon begins to sing "somebody say" and the group responds with breathy vocal effect that supports his vocal melody.
2:46	The song transforms again as Simon drops out and Ladysmith begins to sing a mix of harmonies and special effects such as breathy vocals, mouth clicks, tongue trills, etc.
3:15	Simon returns with "somebody say."
3:35	Ladysmith finishes the song with a brief coda in Zulu language.

This track demonstrates the distinctive features of the vocal style of *isicathamiya*: complex harmony and rhythm, use of dynamics (wide range of volume from soft to loud), bass vocal sounds strongly emphasized, lead vocalist in a high range that can be heard clearly over the rest of the group.

The sound of *isicathamiya* is not only the legacy of Solomon Linda's original song "Mbube," but is quintessential African music. It is music that is densely layered with rich polyphony in the vocal harmonies and is made up of repeating ostinato patterns. The variety of timbres used by the voices—from low, mellow bass voices to the high, shrill lead voice—allows listeners to easily hear those many layers of sound. It is also conversational in its use of call-and-response patterns and some vocal phrases that sound almost more like speech than song.

Ultimately, it is the communal function of the music that is perhaps the most significant. On their journey from the coal mines of South Africa to the concert stages of the global pop music market, Ladysmith Black Mambazo has maintained the value of community from the very beginning and continues into the twenty-first century. In 1999, Joseph Shabalala founded the Ladysmith Black Mambazo Foundation, dedicated to teaching young Zulu children about their traditional culture and music, with an academy that includes a rehearsal hall and recording studio to help enable the Zulu people to keep their now global community strong through music.

11

Music in Latin America

Latin America presents an intriguing melting pot of musical culture that has been historically influenced by other parts of the world and has in turn exerted a powerful influence on the present-day musical landscape of our planet. But any attempt to define or generalize about Latin American music is soon thwarted when one begins to examine the diverse kinds of music that developed in this region. It is neither easy nor especially useful to define Latin American music by identifying any common features shared by some of its most famous musical styles, for example, Brazilian samba, Peruvian panpipes, and Argentinian tango in South America, or Mexican mariachi, Cuban *son,* and Jamaican reggae in North America and the Caribbean. All of these musical styles, however, reflect the dynamic nature of this region of the world and the incredible mixing of cultures that makes Latin America so distinctive.

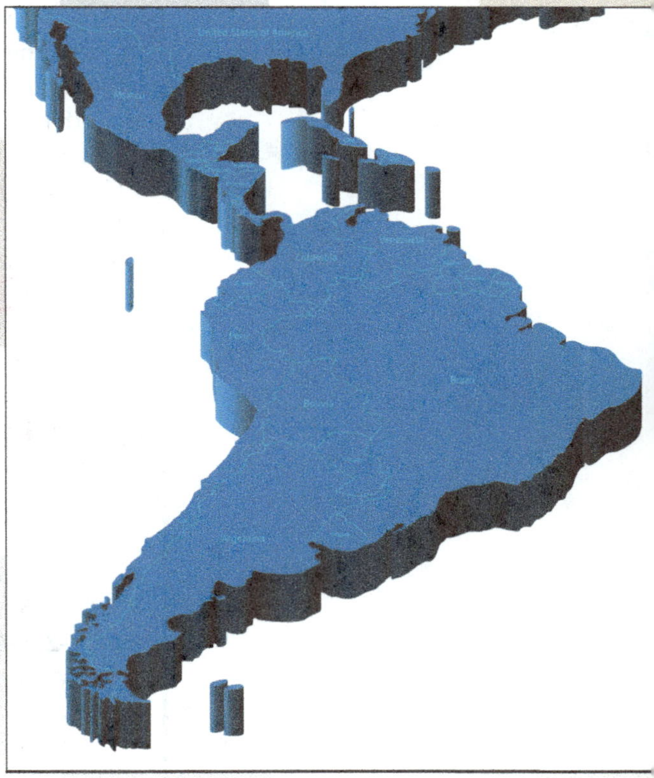

© ildogesto, 2013. Used under license from Shutterstock, Inc.

If there is one word that could be applied to all the music in this chapter, it is **syncretism**—the combining of different, seemingly contradictory cultural forms into a new hybrid form. While this concept may be a part of the creation of all forms of music in the world, it becomes especially relevant when considering the music of Latin America because of its cultural diversity and its long history of clashes between different civilizations. Indigenous Amerindian people make up the earliest civilizations, ranging from rain forest dwellers in the Amazon to the great pre-Columbian civilizations in Peru. Beginning with Christopher Columbus's initial voyages in 1492, European civilization exerted a transformative influence across Latin America, marking the most important turning point in Latin American history and initiating the start of a powerful Spanish and Portuguese influence. As a direct result of this Europeanization of the region, African culture would also alter Latin America with the slave trade of the sixteenth to nineteenth centuries. Given this long history of migration and cultural clash (which includes significant migration from Asia as well), it is not surprising to find music that reflects various degrees of blending of Amerindian, European, and African cultures.

The Indigenous Sound of the Andes

Indigenous Amerindian people make up the oldest strata of musical culture in Latin America. Our first example comes from the Aymara people, who live in the Andes mountain region of western Bolivia, northern Chile, and southern Peru. The Aymara people have lived in this region for 2,000 years and were at one time conquered by the Incan empire around the fifteenth century. After contact with Europe they became subject to the Spanish empire during the sixteenth century. Despite a recent history of subjugation, the Aymara, like related Andean ethnic groups such as the Quechua and the Uru, continue to maintain their indigenous musical culture today.

The music of the Andes is noted for distinctive strings, winds, and percussion. String instruments include guitar-like lutes (*charango*) and harps. Percussion instruments include stick-struck drums of various sizes. Wind instruments are perhaps the most diverse, with various sizes of flutes, recorders, and panpipes. Our listening example features a large ensemble of 15 musicians playing the *pinkillu* (cane duct flute or recorder), an instrument associated with the rainy season, and 12 musicians playing the *caja* (large snare drum). Although duct flutes are usually relatively quiet instruments, this music is loud and boisterous, suitable for Carnival time when it is played outdoors in the village. The Aymara achieve a thick, dense sound by overblowing on the flutes producing higher pitches and playing very fast eighth note triplets on the *caja* drums. The overall sound is what they value as "dense" or "wide unison." In other words, everyone is playing the same pitches, but some are slightly sharper or flatter than others, creating a thick sonic texture.

Although it may be difficult to hear at first, the piece has a simple form throughout that can best be described as AABBCC. Each phrase lasts twenty-four beats of the fast drum pattern and is then repeated. As you listen, try counting to twenty-four in four groups of four beats like this:

> **A:** 1-2-3-4-5-6 / 2-2-3-4-5-6 / 3-2-3-4-5-6/ 4-2-3-4-5-6
> **A:** 1-2-3-4-5-6 / 2-2-3-4-5-6 / 3-2-3-4-5-6/ 4-2-3-4-5-6
> **B:** 1-2-3-4-5-6 / 2-2-3-4-5-6 / 3-2-3-4-5-6/ 4-2-3-4-5-6
> **B:** 1-2-3-4-5-6 / 2-2-3-4-5-6 / 3-2-3-4-5-6/ 4-2-3-4-5-6
> **C:** 1-2-3-4-5-6 / 2-2-3-4-5-6 / 3-2-3-4-5-6/ 4-2-3-4-5-6
> **C:** 1-2-3-4-5-6 / 2-2-3-4-5-6 / 3-2-3-4-5-6/ 4-2-3-4-5-6

You might lose count easily because there are a few extra beats at the end of some of the phrases. But if you tap your finger quickly to the drum and follow along with the chart, you will probably be able to keep track. Especially helpful is the fact that every phrase ends on the same four notes, "da-da-daah-duh," the last being the lowest pitch used.

Guided Listening

Centro Social Conima, 1986: Manuelita

http://www.rhapsody.com/members/wgcve5/playlists/mp.172604071

00:00	The example fades in on A phrase, repeats.
00:13	B phrase lasts 24 beats, then repeats.
00:23	C phrase, repeats.
00:33	A phrase, repeats; notice how the A phrase begins on a higher pitch and uses more higher pitches than the other phrases.
00:46	B phrase, repeats; notice how the B phrase begins on a lower pitch and uses more lower pitches than the other phrases.
00:57	C phrase, repeats; notice how the C phrase starts low, ascends up, and descends back down again.
1:08	A phrase, repeats.
1:20	B phrase, repeats; note the whistle that starts this phrase and reoccurs at certain points in the piece.
1:31	C phrase, repeats.
1:41	A phrase, repeats.
1:53	B phrase, repeats.
2:03	C phrase, repeats.
2:14	A phrase, repeats.

This pattern continues unchanged until the end of the piece when it fades out. After you understand the structure, try to isolate specific parts and notice how loosely some of the musicians are playing their individual parts. Also note how everyone's parts slightly overlap with each other. According to the locals, this is to ensure that there will be "no holes" in the music.

Ethnomusicologist Thomas Turino has studied Aymara musical ensembles such as this one and he has shown how musical structure mirrors social structure. Turino found that in making music in this manner, Aymara musicians promote values of social cohesion important to their culture. The unison playing that is the foundation of the music helps ensure that no single individual stands out, which is an important cultural value maintained by the Aymara. In fact, the thick, blended texture of the overlapping parts that prevents "holes" in the music is a perfect metaphor for social cohesion.

But Turino found that the aesthetic ideal of togetherness was sometimes at odds with actual togetherness in the community. For example, these groups regularly participate in competitions to see which group can create the smoothest, most blended instrumental sound. But a common practice of these social clubs is to be inclusive, meaning that sometimes poor-quality musicians or musicians who never practice are allowed to join at any time. The presence of such substandard musicians can lower the overall quality of the group sound, but this is done in the spirit of maintaining a welcoming community, and so social ideals can be in direct conflict with musical ideals.

"El Condor Pasa": An Iconic Symbol of the Andes

While the Aymara and other indigenous groups are marginalized within modern society, their culture has become iconic of Peru and these ethnic groups have played a major part—willingly or not—in creating a national identity for Peru. The phenomenon of the ethnic majority of a nation appropriating the culture of ethnic minorities for nationalistic purposes occurs all around the world, and when it does occur, music often plays an important role, as is seen in Peru with the song "El Condor Pasa."

In 1913, Peruvian composer and ethnomusicologist Daniel Alomia Robles (1871–1942) composed a song for a *zarzuela* (Spanish operetta or musical play) entitled *El Condor Pasa* (The Condor Passes). The play tells of hardships of the Amerindian people who are exploited by European bosses in the mines of Peru. The song is sung during the finale of the play with words in the Quechua language, in which the singer calls on the great condor of the Andes to take him back to the great Inca kingdom of Machu Picchu. Composed in the style of indigenous Andean songs, "El Condor Pasa" appealed to folk musicians who recorded the song. It was eventually discovered by American pop star Paul Simon, who thought it was a traditional folk song with no known author. Simon added lyrics to the song, and the version recorded by Simon and Garfunkel became a huge hit in 1970. After a lawsuit against him later that year, Simon cleared up the misunderstanding with the Robles estate (he would become more careful about this sort of cultural appropriation later in his career when he encountered Ladysmith Black Mambazo).

As a result of international airplay, the song "El Condor Pasa" is widely known and is iconic of Peru and the Andes. Today in many major cities of the world you can see street musicians playing Andean-style music, and this highly recognizable song will invariably be featured. This recording is by a Peruvian group, Los Indios Paraguayos, and features Amerindian flute playing the lead melody with accompaniment by a *charango* (a small guitarlike instrument). These instruments conjure up the image of the Andes in the minds of many listeners around the world.

Guided Listening

"El Condor Pasa," Composed by Daniel Alomia Robles (1913), Performed by Los Indios Paraguayos

http://www.rhapsody.com/members/wgcve5/playlists/mp.172604071

00:00	Intro on flute, guitar joins.
00:19	Guitar begins to play a steady rhythm.
00:24	A section of the song begins, the flute plays the main melody; the *charanga* lute plays a steady strumming of chords.
00:45	A section repeats.
1:04	B section of the melody, first played with high notes on flute.
1:17	B section repeats with flute playing same melody, but one octave lower.
1:39	Music slows down and pauses.
1:41	A voice is heard and the *charango* begins to rapidly strum chords.
1:45	C section begins a new melody at rapid tempo.
1:54	C section repeats.
2:03	D section.
2:13	D section repeats.
2:29	Music slows down as the song ends.

The Social Movement and Musical Style of *Nueva Cancion*

Another example of how regional folk music has been appropriated for national purposes is the musical genre and social movement known as *nueva cancion* (literally "new song") that swept through South America starting in the 1960s. This was a time of turmoil and change in many countries all around the world, and many musicians explored the folk music of South America as an expression of indigenous, impoverished, peasant-class peoples that are perpetually exploited and oppressed by big business and corrupt governments. Simply by making folk music in this way, many of these artists were seen as implicitly criticizing modern society. Soon the major artists of the movement became directly involved in politics with songs that criticized the Chilean government.

Singer and songwriter Victor Jara (1932–1973) was one of the most influential artists of *nueva cancion* in Chile, where the movement started. His song "El Lazo" (The Lasso) is an example of the kinds of songs musicians sang about peasant people that conjure up images of minorities suffering grueling hardships. This recording of Jara's "El Lazo" by the Chilean group Inti-Illimani utilizes many musical references to the music of ethnic minorities of the Andes in a modern arrangement with guitars, keyboard, acoustic bass, and drums.

Guided Listening

"El Lazo" ("The Lasso"), by Victor Jara (1967), Performed by Inti-Illimani

http://www.rhapsody.com/members/wgcve5/playlists/mp.172604071

00:00 Introduction, sung quietly over a drone on keyboard.
As the sun was setting I found him
in a dark hut in Lonquen.
In an impoverished hut I found him
when the sun was setting in Lonquen.

00:56 Verse 1:
Although his hands were old, they were strong in their plaiting.
They were rough, yet tender like animal skin.

1:11 Verse 2:
The plaited lasso curled like a snake around a tree
And in every pleat was woven his life and bread.

1:26 Verse 3:
How much time is in his hands and gaze?
No one told him that he'd done enough and should not work anymore.

1:41 Bridge: note the change in melody.
The shadows intertwining with the final light of day
The old man weaves verses to bring himself joy.

1:55 Solo on Andean flute (an end-blown notch flute).

2:47 Verse 4:
His lassos traveled south and north, to the hills and to the sea
But the old man never knew what distance meant.

3:00 Verse 5:
His life in woven leather, tied around a tree.
Soon death will come and be woven in.

3:15 Verse 6:
How important is it that the lasso is strong and lasts forever.
Entwined with some country home, the old man rests.

3:32 Bridge:
The shadows intertwining with the final light of day
The old man weaves verses to bring himself joy.

3:45 Flute solo.

4:20 Return to Intro:
As the sun was setting I found him
in a dark hut in Lonquen.
In an impoverished hut I found him
when the sun was setting in Lonquen.

A Cuban stamp commemorating the tenth anniversary of the violent coup that overthrew the socialist government of Salvador Allende. President Allende and many who supported him, including musicians of the *nueva cancion* movement, lost their lives in this tragedy.

This song is Victor Jara's loving tribute to an unknown peasant worker who is an unsung hero of traditional craftsmanship in his old age. The repetition in the melody and instrumental parts contributes to the lyrics that depict the ceaseless repetition of the old man's hard work that lasted his entire lifetime. But there is a foreboding sense that is developed in this song, particularly in the way Inti-Illimani have arranged the Intro with a drone as the sun sets and the old man approaches death, suggesting that his death in an impoverished hut is an injustice to this hero of the common folk.

The story of the Chilean *nueva cancion* artists is even more tragic. As artists such as Victor Jara became politically outspoken, they became heroes of a left-wing movement that led to the election of Salvador Allende's socialist government in 1970. Unfortunately, this new government was short-lived, and military general Augusto Pinochet seized power in a military coup in September 1973 that cost many lives. Not only did Salvador Allende commit suicide during that military takeover, Victor Jara was immediately arrested, tortured, and executed by the military. The group Inti-Illimani was more fortunate, having been in Europe on a world tour during the coup, but they were unable to return to Chile, where *nueva cancion* was then outlawed. They eventually returned to their homeland in 1988 after General Pinochet stepped down from power and democracy was restored.

Samba: The Afro-Brazilian Heritage

Brazilian samba provides another example of how folk music has blended with other forms to become a national symbol. In the case of samba, the music (and the spectacular dance that the music accompanies) comes directly out of Afro-Brazilian culture, rooted in the culture of Africans transplanted to Latin America via slavery.

Samba is a form of dance music that originated in the urban centers of Brazil and has become a national symbol of Brazilian culture in many countries around the world. As an iconic Brazilian cultural form, samba reflects the confluence of African and European music and culture. Originating in urban Rio de Janeiro in the nineteenth century, samba developed into several different forms in many regions throughout Brazil. Perhaps the most famous style of samba is the festival style associated with carnival, the pre-Lent ritual celebrated in many parts of the world with celebratory music.

Our listening example features a large ensemble performing festival-style samba typical of the types of groups, called schools of samba (*escolas de samba*), that participate in samba competitions at carnival time. Not only does this style of music echo the polyrhythmic drumming ensembles of West Africa, but the social organization is African as well. Samba schools are made up of members from a particular neighborhood or urban ghetto (*favela*), thus giving a communal function as these groups try to create a sound that will beat all the competition and bring fame to their neighborhood.

The large ensemble heard here consists of many kinds of drums, including large stick-struck bass drums (*surdo*), smaller stick-struck drums (*repinique*, *tamborim*), hand drums (*hand repique*), friction drums (*cuica*), and tambourines (*pandeiro*). There are also various idiophone percussion instruments such as hand bells (*agogo*), shakers (*ganza*), rasps (*guiro*), jingle sticks (*chocalho*), and a vibraslap (an instrument of wire and wood that makes a rapid "chattering teeth" sound). There are also electric instruments, such as electric bass guitar and keyboard, that come in at the peak of the instrumental buildup. Topping it all off is a prominent whistle that can be heard over everything, thus functioning as a signal caller for the entire group. Although it is very dense and complex, understanding how this piece works is made a little easier because the instruments enter one at a time. This allows you to learn to identify them as they create a thick, layered sound made up of repeating patterns organized by call and response in the manner of so much African music.

Guided Listening

"Batucada Brasileira": Samba Brazilian Batucada Band

http://www.rhapsody.com/members/wgcve5/playlists/mp.172604071

00:00	Introduction section begins with drum roll by solo drummer.
00:02	Joined by stick drum (*repinique*), high-pitched vibraslap sounds every eight beats.
00:09	Bell joins to complete rhythmic pattern.
00:15	Break in rhythmic pattern with stick drum "call" and "response" by hand drum.
00:17	Return to rhythmic pattern played by all, now joined by a rasp.
00:24	Another bell joins in playing two pitches (high-low).
00:30	Another break in the rhythm with stick drum "call" and "response" by hand drum.
00:32	Now stick drum plays solo breaks.
00:37	Entire group of musicians responds with several strong beats.
00:41	Stick drum.
00:45	Group response; listen as the stick drummer and group engage in call and response.
1:21	Samba section begins as entire group starts to play. Note the very lowest-pitch drums (*surdo*) that accent the main duple pulse of the music.
1:33	Break with high-pitched whistle, acting as a signal for group changes.
1:37	Entire group joins in again, this time with electric instruments; note whistle playing in high-low pattern.
2:03	Group drum break.
2:07	Drum group plays.
2:20	Whistle signals another change.
2:22	Melody instruments return with whistle pattern.
2:48	Drum break, followed by drum section.
3:09	Whistle signals another change in texture.
3:11	Drum solo by hand drum with group response accents.
3:18	Low drum begins steady pulse.
3:23	Drum break with call and response.
3:35	Drum group returns.
4:04	Drum break and whistle signals the end of the piece.

Cuban *Son*

If we move northward from South America to the Caribbean, we again find syncretic musical forms that have undergone similar transformations. *Son* music from Cuba has gone from local to national and international popularity to become iconic of the modern nation of Cuba. Built from a combination of European-derived plucked strings and African-derived percussion instruments, the *son* has been described as Cuba's most important genre of music in much the same way as samba is to Brazil. Our listening example clearly displays the mix of European elements and African elements in a performance by a group that has helped boost Cuban traditional music into the world music spotlight in the twenty-first century.

In the late 1990s, American guitarist Ry Cooder traveled to Cuba and assembled a group of older, veteran musicians who had played various styles of Cuban music during the 1940s at a members' club in Havana called the Buena Vista Social Club. Using that name for this group of musicians, most of whom were in their seventies, eighties, and even nineties, Cooder recorded an album and took them on a world tour. Cooder even enlisted German filmmaker Wim Wenders to make the documentary film *Buena Vista Social Club* (1998), which was nominated for an Academy Award and brought renewed attention to Cuban music worldwide.

The Grammy Award–winning group from Cuba, the Buena Vista Social Club, performing in Portugal, 2009.

"El Cuarto de Tula" ("Tula's Bedroom") is a song in the *son* style from the Grammy-winning album *Buena Vista Social Club* (1998). This song reflects the oldest style of *son* in Cuba, in which a soloist alternates with a group that sings a refrain that invokes the kind of call-and-response group music we heard in our chapter on African music. Classified as a *descarga* (Cuban jam style), this *son* features extended improvisations done by several solo singers, a trumpet soloist, and a soloist on the *laoud*, a small, twelve-string plucked lute of European origin. The song structure is held together by the constantly returning group refrain that alternates between soloists, and the piece increases in rhythmic intensity by the driving rhythm so characteristic of African-derived music.

The heartbeat of the *son* is the ***clave*** (literally "key"), a specific rhythm that holds the music together in the same way that the bell holds together the timeline of the West African drum ensemble we heard in the earlier chapter. There are two ways the *clave* can be played:

3+2 *clave*:

1	-	2	-	3	-	4	-	5	-	6	-	7	-	8	-
x			x			x				x		x			

2+3 *clave* (sometimes called "reverse" *clave*):

1	-	2	-	3	-	4	-	5	-	6	-	7	-	8	-
		x		x				x			x			x	

While the *clave* pattern is sometimes played on two sticks (that are also called *clave*), many times this pattern is merely implied in the music, as the musicians are all aware that this beat structures the entire piece—that is, they "feel" the *clave* rhythm instead. Conveniently, the *clave* pattern can be heard on this recording from the beginning of the piece very clearly and can be easily identified as the 2+3 or "reverse *clave*."

Guided Listening

"El Cuarto de Tula" ("Tula's Bedroom"), Buena Vista Social Club

http://www.rhapsody.com/members/wgcve5/playlists/mp.172604071

00:00 Introduction trumpet melody; listen for the "reverse *clave*" pattern.

00:20 First verse about a fire in the neighborhood; when the lyrics mention the arrival of firemen and the sound of sirens (*sirenas*), we hear one singer make a siren sound with a vocal **glissando**.

00:38 A short refrain is sung twice: "ay mama, que paso?" ("what happened?")

00:47 Instrumental intro repeats.

1:06 First verse repeats with same lyrics and "siren" vocal.

1:25 Refrain repeats: "ay mama, que paso?"

1:34 Beginning of improvised section (*montuno*); this section begins with a chorus sings two lines telling us that Tula fell asleep with a burning candle (*candela*).

1:41 Trumpet solo (response to the chorus).

1:51 Chorus repeats.

2:00 Trumpet solo response.

2:10 Chorus repeats.

2:19 Vocal solo improvisation section begins; each vocalist takes a turn improvising a line, singing the names of the others in the performing group and acting as if they are all gathered around watching the fire grow; as the music "heats up," the singers begin to call out for help to put the fire out.

Listen to how each different voice sings one line, followed by a response from the chorus.

4:09 Extended solo on *laoud* begins; note how the soloist plays "against" the main rhythm (using syncopation, emphasizing off-beats); as he plays the vocalists shout encouragement.

5:59 Chorus returns.

(continued)

6:08	Trumpet solo response.
6:16	Chorus.
6:24	Trumpet solo response.
6:34	Chorus.
6:43	Trumpet solo response.
6:51	Chorus.
6:58	Rhythm stops suddenly with a brief flourish on the *laoud.*
7:03	Chorus ends the song.

Salsa: The Sounds of the Caribbean in North America

The United States' reputation as a melting pot of immigrant cultures is represented musically by many syncretic styles, and people from Latin America have made tremendous contributions to this musical mix. Following the incorporation of Puerto Rico as a U.S. territory in 1898 and the Jones-Shafroth Act of 1917 that granted U.S. citizenship to all Puerto Ricans, the twentieth-century boom in immigration from the island led to Puerto Ricans becoming the second largest Hispanic population in the US. The largest population of Puerto Ricans in the U.S. has always been in New York City; today it numbers over one million, and the cultural legacy of New York's Puerto Rican population can be seen in the musical *West Side Story*, which focuses on the clash between Puerto Ricans and whites in poor neighborhoods in New York.

Tito Puente, bandleader, songwriter, and Puerto Rican musical hero, commemorated on a U.S. postal stamp in 2011.

As a result of the "Great Migration" from Puerto Rico to New York after World War II, New York City became the center of a vibrant musical culture in which big bands performed Cuban and Puerto Rican music styles such as *son*, rumba, mambo, and cha-cha-cha. Playing high-energy dance music in large bands for ballrooms filled with dancers, several Latino bandleaders during this time period became big stars: Machito and Mario Bauza from Cuba and Tito Rodriguez from Puerto Rico. But the one musician who best embodied the blend of Latin American and U.S. culture was an American born of Puerto Rican parents in New York City and often referred to as the "king of Latin music," Tito Puente.

From his childhood, in which he beat on pots and pans around the house, to his teens, in which he imitated the jazz drumming of musicians like Gene Krupa, Puente helped establish the distinctive musical style that is sometimes referred to as "Latin Jazz," but is best described by a more all-encompassing term, "salsa." While Puente always rejected the term "salsa" (literally "sauce") to describe his music, the name stuck to describe the dance music that many Latinos continue to make today.

Our listening example is Puente's most famous song, "Oye Como Va," which has been performed and recorded by countless musicians, including a rock version by Carlos Santana, and has become Tito Puente's signature song.

At the heart of the song is a syncopated, *clave*-like riff that is usually played on the piano, but in this recording the organ is used for a special effect. You can hear this riff from the very beginning of the recording:

***Clave*-like riff:**

1	-	2	-	3	-	4	-	5	-	6	-	7	-	8	-
x		x			x		x				x		x		

As this kind of music was, and usually always is, intended for dancing, this basic rhythm is patterned after the cha-cha-cha, a popular dance rhythm that these New York bandleaders played to keep their audiences out on the dance floor.

Guided Listening

"Oye Como Va," Tito Puente

http://www.rhapsody.com/members/wgcve5/playlists/mp.172604071

00:00	The song begins with the *clave*-like riff played on the organ along with off-beat handclaps and wooden sticks.
00:15	Puente and his entire band enter; Puente plays the timbales (a pair of stick-struck drums with skins stretched tightly to create a sharp, ringing sound) with a cowbell attached.
00:23	The flute plays the main melody.
00:38	The band plays a unison phrase (all instruments play the exact same thing together).
00:46	Vocalists enter singing the song.
1:01	Band repeats unison phrase.
1:05	This is the beginning of the improvisation or "mambo" section in which the band carefully builds up layers of phrases; the first phrase is played on the saxophones.
1:20	Trombones enter with a different phrase.
1:36	Trumpet enters with another phrase.
1:51	Unison phrase is played only partially.
1:56	Vocalists repeat the song lyrics.
2:11	Buildup to the next mambo section.
2:19	Mambo section; listen as the different instruments play short repeating figures.
3:06	Return of unison phrase.
3:16	Lots of shouting, followed by a return to the mambo section that continues until the song ends with the unison phrase.

12

Spanish Flamenco

by Steve Mullins, adjunct instructor

© Jack.Q, 2013. Used under license from Shutterstock, Inc.

Spanish flamenco is a music and dance form that can be appreciated on many levels. On the surface, it is very dramatic and emotionally intense. We're likely to notice that first. Less obvious are the complex rhythmic and melodic variations, the playful stretching of rules, the harmonic nuance, and the subtle interactions and cues that guide the performers along a path of improvisation and risk within the fixed traditional structures.

Flamenco originated in southern Spain, primarily in the region known as Andalucía. There are eight Andalucían provinces—Almería, Cádiz, Córdoba, Granada, Huelva, Málaga, Jaén, and Sevilla. Regional styles, which were originally quite diverse, have gradually become unified into a single tradition called flamenco. The consolidated repertoire includes genres that originated locally in many of these areas: for example, the *malagueña* from the city of Málaga, the *granainas* from Granada, the *sevillanas* from Sevilla, the *alegrías* from Cádiz, and so on. Some genres originated in the region of Murcia to the east of Andalucía—these are known as *cantes de levante*, or "songs from the east."[1] The various local styles began to be disseminated throughout Andalucía during the course of the nineteenth century, and by the end of the century a relatively unified tradition was in place. Certain genres have historically been closely identified with Gypsies, and are known as *cante gitano* or Gypsy song, especially the *siguiriyas* and the *soleá* families, two of the four foundational styles of the flamenco repertoire (the others being the *tangos* and *fandangos* families). The *tangos* family is also considered by some to be *cante gitano*, while others include it in the category of *cantes de ida y vuelta*, or "roundtrip songs" (along with the *guajira, columbiana, rumba, milonga*, and the *vidalita*), which exhibit influences from Latin America.

The term *flamenco* first described performances of this repertoire sometime in the middle of the nineteenth century. Most flamenco historians agree that the roots of flamenco are in the song tradition, or *cante*. The other two essential ingredients (which became standard by the second half of the nineteenth century) are

[1]The term *Levant* is often used in Arabic to denote the Eastern Mediterranean region, also known as *Mashriq*. In the flamenco usage, however, it refers to the region east of Andalucia, called Murcia, or to the easternmost regions of Andalucía that border Murcia.

the dance (*baile*) and the guitar (*toque*). Different eras and performance contexts have prioritized these three elements somewhat differently. In some contexts such as the *peña* (private club), *cante* and guitar together (without the dance) is common, whereas in public settings such as the *tablao* or on the theater stage, all three components are considered essential. Modern flamenco (*nueva flamenca*) tends to place far more emphasis on the guitar, de-emphasizing or sometimes omitting the other two elements.

Genre Classifications

At the core of flamenco is the group of approximately forty genres, or song-forms, called *palos*, which constitute the repertoire. The *palos* each have definite and idealized forms that are central and solid. Innovation is allowed, and to some degree encouraged, but only within the strictures established by tradition through the structure of the *palos*. This applies to the repertoire of song-types (*cantes*), and guitar melodies (*falsetas*), both of which are often formalized and formulaic. The term *estilo* (style) in regard to the flamenco *cantes*, or songtypes, refers to specific commonly heard examples or variants of a tune. There are nearly one hundred recognized *estilos* of the genre *soleá*, for example (Kliman).[2] The numerous *estilos* in the repertoire are best understood as "flexible schematic outlines," rather than specific "songs" (Manuel 2010, 107–109). The singer is expected to construct a rendition of a *palo* by putting together a sequence of *estilos*, drawn from their reservoir of traditional repertoire. The guitarist sequences pre-existing *falsetas* in the same way. In both cases, the raw materials of the performance are pre-existing and inherited.

The different genres are often referred to as individual branches of the family tree of flamenco. The "roots" of the tree are debated, but many of the relationships are obvious and widely acknowledged. *Palos* are often categorized based on musical considerations such as rhythmic or harmonic structure. They are also organized based on ethnic or regional origin, and compared on the basis of emotional themes, topics, perceived weight, seriousness, or aesthetic impact.

The Three Components of a Flamenco Performance

El Cante

The singing is considered the original (and to many the most important) component of flamenco. Vocal timbre is very distinctive and expressive in flamenco song. Flamenco-specific terms like *afillá* (raw, hoarse, and "earthy") or *rajo* (intensely expressive) are used to describe timbral qualities. *Cante gitano* (or Gypsy singing) is usually distinguishable from non-Gypsy style on the basis of these qualities; it is *más afillá* (rougher). Flamenco singing is melismatic and highly ornamented. Phrases are frequently extended with long improvised cadenzas, typically expressive of grief or other intense emotions. The poetry is itself very emotionally expressive. The voice is used to amplify that emotion through the use of melismatic vocables and timbre. The term *cante quejío* or "moaned songs" describes this important component. Singers also conduct the interaction of the ensemble to a large extent. The guitarist and dancer(s) follow where the singer leads.

[2]http://perso.orange.es/sonionegro/soleares.htm#andonda1

El Baile

Dance has been seen as a primary component of flamenco for as long as flamenco has been documented (since the mid-nineteenth century). Although most flamenco historians argue that *el cante* predates it, there is little documentation to confirm or deny that. The dance is most representative of flamenco in its public context, as a performance art, while the singing is often more central in private intimate settings. In the early documented history of flamenco, there were more famous dancers than singers or guitarists. The dance is the central visual component of the art form, but also contributes to the sound. Footwork sequences (*zapateado*) are conceived of musically, and considered part of the music. Dancers must have an intimate understanding of the rhythmic cycles and other structural standards of the music, participating in the performance of the music with their feet, while appearing to respond to it with the remainder of their bodies.

El Toque

The third essential member of the flamenco triumvirate is *la guitarra*. In traditional flamenco, guitarists are accompanists first and foremost. It is important, according to most, to complete the apprenticeship in song and dance accompaniment before attempting to be a soloist. The skills involved with these three activities are, indeed, very different. Accompanists of *el cante* must learn to listen very carefully to pitch, following the singer's lead, and providing appropriate chords to harmonize his or her melody. Once a guitarist becomes familiar with a given *palo* and its repertoire of *estilos*, the singer's likely harmonic destinations become very predictable, but the subtle timing and interplay between singer and guitarists remains a sophisticated art. A sense of dialogue is valued, but always led by the singer. Even when a song has been rehearsed and the guitarist is therefore well aware of where the singer is going, it would not have the appropriate sound, or be polite, for the guitarist to arrive there first. The tradition (which did not originally involve such rehearsed standardization) has established standards which involve a sort of "slide-rule effect": the singer slides to a given position, which predetermines the guitarist's reply.

Accompanying the dance involves a different but equally challenging skill set. The dance accompanist must listen very carefully to rhythm, accurately interpreting the changing subdivisions and syncopated accents of the footwork. Guitarists are expected to recognize and respond to syncopated patterns and audible cues (of the dancer's footwork) and to recognize visual cues in the body movements of the dancer.

Solo guitar performance and musical "compositions" for guitar are a relatively recent phenomenon in flamenco, gaining momentum during the course of the twentieth century. The tradition of the "concert flamenco guitarist" began with Ramón Montoya in the early twentieth century, followed by the generation of Sabicas and Niño Ricardo in the mid-century, culminating with Paco de Lucía (and then a host of others) in the last quarter of the century. Modern flamenco generally features the guitar and instrumental composition more than the song or dance.

Performance Contexts

Café Cantantes

The *café cantante* era, beginning in the late nineteenth century and lasting into the 1920s, is often considered the "Golden Age of Flamenco." This is the era when flamenco first became a popular form of public entertainment and first became well documented. *Café Cantantes* (or Singing Cafes) were small venues presenting live flamenco, offering the first opportunity for Gypsy singers to become professional performing artists. It is probably accurate to say that prior to the emergence of the *café cantantes*, the dance had not been so central and defining a component of flamenco as it has been ever since (at least in the public formats).

Ópera Flamenca

The style known as *ópera flamenca* largely supplanted the *café cantante* style in the early twentieth century. This was a much larger-scale theatrical presentation involving travelling variety shows performing in bullrings and theaters. Artists such as Pepe Marchena became famous in this context. The *cante* regained a central role in *ópera flamenca*, but the vocal timbre became less *afillá* (less rough), and the repertoire tended to feature the light or *"chico" palos*. The *cante jondo* (deep song) genres of "Gypsy flamenco" declined, and the spontaneity and intimacy of the flamenco of the *café cantantes* was lost.

Ópera flamenca was popular from about 1915 to 1950. This era has been variously characterized as "a period of dilution" (Serrano 1990:45), "a process of decline" (Edwards, 2000:80), or "the most dreadful, artless and degrading period in flamenco history" (Martínez 2003:68).

Tablaos

From the latter half of the twentieth century to the present, one of the most important or at least most visible contexts for flamenco performance has been the *tablaos*. These successors to the *café cantantes* are clubs and restaurants that provide staged flamenco shows in conjunction with or following a meal, largely for tourists. This context is similar to the *café cantantes*, but with additional theatrical elements from *ópera flamenca* as well—staged lighting, amplification, costuming, and choreography. Flamenco "purists" often criticize the *tablao* context for its touristic approach and lack of spontaneity, especially when compared to the other principal contemporary performance context: the *peña*.

Peñas

Peñas are flamenco clubs found throughout Andalucía. They are often private venues for members only, though they may sponsor flamenco events open to the general public. Some, as Totton describes, "are so exclusive they have a guard on the door to keep out non-members, and even the performers are made to feel like servants allowed into the drawing room at Christmas" (2003, 195). Most *peñas* feature singing, by and between the members—mostly men. The emphasis in this context is on communication and interaction between individuals. Flamenco of the *peña* variety requires direct contact between two people—the singer and the recipient of the song. A singer may communicate to more than one person during the course of the song, but usually only one at a time. A sense of intimate connection is important, and is maintained by eye contact and physical proximity. The quality of attention of the recipient is an important part of this exchange, and if it is deemed lacking, the singer will move to a more deserving recipient, or lose inspiration and stop singing. Singers may perform a capella or with guitar accompaniment. Many *peñas* sponsor more formal public performances, bringing in dancers and instrumentalists, in addition to singers. There are many flamenco aficionados, however, who believe that the intimate performance practice of one man singing to another defines "authentic" flamenco, and that staged performance for the entertainment of audiences is therefore inauthentic. Despite these attitudes, flamenco performance in the twenty-first century has been steadily returning to the theater stage, larger and larger venues, and more formalized theatrical presentations, de-emphasizing singing in favor of the guitar and dance, de-emphasizing intimacy in favor of entertainment.

Modern Theatrical Flamenco

In the late twentieth and early twenty-first centuries, flamenco has become an increasingly popular international art form. Many of the values of *ópera flamenca*, from a century earlier, have returned. Large-scale theatrical productions have again become commonplace. No longer the "light" variety shows of *ópera flamenca*, however, modern theatrical flamenco has moved toward plot, drama, and highly choreographed, highly synchronized virtuosity.

The Music

The different *palos* of flamenco are often related to one another on the basis of musical sound, especially rhythm. One of the most important musical concepts in flamenco is that of *compás*, which is usually described as "rhythmic cycle," as compared to a Western idiomatic concept of meter. *Compás* not only denotes the number of regularly recurring beat groupings (as does meter), but also the accent patterns within each cycle, along with associated harmonic changes and melodic gestures that define the given genre. The *compás* defines the *palo*, and that definition involves more than just rhythm (i.e., the accents involve harmony and melody); these elements are not always separable from the rhythmic aspects.[3]

Flamenco music is often structured in a through-composed manner in which musical sections designed to reveal the formulaic rhythmic and harmonic basis of the *palo* (called *compás* sections) alternate with changing melodic sections (*falsetas*). Aspects of the *compás* are common to different *palos* and establish familial relationships between them. For example, several *palos* utilize a twelve-beat rhythmic cycle, often involving the same series of accents, though they may not begin at the same point in the cycle. The so-called "*compás* clock" is sometimes used to illustrate the rhythmic relationships between different twelve-beat *palos*. Several *palos* begin on beat 1, the one o'clock position, while many others begin one beat sooner, at twelve o'clock. Many flamenco students outside of Spain are confused upon first encountering *palos* such as *bulerías*, which are commonly counted beginning on beat 12. "Why would the first beat of the cycle be called twelve?" is a common question. Most flamenco teachers don't seem to have an answer, beyond

[3]In this sense, it is more comparable to the Balinese conception of colotomic structure, or the Indian tala system.

comments like "That's just how it's done." The *compás* clock does clarify the issue. The beginning of the *bulerías* is beat twelve in relation to other older *palos* such as *soleares*. A rhythmic conception based on a circular or cyclic metaphor does not need to insist on a single starting point; it is an example of what might be called an open form. The difficulty that non-Spaniards have accepting the idea of beginning on "twelve" may be a product of the ethnocentric force of the metaphoric conception of rhythm as linear and metric.

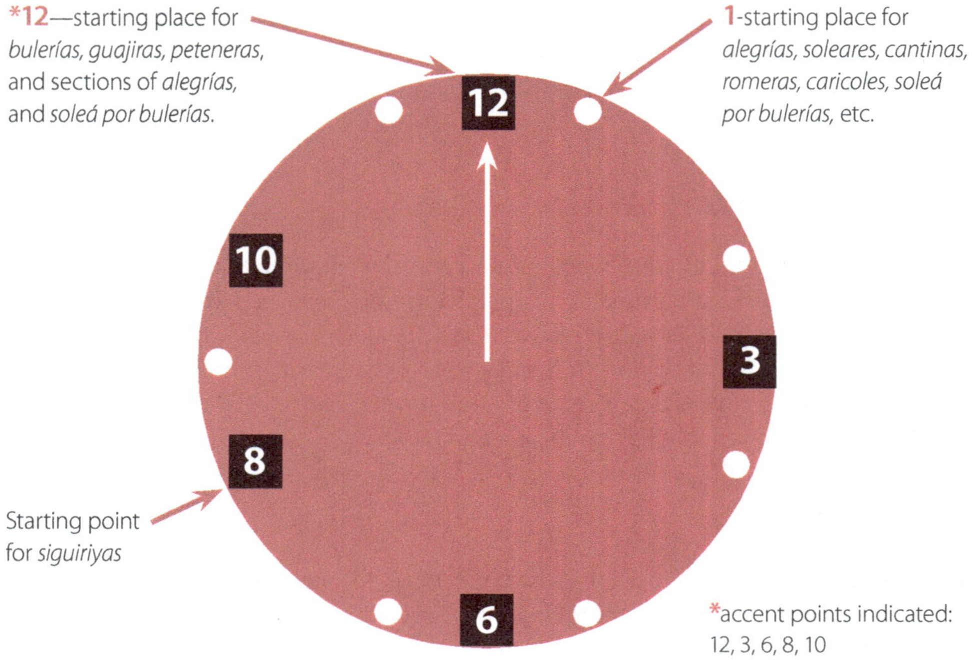

Figure 1. The *Compás Clock.*

The Dance and the Music

The formal "movements" of flamenco dance and flamenco music correspond. The way that energy is shaped in the dance (through tension, counter-tension, and relaxation) has many corollaries in the music. A flamenco musical composition, even without dancers, is structured, in an important sense, by the dance. The through-composed sequential structure of the music, with the typical extended series of contrasting melodic sections, may seem aimless and confusing to uninitiated listeners. It is the conventions of the dance and references to the shape and character of the dance that provide much of the structural integrity to the music. The overall structure of a flamenco dance performance is relatively standardized. Value is placed on wide-ranging energetic contour. Instrumental flamenco is a product of the same values and utilizes similar energetic blueprints. Instrumental flamenco music (in the absence of an actual dancer) manifests "virtual dancers" in the imagination of the flamenco listener.

Flamenco Interaction

The *compás* helps keep the performers working together, regulating their interaction. The movements of the dancer and the sound of the music, express the *compás*. The accents of the rhythmic cycle are clearly evident in the body movement of an accomplished dancer. The guitarist also "marks" the *compás* by tapping the top of the guitar (*golpe*) at the important accent points, while simultaneously playing chords or melodies. *Golpes* are referentials, or markers, designed to help coordinate the members of the ensemble. Dancers and singers listen carefully to the *golpes* of the guitarist in order to remain oriented to the *compás*.[4] This technique has a clear interactive function, but it has also become an integral part of the guitarist's technical arsenal and an important part of the flamenco sound. Guitarists continue to use *golpe* technique when performing solo, with no ensemble to coordinate. Another way that the music typically reinforces the *compás* is through chord changes. There are important conventions about when chords should change, and how they should progress. In *bulerías*, for example, the most important moments for chord changes in the twelve-beat structure are beats 3 and 10; when there are only two chords per cycle they almost invariably fall there. When there are additional chord changes, they usually fall on the other important accent points (beats 12, 6, and 8).[5] Harmonic "movement" corresponds to and helps orient the movements of the dancer.

Possibly the most intimate and omnipresent interaction that takes place in a flamenco performance is between the *palmeros/as* (clappers), and also between the sounds of their clapping and the dancer's footwork. A "groove" of interlocking composite rhythms is established, based on the *compás*. The figure below illustrates one common set of interactive possibilities. The outside circle represents the basic *compás* (including the "markers"/accents). The middle circle represents the interlocking pattern of a second performer, and the inner circle, a third level of rhythmic activity and interlocking interaction.

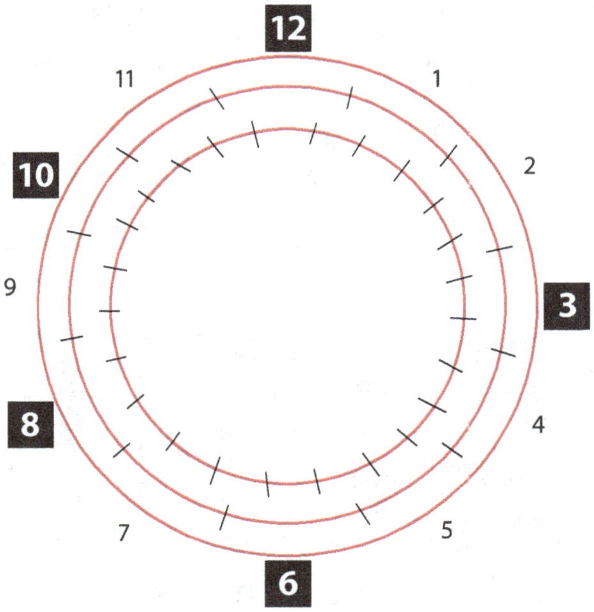

[4]Additional "referentials" are provided by the *palmas* (clapping) when that is present.

[5]It also common for chord changes to be syncopated, either slightly following or anticipating these structural accents.

Three-Part Composite Rhythm

This sort of synchronization depends on all the participants being oriented to the basic *compás*, while constantly referring to each other, constantly aware of the composite nature of their interaction. The ensemble continuously coheres into unified and shifting interlocking patterns. The figure above illustrates possibilities based only on quadruple divisions of the basic beat. The dancer or guitarist may shift to other rhythmic densities, most commonly divisions of three or six, while emphasizing intermittent syncopated accents within those pulses.[6] The ensemble must be attentive to those shifts, accurately interpreting new composite pulses as they are introduced, in order to remain synchronized and oriented to the *compás*.

Performers and audience members are expected to be aware of a considerable amount of information in a flamenco performance—musical formulae, sectional sequences, cues, closing calls, and the like. Competent artists can perform together without rehearsal because they know the established sequence of events and because they are familiar with the interactive vocabulary. Without interactive competence, synchronized transitions from one section to another would not be possible. Competence, in this sense, equates to familiarity with and sensitivity to the formalized system of cues. The most important and obvious cue is the *llamada* or "call," which can be executed by the dancer or guitarist. The dancer's *llamada* is one of the most important and obvious of visual gestures in flamenco dance. It is primarily communicative, but also structural in the sense that it may punctuate sections of the performance. *Llamadas* signal change. They may call the singer to begin, or notify the ensemble that the dancer has finished improvising over a given section and is ready to move on to the next section.

The standard shape of a *llamada* in the dance is very distinctive. A *llamada* in each of the twelve-beat *palos* is one *compás* (twelve beats) long. Each of the image sequences that follow spans one *compás*.

Lia Ochoa executing a *llamada* in *soleá por bulerías*.
Image courtesy of the author.

Jeanette Trujillo-Lucero executing a *llamada* in *alegrías*.
Image courtesy of the author.

[6]The term *contratiempo* (rather than *syncopation*) is normally used in flamenco to describe accents that occur between the basic beats.

The two *llamada* examples above reveal essentially the same shape, abstracted below. The still shots do not necessarily capture the exact same instants in that shape, and the two dancers don't execute it identically (for example, Trujillo doesn't raise her arms as high as Ochoa at the beginning of the gesture), but the overall gesture is the same, and is recognizable to any flamenco artist.

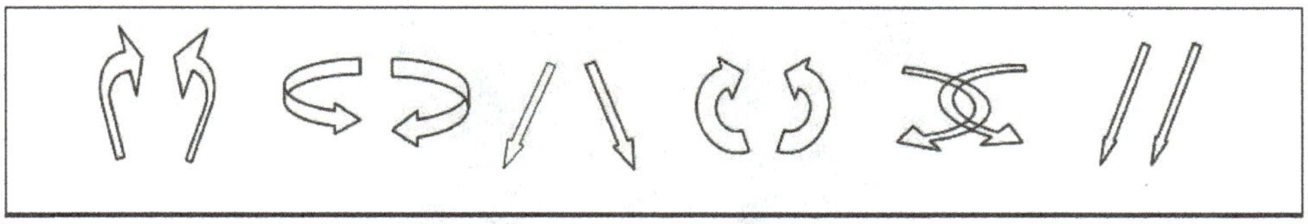

The abstracted arm motions of a *llamada* as illustrated in the photo sequences.
Image courtesy of the author.

Contra

Another important flamenco concept is *contra* or *contratiempo* (translated literally as *against* or *against time*). In flamenco (as in the bullfight) there is a high value placed on opposition, whether it is opposing death (the bull), opposing another performer, or opposing the beat. A good dancer, for example, is expected to demonstrate clear and "clean" *contra*. A good flamenco melody is one that employs the proper amount of *contra*. The term *contratiempo* in common usage means "against the beat." The accenting of "off-beats" (or syncopation) is crucial to establishing a proper flamenco feeling or "*aire*." *Contratiempo* is integral to the basic feel or "groove" of many genres. The *compás* comes to life, so to speak, only when it is activated by the *contratiempo*.

There are other characteristics of the music and dance that have a similar quality of contrariness. Again the music and dance are products of the same values, and may reflect similar oppositional values in the society at large.[7] In the dance, for example, the term *oposiciones* is used to describe the basic flamenco stance, involving the placement or movement of the arms or legs in counter direction to each other. Another important technique is what is referred to as *torcido,* the twisting of the upper body in the opposite direction from the lower body, a technique that is very Spanish and very difficult for most dancers from other traditions.

Torcido.
Image courtesy of the author.

[7]Many authors have discussed the relationship of flamenco to the bullfight, and the way in which both express oppositional attitudes of Spanish society at large (see Gilmore, Landborn).

Braceos (Gina Martínez and Lia Ochoa).
Courtesy of the author.

Another dominant characteristic of flamenco dance that distinguishes it from classical dance is the way in which the arms are often held in a sort of isometric tension, pushing downward against some apparent but unseen force.

Movements of the arms in general are called *braceos,* and it's no coincidence that the verb *bracear* also means, "to struggle." The music often establishes a sense of tension and countertension that is analogous to these dance gestures.

Contra-Harmonía

Flamenco harmony, like flamenco rhythm, is very oppositional, with a strong value placed on clashing opposition. First, there is a tendency (particularly for modern flamenco artists) to embellish chords with neighboring chromatic dissonances, i.e. another chord a half-step away. Modern flamenco borrows harmonic vocabulary from jazz, but the flamenco use of such harmony differs from jazz, in that it is less directional or functional (not as often based on tonal movement by fourth). It is instead used more as a *contra*-device, creating opposition and tension.

In addition to oppositional chords a half-step apart, another important quality of flamenco harmony is the inclusion of dissonant notes within chords. This typically involves "open" (unfretted) guitar strings clashing *against* another fretted tone a step away. Flamenco harmony is idiomatic to the guitar, and this sound of open strings ringing in opposition to neighboring fretted notes is a central feature. Flamenco guitarists typically play in a very limited number of keys (or modes), at least in terms of fingering—often using the capo (*cejilla*) to play in many actual modalities while utilizing the fingerings of very few. This is a way to exploit the tuning of the guitar and its limited possibilities for using strings in this oppositional way. Many of these chords help define specific genres: for example, the central sound of *tarantas* and *tarantos* is what might be called a F#11b9 chord (with f#-a#-c#-e-g-b notes). The fretted f# clashes against the open g-string, and the fretted a# clashes against the open b-string in this idiomatic way. The genre of *granainas* features the sound of a "Bm13" chord, with a d opposing an e, and an f# against the g-string. The designations F#11b9 or Bm13 are borrowed here from jazz vocabulary. These sorts of labels are not generally used by flamenco performers. There isn't a harmonic theory per se. The tuning, number of strings, and physicality of the guitar, along with the value placed on opposition, generate this harmonic vocabulary. An interesting term that *is* sometimes used to describe this sort of harmony is "horned chord," referring to the proximity of the dissonance (like "the horn" of a bull) to the consonance (the bullfighter) , the f# to the g in the chords described above, for example. Flamenco chords often have at least one such "horn." Again this is a musical analog of dance gestures that also relate to the bullfight. An important movement motif in the dance is "arching," and its corresponding implication of *nearness*. This posture represents nearness to the bull, and by implication, nearness to death.

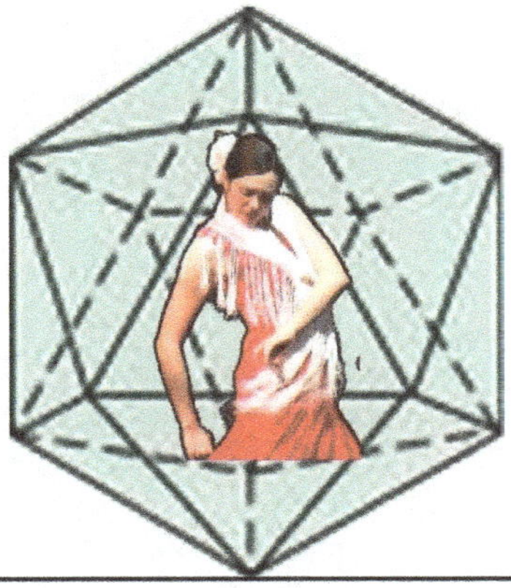

The "horned chords" appeal to a similar oppositional sensibility.
Image courtesy of the author.

Conclusion/Summary

Flamenco is a complex art form with an extensive traditional repertoire. The various genres are structured first and foremost by their *compás*—rhythmic cycle with harmonic characteristics (specific mode and idiomatic dissonances) and standard melodies or melodic formulae. The three main components of a flamenco performance are the singing, dance, and guitar, with varying degrees of emphasis in the different performance contexts. Flamenco involves standardized dance forms, sectional sequences that are navigated by way of a complex system of cues, requiring considerable experience and competence on the part of the performers. There is value placed on risk and improvisation within these structures, and on opposition (or *contra*), evident in the rhythms, harmonies, and dance movements, which are often analogous to one another and to the bullfight. Flamenco is an important expression of Andalucian history and sensibility.

Section IV

Popular Music in America

The Rise of American Popular Music

13

KEY TERMS

Minstrelsy
Vaudeville
Ragtime
Piano roll
Tin Pan Alley
Blues
12-bar blues
Jazz
Swing
Riff
Crooners/Canaries
32-bar Tin Pan Alley AABA Standard
Chorus
Bridge
Hillbilly Music
Rural Blues
Jump Blues
Country and Western

KEY FIGURES

Scott Joplin
W. C. Handy
Bessie Smith
Louis Armstrong
Benny Goodman
Count Basie
Frank Sinatra
Jimmie Rodgers
Robert Johnson
Louis Jordan
Hank Williams

As we learned in Section II of this book, music in Western civilization developed out of an oral tradition rooted in ancient times and transformed into a written one in the modern era. From the 15th to the 20th centuries, notation and printed media enabled a magnificent tradition of composers to achieve fantastic heights in the artistry of music with their published works. This written tradition has become the cornerstone of Western Art Music. Music that was not written down in notation existed outside that tradition and was unable to leave its mark on the history of music. But at the dawn of the 20th century the oral tradition was beginning to bounce back. In Section IV we trace the rise of popular music in America to show how new technology, media, and ideas about art and entertainment allowed for mass-mediated music to develop and eventually occupy the center stage in global popular culture.

The most significant technological change that shifted our attention back to oral/aural culture was the invention of the phonograph by American inventor Thomas Edison in 1877. The cylinder-playing device developed by Edison was replaced in the early 20th century by the gramophone—a machine that played flat, double-sided discs with a spiral groove on a turntable. Things would never be the same again. As monumental a change as photography was for the visual arts, the ability to capture actual musical performances on a disc and then distribute and sell recorded music to a growing public of consumers would change music forever.

The revolution in popular music, however, was much more than just capturing, reproducing, and distributing the *sound* of musical performances. Remember that in Section III on World Music we learned that musical phenomenon consists not only of what we *hear* (Sound), but also what we *see* (Behavior). With the further development of print media and the revolutions of photography, cinema, and television, music became a central player in the mass media of the 20th century that would influence society in profound ways.

Popular Music in the 19th Century

If we examine the rise of popular music in Western culture we can see the rise of the United States as a cultural and economic power in the modern world. In the same way that the history of Western classical music reflects political, social, and cultural developments of European nations, the history of popular music shows us how the United States grew up during the 19th century and came into its own in the 20th century as a nation at the forefront of Western popular culture. In the 19th century the United States was a country filled with European content, but the form of the country was something unique and new—a frontier nation that encouraged entrepreneurship across a vast region with a diverse and dynamically changing population. Not surprisingly this new form of a nation changed the cultural content as well, and it is in popular culture that we see very dramatic shifts.

From the time of the Civil War, America was a highly industrialized society of mass markets. Charismatic performers with talent and popular appeal found immense audiences in America ready to follow their careers. People went in droves to see popular sensations such as Buffalo Bill, opera star Jenny Lind, pianist Louis Moreau Gottschalk, or anyone else who brought something colorful, talented, exotic, topical, and almost anything else to the stage. European musical and cultural products such as the symphony and the opera may have had the elite aura of art for the literate middle class, but the rise of mass entertainment led to a culture in which many forms of popular culture mixed together. This can be seen in the rise of **vaudeville**—a theatrical form made up of a variety of separate performances by musicians, dancers, comedians, magicians, and more that encompassed virtually any kind of art or entertainment. Within this new context, popular entertainment not only *offered* something for everyone, it could be *made* by virtually any American regardless of class or color. American forms of egalitarian entertainment for the masses soon eclipsed European forms of elite art for the few. It should be noted, however, that although America led the way in breaking down many of the barriers between class-based notions of high art vs. mass entertainment (and racial divisions of music production and consumption), American popular music in the 19th century was still fraught with class and racial tensions.

VAUDEVILLE
Popular genre of theatre made up of separate performances that could encompass a wide variety of entertainment, including music, dance, comedy, magic, acrobatics, juggling, etc.

As uncomfortable as it is to consider, the American entertainment form known as **minstrelsy** set the stage for popular music of the 20th century. The minstrel show was a form of popular theatre in which performers wore black face paint as they acted out comical skits, danced, and performed music. From the 1830s to the beginning of the Civil War in the 1860s, white performers wearing black face paint such as Thomas Dartmouth Rice and Dan Emmett became some of the biggest stars in American popular culture. Although anti-black satire increased in minstrel performances in the years leading up to the Civil War, soon black entertainers themselves formed minstrel troupes. African American performers such as Billy Kersands, James Bland, and Wallace King became big stars. In spite of the racism inherent in minstrelsy, this entertainment form nevertheless empowered black performers in many ways. Minstrelsy also gave birth to some of the most famous American songs of the 19th century such as "Oh! Susanna," "Camptown Races," and "My Old Kentucky Home," all composed by Stephen Foster, one of America's most famous songwriters. By the end of the 19th century, minstrelsy declined with the rise of vaudeville, but minstrelsy would cast a long shadow on both black and white performers of American popular music well into the 20th century.

MINSTRELSY
19th century popular theatre consisting of music, dance, and comical skits by performers wearing black face paint.

RAGTIME
A musical genre from 1895–1918 that featured syncopated or "ragged" rhythm. The most famous ragtime composer was Scott Joplin who composed many works for piano.

The music craze that bridged the 19th and 20th centuries was **ragtime**—music so named because of its syncopated or "ragged" rhythm. Originating as dance music in the red-light districts of African American communities, ragtime combined the march music of John Philip Sousa with African-derived rhythms. Ragtime became massively popular following the publication of "Maple Leaf Rag" in 1899 by **Scott Joplin**, an African American pianist and composer who became known as the "King of Ragtime." Although white audiences praised ragtime for its wildness and primitivism, Scott Joplin published 44 original ragtime compositions that displayed the work of a trained and disciplined composer. Joplin portrayed himself with the more dignified image of an artist than the minstrel performers of the earlier part of the century. Ragtime also made use of the cutting edge technology of the time, the player piano—a self-playing piano that used rolls of perforated paper that enabled people to just sit back and listen. This new kind of listening experience foreshadowed what was to come in the next century. The sales of piano rolls and sheet music fueled the ragtime craze until it was replaced by newer forms of syncopated music after 1918, making ragtime a transitional form of popular music that would soon be dominated by new media in the 20th century.

Scott Joplin (1867–1917)

Guided Listening

"Maple Leaf Rag" by Scott Joplin

http://app.rhapsody.com/artist/scott-joplin/album/elite-syncopations-shout-factory-records

This performance is not by a human being—it is a mechanical piano playing a **piano roll**. Note the steady tempo and the different melodic sections of equal length that repeat.

0:00 Section A, begins.
0:21 Section A, repeats.
0:41 Section B, begins with a new theme.
1:01 Section B, repeats.
1:21 Section A, returns, playing the same music heard at the beginning of the piece.
1:40 Section C, begins with a new theme.
2:00 Section C, repeats.
2:20 Section D, begins with a new theme.
2:39 Section D, repeats.

The Rise of the Music Industry in the 20th Century

At the dawn of the 20th century, the center of the popular music industry was New York City. A single block on 28th Street consisting of offices filled with music publishers, composers, and promoters ("song pluggers") became known as **"Tin Pan Alley"**—jokingly named for the clamor of sounds that one could hear emanating from the office windows on any given business day. In true industrial fashion, the composers and lyricists of Tin Pan Alley manufactured songs for the American mass audience, but before the rise of phonograph records, songs were sold as sheet music for people to play on the piano and sing on their own. In order to attract consumers, songs needed to become famous first, usually by a famous

PIANO ROLL

A roll of paper on which was inscribed a musical piece to be played on a "player piano" (self-playing piano). Many early ragtime compositions were sold as piano rolls.

TIN PAN ALLEY

The name of the music industry that emerged in New York City in the late 19th/early 20th centuries, specifically one block on West 28th Street where the offices of music publishers and songwriters were located.

28th Street in New York City today, once known as "Tin Pan Alley."

singer in vaudeville or on Broadway. But getting the song to the singing star required an intermediary. The "song plugger" was a person whose job it was to promote songs to the top stars of the day who would make it famous and create demand for the sheet music.

This "factory" system was a simple, effective, and productive model for the music industry for several decades, but Tin Pan Alley did not survive into the second half of the 20th century. Always responding to constant changes in technology, economic, and cultural trends, the dynamic nature of popular music ultimately sealed the fate of Tin Pan Alley. For the remainder of this chapter we will demonstrate how several different genres of popular music, the media that produced them, and the audiences that were its consumers, all worked together to lay the groundwork for the new phenomenon of rock and roll at mid-century. As we will see in Chapter 14, Rock and Roll would completely alter the structure of the music industry and give birth to American popular music as we know it today.

The Birth of the Blues

BLUES
A genre of music that originated among African Americans in the United States in the 19th century and one of the most widely used forms in American popular music.

In his 1941 autobiography, musician, bandleader, and composer **W. C. Handy** described the unforgettable experience of first hearing a kind of music that would transform popular music in the 20th century:

> A lean, loose-jointed Negro had commenced plunking a guitar beside me while I slept. His clothes were rags; his feet peeped out of his shoes. His face had on it some of the sadness of the ages. As he played, he pressed a knife on the strings of the guitar in a manner popularized by Hawaiian guitarists who used steel bars. The effect was unforgettable (Handy 1957, p. 74).

Based on this experience Handy wrote a song called "Memphis Blues" that he published as sheet music in 1912, the same year that two other similar songs were published, "Dallas Blues" and "Baby Seals Blues." Handy's "Memphis Blues" was adopted by America's leading dance instructors, Vernon and Irene Castle, for their new dance step, the foxtrot. It was also recorded by The Victor Military Band in 1914. A national craze for this music had begun. The blues would soon become a cornerstone of American popular music, the first of a number of rising and falling musical fads that would define popular music in the 20th century and beyond.

Out of this blues craze emerged a royalty of female African American blues singers such as Ma Rainey and Mamie Smith whose "Crazy Blues" has long been credited as the first blues recording by an African American artist. It was supervised by Ralph Peer, a recording engineer and talent scout who would soon emerge as a major figure in the popular music industry. Mamie may have been the first, but "The Empress of the Blues" was **Bessie Smith**, who caught a big break in 1912 after being hired as a dancer on the vaudeville circuit. After years of singing blues and other types of songs in vaudeville shows, Bessie was signed by Columbia Records in 1923. In 1925 she had a hit record with Handy's "St. Louis Blues" accompanied by the great jazz trumpeter **Louis Armstrong.** It was such a hit that it was taken to the big screen in a Hollywood production starring Smith herself. By this point Bessie was the highest paid black entertainer of the day.

Guided Listening

"St. Louis Blues," Bessie Smith (with Louis Armstrong)

http://app.rhapsody.com/artist/various-artists/album/jazz-the-definitive-performances/track/st-louis-blues

The 12-bar blues is one of the most common song forms used in the history of popular music. Many of our examples follow this structure and lyrics often follow an AAB form. This can be diagrammed as follows:

Music:				*Lyrics:*
I	I	I	I	Lyric line A
IV	IV	I	I	Lyric line A repeated
V	IV	I	I (v)	Lyric line B (new line that concludes the phrase)

On the left side of this diagram, the tonic chord (I) is shown in measures of four beats. The top line shows four measures of the tonic (I) chord. The second line shows a harmonic shift to the subdominant chord (IV), which is played for two measures, followed by a return to the tonic chord (I). The third line shows one measure of the dominant chord (V), followed by one measure of the subdominant chord (IV), then two measures of the tonic chord (I) to close the cycle. The parenthesis on the last measure shows how it might feature the dominant chord (V) as a transition setting up the repeating cycle.

On the right side of the diagram is the typical AAB form of lyrics used in the blues. Often the AAB lines map directly onto the first, second, and third lines of the 12-bar form as shown here and heard in this listening example.

W. C. Handy composed this song in 12-bar blues form but with an added section that departs from the form. It is fairly common in blues music for composers and musicians to create different variations of the basic form.

0:05 Bessie Smith begins to sing the first verse in a standard blues form: the first line can be labeled as A and the music is played on the tonic (I) chord.

0:15 As Bessie finishes the first line, Louis Armstrong responds to that line with a melodic phrase on the trumpet.

0:21 Bessie repeats the same words, but the musical accompaniment has shifted to the subdominant (IV) chord and Armstrong responds with another phrase on trumpet.

0:35 Bessie sings the third line (B) over the dominant (V) chord.

0:44 Armstrong follows this with a descending trumpet line that leads the music back to the tonic (I) chord. This marks one cycle of the standard blues pattern of lyrics in the form of AAB and music using I-IV-V chords.

0:50 This pattern begins again with Bessie singing another verse in AAB form, followed by another melodic response from Armstrong.

1:06 Bessie repeats the A line and Armstrong responds.

1:19 Bessie sings line B that concludes the verse.

1:34 New music as Bessie sings a new phrase.

2:28 The music returns to the tonic chord (I) as Bessie sings a verse that includes the title of the song, "St. Louis Blues," and the music features one last cycle of the I-IV-V chord pattern.

12-BAR BLUES

One of the most widely used chord progressions in popular music based on the chords I-IV-V played within a time frame of twelve measures or "bars."

By the 20th century things, however, started to get organized. Handy and Bessie were working in a system buttressed by copyright law, populated by song pluggers, talent scouts (such as Ralph Peer), publishers, and others. These were the types of people who began running the media and more and more could be calling the shots. As the music industry grew and developed it laid down the roots of rock and roll and its media of choice was the record and the recording industry.

In the heyday of the blues there were over 150 competitor labels going after the growing market, including the well-known Columbia which had signed Bessie Smith in 1923 and within a year expand into new, diverse markets, such as the burgeoning "race record" series. This boom for records, exciting as it was, was short-lived. When the stock market crashed in 1929 and the onset of the Great Depression of the 1930s hit, the record labels quickly found themselves vulnerable to competition from other media. Sound production developers were already looking to Hollywood, where "talking pictures" had replaced silent ones. In public places, music lovers were flocking around the new jukebox where it took only a penny to hear a new favorite. Most importantly, it was the radio that would prove to be the cheapest and most immediately accessible media, and thus it was the one most suited for those hard times.

Blues, as we will discuss later, was certainly not to die in the face of a new dominant media, but the whole craze phenomenon for the style itself was over. Of course not everyone felt this so immediately. W. C. Handy, the self-described "Father of the Blues," died decades later a wealthy and well-respected musician and author. Bessie too had prospered in her lifetime, and remains a cherished figure of American music. Her untimely death in 1936, however, was tragic. Severely injured in a car accident in Mississippi, she may have bled to death because no one would take her to a "whites only" hospital. Once so powerful as to cause Columbia and Victor records to establish the niche in a market for African American audiences to compete with Okeh, blues was now in marked decline. This was the dawn of the swing era.

Louis Armstrong (1901–1971)

The Swing Era: 1935–1945

Swing was a social craze that defined American popular culture from 1935 until the mid-1940s—a musical and cultural explosion as significant and as controversial as the birth of rock about 20 years later. What spurred this new craze was the radio. If it weren't for the radio, it seems, bandleader and future "King of Swing" **Benny Goodman** might well have given up after a grueling tour of one night stands. Before 1935 Goodman specialized in a new, hot style of syncopated dance music. Most audiences across the United States were indifferent to it. But after performing on the weekly national radio program *Let's Dance* originating from New York (which happened to air at a more convenient time for listeners on the West Coast), he was greeted by crowds of dancers at the Palomar Ballroom in Los Angeles who had lined up around the block eager to dance to the hot new music of swing.

JAZZ

A genre of music that originated with African Americans in the United States combining various African musical elements with European harmonies.

SWING

A form of jazz music that dominated American popular music in the late 1930s and early 1940s featuring big bands that provided music for dancing.

The electrifying music with which Goodman hit it big featured the arrangements of African American jazz bandleader Fletcher Henderson, who utilized a large ensemble playing at a fast, four-beat tempo. Before Goodman hit it big in mainstream popular music, African American bandleaders such as Chick Webb were also playing hard-driving swing for dancers at places like the Savoy Ballroom in Harlem where swing dance movements were first developed.

But, as Goodman's experience shows, it was the radio that brought this infectious music to the nation. This medium did more than just serve those looking to entertain themselves. It also brought music to the ears of influential intermediaries such as John Hammond who was integral in launching the careers of such diverse stars as Billie Holliday, Pete Seeger, Bob Dylan, Bruce Springsteen, Stevie Ray Vaughn, and even Goodman. Hammond happened to be listening to the radio one night when he heard a radio broadcast from the Kansas City area. What he heard was the music of **Count Basie** who was laying down a type of swing that utilized short-repeating musical patterns called **riffs** that were played over 12-bar blues, allowing his musicians plenty of room to improvise. While Basie's style was highly influential on the later jazz style of bebop, his use of blues singers, especially blues "shouters" such as Jimmy Rushing, gave the blues broad exposure and generated a sound that would eventually be called rhythm and blues, an essential component of rock and roll that came to prominence after World War II.

RIFF

A short musical phrase that is repeated.

CHORUS

The word "chorus" has multiple meanings in American popular music: in terms of song form it refers to a section of words and melody that repeat (also called refrain); in terms of performance it refers to one cycle of the song form (e.g., "play one chorus").

Guided Listening

"Boogie Woogie (I May Be Wrong)" by Count Basie (with Jimmy Rushing)

http://app.rhapsody.com/artist/count-basie/album/the-complete-decca-recordings

In this song from the Swing Era, the Count Basie big band creates danceable music playing the 12-bar blues form in a faster tempo than what we heard on "St. Louis Blues." Bandleader and pianist Count Basie plays an introduction on the piano and piano "breaks" in the rhythm in a dance-oriented piano style known as boogie woogie. This song demonstrates the jazz performance form in which musicians would play through a form such as the 12-bar blues multiple times, featuring vocalists, instrumental soloists, or group arrangements. Each repeat of the cycle is called a **chorus**.

0:00	Song begins with a solo piano introduction by Basie.
0:05	The band joins in playing the 12-bar blues in a fast tempo. Note the use of short repeating patterns (riffs) in the horn section that give rhythmic drive to the music.
0:16	Another solo piano break by Basie.
0:21	The band plays another chorus.
0:33	Vocalist Jimmy Rushing begins to sing an AAB blues chorus.
0:49	Rushing sings another AAB chorus.
1:07	Rushing sings a break over new music.
1:24	Rushing sings "yes, yes" in call and response with the rest of the band.
1:40	Basie plays a chorus on piano.
1:58	Basie takes another chorus on piano.
2:15	Basie plays another solo break, the same one that opened the song.
2:20	Band plays another chorus.
2:32	Basie plays another solo piano break, playing half a phrase and the bass player responds by completing the musical phrase.
2:37	Band plays another chorus as the song fades out.

Something to See: Television and the Crooner Era (1945–55)

Benny Goodman was a star of the swing era, but was he really something to see? And who on the dance floor would care anyway as they were flung around the floor, executing the latest swing dance moves? The musical talent in the swing bands was such that it would be the breeding ground for modern jazz, a form that America would proudly describe as its "classical music." But in the post WWII era, when the new media was television, musicians faced a new problem and that was "looks."

This was a time, to put it bluntly, when anyone with an attractive face or a great style could emerge as a star, that is, as long as they also had spark and talent. The new media invited everyone from the young, operatically trained singer Mario Lanza, who was easily transformed into a pop singing heartthrob, to the seasoned entertainer, trumpeter and singer Louis Armstrong, who would end up on the cover of Time magazine in 1949, the first black musician to do so.

Jazz created many options for musicians, something Dizzy Gillespie, Charlie Parker, and other musicians trained in swing well understood as they pioneered a new style known as bebop and transformed jazz into a form of fine art. Bebop was hip and chic, and even beyond its musical contribution it made its mark on popular culture (our study of bebop will be covered in Chapter 15). Underneath all the black berets and goatees of the beboppers was a sentiment of seething rebellion and coolness that appealed both to disenfranchised African Americans and the youth in general. Its spiritual influence on rock and roll was pivotal. But the birth of cool, for all its importance, crept slowly and decisively into popular culture with a musical style that did not launch a national craze as had the blues and swing. The real limelight was on those willing to be watched. They fall into two categories: jump blues and crooner/canaries.

Jump Blues and Crooner/Canaries

All across the musical spectrum the idea of paring things down seemed to be the best approach to the economic realities. This was the time of the cabaret tax of 1941 that forced clubs to pay 30% of their ticket sales to government coffers, almost single-handedly curbing the dance craze and the large bands and orchestras that catered to it for so long. The small combo was the result of economic necessity. But there is something visually arresting about a combo in which every member has a spotlight. Nobody knew this better than **Louis Jordan**. Lit up with neon lights in his theatrical, televised performances, Louis Jordan introduced the world to the backbeat, the new infectious rhythm that was so crucial to the foundation of rock and roll. But the time was not yet ripe for this most explosive of all musical fads.

JUMP BLUES

A style of blues music played at a faster tempo by small bands featuring horns.

CROONERS/CANARIES

Singers of American popular music in the decades following the invention of the microphone who used the new technology in new expressive ways.

This was instead the heyday for the crooner/canaries; those photogenic singing stars who were easiest on the eyes. But you may well ask: what about the ears? Most rock textbook authors cast the music of the crooners and canaries as vacuous and deserted. And this is true of rock fans too. The Motörhead bassist Lemmy Kilmister is legendary among young people for having lived at a time "before there was rock." As rock star Henry Rollins notes:

> "He said 'I remember when there was only Rosemary Clooney records . . . there was just like your mom's records . . . then we heard Elvis and we never turned back . . . we heard rock and roll and we said that's us'" (Rollins interview in the documentary *Lemmy*, 2010).

32-BAR TIN PAN ALLEY AABA STANDARD

The most common popular song form (along with the 12-bar blues) in American popular music during the first half of the 20th century.

BRIDGE

A contrasting section in American popular song, the most common being the eight-bar B section in a 32-bar AABA form.

Singers like Clooney are charged with making music so boring that rock had to be invented to save popular music. In fact this was an era of great eclecticism and musical refinement. It was at this time that musical artists such as Clooney, Billie Holiday, **Frank Sinatra**, Peggy Lee, and Tony Bennett would explore how the microphone could be treated like a musical instrument. As far as the birth of rock was concerned, what we owe to these crooners and canaries was just as important as the blues and the backbeat. It was *image*—the embodiment of something larger than life, a palpable but unquantifiable form of charisma that somehow could immediately appeal to millions of people. Radio, records, jukeboxes, concert performances, and movies certainly helped musicians build such images over the course of the 20th century (and still do today), but with its reach and its visual element, it was the television that brought all this to a new level in the immediate post-war era.

Guided Listening

" 'S Wonderful" by Frank Sinatra

http://app.rhapsody.com/artist/frank-sinatra/album/frank-sinatra-legacy-hits

The **32-bar Tin Pan Alley Standard AABA** form is one of the most common song forms in popular music of the 20th century. Composed by the songwriting team of George and Ira Gershwin, " 'S Wonderful" follows a cycle of 32 bars (a bar is one measure of four beats) in a form described as AABA. We can diagram the 32-bar AABA structure with slash marks, each mark indicating one four beat bar:

Bar:	*1*	*2*	*3*	*4*	*5*	*6*	*7*	*8*
Sec. A	/	/	/	/	/	/	/	/
A	/	/	/	/	/	/	/	/
B	/	/	/	/	/	/	/	/
A	/	/	/	/	/	/	/	/

The first A section has a melody over a series of chords that last eight bars, then the same music repeats again for eight bars. The B section features a new melody over new chords for eight bars. The A section is played for another eight bars to complete the cycle. In this form, the B section of new music is typically referred to as the **bridge** because it acts as a "bridge" between the second and last A section. The B section is easy to identify because it sounds very different than the rest of the song and a good thing to listen for if you get lost in trying to follow the form.

Try following along with this chart while listening to this version of " 'S Wonderful" by Sinatra, one of the most famous crooners of all time. This recording is very short and the tempo is very fast so you don't need to count every beat, just count each measure or bar as it goes by. The entire song consists of two choruses of the 32-bar AABA form with eight bars of the A section between the two choruses played as an instrumental. Note how Sinatra "croons" his vocal part, singing up close to the microphone to help create a soft and intimate atmosphere. Notice how the melody and the supporting harmonies change in the B section.

0:00 First A section begins.

0:09 Second A section begins with the same music, but new lyrics.

0:19 B section begins with new music as Sinatra sings.

0:28 A section returns with the same lyrics as the first A, but Sinatra phrases it differently this time.

0:38 Eight bars of the A section is played by the band as an instrumental transition.

0:48 The AABA cycle begins again with another "chorus" of the song.

0:57 Second A section of eight bars.

1:06 B section of eight bars.

1:14 A section returns with extra measures added as a "tag" to end the song.

The musical landscape of 1945–55 was no desert; rather it supplied the well-fertilized topsoil for the birth of rock and roll. Yet there quickly comes a point when sophistication and refinement go too far in popular culture. Was rock a simple reaction to all the subtleties that had emerged in the popular music mainstream? To some extent it was just that. One could even go further and suggest that rock was a "retro" movement, one where we find the pendulum *swinging* back to radio and dance (or back to swing!). Just like those crowds that greeted Benny Goodman in the 1930s, there was a youth movement in the 1940s that began clamoring for something new and exciting. But had rock been simply a fashionable "retro" movement, it would never have lasted as long as it did. Outside of all the crazes and spotlights of national popular culture, specifically in the rural south, we find the deepest roots of rock.

Rural Blues

RURAL BLUES
A term for the blues styles that emerged in the rural areas of the Southern United States typically sung solo with accompaniment on guitar or other acoustic instruments.

Far from the limelight of Sinatra, Clooney, and even Bessie Smith were rural itinerant musicians who had begun to populate the southern regions of the United States shortly after the Civil War. Known as songsters, these singers were mainly, but not exclusively, African American men who lived a hard life. The topics of their songs ranged from the ballad legend to contemporary topics. These singers usually accompanied themselves on cheap and portable instruments. Many traveled far and wide, living on the road. From the songs they sang about their experiences they opened up the whole rich panorama of American roots music, which covered everything from mythical ballad figures, including John Henry; US presidents, such as Franklin Roosevelt; to current events such as the Titanic catastrophe.

Perhaps more than anyone else, Huddie William Ledbetter *aka* Lead Belly was the figure that connects the songster tradition to the blues. He not only performed a wide variety of song types, he also played a number of instruments including accordion, piano, and harmonica. He was most famous for his 12-string guitar. He ended up performing for New York intellectuals and students at Harvard and other colleges, but it was the red-light district where he spent most of his career as a musician. His life was full of all the hardships one associates with the "down and out," including prison time, poverty, and racism—to which he responded in his songs— and hard times in general. Whether or not his songs were technically blues, they came across to many as an authentic voice of a rural folk tradition.

The first to become successful as a rural blues star was Blind Lemon Jefferson, who has been referred to as the father of the Texas Blues. Blind from birth, Jefferson was "discovered" as a popular performer on the streets of Dallas, Texas where he drew crowds playing guitar and singing in a high-pitched, moaning style. Jefferson died in 1929 when he was only 36 years old, but his legacy is a lasting one with his songs having been recorded by rock musicians such as Bob Dylan, Dave Matthews, and Nick Cave. Blind Lemon Jefferson demonstrated that there was a market for the more raw style of rural blues. He opened the door for other male performers.

None of these bluesmen had the commercial success of Blind Lemon Jefferson during their lifetimes, but a few of them have become some of the most influential in the history of rock, especially musicians from the Mississippi Delta area who played Delta Blues. Musicians from this small, impoverished area in Western

Robert Johnson (1911–1938)

Mississippi exuded a raw, primitivism in singing and employed a highly rhythmic approach to guitar accompaniment, often using a bottleneck slide, and sometimes playing harmonica. Delta blues legend Charlie (Charley) Patton exemplified this sound with a gravely, growling style of singing blues songs. He was noted for flashy showmanship while playing guitar, long before rock guitarists like Jimi Hendrix made it a standard part of rock performance.

An even more obscure Delta Blues performer during the 1930s became far and away the most influential and widely revered rural blues musician of all time: **Robert Johnson**. An itinerant performer who roamed about the south playing for money on the streets and in restaurants, Johnson epitomized the image of a wandering blues man who shunned stable domestic life to make music on the road. While Johnson's nomadic lifestyle and lack of commercial success from the eleven records released during his brief lifetime has kept historians guessing about the details of his life, the myth about Robert Johnson has taken the place of biography in popular culture. The most well-known story is how Johnson miraculously transformed from a mediocre guitar player into a musical genius overnight by making a "pact with the devil" during a midnight meeting "at the crossroads" (a scene referenced in the movie *Oh Brother Where Art Thou*).

Eric Clapton and Keith Richards emulated Johnson's propulsive guitar playing with his characteristic use of a bottleneck slide. Johnson's songs also became standard material for bands like The Rolling Stones and Cream who turned Johnson's song "Cross Road Blues" into a rock classic. Johnson's lyrics were a primary inspiration for the young Bob Dylan who was especially moved by Johnson's lyrics, citing his use of free association, "sparkling allegories" and "big-ass truths wrapped in the hard shell of nonsensical abstraction" (Dylan, 2004, pg. 285). Johnson delivered his lyrics of sexual frustration, cheating women, violent confrontations, and encounters with devils and evil spirits in a wide-ranging vocal style that shifted effortlessly between soulful note bending, falsetto cries, and speech-like interjections. The sonic result was energetic and passionate, yet gloomy and foreboding. Johnson's early death at the age of 27—which would eventually be viewed superstitiously as an unlucky age at which many famous rock stars would die—seemed an inevitable outcome of the dark universe evoked in his music and seemed to point to the future of rock: its aggressive sound, its individualist ethos, and its danger.

Guided Listening

"Cross Road Blues" by Robert Johnson

http://app.rhapsody.com/artist/robert-johnson/album/the-complete-recordings-41-tracks

A classic 12-bar blues, this song follows the 12-bar blues form with lyrics in the AAB pattern:

Music:				*Lyrics:*
I	I	I	I	Lyric line A
IV	IV	I	I	Lyric line A repeated
V	IV	I	I (v)	Lyric line B (new line that concludes the phrase)

Johnson plays the 12-bar blues form throughout, but in a somewhat rough, uneven form. Because he is playing by himself he does not have to keep a strict count of four beats to every measure. Hence, some measures are a bit longer than others. Nevertheless, he does stick to the pattern of I-IV-V for the entirety of the song.

0:00 Song begins with an introduction played on guitar by Johnson.

0:07 Johnson begins playing the tonic chord (I) and begins to sing an AAB blues chorus.

0:22 Playing the subdominant chord (IV), Johnson repeats the first A line and his guitar "answers."

0:34 Playing the dominant chord (V), he finishes with the B line.

0:43 Begins the next chorus, moving again through the tonic (I) to the subdominant (IV) to the dominant (V). Note the guitar picking and the use of high falsetto voice.

1:15 In the next chorus, note how each A line is sung in a high pitch. He sings falsetto in the second second A line, then the B line is in a lower talking style.

1:43 On the next chorus the voice starts high again.

2:13 The last chorus begins again in high register.

2:33 Johnson finishes with a tag line played on guitar.

Let's sum up the rural situation. It would be difficult to think of anyone more important to the creation of rock and roll than Lead Belly, Blind Lemon Jefferson, Charley Patton, and Robert Johnson. These four musicians, more than any others, did the most to sustain its credibility over time. But let's face it; these were not people who enjoyed anything remotely resembling the extravagant lifestyles of the rock and roll rich and famous. How did they become so important? The answer is quite simple: the phonograph record.

The phonograph, unlike radio and television, changed music history by leaving a permanent mark. Even though they never reached a level of fame of the blues queens or the swing stars and crooners and canaries, the great rural bluesmen of the 30s and 40s did get recorded and this was how they were able to leave such a distinctive stamp on the history of popular music. The limited commercial success of Jefferson's raw style demonstrated that popular music did not have to rely on sophisticated arrangements or recording techniques. It also indicated that there was indeed an audience for regional styles of music. Charlie Patton was not much of a commercial success at all. But he did record for the small Paramount and Vocalion labels from 1929 until his death in 1934 at age 42. Even though few of his records sold during his lifetime his influence on later musicians, especially other blues musicians from the delta, outweighs the fact that he never achieved commercial success. Robert Johnson was certainly the bluesman who was the greatest beneficiary of the phonograph record in terms of legacy. The 29 songs recorded between 1936 and 1937 have become highly influential in the development of rock and it is through those recordings that his legend lives.

Country Music

Legends and traditions are the stuff of country music, and they always were. When we hear the homespun melodies of a loving family on the back porch, the moans and plaints of the un- or under-employed drifter, the yodels of the lonely cowboy, or the sobs of the jilted lover, we like to think we're witnessing something honest, pure, and natural. And many times we do. This doesn't mean, of course, that there weren't people "pulling the strings," helping to bring the "authentic" American sound to the people. On the one hand, because of its respect for tradition and its rural roots, the phonograph played an important role in the cultivation of a country style, just like it did in the blues. But country music was not just left to percolate. Rather it was poised to be the next "big thing" in the years leading up to the 1950s. This had to do with radio and TV, both of which served purposes similar to that of their close cousins in the swing and crooner/canary worlds.

Here we should return to Ralph Peer who we briefly mentioned at the beginning of this chapter. As we noted, he recorded Mamie Smith's path-breaking "Crazy Blues" for Okeh records. After establishing a firm market in what was then called "Race records," Peer turned to the **"hillbilly"** market (on these terms see sidebar). For a time the aspiring country star of the time would have to travel to New York to record his or her music. Peer used a new technique of remote recording, setting up in hotels, warehouses and even in barns—all a far cry from his city studios. Peer combined recording skills with those of the talent scout. Among those he sought out, discovered, and recorded were such rural musicians as Fiddlin' John Carson and Gid Tanner and The Skillet Lickers, whose sides are now regarded as the first country records. It was actually in a hat warehouse in Bristol, Tennessee where Peer recorded two of the founding acts of early country music, **Jimmie Rodgers** and The Carter Family.

HILLBILLY MUSIC

An early term for music performed by rural white performers in the American south that led to the development of country and western music.

Regarded today as the first family of country music, the trio of A. P. Carter, his wife Sara, and sister-in-law Maybelle, *aka* The Carter Family, recorded a string of hit records in the late 1920s. It was under Peer's tutelage that they would bring out "Wildwood Flower," "Keep on the Sunny Side," "Wabash Cannonball," and "Can The Circle Be Unbroken" among other soon-to-be country standards. As the group's leader, A. P. Carter collected songs while traveling around the south, often, along with Peer, copyrighting these songs as he "found" them. Most enduringly, A. P. and his family created a distinctive sound in recordings, featuring Sara's twangy lead vocals with Maybelle's guitar and close vocal harmony. Not surprisingly, the Carter Family's music reflected the diversity of American music at the time, drawing from Anglo-American ballads, Sacred Harp songs, and even Tin Pan Alley song styles. Along with their distinctive sound and wide repertoire, The Carter Family exuded a downhome image too, one that would stand forever as one of the hallmarks of the style, with its celebration of home, family, and togetherness.

Jimmie Rodgers (1897–1933)

In contrast to The Carter Family's downhome country atmosphere, the music and image of Jimmie Rodgers laid the groundwork for the country music image of the rambling drifter that would soon influence country and then rock musicians. Working on the railroads since a teenager, Rodgers picked up guitar skills from railroad workers and hobos, developing his performing skills from a very young age. After being discovered by Ralph Peer at that legendary recording session in 1927, Rodgers became the first major star of country music with a string of hits in the late 1920s and early 1930s that celebrated a rogue lifestyle of hopping freight trains and refusing to settle down, earning him nicknames such as "the singing brakeman." This image was exploited in publicity photos of Rodgers, as well as his appearance in a Hollywood movie short, *The Singing Brakeman*, in which he was dressed to look the part.

Like all the early country music, Rodgers's music was an eclectic product of the American cultural mix. Although his music was not labeled "blues," most of his songs relied heavily on the 12-bar blues form so prominent in African American music. The diversity of the musical mix can easily be heard in his trademark yodel that earned him another nickname: "the blue yodeler." The song "Blue Yodel No. 1 (T for Texas)" from 1927 was one of his biggest hits and a country classic that was covered years later by southern rock band Lynyrd Skynyrd. Rodgers's fame in the world of pop music led to even more eclecticism, recording with legendary jazz trumpeter Louis Armstrong in 1930. The illustrious career of Jimmie Rodgers was brief however, being cut short by his death from tuberculosis in 1933. He would leave a lasting legacy in what was soon to become **Country and Western** music. Like his counterparts of the era making race records—Blind Lemon Jefferson, Charlie Patton, and Robert Johnson—Jimmie Rodgers epitomized the image of the independent, individualistic rambler that would become one of the building blocks of rock and roll.

COUNTRY AND WESTERN
A genre of American popular music that developed out of rural areas of the Southern United States featuring musical elements that began with hillbilly music.

Guided Listening

"Blue Yodel #1 (T for Texas)" by Jimmie Rodgers

http://app.rhapsody.com/artist/jimmie-rodgers/album/the-essential-jimmie-rodgers/track/blue-yodel-1-t-for-texas

Most of Rodgers's hit songs followed the simple formula heard here of 12-bar blues form with an added "yodel" phrase at the end of each chorus.

0:00 Song begins with an introduction played on guitar by Rodgers.
0:05 Rodgers begins to sing an AAB blues verse.
0:28 Rodgers adds a tag to the blues verse with his signature vocal gimmick, a yodel.
0:35 Rodgers begins a new AAB verse.
1:01 Another yodel ends this verse.
1:08 Another verse, also ending with a yodel.
1:40 Another verse in the same manner.
2:10 New chords sound to provide a little contrast.
2:18 Another AAB verse.
2:49 New chords again for contrast.
2:55 Last AAB verse that ends the song.

Gene Autry, known as "the singing cowboy," began his career around the same time after signing with Columbia Records. His records brought the attention of Hollywood and, starting in 1934, he began appearing in Western movies in which he played himself and sang songs while playing his guitar. In so doing, Autry introduced the "Western" part of Country and Western into the mix. After more than 40 films, Autry had a radio show in the 1940s and a television show in the 1950s following the same model of the singing cowboy, an image so successful it spawned another singing cowboy star, Roy Rogers. While the image may have been manufactured by show business, the music was distinctly American in its blending of folk, blues, and Tin Pan Alley with distinctive "country" timbres such as the Hawaiian slide guitar and vocal yodeling.

Just as many southerners migrated to major cities like Chicago, Detroit, Baltimore, Cincinnati, and Los Angeles for greater employment opportunities, country music itself became urbanized after establishing its headquarters in Nashville, Tennessee. Known today as "Music City," Nashville is still the center of country music recording and publishing today and the home of the Country Music Association (CMA) that hosts an annual awards ceremony for the industry. Country musicians had been converging on Nashville since 1925 with the beginnings of the Grand Ole Opry, a stage show and radio broadcast that has long been the premiere showcase for the major stars of country music. When singer Roy Acuff, who had a major hit with his song, "Great Speckled Bird" in 1936, went into song publishing with songwriter Fred Rose, the two formed a publishing company, Acuff-Rose, and set up their headquarters in Nashville. Acuff-Rose hired some of the most famous singers and songwriters of country music, including Hank Williams.

Hank Williams was originally hired by Acuff-Rose as a songwriter, but quickly became one of country music's most famous singing stars in the late 1940s. Unprecedented for country music at the time, Williams had 36 Top Ten Records on the Country and Western charts between his start in 1947 and his death in 1953. Eleven of these songs reached number one, including "Jambalaya (On the Bayou)," "Lovesick Blues," "Your Cheatin' Heart," and "Cold, Cold Heart" which became the first major hit for a young Tony Bennett in 1951 and showing the crossover appeal of Williams's music.

Like Jimmie Rodgers, Hank Williams had a brilliant, short-lived career and a hard-living image that went with it. But unlike Rodgers, the independent, hard-living Hank Williams was more than just a persona. His life reads like the stories of excess one typically hears of rock stars. Because of his chronic back ailment, he regularly used painkillers such as morphine and self-medicated with excessive amounts of alcohol. His frequent intoxication led to his reputation in the business for unreliability, resulting in getting fired from The Grand Ole Opry and having a falling out with Fred Rose shortly before he died from a heart attack brought on by a lethal combination of drugs. Hank Williams died on January 1, 1953 at the age of 29.

Hank Williams (1923–1953)

Guided Listening

"Your Cheatin' Heart" by Hank Williams

http://app.rhapsody.com/artist/hank-williams/album/moanin-the-blues-the-best-of-the-great-hank-williams

Country musicians, like most popular musicians, drew on the most common song forms such as the 12-bar blues and the 32-bar AABA Standard form as heard in this song. Like the Sinatra song heard earlier (but in a much slower tempo), this song follows the Standard AABA form:

	Bar: 1	2	3	4	5	6	7	8
Sec. A	/	/	/	/	/	/	/	/
A	/	/	/	/	/	/	/	/
B	/	/	/	/	/	/	/	/
A	/	/	/	/	/	/	/	/

As with the blues, the 32-bar form is flexible and determined by the performers. In this case, Hank Williams sings one chorus of AABA, followed by an instrumental that uses eight bars of B and eight bars of A, then finishing with a second chorus of the AABA song.

0:00 Song begins with an introduction of four bars.

0:07 AABA begins as Williams sings the title of the song.

0:23 The next A section begins.

0:38 B section begins.

0:53 Final A section.

1:07 An instrumental section features the B section music played with a solo on steel guitar for eight bars . . .

1:24 . . . then eight bars of the A section are played, featuring a violin solo.

1:37 AABA returns with Williams's vocal.

1:52 Second A section

2:07 B section

2:22 A section to end the song.

Country Music on the Cusp of Rock

Country seemed at its height in the mid-1950s just at the moment when rock and roll was born. It is tempting to see the explosion of rock and roll as eclipsing country and Western in the mid-1950s and even a threat to its existence and its values. By the 1950s, Country music had become big business and a "tradition" with its own image and values. For example, the Grand Ole Opry, the symbol of country tradition, forbid the use of drums, as they were not deemed suitable, resulting in musicians such as Bob Wills struggling against these restrictions. Ironically, country music was valued for its "purity" despite the eclecticism of its musical sound. It is easy to see why country music traditionalists would feel threatened by rock and roll. But country music and rock and roll had a symbiotic relationship: they were dependent on each other.

It is clear that country music helped give birth to rock and roll and is one of the essential building blocks when one looks at some of the biggest early rock stars, including Elvis Presley and Bill Haley (once a cowboy yodeler singer) who got their start in what was essentially "country" music—rockabilly. But it was hardly the case that the explosion of Elvis Presley eclipsed mainstream country music. It is significant that Country and Western, for all its success, still sold fewer records than mainstream pop from Tin Pan Alley in the mid-1950s. It was not until rock and roll was born, that country music, and Rhythm and Blues as well, began to successfully invade the mainstream of popular music. Thus, instead of rock and roll "killing" Country and Western music as many people believed when country appeared to be at its height, rock and roll was the next inevitable and crucial development in the changing soundscape of popular music and the biggest challenge to the way the music industry operated until mid-century.

References

Handy, W.C. 1957. *Father of the Blues.* London: Sidgwick and Jackson.

Lemmy. A documentary film directed by Greg Oliver and Wes Orshoski (Damage Case Films), 2010.

Dylan, Bob. 2004. *Chronicles Volume One.* New York: Simon and Schuster.

14 The Birth of Rock and Roll

Key Terms

Blackboard Jungle
Crossover
Sun Records
Backbeat
Rockabilly
Chess Records
Boogie-woogie
Payola scandal
"the day the music died"

Key Figures

Bill Haley
Elvis Presley
Sam Phillips
Jerry Lee Lewis
Chuck Berry
Leonard Chess
Little Richard
Buddy Holly
Alan Freed
Pat Boone

If there is any date that you need to memorize in a rock history class, it's 1955. Just open any encyclopedia or history book or newspaper and you'll discover that this was the very year rock was born. Why 1955? It turns out that musicologist Richard A. Peterson has attempted to answer that very question with a fascinating new look at the way American media had nurtured and responded to the popular musical developments that characterized the first half of the 20th century. As he explains, the big controlling companies thought they had everything under control by licensing popular songs through organizations such as ASCAP. Four major corporations had released more than 80% of all the records that reached the top of the charts. On their national networks studio bands under the network name played the "hit parade" with all the polish and professionalism that money could buy. Firmly under their control were both the television and the radio airwaves, and this was all for the good . . . as long as you liked the music and the way it was played.

Not surprisingly, this system could not sustain itself for very long. One of the assumptions of the "big four" was that America would somehow conform to this uniform taste. They also assumed, as Peterson notes, that radio was on its way out and records were really not that important. While the big corporations were looking elsewhere, the FCC had relaxed some of its restrictions and the independent radio operator suddenly found it easier to get a license. Small-time indie operators who could not afford an in-house orchestra could now broadcast music using records. Today we see these indie operators, such as **Sam Phillips**, Leonard and Phil Chess, Ahmet Ertegun, "Bumps" Blackwell, and Norman Petty as the behind the scenes heroes of the nascent rock era. Their weapon, the record (a disc of grooved vinyl), as we have already seen and will continue to show in this history, stands as the touchstone of popular music in the 20th century. (Since we're talking about dates to memorize, notice here that we did not include the 21st century in this statement.) With new formats, such as the 45 rpm, and new products, such as transistor radios that could be hand-held or fitted onto a car dashboard, audiences could simply subvert all that the big networks were trying to accomplish.

So to answer the question "why 1955?" . . . there were small independent operators on a much lower budget with more flexibility who could reach audiences with alternative content and therefore blindside the big companies. No doubt this notion captures a lot of the changes that were happening and really explains how media as a large institution could change the history of popular music. But what did people say about 1955 and the birth of rock before this was all spelled out? There seem to be two theories that have held over the years. They can be simplified into the economic terms of supply and demand. The demand-side explanation had the premise that the world just erupted.

In purely economic terms, the post-war American society was faced with an interesting problem. The allies won the war and America, more than any other country, got the spoils of war. Everyone had been through some tough times. In America there had been the Great Depression, war rationing, temperance movements, prohibition, xenophobia, and fear of the future. With Hitler, Stalin, and Hiroshima in the recent past, a grim outlook for the future would be understandable . . . but try telling this to the young American of the mid-1950s. Now we're talking about an age group who generally felt naturally inclined to feel positive about themselves. This particular generation was the first to be bombarded with a cornucopia of supermarket shelves full of colorful packaged food, shiny cars on spotless showroom floors, and help-wanted signs with the promise that all this prosperity was well within reach. Never before was there a more clear case of two generations having such different ways of looking at the world.

For all the viability of the demand theory, the most sensible explanation for many was that rock was born at this time because of the great supply. In 1955, many of the most legendary rock and roll stars such as Elvis Presley, Chuck Berry, Fats Domino, Little Richard, and others were just starting to make records. This group of stars embodied all the energy that was wished for, and did much more than just fill a need. They broke open a path. They were at the forefront of a movement that was starving for leaders. Rock and roll musicians, oddly enough, would serve a function that someone like Plato or Socrates wanted to serve as a philosopher—as the wise, trustworthy, and sincere models for behavior in an era in which fashion ruled.

In this chapter, we will explore how a group of stars became leaders of this stature. All this sounds like a complete break with the past and that the sails were out and everything was flowing. But when we end this chapter we will see how fads, even ones as powerful as rock and roll, have their weaknesses. The older generation, it turns out, actually won the first battle of the cultural war over music.

The Wild Ones

In the spring of 1955 a controversial new movie hit the theatres that had teenagers dancing in the aisles and adults fearing for their safety. ***Blackboard Jungle***, a film about a schoolteacher who challenges the violent teenage gang that runs an inner city high school, fed parents' worst fears about juvenile delinquency at the time. Just like an earlier movie from 1953, *The Wild One*, which featured young Marlon Brando as the menacing leader of a biker gang, *The Blackboard Jungle* brought a huge teenage audience to the theatres. But this time there was something new and even more threatening to the adult generation. The opening of the film featured a new song by Bill Haley and the Comets called "Rock Around the Clock." For many teenagers, this was the first time they heard the new music that would be called "Rock and Roll." The beat and sheer volume of this song in the theatres got teenagers out of their seats and dancing. In response to this national craze, some theatres cut this opening part from their screenings, but it did nothing to quell the enthusiasm for the movie or for rock and roll music.

> ***BLACKBOARD JUNGLE***
> A 1955 Hollywood film about juvenile delinquency that is noteworthy for the inclusion of rock and roll for the first time in cinema, Bill Haley's "Rock Around the Clock."

Things did not calm down as "Rock Around the Clock" immediately hit the pop charts. Riots were reported on college campuses from students playing the song in their dormitories. For two consecutive months in the summer of 1955 the song was number one in the United States. In England the film featuring Haley's song had an even more powerful effect. Stories of riots at movie screenings in the UK were so widespread that Beatle John Lennon recalled that when he went to see the movie as a young teen in Liverpool, he was disappointed that a riot did *not* break out. In hindsight, the pandemonium over "Rock Around the Clock" was certainly exaggerated in the media, but rock and roll was clearly a pop phenomenon that seemed to take everyone by surprise. "Rock Around the Clock" was just the beginning of a new sound made by musicians such as Little Richard, Chuck Berry, Jerry Lee Lewis, Buddy Holly, and others that triggered ecstasy in dancing teenagers and shock from horrified parents.

Bill Haley: The "Father" of Rock and Roll

Bill Haley had come on the scene with a cover version of rhythm and blues singer Big Joe Turner's "Shake, Rattle and Roll." Take a moment now and listen to Big Joe Turner's recording [http://app.rhapsody.com/artist/big-joe-turner-jump-blues], then compare it to Bill Haley's rendition [http://app.rhapsody.com/artist/bill-haley-and-the-comets], paying special attention to the lyrics. Much has been made of the differences in the lyrics with the idea that Haley cleaned them up for a wider mainstream audience. It is true that Haley's version removed the voyeurism and pederasty, but to suggest that the song was devoid of sexual elements is misleading. In both songs, rock and roll was a depiction of the sex act and Haley kept the rather risqué images of Turner's version. Haley even added sexual innuendo to the first verse in which Turner comes off literally as a sexist male demanding his breakfast whereas Haley simply wants to "roll" with the female.

Turner's is an adult-oriented, vaudeville seasoned, low-down version of the "Shake, Rattle and Roll" story with all the gender antagonism typical of blues at the time. Turner's male evokes the devil, grits his teeth, threatens the woman and insults her throughout the song. He strikes the dark tone that was typical of an adult story at the time. Indeed all the main genres of the late 1940s/early 1950s had their low-down, serious or depressing aspect. On the hillbilly side, too, were plenty of sad sacks moaning about their cheating wives and their lost jobs. But there were bright spots in the blues as well as the country traditions. Jump blues was certainly a lighter counterpart to the urban styles in Chicago and Western Swing, which was cultivated in Texas and parts of California. Jump blues soon emerged as the more upbeat version of Country and Western.

© catwalker, 2014. Used under license from Shuttershock, Inc.

Just looking at a photo of the Michigan born Bill Haley tells you he was going to favor the fun-loving side of any genre. Not surprisingly, he began his career in Western swing. All of the traits of his chosen style emerge in his version of the Joe Turner song. Haley's bright and cheery, fun-loving protagonist makes some of the complaints we find in Turner's version, but they are delivered with none of the rhythm and blues venom. Rather than leering at the woman, Haley's protagonist is clearly out to flatter her in a way she would appreciate—noticing how her hair is nicely done. If you put this song together with "Rock Around the Clock," you can see that Haley was encouraging kids to enjoy themselves thoroughly and stay out all night to live their teenage dreams. Haley has rightly been called the "Father of Rock." But rather than being a father in the parental sense, he fit much more the role of the permissive, fun-loving uncle.

Elvis Presley: The King of Rock and Roll

In 1945, the very year World War II ended, an unpromising poor, white child whose father was serving time in prison got the chance to sing a song—Red

Foley's country tune "Old Shep"—at a local talent contest. This shy, young man, who soon after would be prone to stage fright and was bullied in school as a "mama's boy," knew throughout this period that he loved music. From his early years he absorbed gospel music with a passion and was soon to be identified as a loner who played the hillbilly music that was, though popular, dismissed as trashy by polite society. If it weren't for music, this young man might have been the quintessential average teenager of the post-war era; one who, coming out of the darkness of the depression and World War II could see the light of a more prosperous future. Thanks to the history of music, this young man became a phenomenon. Instead of being just one of the crowd, he became a true leader of this era: **Elvis Presley**.

When we talk about Elvis Presley, we need to consider two things—the musical archaeology and the iconic status. As far as the musical archaeology goes, Presley's music spanned everything from lowdown hillbilly and blues styles, to the panache of mainstream pop songs with a good dose of both white and black gospel intermixed. By bringing in all these musical elements, Presley made rock and roll a diverse and energetic form. It is hard to overestimate Elvis's musical contribution just on this stylistic diversity alone. But, as far as rock history goes, it would be just as difficult to overestimate the importance of his iconic status. Perhaps to compensate for his shyness, Elvis used fashion—leather jackets, shirts with turned-up collars, long sideburns, and slicked down hair with a ducktail in back—to stand out in a crowd, not as a conformist but rather as a rebel. No other musician better embodied the idea that the new music called rock and roll would pose such a threat to society.

Legend tells us it was at Sam Phillips's Sun Studio one night in July 1954, that the musical mix came together. At the end of the night, after an unproductive recording session, Elvis and his trio started fooling around with "That's All Right," a blues song by African American blues man Arthur Crudup. Scotty Moore, Elvis's guitar player, was combining the finger picking style of country music with note bending based on blues. The bass player, Bill Black, was pulling the strings of the bass so hard it made a slapping sound that energized the rhythm. It seems as if they were just blowing off steam. Perhaps they were exaggerating the features of the blues as a way of entertaining themselves. But Phillips took it all quite seriously. After a long day of trial and error, it was here that the energy Phillips was looking for finally made it into the mix and he began to roll the tape.

This story has become a seminal moment in the history of rock and served its purpose in Rock myth making. Whether it happened exactly as people remember it or not, we'll never know, but we do have that landmark recording, "That's All Right." Once we hear that bass slapping so rhythmically, it is not hard to imagine why Phillips ran the tape. It also isn't hard to imagine what the drummer would do in this new mix. Inspired by jump blues, the drummer's main options would be to play a shuffle or a backbeat. Both of these techniques generated the energy of rock and roll. The shuffle beat brought out all beats of the measure while the backbeat put an emphasis on the second and fourth.

Guided Listening

"That's All Right" by Elvis Presley

http://app.rhapsody.com/artist/elvis-presley/album/the-best-of-elvis-presley/track/thats-all-right

This song is an example of 8-bar blues that can be diagrammed as follows:

I	I	I	I
IV	IV	V	V

In this song Elvis Presley sings new words each time through the top line and a vocal refrain of "That's all right" over the second line. This is from the original **Sun Records** session in which Presley and his band "discovered" the rock and roll sound that would make them famous. After listening to this, you might be surprised to discover there are no drums played on this track—just one acoustic guitar strumming chords, one electric guitar picking individual notes, and one bass player. The drumming sound is coming from the bass player who is slapping the strings.

0:00 Song begins with the strumming of Presley's guitar.
0:06 The 8-bar blues form begins as Elvis sings.
0:13 Elvis sings the refrain over the IV and V chords.
0:26 Another 8-bar chorus begins as Elvis sings.
0:47 The band plays one chorus as an instrumental.
1:09 Elvis begins another verse, followed by the refrain.
1:29 Elvis sings another verse, this time "scat singing" the words.

SUN RECORDS

The independent record label founded in the 1950s by Sam Phillips who launched the careers of many rock and roll stars, including Elvis Presley, Jerry Lee Lewis, Carl Perkins, Roy Orbison, and others.

BACKBEAT

Term used to describe accenting the "off" beats (beats 2 and 4) in a four-bar measure, as commonly heard in early rock and roll.

The **backbeat** is crucial to the rock style, but it represents a marked departure from practices of the past. Rhythm is the way music is marked in time. Most music of the 20th century falls into a rhythmic system in which four equal beats are placed into a measure in which certain beats are emphasized over others, or in musical parlance, are accented. The backbeat does not disturb the measure, but it does dramatically change the pattern of accents within it. The backbeat is precisely the opposite of most Western music of the time in which beats 1 and 3 are emphasized. Thus, the backbeat reversed the expected pattern, adding a kind of musical syncopation. It also invites participation and for this reason, it would be interesting to try to trace this back to African styles of call and response. For example, when you listen to a gospel song, notice how you feel compelled to clap along with it. When you do, and you certainly are invited to, you are clapping on the second and fourth beat. Like swing jazz, but unlike the crooners of mainstream popular music, the participatory elements of clapping, dancing, and even screaming on cue, are part of the phenomenon of rock and roll.

Presley's image was quite a mixture of elements as well. Blessed with classic good looks and a baby face any mother could love, Elvis had the sex appeal and vulnerability that appealed to women of all ages. But when he raised and twitched his upper lip and started shaking his leg—earning him the nickname "Elvis the pelvis"—he seemed to be advertising an almost predatory version of sexual prowess. In any case, it was almost as if he was inviting everyone to join him in a voyeuristic fantasy in which the whole performance could be boiled down to a sensational sex act. Presley had tapped into something very deep-seated in the psyche of adults. With so many dreams at stake in the post-war period, parental fears were at an all-time high. Downward vs. upward social mobility, mixing of race and class, and financial instability due to premature responsibilities, number among the many concerns that parents had for their children, especially their daughters, but it all came down to one basic fear: pre-marital sex.

With all these ingredients in place, Elvis Presley quickly rose to the top of the charts with a string of hit singles. "Blue Moon of Kentucky," was one of his early hits. This song, by bluegrass legend Bill Monroe, shows how close to the country tradition Elvis had always been. His first number one hit, "Heartbreak Hotel," was not only the biggest selling record of 1956, but also reached number one on the Country and Western chart and number five on the R & B chart. Elvis could croon, too. His hit "Love Me Tender" featured an intimate, seductive, vocal recorded close to the microphone that only increased his appeal to women. If any song encapsulated Presley's aggressive male energy it was "Jailhouse Rock," with its hard-hitting, rockabilly beat.

When he wasn't trying to seduce the listener with his voice, Elvis was usually snarling, radiating a kind of aggression that put the transgression of the blues into visual form. Probably no song encapsulates this better than his rendition of "Hound Dog." Originally a song for blues singer Big Mama Thornton and composed by the seasoned Tin Pan Alley songwriting team of Leiber and Stoller, it was replete with all the sexual innuendo that adults had come to expect from the blues. It would have been sure to inspire a smirk and a smile. When Elvis recorded it, they cleaned it up a bit, basically removing the sexual innuendo from the lyrics. What no one seemed to anticipate was how far Elvis could reinstate that sexuality through his pelvic gyrations and twitching of his legs. When TV host Ed Sullivan saw Presley perform, he was convinced Presley was harboring some kind of device in his pants that revealed the outline of his genitals. One wonders if Sam Phillips had any idea such sexual exhibitionism would be the result of his simple wish when he told his secretary that if he could find a white man who had a black sound he could "make a billion dollars."

Sam Phillips ended up making a lot of money, but Elvis Presley was just a steppingstone for Phillips who sold Presley's contract to RCA Records, a major label that was better able to promote Presley and make him into a big star. A smart businessman, Phillips took the money from the RCA Corporation and invested it back into his studio so that he could make stars out of other musicians playing the new music. Thanks to this business deal, some other legendary talents from Sun Studio became big stars such as Roy Orbison, Johnny Cash, Carl Perkins, and **Jerry Lee Lewis**. Lewis and Perkins became known for their southern style of rock and roll known as **rockabilly**—essentially southern flavored rock and roll that was popular in the 1950s and would have several revivals in later decades.

ROCKABILLY
Rock and roll from the Southern United States with a strong country influence that began in the 1950s and has had subsequent revivals.

What many people today don't realize about early rock and roll is that it was driven entirely by small-time, independent operators like Sam Phillips. Big companies, like RCA, did sweep in and grab Elvis Presley to make bundles of money with his music, but the majority of classic rock and roll songs that are historically important today—records by Chuck Berry, Little Richard, Eddie Cochran, Ritchie Valens, and many others—were all released on small independent labels. This is the beginning of a pattern that we will see repeated from the 1950s onward: the independents innovate with what little they have, and the major corporations scramble to capitalize on the new sensation, by either buying the contract of a rising star (such as Elvis) or developing their own talent. Innovation in rock and roll has always come from artists and entrepreneurs operating independently.

You might expect that in the wake of Elvis the major labels would have snatched up all the independents to make a quick fortune. Oddly enough, with the exception of Elvis Presley at RCA, the major record labels avoided hard-core rock and roll in the 1950s, mainly because it was so controversial in American society at the time. Rather than promote talent that might risk moral outrage among American adults, the major corporations began to develop their own talent to sell to teenagers that today sounds watered down when compared to the greatest stars of rock and roll. For the rest of this chapter we will stick with the controversy by focusing on the most important and influential rock musicians of the era. We will examine how this music that pushed the boundaries laid the foundation for popular music in the coming decades and how the controversy over this music continued to stir social fears that worked against the survival of rock and roll in the 1950s.

For the first time in modern society, teenagers in the 1950s were able to have a lifestyle separate from their families and away from parental supervision. The automobile, the car radio, and the drive-in movie theatre, made for a combination that had many adults worried about teenage morality.

Chuck Berry: Rock and Roll Guitar and Teenage Stories

CHESS RECORDS
The independent record label founded in Chicago by brothers Phil and Leonard Chess, specializing in blues, R&B, soul, and early rock and roll music.

The discovery of the legendary guitarist and songwriter **Chuck Berry** can be attributed to **Leonard Chess**, an independent record producer who had set up **Chess Records** in the south side of Chicago in the late 1940s. Chess signed Etta James, Muddy Waters, and other founders of electric rhythm and blues. Like Sam Phillips in Memphis, with whom he was in contact, Chess was searching for a new sound. But rather than seeking a white voice with a black sound, he wanted to bring great black talent to a white audience. His discovery was Chuck Berry, a guitarist and protégé of the jump blues musician T-Bone Walker. A 29-year-old ex-con who did time for armed robbery when he was still a teenager, Berry was that juvenile delinquent parents of teenagers so feared at the time. Yet Leonard Chess saw him as the very person to bridge the gap between black and white music.

Eclectic by nature, Chuck Berry spent the early 1950s performing for black audiences with his partner, the pianist Johnnie Johnson. Although their main fare was blues, they also featured hillbilly tunes as something of a novelty. One such tune, "Ida Red"—recorded in the 1930s by Texas swing artist Bob Wills, country music mogul Roy Acuff, and others—became the basis for Berry's first hit single, "Maybellene." "Ida Red" seems like a peculiar choice for Berry to appropriate. Typical of an old-time ballad, "Ida Red" was a free-form conglomeration of country tropes: downhome living, cheating women, barnyard animals, etc. By the time this amorphous text had reached the mid-20th century it had almost turned into nonsense, strangely combining the hurtfulness of a cheating woman with the comforting sentimentality of a 19th century parlor song description of the home and hearth.

What Chuck Berry did, apparently with Chess's encouragement, was to bring this song right up to date. Realizing they needed a name change because of copyright law, they happened upon "Maybellene" which was the name of a cosmetic firm. Whether or not this was calculated to reach a young female audience, there can be no question that Berry cast the lyrics toward the teenage male. Although a cheating woman is still present in the updated lyrics, the car is the star and dominates each verse. The cozy place of comfort is no longer a parlor, it's now the front seat of a car.

As a lyricist, Chuck Berry had discovered something essential about the new teenage audience. They wanted their own domain outside the home and far from the reach of parental control. Desiring a domain far from the reach of parental control, they flocked to dance halls, movie theatres, malt shops, and any place that catered to them. But it was the car, replete with radio, comfortable seats, and almost enough power to escape the police, that satisfied their quest for autonomy. Chuck Berry, the first great lyricist of rock, provided the soundtrack for this new teenage lifestyle.

"Maybellene" was not simply a country song sung by a black musician. In a country song, instrumental breaks literally provide a break for the singer to take a breath and the audience to let the words sink in. But since the song is now in a car, Berry used the instrumental breaks differently. Thrashing an electric guitar with an abandon unprecedented in popular music at the time, Berry expressed all the energy of a hot rod screaming down the highway in high gear. In live performance, Berry coupled this with showmanship that featured a duck walk that called all the more attention to his instrumental prowess. As far as legacy is concerned,

Guided Listening

"Maybellene" by Chuck Berry

http://app.rhapsody.com/search?query=maybellene

One of Berry's biggest hit records, "Maybellene" is a fast blues song in which the 12-bar form is played for the refrain (in which he sings the words "Maybellene") and each verse that tells the story uses only the tonic chord (I). The tempo is in a fast two-beat style similar to country music. Typical of country music, Berry tells a story, but the story is one geared specifically toward teenagers of the time.

0:00 Berry plays a guitar riff as an intro to the song before the rhythm section enters.

0:05 Berry sings the title of the song in a refrain of AAB lyrics over the 12-bar form.

0:18 Berry begins singing a story about a car race while the band plays the tonic (I) chord.

0:29 Refrain over the 12-bar blues form.

0:42 Second verse sung over the I chord returns to the car race story.

0:54 Refrain.

1:06 Berry plays a guitar solo over the 12-bar blues chords.

1:18 Berry continues his guitar solo for another chorus of 12 bars.

1:30 Refrain.

1:43 Third verse.

1:55 Refrain.

2:08 Berry plays a guitar tag to end the song.

Chuck Berry was the first guitar hero, cited by rock guitarists such as Keith Richards, John Lennon, Ted Nugent, and many others as one of the greatest guitarists of all time.

Little Richard: The Piano Goes Rock and Roll

BOOGIE-WOOGIE

A style of piano-based blues originally designed for dancing that features a steady left-hand bass line.

Rather surprisingly, Berry, one of the greatest rock guitarists of all time, described everything he did in music as based on the piano-driven tradition of **boogie-woogie**. Since the 19th century the piano had always been around. Compared to the guitar, which evoked the wayfaring, migrant musician, the piano maintained respectability. It was a standard feature in churches and civic halls throughout America. Even in the poorest household it represented a reassuring stability for its owners. From all sides, Americans were long used to hearing the live and recorded music of great pianists from Sergei Rachmaninoff, Arthur Rubinstein, to Scott Joplin, George Gershwin, Duke Ellington, and arguably the most phenomenal of all, Art Tatum, who combined the finesse and subtlety of classical music with all the syncopations and infectiousness of popular piano styles.

Not all piano music was so polished, however. As far as rock history goes, there was a boogie-woogie piano tradition that had developed to the point that it could be said to be a proto-rock style. Boogie-woogie was essentially a substitute for a whole band in a setting when dancing was called for and only a piano was available. To simulate the sound of a band, pianists relied on a rhythm-heavy, repetitive left hand which became a hallmark of the style. With fingers flying and sometimes multiple pianists at the bench, this sound could be quite infectious. Intriguingly, this style was so popular that some musicians added the instruments anyway, but they crucially kept the raucous, driving rhythm of the left-hand. In the hands of musicians such as Little Richard and Jerry Lee Lewis that old reassuring piano would be put on equal footing with the energetic rowdiness of the slap bass, backbeat-driven drums, and the electrified guitar.

CROSSOVER

The term used when a pop song appeals to multiple audiences, such as when Elvis Presley's song, "Hound Dog," became a hit on the mainstream pop chart, the R&B chart, and the Country and Western chart at the same time.

Just before the piano exploded as a hard-driving instrument of rock and roll, the great songwriter and pianist Fats Domino from the "Big Easy" (New Orleans, LA) scored his first hit in 1955 with "Ain't That A Shame," making the **crossover** from boogie-woogie into the teenage market seem as mellow and effortless as his hometown's reputation. He followed this with a series of hit singles that have become classics of early rock and roll, such as "Blueberry Hill" and "I'm Walkin." Domino represents one of the less aggressive of the early rock and roll musicians. It is intriguing to watch him in feature films such as *Don't Knock the Rock* (1956) in which the way he sings to the camera seems so obviously to be inviting you into the music making process itself. You almost don't notice the subtle restraint of the partition ropes set up to segregate the black performers from the white audience depicted in the film.

Whereas Fats Domino was essentially smooth and mellow, many independent record producers were looking for something rough and forceful. Ruth Brown, with her 1953 R & B crossover hit, "Mama He Treats Your Daughter Mean," showed how gospel could be the source of this force and energy. Other artists, such as Ray Charles, had crossover success with a blend of rhythm and blues and gospel. But the real breakthrough to a highly charged, aggressive rock and roll piano star came with Richard Wayne Penniman, otherwise known as **Little Richard**.

A gay, black man from Macon, Georgia, Little Richard combined the ecstatic extremism of Pentecostal spirituality with the most risqué, adult entertainment focusing in his songs on explicit detail about sexual encounters, whether hetero- or homosexual. No matter what his sexual orientation it would be difficult at any time in the history of rock to find a musician wilder, more energetic, and more infectious than Little Richard. Rock musicians as diverse as Paul McCartney, Bruce Springsteen, Boy George, and Lemmy Kilmister have praised Little Richard as a path breaker. And everyone knows that there was no musician more energized on stage and off stage than Little Richard.

The story of Little Richard's breakthrough is another one of those "great moments" in rock history when a new sound emerges. At some point in that fateful year of 1955, Specialty Records entrepreneurs Arthur Rupe and Robert "Bumps" Blackwell were looking for what they describe today in Hollywood as a "meets." In this case it was "Fat Domino meets Ray Charles." Blackwell described Little Richard that day as "a cat in this loud shirt with hair waved up six inches above his head . . . talking wild, thinking up stuff just to be different . . . a mega-personality" (White 1994, p. 47). But the "problem was," as he stated, "what he looked like and what he sounded like didn't come together" (ibid. 49). Perhaps the problem was simple: Richard wasn't playing the piano, he was singing instead with the accompaniment of Fats Domino's back-up band, which included a session pianist.

Furthermore, there were no plans at first to record "Tutti Frutti" even though it was one of Little Richard's most successful songs in his nightclub act. This was because "Tutti Frutti," in its original manifestation, was followed by the words "good booty," which contained explicit references to anal sex, and code words for the gay lifestyle that were designed to amuse and entertain an adult audience at their most uninhibited. Blackwell never would have heard this song had he not taken a break with Richard and gone to a bar next door. Probably just to break the tension, Little Richard performed "Tutti Frutti" before an impromptu audience he discovered there, "hamming it up" as he would do in his live act. This was the sound they were looking for.

They immediately returned to the studio to record the song. But two changes needed to be made. First, they could not use those explicit lyrics. Frutti was undoubtedly a reference to a gay man and "booty" referred to the posterior, just as it does today. In any case, any references to women were references to drag queens. All this needed to be toned down. For this, Blackwell brought in a seasoned lyricist and composer, Dorothy LaBostrie, who obviously needed to listen to Little Richard's song in order to fix the lyrics. But once he took it out of the nightclub context, even Little Richard was a bit shy to perform for a woman and so he faced the wall. All this might suggest that the song would be completely toned down, but there was a second change that charged it right back up. This was to put Little Richard on the piano.

Guided Listening

"Tutti Frutti" by Little Richard

http://app.rhapsody.com/members/wgcve5/playlists/mp.172745299

Little Richard's first big hit song is an excellent example of the blues played at a fast tempo to create a distinctive rock and roll sound.

0:00	Richard sings an intro of nonsense syllables.
0:03	Richard begins the 12-bar blues form, singing the refrain with song's title.
0:16	He sings the nonsense syllables as a rhythmic break.
0:18	Richard then sings the first verse of the song over the 12-bar form.
0:29	Richard sings another rhythmic break while the band plays short, stop-time chords to accent this passage.
0:34	Refrain, ending with the break of nonsense words.
0:49	Verse.
1:00	Richard sings another stop-time break.
1:05	Refrain.
1:20	Saxophone solo over the 12-bar form for one chorus.
1:35	Refrain.
1:51	Verse.
2:02	Another stop-time break.
2:07	Refrain with song ending on the break of nonsense words.

From the time of his youth, Little Richard had been singing for the public, both as a church musician and in his own family group of gospel singers that performed publicly. Even at that time, there was evidence that Little Richard was pushing the boundaries of the music, but if you listen to his early recordings, before Specialty and the music of his mentor Billy Wright, the differences in style were not one of type, but of degree. The piano-based boogie-woogie jump blues that Wright cultivated was simply a tamer style than what Little Richard made famous. Little Richard turned it all up, as he did his own stage act. Richard was well aware of the risks he took with his wild, sexually charged show and was concerned that white kids had to hide his records. Rather than tone it down however, he decided that the more outrageous he became the better. For the teenagers of the 1950s that made up his best audience, it was just fun.

Buddy Holly: The Teenage Auteur

Buddy Holly has been described as a "young man in a hurry." Coming on the scene slightly later than the others we've discussed, the young Charles Hardin Holley (later changed to Holly), seemed to have a drive and ambition that embodied all the energy of the others, but was based on a different goal. More than any other, Buddy Holly it seemed, sought control of his destiny. He paid inordinate attention to contracts, exercised greater artistic control in the studio, branched out into different media, and mentored new talent. By the time he died at the peak of his success, he had had a string of hits, he was maintaining a touring schedule described as "insane," he was preparing for film and Broadway roles, and he had laid the foundation for a conglomerate for recording, publishing, and developing new talent.

In 1955 Buddy Holly had yet to take off. Since 1952, Holly had been playing in a country duo with Bob Montgomery, but in 1955 had expanded this into an Elvis-influenced rockabilly band called The Crickets. After opening for Elvis Presley and Bill Haley, Holly began to get noticed and was signed to major label Decca Records. After his initial recordings with Decca went nowhere, Holly soon found himself in the unusual situation of having two recording contracts, one for The Crickets with Brunswick Records and one for himself with Coral Records. Both labels, ironically, were subsidiaries of Decca. The complications that arose from this would plague him for the rest of his short career.

Beginning with "That'll Be the Day," which went to number one on the pop charts, Buddy Holly had several hits in 1957. One of them was the result of another studio experiment with unexpected results. The original idea was to take Holly's song "Cindy Lou" and add a Latin beat for novelty. Realizing this was not working at all, they pushed the drummer, Jerry Allison, to come up with a different beat. He responded with a basic exercise called the paradiddle that all drummers learn early on. The problem was he played it so loudly that he drowned out the other musicians. Once the drums were moved out of the studio and into the hallway, echo was added. Buddy Holly responded with aggressive down strokes on rhythm guitar and The Crickets came up with one of the most enduring classics of rock and roll. Given his contribution on the drums, it was fitting that Jerry Allison encouraged Holly to rename this song "Peggy Sue" after his then girlfriend and future wife and one of the main sources for biographical information on Buddy Holly to this day. If any song is Buddy Holly's signature song, it is probably "Peggy Sue" which reached number three on the pop charts.

Buddy Holly (1936–1959)

Guided Listening

"Peggy Sue" by Buddy Holly

http://app.rhapsody.com/members/wgcve5/playlists/mp.172745299

0:00	Song opens with a four-bar introduction before starting the 12-bar form.
0:07	Over the 12-bar form, Holly sings the first verse.
0:26	Second verse in 12-bar form.
0:45	This third verse still uses the 12-bar form, but Holly does an unexpected chord substitution in a minor key.
1:04	Fourth verse; notice how Holly changes his vocal style for effect. He begins to exaggerate his voice with hiccupping sounds.
1:24	Guitar solo for one chorus. Holly keeps it very simple but engaging, playing the chords with forceful down strokes on his guitar with a fast, syncopated strumming.
1:43	Repeat of the third verse with the minor key chcrd substitution.
2:02	Another verse.
2:21	He sings an extra vocal tag to end the song.

The Death of Rock and Roll

In spite of all its commercial success, it must be remembered that rock and roll was seen by the older generation as a major threat to society. For a frightened older generation, rock and roll was seen as inextricably linked with juvenile delinquency, miscegenation, overt sexuality, and teenage pregnancy. Some even developed the paranoid idea that rock and roll may have been a plot hatched by Soviet communists to weaken the Western nations during this time of Cold War. With politicians and military leaders nervously fingering the triggers of nuclear weapons on both sides of the "iron curtain," rock and roll could even be seen as a threat to national security. As the teenagers danced with greater abandon, many worried Americans wanted it all to stop.

The campaign against rock and roll was actually there from the very beginning, since theatre owners first reacted to teenagers dancing in the aisles to the music of Blackboard Jungle. As early as 1955, DJ Alan Freed publicly railed against those in the industry and the media who opposed rock and roll and accused them of racial discrimination. The man who first applied the words "rock and roll" to the new teenage music on his radio program worked tirelessly throughout the 1950s as its main promoter, promoting shows by leading rock and roll acts. But by 1958 things started to unravel. With tensions high about the social threat of rock and roll, police were always on alert at Freed's rock and roll shows, so it was only a matter of time before disaster would strike. On May 3, 1958 a riot broke out at one of Freed's shows in Boston resulting in scandal and Freed's arrest.

PAYOLA SCANDAL

Scandal in the late 1950s in which many disc jockeys were found guilty of accepting bribes from promoters to play rock and roll records on their radio programs.

Even more damaging than that incident, Freed was one of many in the media implicated in the **payola scandal** in which independent DJs had been found guilty of taking money from record companies and promoters to play rock and roll records on their radio shows. The scandal was a devastating blow to defenders of rock and roll. Detractors could easily argue that rock and roll music was never really any good otherwise it would not have required the bribes. The music was now tainted with corruption and provided further evidence that Western civilization was somehow endangered by rock and roll. Worst of all, rock and roll could be simply dismissed as a shallow and misguided fad that was never meant to last.

"THE DAY THE MUSIC DIED"

February 3, 1959 was a legendary day in the history of rock and roll: pop stars Buddy Holly, Ritchie Valens, and the Big Bopper were all killed in an airplane crash.

In fact, the "fad" of rock and roll did come to an end in a very symbolic way. Just as 1955 is an important date for the birth of rock and roll, so 1959 is memorable for the death of rock and roll. Referred to as **"the day the music died,"** 1959 will forever be remembered by rock historians for the collapse of rock and roll when a perfect storm struck the major artists of the era. The "day the music died" literally refers to February 3, 1959 when an airplane crash ended the lives of Buddy Holly, Latino rock and roller Ritchie Valens, and rising singer The Big Bopper. This could not have come at a worse time for rock and roll fans. Elvis Presley, the number one rock and roll singer, had enlisted in the army and was away in Europe serving in the military from 1958 to 1960. As John Lennon once famously said, Elvis had "died" when he went into the army. This is because Presley would never make teenage rock and roll with such high energy ever again, focusing after 1960 on making movies and eventually Las Vegas style shows.

In 1959 it seemed as if every major star was being edged out of the picture. Since having a sudden religious conversion on an Australian tour in 1957, Little Richard began seriously studying theology and eventually made a decision to stop playing rock and roll. When his contract with Specialty Records expired in 1959, Richard went into a temporary retirement from music. It was as if even Little

Richard was beginning to believe the idea that rock and roll was the music of the devil and must be suppressed. Further evidence of the moral decline caused by rock and roll was the arrest of Chuck Berry in December 1959 on a violation of the Mann Act because he had transported a 14-year old girl across state lines. An even more sensational and damaging morality scandal brought down the great Jerry Lee Lewis who married his 13-year old cousin, resulting in an industry blacklisting of Lewis that halted his skyrocketing career.

But the most insidious nail in the coffin of rock was provided by the music industry itself. By 1959 a new formula for packaging music for teenagers was in place and the industry had by now developed a system for providing teenagers with clean looking teen idols that smiled sweetly and sang the new music. The biggest selling artist of 1959 was not Elvis, Richard, or Berry, but the well-scrubbed, fresh-faced **Pat Boone** who sang cleaned-up cover versions of rock and roll songs to a teenage audience ready to consume pre-packaged pop. To supply music for singers like Pat Boone and rising stars such as Paul Anka and Frankie Avalon, a new Tin Pan Alley was born in the Brill Building of New York with young songwriters writing the songs, song-pluggers promoting the songs, and record executives collecting the royalties on the songs in a music industry reinvigorated by the brief explosion of rock and roll. By the early 1960s it seemed as if nothing had changed and pop music had become as bland as ever. But then rock and roll would have a second coming from England that would provide an even bigger explosion.

References

White, Charles. 1994. *The Life and Times of Little Richard.* New York: Da Capo.

The Art of Modern Jazz 15

KEY TERMS

- New Orleans Jazz
- Swing
- Bebop
- Latin Jazz
- Chorus
- Cool Jazz
- Hard Bop
- Modal Jazz
- Avant-Garde (Free Jazz)
- Fusion

KEY FIGURES

- Coleman Hawkins
- Lester Young
- Charlie Parker
- Dizzy Gillespie
- Thelonious Monk
- Miles Davis
- John Coltrane
- Ornette Coleman
- Herbie Hancock
- Wayne Shorter
- Lester Bowie

Jazz is one of the cornerstones of American popular music. But jazz challenges our very notion of "popular" music as mass-mediated music designed for entertainment. Jazz has always been mass mediated, but the only time the music was massively popular was during the Swing Era of the 1930s and 40s (as discussed in Chapter 13). Actually, it was after World War II when jazz was no longer the top selling genre of popular music, when many of the greatest figures of jazz created the styles that jazz fans know and love today. Consequently, many people think of jazz not as "popular" music, but as a kind of art music performed by highly trained professionals and listened to by aficionados. Thus, jazz itself has a kind of split personality between art and entertainment. This split can be seen historically. Before World War II, jazz began as entertainment in the pleasure districts of New Orleans and grew into Big Band Swing music with a central position in the popular music industry. After World War II, jazz began to develop as a form of art music, progressing over the next four decades through a series of stylistic innovations by each subsequent generation of musicians. Jazz styles originating before 1945, such as **New Orleans Jazz** and **Swing** are categorized together as Classic Jazz or Traditional Jazz. The many styles of jazz created after 1945 are generally referred to as Modern Jazz.

NEW ORLEANS JAZZ

Also known as Dixieland, New Orleans Jazz refers to the earliest jazz style to develop in the city of New Orleans in the first decade of the 20th century before spreading to Chicago and New York after 1910.

SWING

A form of jazz music that dominated American popular music in the late 1930s and early 1940s featuring big bands that provided music for dancing.

BEBOP

A form of jazz music developed during the 1940s that broke with earlier forms of jazz such as Swing and New Orleans Jazz in its emphasis on complex melodies, unexpected rhythmic accents and harmonic substitutions.

The remarkable thing about this division is how suddenly jazz music seemed to change as soon as World War II came to an end. As swing dancer Frankie Manning recalls in Ken Burns's documentary on the history of jazz:

> "I was in the army for five years. I came out in 1947. And I come out of the army and I hear (mimicking fast chaotic music) . . . I just could not get accustomed to that. I said what is this? What's going on, you know?" (Manning quoted in *Jazz: A Film By Ken Burns*, 2001).

What was going on was a new kind of jazz, called **bebop**, the first style of modern jazz characterized by fast tempo, complex melodies, and sudden rhythmic accents to which musicians would play extended improvisations. This music was a complete shock to Frankie because the tempo of the music, the unexpected rhythmic accents and unfamiliar melodies made it completely unsuitable for dancing. Frankie's comment about being away in the army is also significant. A brief gap of time between swing music and bebop was created by a musicians strike and a wartime ban on pressing records due to a shellac shortage, making it seem as if the music had completely transformed after resurfacing from a dormant period near the end of the war.

Historians have had a lot to say about this sudden change, too. Musicologist Scott Deveaux describes how the change from swing to bebop can be described in terms of revolution or evolution. The revolutionary theory of the birth of modern jazz is probably the more widely accepted theory. In this model, musicians playing in swing bands were becoming fed up with playing the standardized arrangements that big bands were built on. Because swing was all about the dancers, musicians had the job of making the most engaging dance music and big bands structured their music entirely around providing that dance friendly formula. Although big band music did feature soloists who improvised within this format, there was a feeling among many musicians that the artistry of their music was getting shortchanged. But the question remains: how could bebop musicians suddenly innovate a new form of music?

The evolutionary theory of the birth of bebop answers this question. According to this model, certain individual musicians playing in big bands (such as saxophonists **Coleman Hawkins** and **Lester Young**, and trumpeter Roy Eldridge to name just a few), gradually began to push the boundaries of what could be done in jazz improvisation. Although they played in dance bands, the most creative musicians could create innovative improvisations with unusual harmonies and complex syncopation in their solos. If one listens to recordings of some of the most acclaimed swing musicians, such as Coleman Hawkins's 1939 hit recording of the song "Body and Soul," one can hear the roots of the musical ideas of bebop that the founders of the music would pursue during the mid-1940s.

Miles Davis Goes in Search of Bird

In 1944 an 18-year-old named **Miles Davis** came to New York to go to school, but things turned out a lot differently than his parents had planned. This young accomplished trumpeter was on his way to begin his studies at the prestigious Julliard School of Music where he would study the techniques and theory of Western Classical Music. But the first thing Davis did when he got to New York was seek out legendary alto saxophonist **Charlie "Yardbird" Parker**. Davis had already met Charlie Parker earlier that year when he came to East St. Louis, Illinois where Miles was finishing high school. Parker and another jazz great, trumpeter Dizzy Gillespie, were both in town playing in Billy Eckstine's Band. Miles Davis was fortunate enough to get called in to play trumpet because one of the trumpet players in the band was ill. So, when Miles Davis arrived in New York seeking new musical experiences, the first thing he did was to track down Charlie Parker. Much to the dismay of his parents, Miles dropped out of Julliard after only a short time, but did manage to refine his trumpet technique and learn a lot about music theory that he found useful. Miles's real school, however, was the nightclub world of jazz that was at that moment in the process of giving birth to bebop, the musical style that would define the future of jazz as art music of the 20th century.

Miles Davis not only found Charlie Parker, he joined Parker's band in the late 1940s and together with Charlie Parker, Dizzy Gillespie, Thelonious Monk, and others founded what has come to be known as Modern Jazz. But this was just the beginning for the young Miles Davis. As the new progressive idea of jazz developed—the notion that musicians must innovate within jazz—new jazz styles developed every few years to challenge the already existing styles. This was a kind of avant-garde movement that was operating at an incredibly fast pace and Miles was responsible for spearheading several of these new styles. Indeed one could teach the whole history of Modern Jazz simply by examining Miles Davis alone as he was always at the center of innovation. We will return to Miles Davis a few more times in this chapter. First, let's examine how Bebop came about.

The Birth of Bebop

Bebop jazz was built first and foremost on musical virtuosity. Alto saxophonist Charlie "Yardbird" Parker is today regarded as the all-time undisputed virtuoso of bebop. Although there were several other key innovators involved, Parker is often credited with single-handedly creating the bebop style during the 1940s through his imaginative improvisation. After World War II, as word spread of the new style and the new star of the saxophone who improvised flurries of notes at high speed, Parker became famous in jazz circles in New York and eventually with musicians and audiences around the country. However, Charlie Parker was not al-

Charlie Parker (1920–1955)

ways considered a virtuoso and it took some time before the new style was fully understood and accepted.

Like many professional musicians who came up in the 1930s, Parker began playing in big bands. The swing era provided many opportunities for musicians. In a big band that played music for dancers, particularly good musicians like Parker might get the opportunity to play a brief solo, but such improvisation was usually tightly controlled in the big band context. As a way to get around these professional restrictions, musicians began to have informal jam sessions in which they would be free to show off their musical skills or "chops." Often called "cutting contests" because of the fierce level of competition, musicians would come to these sessions held in the after hours, after playing their regular gigs and let loose on their instrument. It was at one of these after hours jam sessions in Kansas City's Reno Club in 1937 when Parker got the chance to jam with the great drummer Jo Jones of Count Basie's band and made a distinct impression—except it wasn't the positive kind.

Only 17-years-old at the time, Parker had been experimenting with new ways to improvise over the chord progressions on standard Tin Pan Alley songs. His moment came when he was jamming with Jo Jones on the classic standard tune "I've Got Rhythm" and he got his chance to play a solo. Parker seized the moment to try out one of his ideas—substituting a chord for the one everyone expected to hear. His bold experiment got everyone's attention but unfortunately it caused Parker to first lose track of the underlying melody and then lose the beat until he ultimately had to stop playing. Jo Jones threw a cymbal at Parker's feet which came down with a crash to which the group responded with laughter. Parker left this jam session in shame, but that did not stop his experimentation. Especially after he moved to New York and became a part of the most active jazz scene in the country.

After hours jam sessions became a regular part of musical life in New York City in the early 1940s. For many working musicians, jamming for the creativity and the sheer fun of playing after work became a regular practice. The regular jam sessions at Monroe's and Minton's Playhouse were instrumental to the development of the new style of bebop. It was here that Parker, trumpeter Dizzy Gillespie, pianist Thelonious Monk, drummer Max Roach, and others forged a new style that was decidedly anti-entertainment. Dissatisfied with their roles as music "workers" in big bands playing for social dance, their new music would be treated not only as an art form that belonged to them, the skill it took to play this fast paced, complex music would make it a musical form that would be exclusively their own, at least for the time being.

The very name bebop epitomized the new sound as it was derived from musical practice. Words like "bebop" and "reebop" were actually onomatopoeically expressing the sounds made in the music, with long complicated strings of notes often ending with a sudden stop that sounded like "bee-bop." As beboppers were routinely jamming and creating new melodies to go on top of chord changes of Tin Pan Alley standard tunes, there were too many melodies to remember so some songs were just referred to as "bebop." In our first listening example you can hear the appearance of this characteristic bebop phrase.

Guided Listening

"Koko" (Original Take 2) by Charlie Parker (rec. 1945)

http://app.rhapsody.com/artist/charlie-parker/album/the-charlie-parker-story-savoy-jazz

This recording of "Koko" demonstrates many of the features of bebop. The "song" or "head melody" written by Parker is new, but the chords used are the same as the song "Cherokee," an important song for Parker who began improvising on it in search of his new style of playing. The recording also features the co-founder of bebop, trumpeter Dizzy Gillespie. They are joined by Argonne Thornton on piano, Curly Russell on bass, and Max Roach on the drums. Miles Davis was in the studio recording with the band that day, but did not appear on this particular song.

The song follows the 32-bar AABA structure that we discussed in Chapter 13. This can be diagrammed as follows, with each slash mark indicating one four-beat bar:

	Bar: 1	2	3	4	5	6	7	8
Sec. A	/	/	/	/	/	/	/	/
A	/	/	/	/	/	/	/	/
B	/	/	/	/	/	/	/	/
A	/	/	/	/	/	/	/	/

Because bebop musicians were intentionally trying to make things complicated, it can be difficult to follow, especially since the "head melody" played at the beginning is so confusing, mixing unison playing with solo improvisation. If you count really fast, however, you might be able to follow the structure of the song. The AABA pattern begins at 0:25.

0:00 An introduction is played by Parker on saxophone and Gillespie on trumpet playing a melody in unison.

0:07 Gillespie plays an improvised solo on trumpet with a Harmon mute placed in the bell of his trumpet, giving it a muted sound.

0:12 Parker responds with an improvised solo on saxophone.

0:19 Parker and Gillespie play in unison again . . .

0:21 . . . and play the sound "be-bop" in unison.

0:23 . . . and a quick flurry of notes in unison to lead into the 32-bar form.

0:25 Section A begins with the chords of "Cherokee" as Charlie Parker plays an improvised saxophone solo on top of these chords.

0:38 Section A again as Parker's solo continues.

0:51 Section B begins.

1:03 Section A again.

1:16 The AABA form begins again as Parker "takes another chorus."

1:42 Here Parker is soloing over the B section of the form.

2:08 Max Roach begins a drum solo which he plays for exactly 16 bars.

2:30 The introduction is restated by Parker and Gillespie leading to the end of the song.

Dizzy Gillespie: Popularizing Bebop

Along with Charlie Parker, **Dizzy Gillespie** was the other great co-founder and improviser of the new style of bebop. Dizzy Gillespie helped define the bebop style of playing with his dynamic trumpet style featuring wide-ranging interval leaps and rapid bursts of notes, often followed by sudden, unexpected pauses. He was such a virtuoso of the trumpet that many other trumpet players of the time chose not to copy him and instead copied other trumpeters with simpler playing styles. Another aspect of his role in the early development of bebop was as a teacher and theorist. Compared to the more intuitive and spontaneous approach of Charlie Parker to harmonic experimentation, Gillespie could articulate the theory behind the harmonies. In jam sessions he would sometimes sit at the piano and explain to others about how jazz harmonies worked—how to substitute the usual chord of a song with a new chord. This kind of chord substitution helped create the sense of surprise that was highly valued by the musicians.

Although Gillespie embodied the sound and style of bebop better than any of his contemporaries, he was actually very concerned that the beboppers' commitment to high art would marginalize the new music so he sought to popularize bebop and keep it as entertaining as possible. Understanding that popular music is as visual as it is aural, Gillespie exaggerated the look of the bebopper by wearing a beret, growing a goatee, and wearing thick, horn-rimmed glasses giving him the look of a serious—if somewhat comic—performing artist. While bebop musicians had carefully crafted the serious art of the small ensemble to counter big band entertainment, Gillespie formed a bebop big band to try and popularize the music. As bandleader and front man he pulled out all the stops to entertain audiences, singing and dancing in a comic style.

Gillespie never actually succeeded in making bebop mass entertainment with his big band. By the late 1940s, many African Americans had moved away from jazz and were listening to the Rhythm and Blues of Louis Jordan, Wynonie Harris, Etta James, and others. Bebop would forever be reserved for an audience of aficionados, be they black or white, and there was nothing Dizzy Gillespie could do to bring their music to center stage in popular music. Bebop would not have any real hit records, but its influence on jazz and American culture was immense. While the early style of fast, frenetic bebop was short-lived, the music became an important influence on the literary underground of the late 1940s, becoming the music of choice for the beat generation of writers. Jack Kerouac, Allen Ginsberg, and other writers celebrated the early bebop of Parker and Gillespie in their novels and poetry, connecting the freedom and spontaneity of the music to their writing style and personal philosophies (although most of the bebop musicians distanced themselves somewhat from the hipster crowd, not seeing a connection between their disciplined music and the beat generation's wildness).

If bebop had any failures, it was in areas other than the music. Unfortunately, the bebop environment in which musicians identified themselves as cultural outsiders led many of the musicians to abuse drugs. Especially damaging was heroin, a drug that not only ruined many musical performances, but led to the premature deaths of many musicians. The most significant premature death was Charlie Parker himself who died in 1955 at age 34 from a heart attack. His body was ravaged by years of heroin abuse and alcohol. For a time many musicians were addicted to heroin in emulation of Charlie Parker, but it became clear to drug addicted musicians such as Miles Davis that it would be necessary to break free of the heroin habit if one were to truly progress in jazz.

Guided Listening

"Manteca" by Dizzy Gillespie and His Orchestra (rec. 1947)

http://app.rhapsody.com/artist/dizzy-gillespie/album/the-complete-rca-victor-recordings-1937-1949/track/manteca

As a popularizer, Gillespie was more successful with another innovation that had a longer lasting impact on jazz. In the late 1940s, he began to combine bebop with Latin music and created the genre of **Latin Jazz**. "Manteca" is one of Gillespie's most famous songs, composed with Cuban percussionist Chano Pozo and arranger Gil Fuller. Pozo can be heard shouting the name of the song, "Manteca," which literally means cooking lard in Spanish, but it was actually a code word for marijuana among bebop musicians and hipsters at the time.

0:00 Introduction on the bass and the bongos.

0:08 Saxophone enters playing a two-note riff and is gradually joined by the rest of the brass section of Gillespie's orchestra.

0:19 Gillespie's virtuosic trumpet improvisation begins here.

0:38 The first chorus of the "song" is heard here with a phrase played by the saxophones to which the brass instruments respond.

0:49 The same pattern of call and response is repeated here.

1:00 A bridge section begins with a melody, followed by a trumpet solo by Gillespie.

1:22 Return to the A section of the song.

1:34 Return to the same music as heard in the introduction.

1:48 Second chorus begins with a solo on the tenor saxophone.

2:10 The bridge is heard again with another trumpet solo by Gillespie.

2:33 Back to the call and response pattern.

2:44 Return to the intro music.

LATIN JAZZ

Jazz that uses Latin American rhythms, as heard in the Latin music of Dizzy Gillespie and Tito Puente.

Thelonious Monk: Modern Jazz Composition and Improvisation

The early beboppers had laid the groundwork for how the model of composition and improvisation would function in most modern jazz to come in the ensuing decades. This new model, despite being based on something as avant-garde sounding as bebop, maintained the stability of the song at the center of it all. Standard pop songs were not to be abandoned, but used for their chord changes which were seen as flexible and could be altered by the performer or composer. Jazz musicians might play popular melodies from Broadway shows or blues songs or they might create new melodies based on standard chord progressions, but the song would always be the basis for the improvising jazz musician. The standard jazz approach that still exists today

Thelonious Monk (1917–1982)

CHORUS

The word "chorus" has multiple meanings in American popular music: in terms of song form it refers to a section of words and melody that repeat (also called refrain); in terms of performance it refers to one cycle of the song form (e.g., "play one chorus").

is for the bandleader to first "call the tune" so that every musician in the group knows what to play. The musicians begin by playing the song or "head" melody as a group one or two times, then each soloist would take turns improvising over the chord progression, always keeping track of the melody implied in the background. After each soloist takes a turn improvising over any number of cycles of the melody—called a **chorus**—the group once again plays the head melody one more time to finish the piece.

Guided Listening

"Epistrophy" by Thelonious Monk with John Coltrane

http://app.rhapsody.com/artist/thelonious-monk/album/thelonious-monk-with-john-coltrane

This is an example of a classic composition in modern jazz by one of the founders of bebop, Thelonious Sphere Monk. This recording features two of the most famous soloists from two different historical eras playing tenor saxophones: **Coleman Hawkins** was one of the pioneers of jazz improvisation who inspired the beboppers and John Coltrane was younger, coming on the scene in the late 1940s and becoming one the biggest stars of avant-garde jazz of the 1950s and 1960s.

The melody of "Epistrophy" is not your typical Tin Pan Alley pop song, but it does follow the standard form of 32 bars in an AABA structure and its strange melody with odd phrasing is a well-known bebop tune. What you hear in this example is four choruses of "Epistrophy": one opening chorus of the melody played as a group, one solo chorus by the tenor saxophonist, one solo chorus by the trumpet player, and one final chorus of the melody by the group. See if you can follow along with the 32-bar form which is much slower than "Koko" that we heard earlier.

	Bar: 1	*2*	*3*	*4*	*5*	*6*	*7*	*8*
Sec. A	/	/	/	/	/	/	/	/
A	/	/	/	/	/	/	/	/
B	/	/	/	/	/	/	/	/
A	/	/	/	/	/	/	/	/

Because bebop musicians were intentionally trying to make things complicated, it can be difficult to follow, especially since the "head melody" played at the beginning is so confusing, mixing unison playing with solo improvisation. If you count really fast, however, you might be able to follow the structure of the song. The AABA pattern begins at 0:25.

0:00 Drum solo introduction.

0:05 The entire group begins playing the "head" melody of "Epistrophy" composed by Thelonious Monk. Like a standard Tin Pan Alley song, it lasts 32 bars and is divided into four sections of 8 bars each. The first 8 bars repeat once, followed by 8 bars of new music, then the first 8 bars repeat again to finish the cycle.

0:17 Another 8 bars of A are played.

0:29 The B section features new chords.

0:40 The A section chords and melody return.

0:51 The cycle begins again and the first soloist, John Coltrane on tenor saxophone, plays an improvisation over the chords of the song. Coltrane plays one chorus.

1:35 Without a pause, the saxophone player stops and the trumpet player, Ray Copeland, begins a solo at the beginning of the 32-bar cycle. The trumpeter plays one chorus.

2:19 The entire ensemble plays the head melody one last time. Listen for the drummer playing a rapid, repeating pattern on hi-hat cymbals that pulls against the regular rhythm of the piece.

Cool Jazz: Miles Davis Finds His Own Sound

Miles Davis (1926–1991)

Miles Davis may have been there at the beginning, playing the new jazz in Charlie Parker's band, but it took him a while to find his sound. Finding the right sound for playing bebop on trumpet was no easy task. The leading bebop trumpet player in the early days was Dizzy Gillespie, but his skill level was so advanced and his high-flying, acrobatic style was so extremely difficult to copy that very few trumpet players ever did copy Dizzy. Miles Davis developed his own sound by going in the opposite direction. Instead of blowing flurries of intense, high register notes at breakneck speed, Miles played in a more relaxed manner with a slower tempo and left open spaces in his solos. In the late 1940s he was beginning to find a sound that was not so "hot" as Dizzy Gillespie's playing style. In fact, his style could best be described as "cool"—a laid-back style built on an economical approach to playing just the right note at the right time, a style that could be even more intense emotionally than if he had played at a faster tempo.

Davis not only began developing his own playing style, he helped develop a new style of music to suit his playing style. **Cool jazz** was a style characterized by more relaxed tempos and a lighter tone than heard in early bebop. Unlike early bebop that shocked listeners with melodies that seemed to go in unexpected directions and sudden rhythmic accents, cool jazz tended to be more calm and even, giving a feeling of relaxation to the listener. Although entirely different in tone than bebop, cool jazz was still art music and maintained a kind of sophisticated, cerebral approach to extending the boundaries of jazz. Miles Davis made a series of recordings in 1949–50 with an expanded 9-piece band (nonet) that expanded the timbral palette of jazz. Miles took a typical bebop quintet of trumpet, alto sax, piano, bass, and drums and added trombone, baritone sax, tuba, and French horn, suggesting something more akin to a wind ensemble in classical music. These recordings were released individually on 78 rpm records in the early 1950s and eventually packaged as an album released in 1957 titled *The Birth of the Cool.* With the launching of Cool Jazz, Miles Davis began a lifelong career of innovating new styles with young players who would then go on to further develop the style launched by Miles. Further developments of Cool Jazz feature groups such as the Modern Jazz Quartet led by pianist John Lewis who played on *The Birth of the Cool* and went on to experiment with including classical music in jazz, one of the unique aspects of the cool jazz style.

COOL JAZZ

A style of jazz created in the wake of bebop that features more relaxed tempos and a lighter tone than early bebop.

Guided Listening

"Jeru" by Miles Davis and His Orchestra (rec. 1949)

http://app.rhapsody.com/artist/miles-davis/album/the-masters-of-jazz-33-best-of-miles-davis

"Jeru" is a composition written by baritone saxophonist Gerry Mulligan and recorded by the nine-piece band Miles assembled for the recordings that resulted in the album *Birth of the Cool* (released in 1957). This recording features the nine-piece band (nonet) that Miles Davis put together to create a new, smoother sounding jazz than early bebop, but a sound that was even more complex.

The structure of this piece is a departure from the usual song structure. The form of this song is AABA, but using a different form than we have heard so far. The A phrases are eight bars long, but the B phrase is 12 bars in length with the middle four bars switching to triple meter. Furthermore, the head melody played at the end of the song is not the same as the head melody played at the beginning (but the B phrase is the same).

0:00	The entire band plays the melody of A.
0:10	The band repeats A.
0:21	B section is played with the first four bars in 4/4 meter . . .
0:27	. . . then four bars in 3/4 meter
0:30	. . . then the last four bars in 4/4 are played with the baritone saxophone in the lead.
0:36	A section returns.
0:48	Miles Davis plays a trumpet solo over a regular 32-bar form of AABA.
1:31	Full band reenters playing an arrangement in stop-time that sounds like triple meter.
1:35	Mulligan plays a solo.
1:41	The stop-time arrangement is repeated.
1:47	Mulligan solos again.
2:13	Final chorus is played, but the melody is completely different from the first melody heard at the beginning of the song.
2:35	The B section from earlier is heard again with the middle four bars in triple meter.
2:50	The final A section is heard with an extension of four bars at the end.

Hard Bop: Infusing Jazz with Soul

Typical of progressive forms of music, modern jazz was always in a constant state of development from the 1940s to the 1970s. New styles, such as Cool Jazz, invited jazz musicians to innovate further. Some musicians chose to extend the new style just developed and other musicians reacted against the new style by creating a contrasting style. Thus, not long after Cool Jazz became popular in jazz circles (especially in California where the laid back style became known as West Coast Jazz), some jazz musicians turned a different direction. The response to West Coast Cool Jazz came from musicians based on the East Coast who viewed the expanded instrumentation and classical borrowing of Cool jazz as mere gimmicks.

HARD BOP

A style of jazz originating in the 1950s that focused on African American styles of popular music such as the blues, gospel, and R&B.

Hard Bop was a style of jazz that focused on African American styles of popular music such as the blues, gospel, and R & B. Effectively bringing jazz back to its African American roots, many Hard Bop songs featured simple melodies, catchy riffs, and steady rhythmic grooves, inviting dancing and thus moving jazz back toward mainstream popular music. Despite the name, the music was not necessarily "hard" (in the way one might think of "hard rock"), but it was certainly more physical with its danceable, hotter rhythms drawn from R & B, gospel, or Latin music.

Guided Listening

"Moanin'" by Art Blakey and the Jazz Messengers (rec. 1958)

http://app.rhapsody.com/artist/art-blakey/album/moanin-ep

Art Blakey was the most famous of Hard Bop jazz musicians and a bandleader for several decades. His band, The Jazz Messengers, had a constantly changing line-up of young up-and-coming jazz musicians, many of whom would go on to lead their own groups. This recording features a rhythm section made up of Blakey on the drums, Jymie Merritt on bass, and Bobby Timmons on piano who composed this song. The front-line musicians are Lee Morgan on trumpet and Benny Golson on tenor saxophone.

"Moanin'" is an example of Hard Bop that shows the influence of gospel music based on a catchy melody featuring a call and response phrase. The melody is made up of a phrase that functions as the "call," suggesting a gospel preacher calling to the congregation, followed by a two-note "response" (as if the congregation is saying "amen" or "yes, Lord!"). In vocal versions of this song, the singers actually respond with the words "yes, Lord." Unlike the more complex example of cool jazz we heard from Miles Davis, "Moanin'" keeps everything simple by following the standard 32-bar AABA form, stating the head at the beginning and end of the song, and giving each soloist plenty of time to play improvised solos in between. Compared to "Jeru" and Charlie Parker's "Koko," "Moanin'" is very easy to follow—what is sometimes called "straight ahead."

0:00 First A phrase of 8 bars: the piano states the first phrase . . .

0:03 . . . and the band responds with two notes.

0:15 Second A phrase: this time the trumpet and the saxophone state the call and the piano, bass, and drums respond.

0:31 The B section, or bridge, features new music that is accentuated by the swinging rhythm that starts here, provided by Blakey's drums and Merritt's "walking" bass.

0:44 Return to the 8-bar A phrase played the same as the first at the beginning, led by the piano.

1:00 The first solo is taken by trumpeter Lee Morgan who plays two choruses of 32 bars.
Note the bluesy notes and funky riffs (repeating notes) played by Morgan which were common features in Hard Bop improvisation.

3:04 The next solo is taken by saxophonist Benny Golson who begins by copying the same notes that Morgan plays at the end of his solo. Golson also plays two choruses of the 32-bar form.

4:03 Note how Golson's second chorus shifts to the higher register of the saxophone.

5:04 The next solo is taken by pianist Bobby Timmons who also plays in a bluesy, funky style with lots of repeating riffs. He also plays a number of descending glissandos.

7:03 The final solo is by Merritt on bass who takes only one chorus of the 32-bar form.

8:00 Finally the band returns to the very beginning of the song with the piano-led A phrase, the horn-led A phrase, the swinging B section, and final return to the piano-led A phrase.

8:56 To end the song, the band plays the first four bars of the B section three times and Timmons ends with bluesy piano flourishes.

Modal Jazz: Miles Innovates Again

In the late 1950s, Miles Davis innovated again. This time Miles was responding to the standardization of modern jazz, specifically reacting against the usual chord progressions used in jazz. In spite of all the creativity required of musicians in order to improvise over the chord progressions of popular songs, the predictability of those chord progressions made it easy for musicians to lapse into equally predictable musical phrases. Miles Davis—who was getting a reputation for bringing out the best in the players he hired for his band—found a new way to avoid those same old chord progressions and jolt good musicians out of any lazy habits of improvisation.

In the spring of 1959, Miles had assembled a band of some of the top improvisers in jazz at the time and brought them into Columbia Records's 30th Street Studio. The band included the rhythm section of bassist Paul Chambers, drummer

Jimmy Cobb, and a phenomenal young pianist, Bill Evans. The melodic front line of this group consisted of Miles on trumpet, along with alto saxophonist Julian "Cannonball" Adderley, and tenor saxophonist John Coltrane. Miles had called this stellar group of musicians into the recording studio with no prior rehearsal—he planned to record them in the most spontaneous way possible. When the session began he handed each musician small bits of paper on which were written the most minimal instructions—scales and melody lines that would be the basis for their improvisation. Miles's plan to record the entire album as a first take did not actually pan out, but the performances he got from his musicians were not only spontaneous, they resulted in the remarkable recordings that would become the most famous jazz album of all time, *Kind of Blue* (1959).

MODAL JAZZ

A style of jazz in which musicians improvise on modes instead of the usual chord progressions of popular songs.

Miles's innovation became known as **modal jazz**—a style of jazz in which musicians would improvise on modes instead of the usual chord progressions of popular songs as jazz musicians had been doing from the beginning. The small slips of paper that Miles had given his performers indicated the mode or set of pitches that they should use in their improvisations. More importantly, Miles kept the structure of each piece very simple by reducing the number of chords used. Instead of a typical pop song in which many chords occur and change frequently—once every four beats or even two or three times within a single four-beat measure—the pieces Miles composed might feature a single chord played for eight or sixteen measures to give each soloist plenty of time to "explore" the mode in their improvisation. Underlying this slow moving harmonic rhythm might be pedal points or drones—repeating notes that seem to "hum" a sturdy foundation upon which musicians could build compelling solos without lapsing into any cliché phrases. Furthermore, the result was as successful commercially as it was creatively and Miles Davis became the highest paid musician in jazz of that era.

Guided Listening

"So What" by Miles Davis (rec. 1959)

http://app.rhapsody.com/artist/miles-davis/album/kind-of-blue-bonus-tracks

"So What" is the first track on Miles Davis's landmark album Kind of Blue (1959). In his effort to avoid all clichés of jazz improvisation, he composed this song on a very simple formula. Although the song is structured with a 32-bar AABA form, it uses only two chords in the entire song, D minor 7 (for the A phrase) and Eb minor 7 (for the B phrase). Such a subtle shift of just a half-step up and down between A and B was very unusual and had no precedence in popular music at the time. Consequently, instead of improvising on the chords of a song, each soloist improvises in a mode, in this case the Dorian mode, one of the ancient Greek or "church" modes that we mentioned back in Chapter Two on Medieval Music. With only two chords to worry about, each soloist has a chance to relax and "explore the mode," in much the same way improvisers do in Indian classical music or the Arab world (as we mentioned in Chapter 9 on Asian Music). On this classic recording, Miles Davis's stellar line up of musicians each came up with stunningly original solos by playing in the Dorian mode.

0:00 An introduction is played by Bill Evans on piano, accompanied by Paul Chambers on the bass before the 32-bar form begins. Chambers finishes the introduction which leads into his opening statement of the melody.

0:33 The first A phrase begins: Chambers states the melody on the bass as a call . . .

0:35 . . . and the piano responds with a phrase that sounds like "so what!"

0:47 Chambers continues the call in the second A phrase and the entire band responds.

1:02 Chambers continues the call in the B phrase, just one half-step higher than the A phrase and the band responds.

1:16	Chambers goes back down a half step for the A phrase again and the band responds.
1:30	Miles takes the first solo on trumpet, playing in the Dorian mode in the A section . . .
1:59	. . . and shifts up a half step for the B section . . .
2:14	. . . and back down again to play along with the A section.
2:28	Miles begins another chorus. Notice how seamlessly it sounds because there is no chord change between repetitions of the AABA pattern. Also notice how laid back and relaxed Miles Davis's trumpet solo sounds. This is very characteristic of the "cool" sound that made Miles so famous.
3:26	The next soloist is John Coltrane on tenor saxophone who starts at the beginning of the 32-bar cycle. He plays two choruses of 32 bars.
5:16	The next soloist is Cannonball Adderley on alto saxophone, which is in a higher register than the tenor sax and is easy to miss if you don't listen carefully. Adderley plays two choruses.
7:05	The next chorus features Bill Evans on the piano with "so what" responses played by the band. Evans phrases his part so it sounds like he is responding to the others.
8:03	Evans then plays one extra A phrase as a transition back to the head melody.
8:15	Chambers states the call of the opening melody with the band responding through the 32-bar AABA form. Atypical of jazz of the time, the track fades out.

Freedom and the Avant-Garde in Jazz

One of the reasons for the success of modal jazz was that the method of using harmonic simplicity to inspire creativity resonated with one of the most important values underlying jazz—freedom. The same can be said of early bebop. When Parker, Gillespie, Monk, and others created bebop, the greater freedom of musical expression they were seeking was also a freedom of social expression. Playing music in a society in which African Americans were still treated as second-class citizens and subjected to relentless racial discrimination (especially in the Southern states where they often toured and suffered humiliation regularly on the road), the need for freedom in music and in everyday life was paramount. It is easy to think of these new freedoms in jazz music as a metaphor for the freedom African Americans sought in everyday life. The modal jazz approach of Miles Davis had "freed" jazz musicians from the boundaries of the conventional pop song by casting off harmonic structure that could be seen as restricting human expression. For those in search of greater freedom, other key elements of music—such as rhythm, pitch, and timbre—could also be liberated and in the late 1950s the time was right.

African Americans' dissatisfaction with living in a society that was still segregated after World War II—a war in which black soldiers fought and died alongside white soldiers—had reached its zenith in the 1950s. The growing civil rights movement led by Dr. Martin Luther King, Jr. of the1950s set the stage for a volatile political climate in the 1960s and music played a significant part, especially modern jazz. As Dr. King gave speech after speech calling for "freedom," jazz musicians responded with greater efforts toward musical freedom in which there would be no more shackles on expression. As the rhetoric of the time period heated up, so did the music, with passion and intensity as an avant-garde revolution took hold.

Jazz in the 1960s was dominated by **Avant-Garde**—a term for various kinds of jazz that in different ways abandon musical conventions of harmony, rhythm, melody, and form in favor of free expression for improvisers and unhindered experimentation. The French term "avant-garde"—literally the advance troops that attack before the regular forces are launched—had been applied to various art movements since the 19th century that have violently attacked convention. This

AVANT-GARDE (FREE JAZZ)
Jazz that abandons musical conventions of harmony, rhythm, melody, and form in favor of free expression for improvisers and open experimentation.

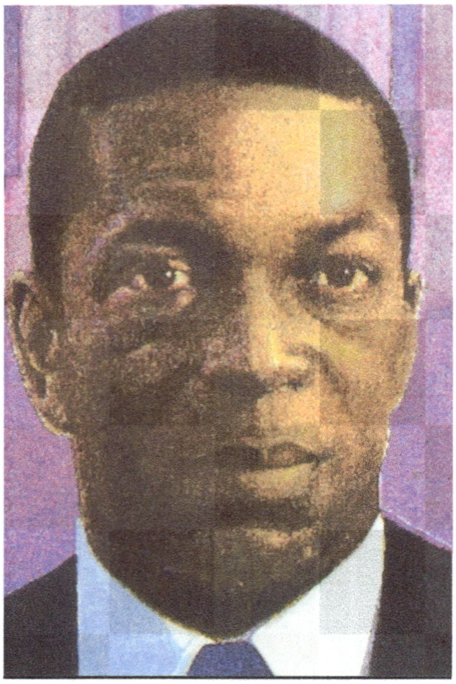

John Coltrane (1926–1967)

term suggesting confrontation was aptly applied to the radical jazz movement of the 1960s. Since all conventions could be abandoned, it became difficult for musicians to agree on a name for the new music. Some simply called it "The New Thing." But the most enduring term became **Free Jazz**, after the title of the landmark album *Free Jazz: A Collective Improvisation* (1961) by saxophonist **Ornette Coleman** consisting of a single group improvisation that followed no key signature or conventional harmony.

Many detractors thought the new jazz had gone too far and believed if musicians abandoned even the most cherished sonic features of jazz, such as swing rhythm, it should not be called "jazz" anymore. In fact, some avant-garde jazz musicians agreed with this. Trumpeter **Lester Bowie** of the Art Ensemble of Chicago argued that the word "jazz" was tainted because of its history as music of the American brothel and insisted that they played "Great Black Music" (in keeping with the name of his band). Thus, free jazz of all kinds in the 1960s was highly politicized, with musicians stating claims of serious artistry independent of the crudities of entertainment, using music for political statements against the racism of American society (as exemplified by the music of Charles Mingus), and making powerful spiritual statements that went much further than many thought jazz could ever go.

Guided Listening

"Acknowledgement" by John Coltrane from the album *A Love Supreme* (rec. 1964, released 1965)

http://app.rhapsody.com/artist/john-coltrane/album/a-love-supreme-bonus-tracks

Regarded as one of the masterpieces of avant-garde jazz and John Coltrane's most significant work, the album A Love Supreme epitomized John Coltrane's belief in the universal spiritual power of music. The recording features his most famous quartet with Coltrane on tenor saxophone, McCoy Tyner on piano, Jimmy Garrison on bass, and Elvis Jones on the drums. "Acknowledgement" is the first part of this large, four-part composition for jazz quartet that takes up the entirety of the album. Influenced by Miles Davis's modal jazz, but also by Indian classical improvisation, Coltrane structures this piece according to modes instead of the usual chords of popular songs. Coltrane bases his entire composition on a four-note motive that is as famous in jazz as Beethoven's four-note motive (short-short-short-long) is in Western classical music.

0:00 The work begins in a solemn manner with a single stroke of a gong, followed immediately by Coltrane on tenor saxophone. Coltrane plays in free meter, similar to the raga style of modal improvisation we heard in Classical Indian music, an important influence on Coltrane at this time.

0:31 Bassist Jimmy Garrison begins to play the four-note motive of A Love Supreme, which was conceived by Coltrane as a kind of mantra (a repetitious spiritual chant). Gradually the bass player is joined by the drummer, then the pianist.

1:04 Coltrane begins his solo in the F Dorian mode, but periodically strays away from the mode to play completely free from any harmonic restriction. Coltrane's solo contains references to the four-note motive of the piece.

3:45 Coltrane begins to move to highest register of his instrument and seems to be reaching for some kind of spiritual goal in his solo.

4:54 Coltrane methodically plays the four-note Love Supreme motive twelve times in all twelve keys. He eventually returns to the original key of the piece.

6:06 Coltrane and Jimmy Garrison begin to chant the four-note motive, singing the mantra "A Love Supreme."

6:36 The motive drops down a whole step to Eb. The vocal drops out and one by one each instrument drops out, leaving the bass alone to play the motive to the end of this first section of this large-scale composition.

Fusion Jazz: Miles Davis Responds to Rock

By the 1960s, modern jazz had achieved the status the musicians had been after since the early beginnings of bebop. Miles Davis, who had once been unhappy with the inequity between the socially respectable classical music of the Julliard conservatory and the maligned modern jazz of the New York nightclubs, could finally claim victory for jazz as great art music in the 1960s. Jazz had made its mark on the American cultural landscape. After many stylistic innovations musicians were capable of taking the art of jazz anywhere they wanted to go. But something else was troubling Miles Davis. Jazz was just not that popular anymore.

While bebop had been developing into the art of modern jazz, finalizing the divorce from dancing, blues music had bolstered its rhythmic elements, transforming into vigorous R & B music that claimed the center stage of popularity for African American audiences. Black popular music in the 1960s was dominated by the soul music of James Brown, Wilson Pickett, Otis Redding, and many others. No longer in the mainstream of popular music, jazz had an American audience, but it tended to be older listeners, many of them white and middle-class. In the meantime, young, white audiences had flocked to the new sounds of rock and roll. With jazz in danger of disappearing into a bottomless vortex of the avant-garde on the one hand or dying out entirely as old-fashioned music on the other, Miles Davis decided to innovate again. Miles Davis began merging jazz with rock to once again create a new form of music.

Fusion jazz, or simply **Fusion**, is the term for jazz that incorporates elements of rock, R & B, and funk into jazz, drawing to various degrees on the rhythm, timbre, or form of other kinds of pop music. Miles Davis's move toward a fusion of jazz and rock was not sudden. In fact, when he began his fusion experiments he had been leading one of the most celebrated avant-garde bands in jazz history, a quintet featuring **Herbie Hancock** on piano, **Wayne Shorter** on saxophone, Ron Carter on bass, and Tony Williams on drums. When Hancock arrived at the studio he asked Miles, "where's the piano," and then Miles introduced Herbie to the electric piano, introducing a timbre to jazz that would define the fusion sound in the 1970s. Similarly, bassist Ron Carter was asked to play electric bass guitar on one song on the album, another instrument that would transform the sound of jazz. Davis's next album, *In A Silent Way* (1969), further developed the fusion genre, this time including electric guitarist John McLaughlin. Davis's next album, *Bitches Brew* (1970), became his most successful fusion album, this time with Miles adding electronic effects to his trumpet and featuring long tracks based on extended rock drumming grooves.

FUSION
Jazz that incorporates elements of rock, R&B, and funk into jazz, drawing to various degrees on the rhythm, timbre or form of other kinds of pop music.

While fusion was certainly commercially successful music that led to Davis performing in large rock venues, the music was still in an avant-garde mode with a lot of free form improvising like jazz and yet it was clearly something different from rock music. Fusion was popular, but among many jazz fans it was just as controversial as Free Jazz, with many listeners choosing to stick with Cool or Hard Bop styles. Many rejected the new music of Miles Davis, but Miles never looked back. After the success of *Bitches Brew*, Miles Davis released numerous albums exploring fusion jazz during the 1970s and most of his records sold well. As it usually happened with ensembles organized by Davis, nearly every musician who played on his early fusion albums went on to create their own groups to great acclaim. Some of these groups became the best known jazz fusion groups of the 1970s with names that sounded like rock bands: The Mahavishnu Orchestra (John McLaughlin), Weather Report (Wayne Shorter, Joe Zawinul), and Return to Forever (Chick Corea).

Guided Listening

"Bitches Brew" by Miles Davis (rec. 1969, released 1970)

http://app.rhapsody.com/artist/miles-davis/album/bitches-brew-legacy-edition/track/bitches-brew

"Bitches Brew" is the title track from Miles Davis's best-selling fusion album. Davis's large ensemble is filled with future stars of 1970s fusion jazz, including Wayne Shorter on soprano saxophone (the higher register horn proved to be effective competing with electric instruments), Bennie Maupin on bass clarinet, Chick Corea and Joe Zawinul on electric pianos, John McLaughlin on electric guitar, Dave Holland on bass, Harvey Brooks on electric bass, Jack DeJohnette and Lenny White on drums, and Don Alias and Jim Riley on percussion. Typical of rock albums of the late 1960s and early 1970s, "Bitches Brew" is a long track at 27 minutes, taking up one entire side of the vinyl double album.

0:00 The work opens with a free meter introduction played on the electric pianos by Chick Corea and Josef Zawinul with additional percussion.

0:42 Miles Davis enters on trumpet which is treated with an electronic delay device.

1:23 Listen closely to hear Miles's trumpet overdubbed an octave below the high trumpet sound in the foreground.

2:50 Bassist Harvey Brooks begins a repeating pattern on electric bass, accompanied by Bennie Maupin on bass clarinet, while Miles Davis snaps his fingers.

3:32 The other musicians in the rhythm section join in.

3:53 Miles Davis begins to play a trumpet solo over the repeating groove built up by the rest of the band. Unlike jazz in the usual AABA form, it is unclear how long a solo will last and when a new solo will begin. This open-ended approach was precisely what Miles was after.

6:35 John McLaughlin takes a guitar solo.

7:30 Music quiets down again.

7:45 An electric piano solo seems to start . . .

8:00 . . . but then the electric guitar reenters and seems to pick up where it left off.

8:57 Miles reenters on trumpet.

As you listen to the rest of the track, note how free and open the whole piece sounds, allowing the listener to get lost in the endless swirl of sounds, very similar to the psychedelic rock music that was common in rock music at the time.

This chapter has shown us just how rapidly a genre of popular music such as jazz can develop from popular entertainment to a form of art, going through a whirlwind of stylistic development in a relatively brief span of time. In just 25 years, jazz experienced the kinds of style changes that took several centuries in Western classical music. This is undoubtedly due to the rapid development in technology and socio-cultural change of the post-WWII era. Music in the modern era certainly evolves much faster than ever before. In our next chapter we will examine rock, a music that experienced the artistic revolution even faster than jazz, transforming from the teenage entertainment of rock and roll to the art of rock in the span of just one decade.

References

Burns, Ken. 2001. *Jazz: A Film By Ken Burns.*

16 The Development of Rock

Key Terms

- Counterculture
- Skiffle
- Beatlemania
- Folk Rock
- Psychedelic Rock
- Progressive Rock
- Hard Rock
- Concept Album
- Woodstock
- Altamont

Key Figures

- The Beatles
- Bob Dylan
- The Rolling Stones
- The Beach Boys
- The Who
- Pink Floyd
- The Moody Blues
- Jimi Hendrix
- Led Zeppelin
- The Grateful Dead
- Jefferson Airplane

In the late autumn of 1963, America was waiting for **The Beatles**. Perhaps the darkest time period of a decade that would have many more dark moments, Americans were headed for a bleak and depressing Christmas that year. In the wake of President John F. Kennedy's assassination and the massive social despair of the nation, many Americans planned for a very subdued Christmas celebration. All the youthful promise that Kennedy had initiated when he said, "ask not what your country can do for you, but what you can do for your country," was seemingly obliterated in Dallas, Texas on November 22, 1963. While it can be said that America was waiting for The Beatles, it was actually The Beatles who were waiting for America—waiting for a number one hit single.

In 1963 The Beatles had taken their native England by storm, not only becoming the top act in their home country, but had triggered a social phenomenon called **Beatlemania** that had turned them into massive pop stars who were literally chased through the streets by adoring fans who were fans in the true sense of the word: fanatical. Given their instant success in the UK they surely could have come to the United States anytime and the boys from Liverpool might have welcomed a rest from the pressures of such adulation as they were seeing in England. But America loomed large for The Beatles. They knew they owed their entire existence to American music. They idolized the greats of 1950s rock and roll: Elvis Presley, Little Richard, Chuck Berry, and Buddy Holly. The Beatles had modeled their music on the American Rock and Roll that some had forgotten about since it came to an abrupt end in 1959. In the United States rock and roll was also in a dark age of soft, Tin Pan Alley, formula-driven pop and The Beatles would be the phenomenon to sweep it all away.

BEATLEMANIA
The media term for the social phenomenon of fan frenzy over The Beatles during the early years of their career.

They badly wanted to make it in America, but they wanted to go with a Number One hit record. On January 18, 1964 they got what they wanted. That was the day "I Want to Hold Your Hand" reached Number One on the Billboard Hot 100 chart. In February The Beatles arrived at New York's Kennedy Airport and found that Beatlemania was alive and well in the United States and even bigger than what they had experienced in the UK. American youth went absolutely crazy over The Beatles and the country—for the time being anyway—was knocked out of its doldrums. Hard core rock and roll had come back to America by way of England, but this time it would be more than just a fad. The songs of The Beatles, with their driving beats, singable melodies, and beautiful harmonies, would transform rock and roll and alter the cultural landscape of the Western world in ways no one could have predicted.

The music of The Beatles is at the heart of the development of rock music in the 1960s. While they were not everything that was happening, they were certainly at the hub of everything that was happening. The Beatles can be credited with many stylistic and technical innovations in popular music during the 1960s and, mainly because of their position as musical and cultural leaders were responsible for popularizing the innovations of others as well. This chapter will ex-

Suggested Listening

"I Want to Hold Your Hand" by The Beatles [not available on Rhapsody]

One of many hit singles by The Beatles during their career, "I Want to Hold Your Hand" was their first number one hit in the United States and a good example of the high energy sound that had been missing in rock and roll since the end of the 1950s. Although the music and the lyrics sound quite innocent today, Bob Dylan and others have said that they thought the line "I can't hide" was actually "I get high" and believed it was a secret drug reference. From the very beginning The Beatles were immediately linked to the counterculture.

amine the music of The Beatles and other rock musicians of the 1960s to show how rock and roll was revived with a new image and a new sound that led to the abbreviated term "rock"—a form of popular music that was no longer limited to mass entertainment for teenagers. Rock music in the 1960s developed alongside the rise of the **counterculture**—a social movement in opposition to mainstream society—and soon became a vehicle for making serious artistic statements about the world through popular music.

COUNTERCULTURE
A post-WWII social movement in opposition to mainstream society that reached a peak during the 1960s.

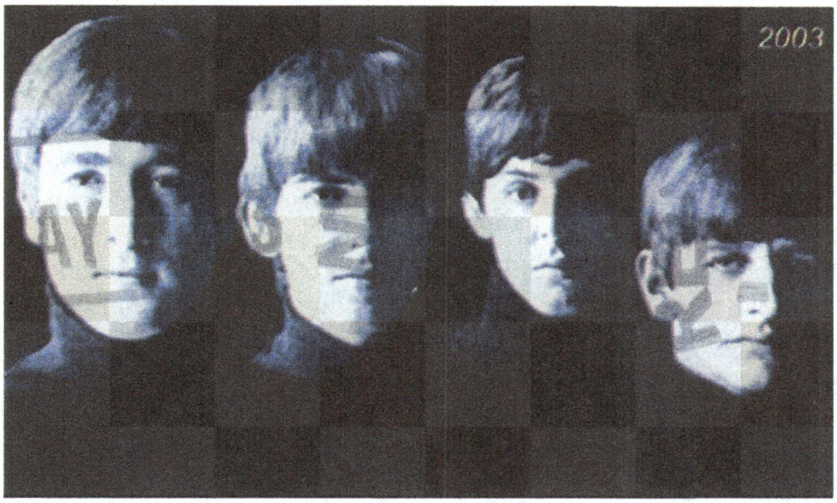

Where Did The Beatles Come From?

The shockwaves of the 1950s rock and roll explosion were also felt outside of the United States. In the late 1950s, the rock and roll of Bill Haley, Elvis Presley, Little Richard, Jerry Lee Lewis, and others crossed the Atlantic via records, movies, and concert appearances. Rock and roll eventually reached the port city of Liverpool, England, the hometown of John Lennon, Paul McCartney, George Harrison, and Richard Starkey (AKA Ringo Starr) who would become the "Fab Four" by 1962. The appearance of American rock and roll in England could not have come at a more opportune time. Since 1954, British teenagers were going crazy over **skiffle**—a genre of American folk music with blues and jazz influences that had disappeared in the United States after the 1940s. With the revival of skiffle in England, teenagers were forming makeshift ensembles using various homemade instruments such as washboards, washtub bass, jugs, kazoos, as well as guitars and banjos. Because of the skiffle craze, the sale of guitars in England skyrocketed and many kids took guitar lessons. But the real beauty of skiffle was that it was simple, anybody could play and many kids began copying American rock and roll songs in their groups. In 1956 John Lennon formed a skiffle band called The Quarrymen and American rock and roll songs were an essential part of the mix. At one performance in 1957, Lennon met Paul McCartney who was asked to join the band. George Harrison joined the following year and by 1960 the group began playing under a new name inspired by Buddy Holly and the Crickets: The Beatles.

SKIFFLE
A genre of American folk music with blues and jazz influences that disappeared in the US, but was revived in the UK in the 1950s where it helped launch rock and roll.

There are many images that come to mind when one thinks of The Beatles. Their early image was as a group of charming (but somewhat sharp-tongued) young lads who had long hair but were well-dressed and drove fans—especially female fans—into fits of wild ecstasy, seen in film footage of the time from concert and TV appearances. But it is important to realize how consciously constructed this pop image was. When The Beatles first started out they played a tough style of 1950s big beat rock and roll and really looked the part. Photos of their early years performing in Hamburg show them in leather jackets with long greased back hair, looking very much like the rock and roll juvenile delinquents that parents were afraid of during the 1950s. Shortly after returning to the UK in the early 1960s, The Beatles met manager Brian Epstein who recognized their obvious popularity and impeccable talent, but knew that if he presented them with a cleaner image he would have something truly phenomenal. It was here that the idea of the rock band was born.

The enormous and immediate success of The Beatles in the United States launched the "British Invasion," in which numerous bands came to the United States to tour, performing in large concert halls for adoring fans. Many of these groups, such as The Dave Clark Five and Herman's Hermits, were packaged as teen idols who were "the next big thing" much like The Beatles, but the success of some of these groups was only temporary and many of these bands have since faded into obscurity. But some of the UK bands of the British invasion had more lasting qualities and have become historically important in the history of rock. The difference between the flash-in-the-pan groups and the groups that became part of the canon of what is today called "classic rock" had everything to do with the new model of the music business that was a result of The Beatles revolution.

Keith Richards and Mick Jagger of The Rolling Stones.

The advent of The Beatles marked the beginning of a new era for popular music. In this new era, the half-century old Tin Pan Alley model of the music industry—in which songwriters created standardized songs to be sold to performers—would completely disappear. The Beatles may have been four working class lads from Liverpool in love with copying 1950s rock and roll, but the group immediately began writing their own original songs. Their success at writing well-crafted songs with catchy melodies, rich vocal harmonies, and imaginative new instrumental textures, all performed with consummate musicianship, inspired virtually every young musician of their generation. Soon rock bands popped up everywhere in the UK and the United States and the idea took hold that if you wanted to be taken seriously as an artist you had to write your own songs. The rock band that wrote their own songs became the new model, cutting out the Tin Pan Alley middleman and a new kind of music industry developed in which rock bands as self-contained units would be developed, recorded, and promoted.

Bands of the British Invasion: The Rolling Stones

After The Beatles spearheaded the "British Invasion" in 1964, there were numerous other bands from England who followed their lead. The most famous being **The Rolling Stones**, a band that formed in London in 1962 with Mick Jagger, Keith Richards, Brian Jones, Bill Wyman, and Charlie Watts. After achieving a modest success in the UK, in June of 1964 The Rolling Stones "invaded" America just as The Beatles did, but to considerably less fanfare. Dubbed a "disaster" by bassist Bill Wyman, the Rolling Stones went to America without first having a hit single in the United States, a mistake The Beatles had been careful to avoid. But there was something else behind the initial "failure" of the Stones.

The Rolling Stones were part of a subculture in England devoted to American blues music. While they loved rock and rollers like Chuck Berry and Buddy Holly, they started out as a blues band, imitating the Chicago electric blues of Muddy Waters, Howlin' Wolf, Jimmy Reed, and others. So great was their admiration for the American blues singers that they felt a little embarrassed to be playing this music for Americans, but to their surprise, none of the kids who came to their shows had ever heard American blues before. So for American teenagers, the music was certainly fresh and the Stones played many more familiar rock and roll songs in their concerts. But the real problem was that The Rolling Stones, like many of their counterparts in the UK, were not writing their own songs. Friends with The Beatles, the Rolling Stones even consulted John Lennon and Paul McCartney who lent them a hand by writing a song for them, "I Want to Be Your Man." Soon Mick Jagger and Keith Richards, emulating their mentors Lennon and McCartney, began writing songs together. After a few initial singles penned by the songwriting team of Jagger and Richards, The Rolling Stones finally broke through in 1965 with their first international Number One hit, "Satisfaction."

Guided Listening

"(I Can't Get No) Satisfaction" by The Rolling Stones

http://app.rhapsody.com/artist/the-rolling-stones/album/out-of-our-heads-us-abkco/track/i-cant-get-no-satisfaction

One of the most successful and well-known songs by The Rolling Stones, this song is a good example of rock music that is structured around a riff instead of a conventional song form. Keith Richards famously came up with this guitar riff after waking up in the middle of the night, recording it, and going back to sleep. When he played it in the recording studio, he added a distorted fuzz tone to his guitar, creating one of the most recognizable rock hits of the 1960s.

What was truly new in 1965, was the open structure of this song. There are only a few chord changes in this song that is otherwise nothing more than a constantly repeating riff. What maintains the listener's interest is the power of the vocals, the story of frustration told in the lyrics, and the relentless drive of the music.

0:00 The first sound heard is Keith Richards's fuzz-tone guitar riff. He is joined by bass player Bill Wyman playing the same riff on bass guitar, followed by the steady drumbeat of Charlie Watts.

0:14 Vocalist Mick Jagger begins singing the refrain featuring the title of the song.

0:27 The only variation in chords in the song occur during this brief passage that builds up to a vocal climax that ends the refrain.

0:42 Jagger begins to sing a story over the repeating riff; the verse ends when Jagger begins to sing the song's title . . .

1:04 . . . then all instruments drop out except the drums and tambourine that play a rhythmic break.

1:07 Instruments and vocalist come back in with a passage that leads back to the refrain.

1:14 Refrain

1:28 Chord changes again building up to the climax of the refrain.

1:42 Jagger begins another verse/story.

2:03 Another drum break, then instruments return.

2:15 Refrain.

2:28 Chord changes again leading up to the climax.

2:42 Jagger sings a third and final verse.

3:04 Drum break.

3:12 Jagger repeats the refrain and extends it as the song fades out.

After this enormous hit, The Rolling Stones went on to a decades-long career that led them to be dubbed, "The Greatest Rock and Roll Band in the World." Such a moniker is obviously open to debate, but no one can argue with the band's success and longevity, considering that they are still together after more than 50 years in the music business.

Comparing The Rolling Stones with The Beatles reveals two groups that formed at virtually the same time, both cashing in on the same rock and roll revival, but they represent two different models of the rock band. Whereas The Beatles were working class toughs from Liverpool who were "cleaned up" by their Manager Brian Epstein, The Rolling Stones, ironically, were actually respectable middle-class boys from London who were "groomed" to look tough by their Manager Andrew Loog Oldham. A former employee of Brian Epstein, Andrew Oldham took a different approach to publicizing a rock band, preferring to make them appear dangerous.

This smooth/rough contrast in image can be extended to the music as well. While The Beatles's music featured well-crafted melodies with group vocal harmonies over somewhat complex song forms, The Rolling Stones favored simpler, riff-based structures with rougher, more bluesy solo vocals by Mick Jagger. In terms of ancient Greek aesthetics, one could describe The Beatles's music, especially that of their later albums, as Apollonian—striving for perfection, balance, and elegance—and the music of The Rolling Stones as Dionysian—willfully rough, crude, and wild. As we look back on several decades of rock bands, it seems as if most rock bands follow one of these two models established by these two bands back in the 1960s.

Bob Dylan Meets The Beatles

The British Invasion was never a one-way street. While the young British musicians were busy selling 1950s American music back to American youth, they were still absorbing contemporary American influences. Indeed the dynamism of rock during the 1960s was rooted in the interchange between British and American musicians who were crafting music that suddenly stood for something meaningful. Furthermore, the counterculture played an important role in creating a feeling of community that was expressed through the music that young people shared. Leading the charge, The Beatles never stopped absorbing influences from American musicians and in doing so continued to revolutionize rock and roll by moving beyond the teen idol world of Beatlemania pop. In fact, the transformation of rock and roll as teenage entertainment into the sophisticated art of rock can be traced to a fateful meeting in 1964 between The Beatles and the young American folk singer, **Bob Dylan**.

Born Robert Zimmerman in Duluth, Minnesota in 1941, Bob Dylan was also a teenager during the rock and roll explosion of the 1950s. But in addition to idolizing the great rock and roll stars of the day, Dylan absorbed the many varieties of American folk music, ranging from the rural blues of Robert Johnson to the folk ballads of Woody Guthrie. The young Zimmerman was so obsessed with folk music that he dropped out of his freshman year at the University of Minnesota and made his way to New York City with his sights set on the heart of a booming folk movement in the countercultural enclave of Greenwich Village. Changing his name to Bob Dylan, he created a mythical persona that was every bit as fabricated as The Beatles's "clean" image and before long, Bob Dylan was hailed in the mainstream media as the star of New York's underground folk movement.

Now in his 70s, Bob Dylan continues to perform live in what he calls his "never-ending tour."

Another reason Bob Dylan was so drawn to New York was that he was also in search of his hero Woody Guthrie who had been permanently hospitalized with a terminal disease. Woody Guthrie was a legendary folk singer and songwriter active in the 1930s and 1940s who became known for writing simple, clever songs with powerful social messages (like the message that he wrote on his guitar: "this machine kills fascists"). The young Bob Dylan visited Guthrie in the hospital during the last years of his life and received his message loud and clear. Dylan would go on to write some of the most famous social message songs of the century—songs that combined simple chords, strong melodies and vivid lyrics that were intellectually compelling and emotionally charged. Consequently, many young people who heard Bob Dylan's songs were even more moved by his words than those of John F. Kennedy. Mixing the social consciousness of folk music with the underground beat poetry of Allen Ginsberg, Bob Dylan gave the counterculture a new young voice by the mid-1960s.

Enter The Beatles. On another whirlwind tour of America in the summer of 1964, The Beatles met Bob Dylan at their New York hotel. Much has been made of this fateful meeting in which Bob Dylan introduced John, Paul, George, and Ringo to marijuana. Although it turned out that two of The Beatles had tried it some time earlier, the symbolism of this meeting is what is most important. The Beatles represented the newest music of the baby boom youth and Bob Dylan represented that same generation's voice of conscience. As a result of each other's influence, their music would coalesce into something even more powerful. Bob Dylan would reach a massive level of popularity as he began to play rock music (and alienate the conservative folk music fans in the process). Bob Dylan represents the beginning of what grew into the genre known as **folk rock** by the end of the 1960s. From the mid-1960s on, The Beatles would begin to write songs that would express the conscience of youth and present themselves as artists. This was the pivotal point when good time rock and roll transformed into the art of rock.

FOLK ROCK

A musical genre that emerged in the 1960s combining elements of folk music with rock.

Guided Listening

"Like a Rolling Stone" by Bob Dylan

http://app.rhapsody.com/artist/bob-dylan/album/highway-61-revisited-columbia/track/like-a-rolling-stone

An anthem for the young generation, "Like a Rolling Stone" is an example of Dylan's new electric music that earned him crossover popularity among rock fans and disdain from many folk music purists of the time. One of his biggest hit songs, this song helped give him the reputation as poet and intellectual leader of the countercultural youth. Especially striking is his accusatory tone in which he is directly addressing the listener and it is not a positive message.

0:00 After a single hit of the snare drum, the band joins in to play an introduction.

0:13 Bob Dylan sings the first line of the first verse, telling a story of a young person from a middle-class family who is going off to live on their own. The rising chord progression of the verse creates a build-up of tension that climaxes at the end when he shouts accusingly at the character in the song.

0:23 Dylan sings another line over the rising chord progression.

0:33 A two-chord progression begins here to contrast with the first progression . . .

0:43 . . . then it starts to descend . . .

0:52 . . . then the chords begin to rise again as Dylan builds up to a vocal climax.

1:01 Dylan sings the refrain of the song over another rising chord progression finishing with the title of the song.

1:34 Second verse follows the same pattern as the first, beginning with the rising chord progression . . .

1:55 . . . then the two chord progression . . .

2:05 . . . then the descending chords.

2:25 Refrain.

3:03 Third verse follows the same pattern.

3:53 Refrain.

4:31 Fourth and final verse.

5:20 Refrain.

Suggested Listening

"You've Got to Hide Your Love Away" by The Beatles [not available on Rhapsody]

From their second motion picture, *Help* (1965), this song reflects the more introspective songwriting of Lennon and McCartney influenced by Bob Dylan. This song also reveals the folk influence.

Bob Dylan's influence can be heard directly in The Beatles music from 1964 on, especially in the introspective songs of Lennon and McCartney that are usually credited to John Lennon. Lennon began to write songs with direct messages that expressed his personal feelings such as "I'm a Loser," "Help," and "You've Got to Hide Your Love Away." Lennon would write story songs inspired by Dylan's folk music such as "Norwegian Wood" to which Bob Dylan wrote a response song, "4th Time Around." Most importantly, The Beatles began to follow Dylan's lead in making record albums that functioned as musical and social expressions of who they were as individuals and what they felt about life. This led to another creative exchange with another American group, The Beach Boys.

Brian Wilson, singer and composer of The Beach Boys, performing at Red Rocks in 2012 for the 50th Anniversary tour of The Beach Boys.

Brian Wilson and The Beach Boys

Carl, Dennis, and Brian Wilson, three brothers from Hawthorne, California, got started in the music business at roughly the same time as The Beatles and also found immediate success. Together with their cousin, Mike Love, they began to play rock and roll inspired by the doo-wop vocal harmony groups of the 1950s. In search of a gimmick to write songs about and create an image, someone suggested the recent surfing craze, and the band became **The Beach Boys**. Their upbeat songs about surfing sung in smooth four-part harmonies became an instant success due in part to the excellent vocal arrangements and clever pop songwriting of Brian Wilson. Although the music could have easily lapsed into a predictable pop formula, it was Brian Wilson who did not let that happen. Brian Wilson was listening closely to The Beatles.

Wilson had heard The Beatles's album *Rubber Soul* (1965), an album that explored a diversity of styles, referencing soul music, country and western, and even Greek folk music. Inspired by the idea that a record album could sound like a total artistic statement, Wilson set to work on a record album that he described as a "teenager's letter to God." Taking the reins of the group while the rest of the Beach Boys were on tour without him (Brian had developed a debilitating fear of flying and being in public that kept him at home), Wilson worked in the recording studio with a large ensemble of session musicians. Wilson strove constantly to orchestrate, rehearse, and record the musical "visions" he heard in his head, what he often referred to as his "pet sounds." After the rest of the group returned home, the complex instrumental music for the album *Pet Sounds* (1966) was completed, only needing the characteristic harmonies of the rest of The Beach Boys to be added on top. The other members of the group were somewhat taken aback by Wilson's dictatorial approach, but Wilson was on a mission to outdo The Beatles and would let nothing stand in his way. The Beach Boys were even visited during one of these sessions by somewhat competitive Paul McCartney who acknowledged that The Beach Boys were indeed creating something musically important.

Guided Listening

"God Only Knows" by The Beach Boys

http://app.rhapsody.com/artist/the-beach-boys/album/pet-sounds/track/god-only-knows

The most well-known song from the album Pet Sounds, released in January 1966, "God Only Knows," was unusual for its serious subject matter. Lyricist Peter Asher writes from the perspective of a person contemplating life after death to his/her lover, mentioning the word "God" which was unusual for pop songs until then. The searching lyrics were musically illustrated by Brian Wilson's imaginative songwriting in which he used chords with ambiguous tonality. What makes the music sound so uncertain is that the chords are not in root position, making it unclear what key the song is actually in.

0:00	Instrumental introduction serves as a brief fanfare by a small orchestra.
0:17	First verse; the chords used in this verse are tonally ambiguous making it unclear which key the song is in. This supports the sense of searching expressed in the lyrics. The chords seem to wander, not settling on a key, until . . .
0:33	. . . the refrain in which the title is sung, featuring descending chords that sound more clear and stable, as if the singer has reached his goal.
0:41	The second verse also features the wandering, uncertain chords leading to . . .
0:58	. . . the refrain again with the chords reaching their goal.
1:03	Instrumental break with a completely contrasting rhythm and harmony.
1:11	Wordless vocal passage with several voices singing in counterpoint over the ambiguous chords of the verse.
1:29	Refrain.
1:34	A third verse.
1:51	Refrain.
1:59	Refrain stated again, but extended this time into a complex vocal passage. Wilson layers multiple voices singing different parts of the refrain in counterpoint as the track fades out.

Although now hailed as one of the greatest albums of all time, in 1966 *Pet Sounds* did not achieve the commercial success the band had hoped for and Brian Wilson's mental problems would soon get a lot worse. Extremely competitive with The Beatles, Wilson was stunned by the next Beatles album to be released later that year, *Revolver*, which marked a breakthrough in the way rock musicians used the recording studio and an expanded palette of musical instruments and special effects. Undaunted, Wilson set to work on his own psychedelic masterpiece for The Beach Boys, "Good Vibrations," a song that was so complicated this "pocket symphony" took months to record. Released in October of 1966, "Good Vibrations" became a million-selling single that hit Number One in the UK. Despite this success, Brian Wilson was still not satisfied because he had a lot working against him, most of all his fragile mental state that would bring him down in the next few years. In this new serious age of rock, his band was burdened with an image that was too clean-cut for teenagers in the rock counterculture to take seriously and thus Wilson felt he had to work even harder than ever to beat his competition. Meanwhile, The Beatles kept pushing the envelope of what could be done in rock music.

Suggested Listening

"Tomorrow Never Knows" by The Beatles [not available on Rhapsody]

The last track on their album Revolver (1966), "Tomorrow Never Knows" is a song that The Beatles never played live on stage and at the time could only be "performed" in the recording studio. The song makes use of multi-track recording, varispeed recording that changes the pitch, backwards tape effects and electronic tape loops. Also featured are Indian instruments. The final vocal section was produced with a revolving Leslie speaker cabinet in an effort to try and produce what John Lennon wanted for the track: a thousand Tibetan monks chanting!

The Album as Musical Statement: *Sgt. Pepper's Lonely Hearts Club Band* (1967)

One of the marks of a great composer or artist is when historians divide the artist's career into periods that tell us not only about their career path, but helps us understand historical trends in art. Just as Beethoven was discussed in terms of distinct artistic periods (Early-Heroic-Late), The Beatles's career is commonly divided into two periods: The Beatlemania Period from 1963 to mid-1966 and the Studio Period from late 1966 to 1970.

The Beatlemania Period encompasses the massive worldwide adulation the band had while constantly touring the world and releasing about two record albums a year, plus many singles, all recorded whenever they could fit recording time into their hectic schedule. The band accomplished a lot during this first era, but there were many problems that exacerbated things almost to the point of destroying the band. To begin with, the pace of touring was too much, allowing little time in the studio to record music that was getting more ambitious and complicated every year. While the technology in the studio was rapidly developing, the technology of amplification on the concert stage was lagging, preventing audiences (and The Beatles themselves) from even hearing the music they were playing. And it did not help matters any that audiences continued to scream non-stop during performances. The disparity between such poor concert conditions and their excellence in the studio meant The Beatles could not play any of their new material from the *Revolver* album onstage. Their concerts were becoming absurd and meaningless charades.

Thus, The Beatles's Studio Era began with their decision in 1966 to stop touring and performing live concerts altogether. From late 1966 onward the band would be able to take more time to develop and record songs, eventually perfecting the long-playing record album as an artistic statement. Their first album of this new era was *Sgt. Pepper's Lonely Hearts Club Band* (1967). *Sgt. Pepper's*, as it is commonly referred to, is often credited as one of the first examples of a **concept album**—a record album in which the music and/or the lyrics are

CONCEPT ALBUM
A record album in which the music and/or the lyrics are organized according to a concept or theme.

organized according to a concept or theme. Although there is some debate about this as several members of The Beatles have claimed that their album was simply a collection of songs, the album was clearly organized around a conceptual frame that led listeners to treat the record as a total artistic statement.

Suggested Listening

"Sgt. Pepper's Lonely Hearts Club Band" and "With A Little Help from My Friends" by The Beatles [not available on Rhapsody]

To get a sense of the conceptual frame of their 1967 album, listen to these first two tracks. Unusual for the time was the creation of a fictional live audience that appears on the first track and an overlap between the first two songs. The last verse of the first song (sung by Paul McCartney) introduces the fictional character, Billy Shears, who sings the second song (Ringo Starr).

The concept behind the album was an idea of Paul McCartney's in which the group would present a record to the audience that appeared to be made by a fictional band called "Sgt. Pepper's Lonely Hearts Club Band." The album begins with the title track featuring a fictional performance complete with audience sounds and horn arrangements suggesting that a band that is not The Beatles is making the music. The frame of the fictional performance is sustained by overlapping into the second song on the album, "With A Little Help from My Friends," but after that song the audio markers of the fictional performance disappear. The rest of the album features a collection of songs that draw from a variety of musical styles and instrumental textures with studio and electronic effects. Although the album is made up of distinctly separate songs with widely ranging subject matter—teen runaways, circuses, couples growing old, the meaning of existence—listeners got the message from the beginning that this album should be listened to as a whole. This is affirmed near the end of the second side of the album when the fictional concert performance returns with the theme music of the title track. And then The Beatles saved their most ambitious track for the very end after "the concert" comes to an end with the Lennon and McCartney collaboration, "A Day in the Life." The mammoth multi-piano chord that concludes the song is followed unexpectedly by a short snippet of additional music pressed into a "run-out groove," essentially a groove that will play forever.

Sgt. Pepper became the new model for the rock album as an integrated whole. Similar to Wagner's idea of the *gesamtkunstwerk* (total art work) discussed in our earlier unit on the 19th century, record albums in this new medium would feature music, lyrics, and cover art that are all designed to contribute to an overarching idea that was meaningful. In fact, the album's cover art was as equally important as the music and lyrics. The cover depicts a funeral for the old Beatles—portrayed as lifeless wax mannequins—in reference to the passing Beatlemania era they had just left behind. Attending the funeral on the cover are The Beatles in their new Sgt. Pepper guises and a cavalcade of famous faces behind them that tell the audience who The Beatles were inspired by, such as avant-garde composer Karlheinz Stockhausen, writer Edgar Allan Poe, actors Marlon Brando (from *The Wild One*), James Dean (from *Rebel Without A Cause*), and actress Marilyn Monroe. Perhaps more importantly, the photo collage included some of the most important underground countercultural figures of the time, such as comedian Lenny Bruce, beat writer William S. Burroughs, and occultist Aleister Crowley. The implicit message to fans was that these were the kinds of people fans should be following. Such a message-laden album cover confirmed The Beatles's status as intellectual leaders of a generation.

Scenes and Styles of Rock in the Late 1960s

After The Beatles "retired" to the studio to make record albums as art, you might think that other rock bands would have followed their lead. In fact, the opposite happened. In the wake of Beatlemania many bands were formed and in the wake of *Sgt. Pepper's* even more bands appeared as a movement of rock music took hold in popular culture. This new generation of bands in the late 1960s began to establish a pattern for the production of rock music that we still see in practice today. Bands went into the studio striving to live up to the ambitions of *Sgt. Pepper's* by creating their own distinctive record album and then went out onto the road to promote that album. While The Beatles were extremely disappointed and disillusioned at the limitations of presenting rock music in large auditoriums and stadiums, the new generation of rock musicians took on this challenge and by the 1970s, the art of the rock concert was developed to the highest level by the likes of **The Who**, **Pink Floyd**, David Bowie, **Led Zeppelin**, Black Sabbath, and countless others.

How did the modern rock concert get started? Again, the counterculture of the 1960s played a pivotal role. It is important to note that when The Beatles made their *Sgt. Pepper's* masterpiece in 1967, they were simply capturing the spirit of the counterculture that was already integrated into rock music. The Beatles simply packaged the countercultural message in their own distinctive way that got the attention of the mainstream media. It was actually in the underground where the countercultural side of rock had first started to develop a few years earlier across the Atlantic and out on the West Coast of California.

San Francisco was a bastion of the counterculture in the 1950s. It was a city frequented by beat poets and writers such as Allen Ginsberg and Jack Kerouac and a burgeoning rock scene with strong links to the 50s counterculture that got started in the mid-1960s. Under the inspiration of the beat generation and the recently invented hallucinogenic drug LSD-25, Author Ken Kesey created a series of countercultural events he called The Acid Tests. Although Kesey avoided stating any goal of these events, the overall concept of these free-form "freak out" events was that they were meant to oppose a mainstream American society. The counterculture objected to an American lifestyle that encouraged normative behaviors of company employment, conventional marriage, and conspicuous consumer spending. Such a lifestyle seemed absurd in the face of political realities such as America's increasing military involvement in Vietnam and the persistence of racism throughout the United States. The counterculture's proposed solution was to focus instead on a quest for an altered state of reality through a spirituality that involved experimentation with alternative forms of community, sexual behavior, and rock music itself.

The early countercultural events in San Francisco became a breeding ground for **psychedelic rock**—a type of rock influenced by consciousness-altering experimentation with drugs and meditation. Markers of this style are the use of new recording techniques and instrumentation—such as backwards tape effects and Indian instruments and modes as The Beatles had done—as

PSYCHEDELIC ROCK
A style of rock that emerged in the late 1960s influenced by consciousness-altering experimentation with drugs and meditation.

well as a new emphasis on extended improvisation. Many psychedelic rock songs last much longer than the usual three minutes in length and may not follow the usual verse-chorus form. In fact, the early psychedelic events in 1965–66 San Francisco were important for this experimentation precisely because the earliest bands did not yet have recording contracts and their music was not constrained by the boundaries of vinyl records, not even the LP. Psychedelic jams often went on for hours to match the extended time length of the psychedelic experience itself.

Guided Listening

"White Rabbit" by Jefferson Airplane

http://app.rhapsody.com/artist/jefferson-airplane/album/the-essential-jefferson-airplane

Written by lead singer Grace Slick, "White Rabbit" uses imagery from Lewis Carroll's Alice in Wonderland to convey the experience of hallucinogenic drugs that were becoming popular in the late 1960s, especially in San Francisco where Jefferson Airplane was based. As a way of musically depicting the drug experience, this song uses a bolero-like form in a slow crescendo leading to a final climax. Songwriter Grace Slick claimed the bolero as her main inspiration recorded by Miles Davis on his album Sketches of Spain (1960) and it also sounds like the more famous piece called Bolero by French composer Ravel. Another similarity to Miles Davis is the use of modal playing by the band. In the same way that Miles Davis explored modal playing to free his soloists, psychedelic musicians also used modal playing to create a similar sense of freedom.

0:00	Song begins with just the bass guitar.
0:05	Drums join in giving it a bolero-like rhythm.
0:09	Electric guitar begins playing a relaxed line over only two chords that alternate, allowing the guitar to play freely in Phrygian mode.
0:28	Singer and songwriter Grace Slick begins the vocal, singing the first verse.
0:46	Two new chords are introduced as Slick sings a refrain.
0:54	Music shifts back to the two Phrygian chords of the beginning and Slick sings another verse.
1:13	Two chord refrain again.
1:22	Two new chords appear with a new vocal melody.
1:39	Music shifts back to the Phrygian chords again, but Slick briefly sings the refrain followed by another verse.
2:07	Dramatic shift to a new chord as Slick sings the climactic "message" of the song.

The psychedelic music culture was an underground phenomenon not limited to San Francisco. The same subcultures were happening in other major urban centers and the music that emerged in these areas came to define the "scene" of that particular location. In contrast to the loose improvisational approach of **The Grateful Dead** and **Jefferson Airplane** that was the San Francisco sound, Southern California featured a diversity of bands now included under the broad term of psychedelic rock. The dark, bluesy poetry sound of The Doors, featuring lead singer Jim Morrison contrasts with the folk-inspired rock of The Byrds and Buffalo Springfield, all bands that performed on Hollywood's Sunset Strip. Southern California was also home to the more avant-garde sounds of Frank Zappa's Mothers of Invention and Captain Beefheart. In Southern California and across the country there were numerous "garage bands" that played psychedelic music that led to later punk rock in the 1970s, such as Detroit's The Stooges and MC5. In New York City there was yet another completely different variant of psychedelic music in the circle of Pop artist Andy

Warhol who produced The Velvet Underground. Led by singer/songwriter Lou Reed and Welsh avant-gardist John Cale, The Velvet Underground was a proto-punk group that dabbled in avant-garde noise and drone music that would influence future generations of punk and post-punk musicians in the 1970s and 1980s.

Naturally, a psychedelic scene developed in London, the home base of the British Invasion. The Beatles were just the tip of the iceberg of psychedelic experimentation in 1967. While *Sgt. Pepper* was the number one album, the number one single throughout the early summer of 1967 (dubbed "the summer of love" in the youth culture) was "A Whiter Shade of Pale," a song by London band Procol Harum. The band merged a melody by Bach with American R & B, featuring Dylan-inspired surrealist lyrics. Other mainstays of the London underground scene at clubs such as UFO and others were groups such as Pink Floyd and Soft Machine, two bands that specialized in extended psychedelic "freak outs" for dancing or just listening. All three of these psychedelic rock groups—the classically inspired Procol Harum, the space rock of Pink Floyd, and the jazz rock of Soft Machine—contributed to the early development of **progressive rock**—a style of rock that features extended forms, instrumental virtuosity, and a diversity of musical influences to expand the range of rock music (see Chapter 17). This expansion of the instrumental colors of the rock palette fully bloomed with the album *Days of Future Passed* (1967) by **The Moody Blues** who performed their entire concept album with the London Festival Orchestra.

PROGRESSIVE ROCK

A style of rock that features extended forms, instrumental virtuosity and a diversity of musical influences to expand the range of rock music.

Rock Concerts and Tribal Gatherings

As ambitious as rock albums were becoming by the end of the 1960s, concerts did not take a back seat to the album. Instead rock musicians rose to the challenge of presenting their new music in public through concert performances and touring. Early British Invasion bands such as The Rolling Stones and later ones such as The Who made concert tours a regular practice. As audiences and arenas got bigger, so did the demand for more sophisticated equipment and amplification systems. With the rise of **hard rock** played by touring bands, it was necessary for sound equipment to provide lots of power and volume to large venues such as sports arenas. The year 1968 saw the formation of the ultimate hard rock band, Led Zeppelin, a supergroup formed by Yardbirds guitarist Jimmy Page out of the remains of his old British invasion group. Along with singer Robert Plant, drummer Jon Bonham, and bassist/keyboardist John Paul Jones, Led Zeppelin set the model for how bands would proceed in the 1970s: spend a year (or more) writing and recording an album, then go out on tour to promote the new album, mixing in songs from previous albums. With each successful album of songs, the fan base could continue to expand and ever larger arenas could be booked for concerts.

HARD ROCK

A style of rock characterized by harder and louder instruments and vocals especially electric guitar.

Led Zeppelin also serves as the best example of the importance of the record album in the new model of rock music. Because of its ability to encompass extended song forms and contain greater thematic complexity, the long-playing album became more important than the single. While the record industry did not yet understand this, Led Zeppelin did. The band made a decision to never release any singles despite the urging of their record label, Atlantic Records. Nearly having a falling out with Atlantic at first because of this practice, Led Zeppelin nevertheless consistently topped album sales without ever releasing any singles.

They even released an album in 1971, known by many today as *Led Zeppelin IV*, that had no title and no identifying text of any kind on the jacket, trusting that their fans would simply find the record and buy it. Such experimentation with obscurity never stopped Led Zeppelin from becoming the top concert draw in the 1970s. In the age of Led Zeppelin, the artists would call the shots.

The birth of the rock concert as we know it today actually came out of the "death" of the counterculture that had grown up around rock at the end of the 1960s. Starting with the Monterey Pop Festival of 1967—that introduced The Who and **Jimi Hendrix** to American audiences—rock festivals became symbolic that a new culture was emerging out of the rock revolution. In the late 1960s, this new culture demanded that rock music live up to some very high ideals as expressed in the artistry of the music reaching its peak at **Woodstock**, the largest rock festival of this era held in New York in July 1969. Organizers of Woodstock had originally planned to make money off this event, but the three-day concert became a magnet for a generation, drawing so many people to the site that it became a free event. The tiny town of Woodstock, New York temporarily swelled to become a new city of nearly half a million people. At the time the festival stood for the ideals of a new generation in which rock was believed to be a force of peace, love, and social change through the expression of an alternative lifestyle. But this alternative was hardly the utopia many believed it to be.

WOODSTOCK

The first and most famous large-scale rock music festival held in New York, August 15–18, 1969 before an estimated audience of over 400,000.

When bands tried to live up to the free spirit of festivals, such as the free festival at **Altamont** organized by The Rolling Stones in Northern California (December 1969), the results revealed the dark side of the 1960s countercultural dream. As documented in the film *Gimme Shelter* (1970), the chaotic Altamont Festival was marred by poor planning, resulting in a Hells Angels biker gang violently "protecting" the stage and the murder of a would-be assassin in the audience. Even more of a harbinger of things to come was the mammoth rock festival held at The Isle of Wight in 1970 that became a battleground between organizers who were trying to make money off selling tickets and counterculture hippies who insisted that these events be completely free of capitalism. Such idealism soon faded as a new, profit-oriented rock concert culture developed in the 1970s.

ALTAMONT

A free festival concert organized by The Rolling Stones held in Altamont, California on December 6, 1969, and noted for its violence.

Suggested Listening

"The Star Spangled Banner" by Jimi Hendrix (recorded live at the Woodstock Festival, NY, 1969)

http://app.rhapsody.com/artist/jimi-hendrix/album/experience-hendrix-the-best-of-jimi-hendrix
or on YouTube
https://www.youtube.com/watch?v=i0WG-ZUUOsg

Another example of **intertextuality** or "code-switching" in music (see Chapter 8), Jimi Hendrix played the American national anthem in a new way and in an unexpected context that effectively "switches" the codes by which we usually interpret this song. Typically performed by a military band or solo singer at a sporting event, when Hendrix played this version on an electric guitar at the biggest rock festival of all time, symbolic of the peace movement at the height of the Vietnam War, it provoked many different reactions and interpretations.

Listen to this version or watch it on YouTube and pay careful attention to the way Hendrix uses his heavily distorted guitar to do **word painting**—musically enhance the words of the song. There are no words sung here, but you can think of the words as you listen and watch. What kinds of musical effects does he do and how do these effects enhance the words of the song? Do certain special effects or additional tunes that he adds correspond to the words or suggest some vivid image? Is this a political statement? Is Hendrix being critical of the United States or is this a patriotic statement of support for the country of his birth? How do you think the audience interpreted this performance? How do you think the older generation who were critical of the counterculture would have interpreted this performance?

Conclusion: A New Era of Rock

It may not be an overstatement to say that more changes came about in music in the 1960s than any other decade of the 20th century. The change in musicians' artistry and the musical industry that developed around this artistry was profound and not just limited to rock. African American musical forms such as jazz and soul also underwent monumental changes, emerging as new forms in the 1970s. At the beginning of the 1960s, teenage rock and roll had faded with the end of the 1950s, but the 1960s marked a new revival of rock as an art form. With ever more ambitious record album production and more sophisticated concert performances that would become visual as well as sonic spectacles, rock music had finally arrived as music that was no longer a fad and demanded to be taken seriously. As always, the media seemed to be trying to catch up with all the new developments. The record industry had changed to accommodate rock musicians as artists with the needs of free expression. And as songs and records became longer, radio also changed with FM stations becoming the place for listeners to hear entire albums played with higher quality stereo sound.

We can conclude this chapter by mentioning just two of the many albums released in 1969 that typified the new era of rock. Guitarist and songwriter Pete Townsend conceived of a "rock opera" called *Tommy* that was released as a concept album by The Who and it was staged at the Metropolitan Opera in New York that same year. The narrative of a boy who has gone "deaf, dumb, and blind" is told through recurring musical themes worthy of 19th century Wagnerian opera. Another example is *Abby Road* (1969), the final album recorded by The Beatles before disbanding in 1970. This album concludes with an extended suite of songs that form a grand finale to their career and a musical map for other bands to follow.

Roger Daltrey, lead singer of The Who.

Guided Listening

"Baba O'Riley" by The Who (rec. 1971)

http://app.rhapsody.com/artist/the-who/album/whos-next-bonus-tracks

This is one of the most well-known songs by The Who: Roger Daltrey (vocals); Pete Townshend (guitar, synthesizer); John Entwistle (bass); and Keith Moon (drums). The unusual title refers to two people important to composer Pete Townshend: his guru, Indian teacher Meher Baba, and American avant-gardist composer Terry Riley, who is referenced musically in the minimalist introduction to the song.

0:00	Intro on synthesizer; in the style of American "minimalist" music.
0:33	Main song begins; piano introduces chord progression (I-V-IV).
0:48	Drums enter.
1:06	Verse sung by Roger Daltrey as the bass guitar joins in.
1:40	Townsend enters with "power chords" on guitar.
2:00	Transition section begins as the steady drum beat stops and drummer Keith Moon accents the guitar chords.
2:08	Pete Townsend sings a passage for eight measures ("middle eight") over the opening synthesizer.
2:23	Instruments return and Daltrey sings another verse.
2:57	Brief passage played by Townsend on lead guitar without drums and bass.
3:04	Final verse sung by Daltrey; note the ornamented bass guitar supporting the verse.
3:23	Transition section with loud guitar chords and lead guitar.
2:00	Section C, repeats.
2:20	Section D, begins with a new theme.
3:50	Closing section: a violin enters and begins to play in the style of an Irish dance tune with synthesizer in background; the drums join in and the tempo gradually increases until the music reaches a climax.

17

Musical Ambition, Cultural Accreditation and the Nasty Side of Progressive Rock[1]

Popular Music (2008) Volume 27, Issue 3, pp. 433–455.

> *"Nice nasties are de riguer these days"*
>
> —*GUARDIAN WEEKLY*, 8 AUGUST 1970

ABSTRACT

Progressive rock of the early 1970s has been demonized as a nadir in the history of rock primarily because of the ambitions of progressive rock musicians. Critics have interpreted these ambitions as attempts to elevate rock music to the level of high art in order to gain cultural accreditation from an unspecified cultural elite. This interpretation is further compounded by the common notion that progressive rock's subject matter is dominated more by individualistic quests for spirituality than by socio-political critique, resulting in a stereotype of progressive rock as apolitical, pretentious and conventionally upwardly mobile. Critics who have propagated this stereotype—including some musicologists—have misunderstood the countercultural politics of young musicians during this era and have overlooked the highly developed musical poetics of progressive rock that were in fact highly politicized. This paper examines four of the leading progressive rock bands of the early 1970s—Emerson, Lake and Palmer, King Crimson, Genesis and Yes—and reveals the nasty side of progressive rock: a scathing criticism of rampant militarism and social conformity that runs counter to the prevailing narrative in which the genre is dismissed as an escapist fantasy with an elitist agenda.

Progressive rock of the 1970s is generally regarded as a movement founded by a group of musicians of the British counter-culture inspired by the experimental and psychedelic rock of the Beatles, Jimi Hendrix and Cream, among others.[2] At its height progressive rock bands such as Emerson, Lake and Palmer, Yes and Genesis commanded the music industry's most lavishly remunerative deals as they introduced formal structures and instrumentation of classical music, jazz and world music into rock to sculpt pop record albums into complex, multi-movement works on a scale that was unprecedented in their stylistic tradition. There were also less visible groups, such as Van der Graaf Generator, Henry Cow, Magma and Faust, who created aggressive pan-tonal works with apocalyptic lyrics and dystopian imagery to pave the way for experiments in extreme rock music by latter-day groups such as Mars Volta[3] and John Zorn's Naked City, who have drawn controversy over their depictions of systematic human torture, execution and criminal violence. In various ways all of the aforementioned progressive groups of the 1970s took the lead in developing a musical language to express such unsettling positions. It is not surprising that progressive metal bands such as Tool, Primus, and Opeth, who stand among the most provocative of recent artists, share a stylistic affinity, as well as a common label, with progressive rock of the 1970s. But critics and students of progressive rock have not appreciated this aspect of the movement. Instead, there is a strange sense of calmness that has colored treatments of the style, one that has haunted its reception to this day. Through the perpetration of a myth that the musical ambitions of progressive artists ran counter to the aesthetics of rock, the disturbing nature of its identity as "progressive" has been lost. We contend that this peculiar critical omission belies a fundamental misconception about the motivations behind this music.

Of all popular styles of music progressive rock is the only one characterized by its musical ambition. The *Oxford English Dictionary* defines the word ambition itself as "the ardent desire to rise to high position, or to attain rank, influence, distinction or other preferment" and lists another connotation of "ostentation, display of the outward tokens of position, as riches, dress, vain-glory, pomp" (1989, *sv.* "ambition"). The derisory tone here notwithstanding, there is no denying that the term fits well the flamboyant behavior of Keith Emerson, Rick Wakeman and other young progressive rock stars who were enjoying sexual and exhibitionistic triumphs that surely made them the envy of their peers. But rather than to consider their outward displays of ostentation in fashion and attitude, rock critics and musicologists alike have located the socio-political ambitions of progressive rockers precisely in their musical activities, in the "appropriation of nonpopular musical forms . . . European 'classical' music, jazz and avant-garde music" (Weinstein 2002, p. 91). Not only is it typical to see this as "an expression of a sociocultural movement, specifically an attempt to put forth value for the upper-middle class" (ibid., p. 92) it is also commonly asserted that the upper-middle class supposedly involved here was a musical establishment run by adults. In this scenario the ambitions of these progressive rockers were directed toward a single goal—to be "accepted by their elders" (Hatch and Milward 1987, p. 150).[4]

We begin by questioning the objective behind this musical ambition: Was it really directed toward the approbation of adults? To answer this we turn first to the often-cited liner notes of the album *Acquiring the Taste* by the progressive band Gentle Giant. The authors used this forum to pompously state that "it is our goal to expand the frontiers of contemporary popular music at the risk of being unpopular . . . From the outset we have abandoned all preconceived thoughts on blatant commercialism. Instead we hope to give you something far more substantial and fulfilling. All you need to do is sit back, and acquire the taste" (Gentle Giant 1971). Commentators have had a field day with this statement. Here, from the mouths of the musicians themselves, was an expression of all the elitism and pretension that betrayed rock's supposed adolescent populism, or, in the memorable words with which Lester Bangs described progressive rock's classical fusions, "the insidious befoulment of all that was gutter pure in rock" (Bangs 2002, p. 50). But a look at the context of the statement by Gentle Giant reveals a more complicated situation. The band chose to illustrate the same album with cover art that so thoroughly deflates their high-toned note inside that it seems to meet Bangs right there in the gutter he found so free of corrupting elements. Surely the same adult members of the elite who would appreciate the high art tone of the liner notes would be put off by the cover of the same album that shows a tongue about to "acquire the taste" of a peach that resembles a person's buttocks.

With this bathroom humor, Gentle Giant opens the door to the nasty side of progressive rock. By nasty we mean everything that might be considered bad form in musical establishment circles: from images of tongues salivating near buttocks to offensive on-stage antics—such as flag burnings—to excruciatingly loud and dissonant depictions of warfare and detailed narratives of human castration. At the core of all this nastiness, we believe, was something confrontational, populist and political. In the wake of urban riots, political assassinations, and student massacres on college campuses in the late 1960s, many in the youth culture turned to the nasty side of political intercourse. Regardless of their personal political beliefs, progressive rock musicians at the time were associated with this countercultural movement, one that lashed out against any form of authority—political or cultural—in ways that were intended to be malevolent, disruptive and foul.[5] Admittedly, it is not easy to discuss these things in the forum of a scholarly journal. However, we see as a paradigm of distortion the neglect of Gentle Giant's image of buttocks in favor of their pretentious statement about "art." Since the time of progressive rock, the mere presence of any trappings of classical music or "adult" intellectual culture has caused many to see it as an "imperturbable" style of music (Atton 2001, p. 29). In this paper we attempt to shift the paradigm and draw attention back to the "nastier" side of the progressive rock movement. In revisiting certain key works, we hope to show how a particular brand of politics was voiced through even the most popular bands like ELP, King Crimson, Genesis and Yes. Following this we consider the causes and outcomes of the critical derision of "the single most deplored genre of postwar pop music,"[6] questioning the validity of this trope of condemnation that informs most narratives of rock.

Emerson, Lake and Palmer: Road Warriors Branded As War Criminals

One group from the early 1970s well known for its vain-glory, pomp and ostentation was Emerson, Lake and Palmer (ELP). Musical ambition was perhaps what made ELP so iconic of progressive rock in that they, more than any other group, "rocked the classics" in the literal sense. Certainly the repertoire tackled by ELP was ambitious (Mussorgsky, Copland, Ginastera), but the group's style of playing the classics with extremes of volume, distortion, rapid tempos and amplified feedback made for a collision of high and low culture that has created some confusion among critics negotiating the populist aesthetics of rock.

Historians of progressive rock found the answer to the critical quandary posed by ELP's classical appropriations in a 1974 essay by Lester Bangs in which he labels ELP "war criminals." The reliance on Bangs for an assessment of this view has been considerable, to the point where an edifice of sorts has been built upon a phrase, for it is treated almost as a metaphor for the critical disdain of progressive rock as a whole. But the position Bangs takes in this article is actually ambivalent. Bangs wrote admirably of Keith Emerson as one who "could churn it out so relentlessly" and recalled with obvious pleasure the nasty side of Emerson's concert behavior, describing how the keyboardist:

> vaulted off the stage waving what looked like a theremin around, nearly decapitating several coeds and a rentacop to forzak of supra-WHIIINE! Reclambering onstage, he capped even his own show by wiping his ass with it: WZZEEEEEE! (Bangs 2002, p. 48).[7]

Despite this admiring stance, Bangs does confront the lines of class-based authenticity that were crossed in ELP's "Classical Fusion," noting with contempt its mix of supposedly high and low cultural signals. Perhaps, though, he felt compelled to adopt a critical stance after Emerson refused to attend his interview, adding perhaps to the critic's grudging respect for this arrogant, youthful star. In any case, after baiting the other members of the band during the interview for this article (and facetiously complimenting them on their polite manners), Bangs snared them on their musical ambitions: he forced them to admit that they hoped their audiences would seek out more music from the classical repertory after seeing their show. However, Lake and Palmer conceded readily that the main point of their fusion exercise was to entertain their audiences, not to enlighten them. To counter this, Bangs departed from the precocious adolescent image he liked to portray in his writing and adopted the attitude of the supposed adult that progressive rockers were out to please. In this guise the critic himself seemed more intent on protecting the purity of the Classical repertory than the band members. It was uncharacteristic of Bangs to miss the opportunity here to point out the blatant iconoclasm demonstrated by the group's "insidious befoulment" of the classics. Musical matters aside, Bangs clearly admired the rock band for all its "riches, dress, vain-glory and pomp" and he knew his readers would not take him seriously when he defended Richard Nixon's concerns about the energy crisis of the time, which ELP flouted grossly with their truckloads of volume-enhancing, electricity-wasting gear. It was in this context of a "mock defense" that Bangs voiced his memorable quip against ELP, labeling them "war criminals."[8]

Recent commentators who have preferred to find in Bangs's essay a condemnation rather than a grudging admiration for ELP have missed the reviewer's rather accurate characterization of Emerson's outlandishly aggressive stage persona and ambitious position as a musical appropriator. The origins of the ELP style are in Emerson's first rock band, The Nice, for which he gained a reputation for classical fusions and onstage antics. At his Albert Hall debut in 1968 with The Nice Emerson violently whip-lashed his band mates, repeatedly stabbed an American flag and burnt it on stage all the while performing an oddly duple-metered version of Leonard Bernstein's "America," resulting in a lifetime ban from the venue. Subsequently, publicists for The Nice cast this ban from the Albert Hall as a badge of honor, announcing it with pride in the liner notes of a re-released CD *The Best of the Nice* (1994). Emerson continued this tradition of bombastic showmanship in the 1970s, performing with ELP at the largest stadia of the time and before huge crowds of fans, few of them much older than the musicians themselves. As he achieved super-stardom in North America with ELP, Emerson kept his anti-war messages before the public.

In 1971, at the height of America's war in Southeast Asia, ELP released the album *Tarkus*, featuring the multi-movement suite of the same name. With its distorted, rapid-fire organ in constantly shifting meters and cover art of cybernetic and mythological warrior creatures, *Tarkus* decries the brutality of mechanized warfare and the hypocrisy that stands behind it. As was typical of rock albums of the era, the music, lyrics and album cover art of *Tarkus* were intended to be read in collusion. The vivid visual imagery of the album cover depicts a character commonly interpreted as Tarkus, a high-tech war machine that engages in battles with other similar machines until it is defeated by a Manticore, a mythological creature of Asian origin. It is hardly surprising that people at the time interpreted the Tarkus machine and the Manticore beast as metaphors for the United States' high-tech military and Vietnam's low-tech culture. Certainly the work had a sharp and bloody edge and if it were an analogy for Vietnam, it was an apt one. Not only does it stand as an astute military analysis of the situation in Vietnam at the time, it also was highly prophetic: the heavily armored Tarkus is finally defeated by a low-tech enemy that gets close enough to find its weak spot in the same manner that the guerilla warfare of the civilian-led Viet Cong defeated the US military machine. Furthermore, the return of the opening section suggests that Tarkus might have only been momentarily defeated, and could be interpreted as the ultimate invincibility of the high-tech US armada against a technologically weaker world enemy.

Given the counter-cultural significance of this Vietnam War analogy, it is surprising that Edward Macan, who argued so strenuously and effectively for the counter-cultural foundation of progressive rock, takes note of it, yet pushes this work out of the political arena:

> It is the nature of the concept album, however, that one can interpret a given album's concept in a more specific sense if one wishes. For instance, I have heard it argued that Tarkus represents the United States, since the armadillo is an American animal; that Manticore, with its origins in Persian and perhaps ultimately Indian mythology, symbolizes Southern Asia; that the sixth movement, "Battle-

> field," is actually about the Vietnam War; and that the entire piece is therefore an antiwar protest. On one level, I rather doubt it. While Keith Emerson was once involved in a flag-burning incident during his days with the Nice, by the early 1970s he admitted to having lost interest in protest politics. Furthermore, since Vietnam protest songs were not uncommon around 1970, resorting to a veiled or hidden protest would have been quite unnecessary. (Macan 1997, p. 90)

Why is Macan so doubtful of an anti-war interpretation? He apologetically describes Keith Emerson, the onstage agitator who reveled in his anti-American tirade at the Royal Albert Hall, as someone who was "once involved in a flag-burning incident" (ibid.). While Macan relies heavily on Emerson's statements to the press in the early 1970s, we don't see any discontinuity between the 1960s agitator and the 1970s musician who packaged his political statements in musical form, no matter what he said to the press. Here, of course, we are all relying to some extent on the complexities involved with authorial intentionality. However, Macan's suggestion that anti-war songs of this era were more explicit than usual at this time simply miscasts the evidence. Many anti-war songs of the period had universal messages, such as "Imagine" by John Lennon, "Wooden Ships" by Crosby, Stills, Nash and Young and "War Pigs" by Black Sabbath to name just a few. Furthermore, the anti-war message of *Tarkus* is neither "veiled" nor "hidden." In his subsequent analysis of *Tarkus*, Macan dispenses with the idea that he, to his credit, develops throughout his book: that lyrics, cover art and music are collusive in progressive rock albums. Instead Macan seeks "to examine how the piece is organized on a purely musical basis" (ibid., p. 91). This undersells the powerful musical, lyrical and visual poetics of this album package that was listened to and studied for hours on end by war-conscious American youth in the pre-MTV days of rock.

In *Tarkus* the subject of war is treated openly and directly, especially in Greg Lake's mournful lament, "The Battlefield," with its funereal organ by Emerson. Here ELP's rather unambiguous disdain of militarism is not only proclaimed in the folk-inspired lyrics, but is also embedded in the music. At the end of "The Battlefield," the somber mood of the funeral is transformed into a clever satire of militarism in the next section of the piece, "Aquatarkus." This instrumental section features a mocking military march with a deliberately nasal trumpet sound on Emerson's synthesizer accompanied by a militaristic snare drum beat played by Carl Palmer. It is interesting that this satire was dropped on ELP's live concert rendition of *Tarkus* performed on the 1974 US tour.[9] In their live version of "Aquatarkus," the humorous synthesized trumpet sound was dropped and the militaristic snare drum was replaced by Palmer's fuller sounding groove on the drum kit as the band turned this section into an extended virtuosic jam.

What was the reason for this change in the song? Obviously ELP happily took advantage of any opportunity to show off their skills, but perhaps they made this change thinking that such a silly sounding musical joke would not work in US Stadium shows. However, the anti-war message of *Tarkus* was emphasized rather than diminished on this live version from the US tour as Greg Lake inserted the chorus of King Crimson's anti-war anthem "Epitaph" at the end of "The Battlefield," just before the group launches into the revised, crowd-pleasing jam of "Aquatarkus." All this indicates that ELP's quest was not simply to forward an elitist musical agenda but rather to pronounce a political message to an audience that they surely assumed would appreciate it. At the same time, they made sure to provide that same audience with their money's worth of over-the-top, circus-like musical productions that placed entertainment, not high art, at center stage. Although ELP today, like Sting, Bono and so many others, would probably want to be regarded as artists, at the time they were playing up to the image of pop star entertainers instead.

Suggested Listening

"Tarkus" by Emerson, Lake and Palmer (recorded live in 1974)

http://app.rhapsody.com/artist/emerson-lake-and-palmer/album/welcome-back-my-friends-to-the-show-that-never-ends-ladies-a-razor-and-tie-label

King Crimson: Napalm Fire, Sonic Violence and Musical Karate

If one were to attack a progressive rock musician for being overly intellectual and prone to bombastic statements of seriousness, then one could perhaps look no further than guitarist Robert Fripp of the seminal progressive rock group King Crimson. However much Fripp's erudite, professorial image has made him an easy target as a negative progressive rock stereotype, he continues to argue against the anti-intellectual stance in rock and questions whether he should "act dumb in order to be a rock musician" (Tamm 1991, p. 20). Fripp believes rock's greatest value is found in the spontaneous communication that can occur between musicians and their audiences and claimed that rock music had tremendous political power:

> Music is a high-order language system; i.e., it is a meta-language. The function of a meta-language is to express solutions to problems posed in a lower-order language system. . .if one were interested in political change one would not enter political life, one would go into music. (Fripp quoted in Tamm 1991, p. 128)

Fripp's vehicle for this political "meta-language" was his band King Crimson whose debut concept album in 1969, *In the Court of the Crimson King*, set the tone for 1970s progressive rock with a screaming red face on the front cover (see Figure 2) and the tormented expressionism of the opening song, "21st Century Schizoid Man." The song's lyrics about napalmed innocents and barbed wire were matched by a hitherto unprecedented sonic violence in rock music, fitting stylistically as well as chronologically between the expressionistic works of Penderecki and Crumb. In addition to heavy metal guitar and pounding bass this song featured a distorted saxophone solo by Ian McDonald, who forced himself into contorted positions while recording it in the studio in an effort to make it sound suitably angst-ridden (Smith 2001, p. 60). This first incarnation of King Crimson that created such anti-war anthems as "Schizoid Man" and "Epitaph" quickly dissolved in 1970 after their first album, but Fripp maintained this confrontational style of music—what Genesis guitarist Steve Hackett aptly described as "musical karate" (Stump 1997, p. 180)—in subsequent versions of the group he continued to call King Crimson.

After supervising numerous personnel changes, Fripp settled on a new line-up in 1972 that has come to be viewed by many fans and critics as King Crimson's zenith. Consisting of Fripp, bassist John Wetton, violinist David Cross, percussionist Jamie Muir and former Yes drummer Bill Bruford, this dynamic group of musicians was perhaps best able to realize Fripp's ideal of collective composition and improvisation. Fulfilling Fripp's notion of creating music as a "high order language system," this group produced social critique without the use of lyrics or a program, the best example of this being the title track of the 1972 album *Larks' Tongues in Aspic* (hereafter *LTA*). Part One and Part Two of *LTA* are two extended instrumental tracks that were collectively composed and improvised by the band in front of live audiences prior to the final recording of the completed pieces. The final result of this avant-garde jazz-like approach to rock composition is a musical battlefield, with guitar, violin and bass using all manner of distortion and wah-wah pedal effects, and an enormous battery of drums and percussion that pushes King Crimson's violent imagery to new levels without the use of lyrics. In the absence of any specific programmatic narrative, Gregory Karl interprets this piece as an abstract narrative of an individual struggling through crisis towards victory, which he sees as a trope that characterizes King Crimson's more agonized recordings (Karl 2002).[10]

An alternative interpretation to *LTA* as a narrative of "individual in crisis"—which one might surmise if it were composed solely by Fripp—that is more in keeping with the band's collective approach to "musical karate" is a more fractured and embattled narrative of "society in crisis." Such an interpretation is particularly appropriate to the long Part One of *LTA* that is structured according to the dynamic contrast of acoustic and electric timbres that Macan (1997) identifies as central to progressive rock, but appears here as full-blown sonic violence with walls of distorted electric guitar, violin and bass obliterating delicate passages of acoustic strings and percussion. The lyrics of humankind's doom that filled earlier King Crimson albums of apocalyptic prophecy are gone, but the listener of *LTA* must negotiate with an even more harrowing roller coaster ride of tension and release, with clashing dissonance, contrary meters and noisy timbres set against highly evocative and gentle passages of "Eastern-sounding" strings and percussion. King Crimson pushed progressive rock ever outward with their broad appropriation of non-Western music in this 1972 work. They created with these new sounds a frightening model of society that juxtaposed a traditional, pastoral life with a frighteningly mechanized, alienated and mass-mediated force that had the power to destroy anything in its path.

Instead of direct references to wars then raging in Southeast Asia, King Crimson's epic depicts battle in a more abstract sense, as a clash of cultures through a dynamic use of instruments and musical sections in warring opposition. The cultural crisis of *LTA* begins with a quiet opening section featuring an African lamellophone (*mbira*) played by Jamie Muir, accompanied by David Cross' violin ostinato that suggests an exotic Eden that is gradually overtaken by a massing of small bells and chimes overdubbed from Muir's percussion arsenal. This quiet, yet unsettling, opening is followed by the slow fade-in of an insistent pulse of double-stops on the acoustic violin that slowly builds in volume, gradually rises in pitch and is eventually joined by a distorted electric guitar line. This malevolent sounding duo ushers in a full electric ensemble of distorted guitar, bass and drum kit that comes in two successive waves of sonic assault on the listener. Heightening the sense of violent assault during the build-up leading to the second wave of attacks, Muir overdubs several squawking bicycle horns that shriek hysterically in the face of this sonic attack, conjuring a vivid image of innocent slaughter. Throughout *LTA* Parts One and Two, as well as the entire album, Muir's various acoustic sound devices (scratched balloons, rubbed glass, feet sloshing through mud, etc.) provide many humanizing elements amidst all the electric timbres, creating an unnerving effect for the listener.

Extreme contrasts in which the gentle is delicately placed before the crushing, mechanized assault of the powerful continue through the rest of this piece. An extended development section based on a frantic, ascending, guitar cadenza by Fripp eventually builds up into a firestorm of rapid-fire guitar chord tremolando and crashing percussion. It is finally relieved by a quiet interlude featuring violin, quiet electric guitar and autoharp. As the pastoral section ends with a soft, Asian-sounding pentatonic melody, the listener is safely returned to the pre-mechanized paradise that began the piece. At this point the work gently fades to silence. Any sense that this might lead to a peaceful ending proves false as the silence is broken by the slow fade-in of the earlier pulsating theme, which crawls back in, this time with the double-stop part played on electric guitar and a new melody on the violin. As this insistent duo of guitar and violin gradually ascends in pitch and builds in volume, human voices are heard for the first time on the album. But these voices—one female and one male—seem disembodied and extremely agitated. It sounds as if a quarrel or the report of a crisis is being broadcast over radio or television. As the tension continues to build, these voices chatter incomprehensibly until the male voice is heard to shout the word "dead!" Several male voices are then heard murmuring incomprehensibly in monotones, suggesting a ritual chant in the aftermath of some kind of death scene. While it is not necessary to map any of these images to any specific war, listeners of King Crimson in the Vietnam era were certainly confronted by an assault of rock music that matched or exceeded the power of "high art" works such as Crumb's Vietnam-inspired *Black Angels*.

Suggested Listening

"The Court of the Crimson King" by King Crimson, from their first album, *In the Court of the Crimson King* (1969)

http://app.rhapsody.com/search/track?query=the+court+of+the+crimson+king

From Genesis to Castration: A Nasty Reading of the Apocalypse and English Society

Genesis, one of progressive rock's most successful bands, was founded at the illustrious Charterhouse school in the mid-1960s. Histories of the band invariably mention this when they cast the group into an elite "world of public schools and comfortable upbringings" (Atton 2001, p. 31). After an initial folk-influenced phase that lasted until about 1971, founding members Peter Gabriel, Tony Banks and Mike Rutherford engaged two King Crimson-influenced rock musicians, Steve Hackett and Phil Collins, to develop a noticeably harder-edged sound (Thompson 2005, pp. 1–66). Unabashedly intellectual, Genesis cast all sorts of literary and musical references over the course of several albums to create a sense of overriding narrative in the band's output. This Romantic proclivity for cyclicism is particularly evident in a stretch of music that extended from the last track of their 1972 LP *Foxtrot*—a multi-movement suite entitled "Supper's Ready"—to the last track of a four-sided album, *The Lamb Lies Down on Broadway* of 1974. Over this span the band drew together ideas from the Apocalypse of the New Testament; poems of William Blake, T. S. Eliot, John Keats and John Bunyan (and others); Ovidian and Greek myths and early Egyptian history; Stravinskian, classical and romantic musical forms and processes; broadside ballad-styled poetry; Brill Building pop lyrics and surreal imagery. What has not been sufficiently recognized is that this group of social elites used their intellectual prowess to express their virulent condemnation of English and American society and mores.[11]

In "Supper's Ready" many of the themes are introduced in the semi-innocent guise of a surreal dream: for example in a section "Willow Farm" a linguistic sex change—"dad to dam to dum to mum"—prefigures the appearance of the Greek mythical figure Tiresias in the song "Cinema Show" on the next LP, *Selling England by the Pound*, as perhaps does also the gruesome castration scene near the close of *The Lamb*. Old, and cast into modern times like Eliot's Tiresias, who "throbbed like a Taxi" in *The Waste Land* (Eliot 1922, III: 217), Gabriel's Tiresias shares his wisdom with an English working class couple about sexual experiences from both male and female points of view. The couple is cast promisingly as Romeo and Juliet, but they are bleakly drawn and clearly need the consolation Tiresias provides. Similarly, John, the author of the Apocalypse that is re-told in "Supper's Ready," returns as a supporting character in *The Lamb* alongside the star "Rael" who is "real," *Gab*riel and *Is*Rael by the end of this *sur*real re-casting of (John!) Bunyan's *Pilgrim's Progress.*[12]

Genesis couched these overarching literary themes in music of similar sophistication. For example, near the end of "Supper's Ready" the bassist and guitarist (Rutherford and Hackett) perform an extended instrumental ostinato on E with displaced accents quite similar to Stravinsky's *Rite of Spring* (Spicer 2000, p. 96). Over this Banks plays a carefully crafted keyboard solo that builds to a climactic point of harmonic tension with a chord in first inversion, or 6th chord (a C major chord over the E), to prepare the return of Gabriel who sings "666."[13] After this "Pythagoras" joins seven trumpeters and writes the lyrics in blood as the narrator awakens from his dream of the Apocalypse. The piece ends soon after this with a reprise of the opening theme to help create the notion that the narrator and his wife are fully awake (or "real") when they hear an angel sing about the coming of the "New Jerusalem." In the context of this album it is not clear if Gabriel wished to cast England as this Jerusalem or to adopt the tone of deep national concern so clear in Blake's poem by that name. But we are given warning that the story is not over, as the lyric sheet of this album ends with the word "(Continued)."

The next album confirms that England was and will be the subject as it is unambiguously entitled *Selling England by the Pound*. This LP imitates a collection of ballads.[14] There are news items depicted in song, one work is a musical illustration of a visual image (like many ballads) and Gabriel opens the album singing monophonically to imitate the older genre. Throughout the puns are almost unbearable, but the point is not lost. "Dancing with the Moonlit Knight," the first track, begins with a question, "Can you tell me where my country lies?" and the answer to all the possible meanings of "lie" seem to point to the United States and especially to its then-new supermarkets that were spreading to England and bringing with them all the impersonal relationships that could destroy a community.[15] By the end of the album the supermarket puns are all too obvious, although the United

States itself has never been explicitly mentioned by name. But just as they connected the end of 'Supper's Ready" with *Selling England*, they immediately answer the question posed by *Selling England* with their next album, *The Lamb Lies Down on Broadway*. Reading England as the "Lamb," we now know where it *lies*, in New York City "down on Broadway."

Suggested Listening

"Dancing with the Moonlit Knight" by Genesis, from the album *Selling England By the Pound* (1973)

http://app.rhapsody.com/artist/genesis/album/selling-england-by-the-pound

There is a patronizingly affectionate tone throughout *Selling England*, but Genesis does not extend many compliments to the British themselves. In the second track, "I Know What I Like," for example, the refrain seems to suggest rather pointedly the closed mindedness of a numbed nation with the phrase "I know what I like and I like what I know." In *Lamb*, America (or, on one level, Babylon), which this group knew less intimately, gets none of the affection of *Selling England* and is treated instead from the start with cool detachment. If we might borrow a Verdian term for musical character and describe *Selling England's* tinta[16] as the ballad, *The Lamb* is colored by the purposely-vague impressionism of Debussy and early Ravel. In any case, distinctly absent are many direct references to American music, an un-Genesis-like omission that is made all the more prominent by the constant barrage of direct quotations from pop songs like "Raindrops keep falling on my head" and "Runaway" in the album's lyrics (Lieber and Stoller's "On Broadway," is perhaps the one exception). If Genesis kept its musical distance from this country Gabriel was trenchant in his socio-political critique in the lyrics. In a powerful quiet scene wherein the character Rael dies, Gabriel makes a viciously sarcastic comment on US history in a brutal "Death American Style" parade of images, as follows: "Groucho, with his movies trailing, stands alone with his punch line failing. Ku Klux Klan serve hot soul food and the band plays 'In the Mood'/ The cheerleader waves her cyanide wand, there's a smell of peach blossom and bitter almond. Caryl Chessman [capital punishment victim] sniffs the air and leads the parade, he knows in a scent, you can bottle all you made." Later, the hero, already dead, is literally emasculated.

Gabriel was as mercilessly explicative about his work as he was gruesome in his details about such matters as death and—even worse for the male members of the audience—castration, using grotesque stories between songs, choreography and costumes, concert programs, liner notes and even the press itself to send one message after the other in an ever-changing *roman a clef*. In a number of ways Gabriel went as far as he could when he got to the point of castration. Given the make-up of the mainstream progressive rock audience at the time—"male adolescents . . . who . . . shared similar cultural backgrounds, though they might not come from the same privileged backgrounds" (Atton, 2001, p. 31)—the unforgiving emasculation scene in *Lamb* shows a blatant disregard for the "cock rock" sensibilities of contemporary audiences.[17] Gabriel was willing at this time to turn his nasty political commentary inward, toward the very youth culture from which he himself had emerged. As a new generation was entering the rock audience, those of Gabriel's age were no longer part of a single "youth" culture of hippies. Progressive rockers such as Gabriel could now direct their attention toward a new and vicious criticism of their younger audiences, as Ian Anderson of Jethro Tull did in his similarly audience-defying quip about his anti-hero "Little Milton" of *Thick as a Brick* whose "sperm is in the gutter and [whose] love is in the sink."

The Threat of Peace and Love in the Music of Yes

It is with the idea of art as a challenge rather than a comfortable status symbol that even groups like Yes, well known for its Aquarian image, join this set of nasty mainstream progressive rockers that we have discussed thus far. Although much has been said about Yes's cohesive musical structures, its use of eclectic musical sources, its peculiar approach to language, its multi-disciplinary utopian visions (that extended especially to album cover art), its spiritual quests and even (obliquely) its politics and its androgynous image, there seems still to be some basic confusion about the overall synthetic image this band created.[18] It cannot be denied that Yes was a band with an affirmative mission, but a closer look shows they too had a provocative side. Certainly one might detect some stubbornness. When criticisms of the movement's excesses were becoming more pointed, Yes sought to create longer and longer spans of cohesive music, abandoning song-form altogether at times in favor of huge cyclic forms common to late-romantic music. Although it is tempting simply to recall the scene in Ken Russell's *Liztomania* with Rick Wakeman urinating in a fireplace, a stronger case for Yes's nasty side rests with their art and the nature of their activism as an affirmative ethos in the progressive style.

By the time of their 1973 *Tales from Topographic Oceans* Yes had achieved something that would seem rather remarkable in rock history (indeed, in the history of any musical style). Jennifer Rycenga has aptly described this achievement as a "spiritual experience in the music" and categorizes their particular kind of spirituality as "panentheistic neopagan immanent cosmology" (Rycenga 2002, p. 145). The string of terms needed to describe the musical-poetics of Yes's spirituality would seem to reduce the impact of the band's basic achievement and confirm instead the critical notion that the musicians had lost touch with their audience, that it had somehow wandered off on an elaborate spiritual quest so personalized as to lose meaning altogether along with any political effectiveness. The complexity of this definitive terminology notwithstanding, the source of Yes spirituality had a direct political basis. As early works by Yes confirm, the band was fundamentally influenced by commonly held, radical ideas of peace and love that were raging especially in the United States. The confrontational nature of these messages has subsequently faded from memory, but at the time there were some who saw the wearing of a peace medallion as tantamount to an allegiance to the communist societies who were engaged with the United States and their allies in a cold war. Yes approached these ideas in ways that reveal the defiance that originally lay behind them.

Yes's *Time and a Word* of 1969–1970 displays many psychedelic trappings and progressive sins—its two covers (of works by Richie Havens and Stephen Stills), its orchestral excesses and its lapses into anthem-like bombast. The album also provides insights into Yes's image in the early stages of the band's development.

Some of the works, like "Astral Traveller," show well the link with *The Yes Album* works like "Starship Trooper," for example (Martin 1996, p. 31). Others betray the radical side of the band's image and its aggressiveness.

These latter features appear clearly in the track "Then," which explores systematically the ways music can cause suspense in a nearly cinematic fashion. The musical drama reaches its peak when the penultimate word is drawn out to the point where we are shocked by the Haydnesque timpani stroke that punctuates brutally the last word of the song. With this sonic blast the song ends ominously with the word "Then," leaving intact the portent and threat of an unknown future. Like many horror tales, the piece as a whole projects a sense of "us" and "them." Specifically, the song promotes the idea of a "New Day" of peace and love and it threatens with obliteration anyone who would stand opposed to it. Thus the group making the threat here, interestingly, is the peaceful one, an "us" instead of a "them." The oppositional group is not described in any detail, but one feature of the New Day is surely that it would not be ruled by traditional authoritarian figures and their ideas. Underlying all this, we believe, is Yes's confident message about the power of the youth culture and the significance of their slogans of love and peace. They reiterate the message, in literal terms, in "The Prophet," also on *Time and a Word*. Here "peace" is mentioned as the most important spiritual characteristic and, again, a clear warning is voiced for those on the outside: "that some will die but only those who doubt."

After *Time and a Word* Yes developed further their already sharply honed musical rhetoric as they produced one impressive album after another. In creating expansive imaginary worlds of unprecedented dimensions—which culminated in the four sided *Tales*—they continued to manipulate their listeners by shaping expectations through methods of varied repetition, musical traits that John Covach (1997), John R. Palmer (2001) and others have shown in detail through meticulous musical analyses. It seems possible that in the process they had indeed forsaken some of the more obvious political trappings—the confrontational peace and love—of the psychedelic era, but it seems also possible that these notions still buttressed the group's on-going work and development. Certainly the later work, with its clarity of purpose and polish, betrays the traits we might expect of the true believer and perhaps even the savvy to use codes that would keep the critics unsure of their purposes.

In describing the lyrics of "I've seen all good people" from *The Yes Album* Jon Anderson has suggested that they might be without meaning.[19] Nonetheless, to us they form a vital link between Yes's progressive musical-poetics and its psychedelic past of *Time and a Word*. In the "a" section, "Your Move," we find the same themes of peace and love that were featured in "Then" and "The Prophet," as well as a sense that "time" in particular will be manipulated to the point where it seems to function dramatically as this band's way to use musical poetics to pronounce a call to action. Indeed, in the particular line Anderson dismissed as chosen merely for its sonic qualities—"'Cause it's time, it's time in time with your time, and its news is captured,/for the Queen to use"—we find a potent expression of Yes's musical poetics. First, the word "time" itself is repeated to the extent that the surrounding words tend to lose their semantic role within the phrase. In this way the word dominates musical "time" and becomes a performative force, compelling one to act, or, at least, to read the word "cause" itself as a pun that suggests the political "cause" as well as the contracted conjunction. Secondly, time is again associated with urgency. Before it was an immanent "then," in this instance, with the word "news," a favorite word of the gospel preacher, the time is now. The word news itself is emphasized by its rhythm position as the last of a string of antecedents (all the others emphasizing "time") that end on a climax with the word "captured."

A politicized reading of the time issue is further bolstered by an intriguing passage that provides a link to peace, one where Anderson again uses nonsense syllables (scat) for dramatic purpose. This is how the lyrics appeared on the page of a reissued CD:

> Diddit diddit diddit diddit diddit diddit diddit didda.
> Diddit diddit diddit diddit diddit diddit diddit didda.
> Diddit diddit diddit diddit diddit diddit diddit didda.
> Diddit diddit diddit diddit diddit diddit diddit didda.

Unstated in the poetic rendition of this passage are two lines interpolated from John Lennon's anthem: "all we are saying/ is give peace a chance" (Martin 1996, p. 80–81). Musically, the Lennon quote is placed in the background and is almost drowned out in the mix by the ominous chordal sequence Tony Kaye performs on a particularly resonant pipe organ. This mix tends to obscure the Lennon reference somewhat, but not to the point of its being lost. Instead there is an overall effect that suggests that one should hear the lines as if it were subliminal, yet important too, as the organ adds much in the way of musical seriousness to otherwise innocuous lyrics which do, however, suggest the ticking of time, and even Morse code. We are further drawn into the hidden theme when the Lennon song, "Instant Karma," is mentioned elsewhere in the lyrics. Two layers are very clear. Overtly the song is about something rather innocent: a game of chess. But all the codes and hidden meanings suggest that there is another game going on here too. And, in this game, we are not told what to do, but the section's very title assures us that we are expected to play, to make *our* "move" toward the political causes associated with peace as proclaimed by Lennon and the so-called psychedelic left he came to represent.[20]

Suggested Listening

"I've Seen All Good People: Your Move/All Good People" by Yes, from the album *The Yes Album* (1971)

http://app.rhapsody.com/artist/yes/album/the-yes-album-bonus-tracks

The messages may have been slightly obscured, but to some listeners, at least, Yes of the early 1970s, after *Time,* was still working for one side in a divided society, which was surely John Lennon's psychedelic left. Others, who opposed that position, presumably still saw them as a force to fear and oppose. Indeed, as it so resembled a form of religious magnetism, Yes's more ambitious musical poetics (rather than their purely linguistic traits) might be said to be the most insidious of all the progressive voices of the era, at least from the point of view of an establishment that opposed their radical viewpoint. To those engaged, friend and enemy, Yes's spiritual worlds "remain[ed as] incurably earthbound" as Freud's view of the imagination itself (quoted in Kumar 1990, p. 1). If in hindsight Yes's *Tales* smacks of the personal (and pointless) spiritual journey so common to the New Age, it is important to remember that this was the group who once tried, through its impressive array of musical skills, to yoke its listeners into the very midst of a social and political battlefield over the politically loaded issues of love and a new day of peace.

And a few still remember it the old way. For example, the progressive rock anthologist Bradley Smith aptly described this confrontational side of Yes in his depiction of all progressive music:

> rebellion required forms that the older generations not only disliked but couldn't understand. Volume, abstract lyrics, weird studio effects, new instruments, and lengthy jams were utilized in a conscious break with the past. To most proponents of the new music the traditional song form—the easily understood 2- to 5-minute love song—became the enemy, representative of the repressive, ugly ignorant society unable to deal honestly with its problems. Both the content (the lyrics) and form (the music) had to change. (Smith 1997, p. 12).

As an aficionado, Smith can speak confidently about the rebellious nature of progressive rock. But musicologists must struggle with the widely promoted narratives of rock music that tend to place this movement into that very adult culture Smith saw as its enemy. In the following section we will argue that today's critics and historians—both in the popular press and in academia—have promulgated an idea of cultural accreditation for progressive musicians that had little to do with youth culture. Only when we look beyond this notion to the media controlled by the bands themselves (in their own image-making and musical output) do we find the nasty side that truly characterized this movement. From this perspective it seems appropriate now to suggest that we have accepted too readily an anachronistic reading of the rock press and its role at the time. It may now have the powers attributed to it by critics, but in the 1970s it was still finding its own voice in the rock world.

Critical Derision of Progressive Rock and the Myth of Cultural Accreditation

Although in the euphoria of the late 1960s rock was celebrated by some as coming of age in a newly expanding medium that "incorporates everything from blues to Indian classical raga, from Bach to Stockhausen" (Eisen 1969, *xi*), critics began to develop aesthetic values for rock during the 1970s that rejected such eclecticism. By the 1980s, critics looked back on the late 1960s with disdain for ambitious musical experiments that seemed to them pretentious and somehow commercially driven:

> Behind lengthy improvisations such as Cream's 'Spoonful' . . . lay the theme of individual spontaneity, exploration and extension. The musical basics of pop now thoroughly mastered, rock was apparently ready for greater things. Its 'authenticity' was to be discovered in the 'natural' expression of an artistic autonomy freed from commercial restraints . . . The confused but fruitful energies surrounding rock in the late 1960s were transformed into the stilled, but highly marketable, waters of 'Art'. (Chambers 1983, p. 111)

According to this narrative, the new "art" of rock, in addition to being highly marketable offered another promise to ambitious young musicians:

> There was also the chance that such creations would elevate the status of their composers and performers—and by implication, pop music in general—to a level comparable with that of the European classical music of the past, and thus lead to acceptance within the circles of the musical establishment. (Hatch and Millward 1987, p. 148)

These authors suggest that musical eclecticism and creative autonomy served rock musicians' desires for socio-economic advancement.

Bernard Gendron refers to this legitimization process as "cultural accreditation" in his study of the relationship between popular music and the avant-garde (2002). According to Gendron, at the forefront of this movement was the Beatles, who had their work validated by literary critics, musicologists and the mainstream press, transforming their "Beatlemania Lows," in which they were first treated as a menace to Western Civilization,[21] into a triumphant anointment by the cultural establishment (ibid., pp. 161–224). Gendron's thesis, however, is built on the assumption that the highbrow cultural establishment had the power to bestow some apparently coveted form of cultural accreditation upon young rock stars.[22] This begs the question of who in fact possessed the most cultural capital in the late 1960s: the highbrow cultural critics or the Beatles themselves.

The economic and cultural capital of the time belonged not to highbrow critics and adults in some kind of "musical establishment," but to the Beatles themselves and it was theirs to bestow upon others. For example, the effect of Paul McCartney's pronouncements of the influence of Stockhausen on the Beatles' music and the appearance of the composer's face on the album cover of *Sgt. Pepper* was surely a boost to Stockhausen's cultural capital, aiding the expansion of his appeal into the hippie culture. Stockhausen's subsequent spiritualistic hippie persona, Leonard Bernstein's extended sideburns and "symphonic" albums of Beatles' songs were all markers of affinity between the classical "long-hair" musicians—as they were sometimes called by the older generation—and their younger rock and roll counterparts. Lest they be confused with "straight" establishment culture, many artists and writers in high culture during the late 1960s went to great lengths to identify themselves with the hippies and gain legitimacy from the culture of rock. The Beatles were even poised to consummate their role as cultural referees of the avant-garde with the formation of a special label, Zapple Records, which had plans to release recordings by the most cutting edge artists and thinkers of the time (Inglis 2000, p. 12). As the intellectual leaders of rock, it was the Beatles then who inspired nascent progressive rock groups like the Moody Blues and Procol Harum to orchestrate rock and use concept albums as tools for cultural criticism, setting the stage for the progressive rock musicians of the 1970s. On a social level, Beatles fans, i.e., young people, as many seem to have forgotten, had everything to offer to the up and coming rock star who knew he or she might attain instant success, new wealth, and a supremely enviable bohemian lifestyle of virtually unhindered sexual gratification and ego fulfillment.[23]

Many young musicians of the 1970s found rock in the post-*Sgt. Pepper* era to be the superior medium for direct expression in music. This was true whether they were formally trained or self-taught, or upper-, middle- or working-class.[24] If some rock musicians lamented the lack of a vibrant culture of classical music—as suggested by classically trained rock musician John Cale's progressive rock album title, *The Academy in Peril*—the antidote was certainly not to be found in the conservatism of classical music, but in the unbridled energy of rock. In describing the "Utopian freedom" of "our music" in the liner notes to the Nice's *Five Bridges* in 1969, the classically-trained Keith Emerson made it clear that he identified not with the orchestra, but with the rock trio "representing the non-establishment" with a "complete trust in a rebellious spirit" (Emerson quoted in Covach 1997, p. 7). Similar sentiments were expressed by another leader of the progressive rock movement, Jon Anderson of Yes, who, like Robert Fripp, also came from a working class background with no formal musical training: "We're not trying to get into classical music, but get what classical music does to you" (Anderson quoted in Bowman 2002, p. 186).[25] As with the Beatles before them, some progressive rock bands of the 1970s had highbrows courting *them*, such as the invitation extended to The Soft Machine to perform at the prestigious Proms concert at Royal Albert Hall in 1970. Soft Machine drummer Robert Wyatt surmised that the Proms concert was a "failed effort to make us respectable, and had it succeeded I think it could have done a lot more damage" (Bennett 2005, p. 217).

If cultural accreditation was not a concern of the musicians, it certainly was not a concern of audiences for progressive rock. Progressive rock found its strongest following among—but was not limited to—the hippie counterculture during the late 1960s/early 1970s that opposed both elite and mainstream popular culture.[26] Upwardly mobile status seeking was rejected as contrary to the value of personal and spiritual honesty of the authentic, uncompromised self that could be free from the constraints of materialistic society. As evident in an ethnography of the counterculture in the early 1970s by Paul Willis (1978), hippies did not worship progressive musicians from a distance or think of them as wealthy, overtrained musical snobs, but rather as members of their own group. The hippies studied by Willis identified progressive rock musicians of the time as sharing the same countercultural values and interpreting life in a similar way (ibid., pp. 163–165). In spite of any economic disparities between ordinary fans and their suddenly wealthy heroes, the musicians' credibility with fans as fellow "heads" rested entirely on musicians exercising their creative freedom to speak out against society. Any appeals to upper class "square" society on the part of progressive rockers would have done little more than alienate their countercultural fan base just as Robert Wyatt had feared about his band's appearance at the Proms concert.

In spite of—or perhaps because of—their roles as creative leaders of the counter-culture, progressive rock musicians have come to play a different role in histories of rock. Instead of being remembered for their roles as anti-establishment provocateurs, now they have been recast as upwardly mobile rock stars for the purposes of a narrative in which they serve more infamously as the "artists" who took rock beyond its boundaries of acceptability. Many critics have described 1967 as the zenith of the maturation of rock and the beginning of a decline for the music.[27] According to this narrative, a kind of "dark age" of rock extends from 1968 to about 1976 when punk rock emerged and revived the cultural values of rock and roll that had supposedly been lost during this dearth of authentic music.[28] As progressive rock has proven to be such a useful foil to construct an aesthetics of rock, it is no mere coincidence that progressive rock's reign from 1968–1976 is also the time period during which rock criticism fully matured in magazines such as *Rolling Stone*, *Creem*, *New Musical Express* and *Melody Maker*.

Rock critics at the time of the Beatles' *Sgt. Pepper* album, like rock musicians, drew their validation not from any appeals to highbrow culture, but from the power of the youth counterculture.[29] This was especially true of *Rolling Stone* magazine, which began in 1967 as an underground paper before evolving into the industry leader of rock criticism by the mid-1970s. As a voice of the counterculture, *Rolling Stone* set out to cover not only rock music, but also the "things and attitudes that the music embraces" (Frith 1981, p. 169). It was the music, however, that best represented the ideology of the youth culture and provided the main focus of the magazine in its early years. Especially important in this respect were record albums that served as social statements in this era of greater creative freedom for rock musicians in the recording studio. The authoritative power of rock albums as countercultural criticisms of mainstream society is evident in *Rolling Stone* magazine's absence of general coverage of political affairs in favor of music coverage since its founding in 1967 until a format change in 1973 that introduced general political coverage into the magazine (ibid., p. 171). Up until that time, for many in the counterculture, rock music was seen as the only way of making sense of the social turmoil of the era and it was this music that validated the work of rock critics as mediators of countercultural messages.

Emboldened by the power of rock as message music, rock critics wasted no time exerting their own power as an elite group of arbiters of public taste in the rapidly developing rock industry. As early as 1967 critic Robert Christgau began to rail against the rising tide of "avant-garde pop" by arguing that it was "elevated by an ignorant audience that applauds the 'new' whether it is bogus or not."[30] Just at the moment when rock musicians began to take up the challenge by the Beatles to expand rock towards an all-inclusive utopian music, some in the rock press began to attack any further eclectic experimentation in rock. This move by the press to maintain stylistic purity in rock required what John Sheinbaum has described as an "inversion of musical values," a rejection of highbrow musical values in favor of lowbrow musical values, such as valuing repetition over musical development, stimulation of the body over stimulation of the mind, simple structures over complicated ones, and music of the lower class over music of the middle- and upper-class (Sheinbaum 2002, p. 24). Although Sheinbaum demonstrates that bands such as Yes employed musical values from both sides of the high art/low art spectrum, it was precisely the musical ambitions to bridge the gap between high and low by Yes and other progressive rock bands that violated the "gutter purity" so valued by rock critics.

In the Beatles's wake the rock press was a new phenomenon. Now it seems to have all the power and influence that Gendron attributed to it in the 1970s. Not only are major bands such as ELP, King Crimson, Genesis and Yes missing from *Rolling Stone* magazine's most recent canonic list of the 500 greatest record albums, but these bands have yet to be inducted into the Rock and Roll Hall of Fame, which also constructs its rock canon exclusively on lowbrow musical values that have informed the "museumization" of rock in the past two decades. Progressive rock seems condemned to the margins by what Bill Martin refers to as "blues orthodoxy" (Martin 1998, p. 22–23) in the same way that avant-garde and fusion jazz have been marginalized in histories of jazz by neo-conservative traditionalists. A similar kind of marginalization occurs among musicologists who have written about the progressive rock style. Grounded in an old musicology that privileges an analytical process based on high art music, yet eager to embrace new ideas about cultural studies, musicologists who study progressive rock have been pushed into a quandary. Here they have the opportunity to apply a well-honed vocabulary based on "high art" musical qualities that tend to isolate music from its context, but it's the wrong vocabulary for a music that was designed to promulgate a political message. The ultimate effect is that a once vibrant, nasty genre of "prog" has now been cast as an imperturbable form of elitism.

Perhaps the most pernicious effects of the cultural accreditation myth on progressive rock's place in rock history is the hegemony that can be found in the attitudes of some of the major figures of progressive rock themselves, who have eagerly disassociated themselves with the 1970s style they helped to create. In spite of increasing public acceptance of nostalgia in rock, progressive rock pioneers such as Peter Gabriel and Robert Fripp have worked hard to create a distance between 1970s progressive rock and their present-day careers. Pushing ever forward, Peter Gabriel has dismissed his impressive work in early Genesis as a kind of musical immaturity and Robert Fripp bristles at any association with the progressive style that he helped to create. Almost as if in exchange for aiding in the blackballing of progressive rock, Gabriel and Fripp are highly regarded by critics as artists who continue to innovate. Among veterans of the 1970s progressive rock underground, where one might expect to find a desire for rehabilitation of the era's musical legacy, the same narrative appears. Chris Cutler, who helped pioneer an avant-garde approach to progressive rock as drummer with the group Henry Cow, has even written an essay on the history of British (progressive) rock that is a textbook example of the dark ages approach to rock history, positioning his own group as one of the few beacons of authentic activity during the 1968–1976 era (Cutler 1993, pp. 106–135). Like Fripp and Gabriel, Cutler celebrates the arrival of punk in the late 1970s as a welcome response to the excesses of the decade (ibid., pp. 124–126). Meanwhile, for former progressive rock musicians who have found success and stardom in simpler, mainstream pop, such as Phil Collins and his band-mates in Genesis, the history of progressive rock is nearly invisible, nothing more than a rite of passage into the big leagues.[31]

One of the few attempts to change the prevailing view has come from Emerson, Lake and Palmer, a band whose music catalog and recent reunion performances are heavily invested in nostalgia of 1970s rock excess and bombast. In the 1996 reissue of their landmark progressive rock album, *Brain Salad Surgery*, all three musicians describe the group's role during the progressive rock era as crude, anti-social and antagonistic, recalling with pride such immature behavior as destroying hotel rooms and throwing up in airports (McCulley 1996). Just as Emerson had expressed back in 1969, the group aligns itself not with the hallowed tradition of classical music, but with the adolescent indulgence of rock's gutter. Rather than pointing to the untold hours of practice and preparation they underwent to perform Ginastera concertos and Prokofiev's symphonic works for huge audiences of contemporaries in vast stadiums, they emphasize that the band was "bloody dark and aggressive . . . aggressive to each other, aggressive in the music, aggressive in performance" (ibid., p. 12). Anxious to show that they foreshadowed punk stars like Johnny Rotten, who replaced them at the forefront of rock's avant-garde, ELP has clearly come to understand that rock critics are now a more powerful authenticating force in popular music than they were in the 1970s.

With their own propaganda efforts ELP has helped uncover a nasty side of the progressive movement that has indeed been sorely neglected.[32] Our research suggests that ELP is not the only victim of this myopic treatment. What we have tried to offer in its stead is a view of Gentle Giant's *Acquiring the Taste* that emphasizes the tongue next to a buttocks instead of a pretentious statement of artistic values; a view of King Crimson that credits their sonic expressionism as political force rather than some kind of quiet intellectualism; a view of Genesis that looks beyond the assumed world views of their elite background and into the disturbing world views that they actually promulgated and, finally, a view that shows Yes not as a precursor to the gentle New Age, but a social force enacting a palpable threat to the inflexible society of their elders. We need not reiterate here all the provocative nature of ELP when they were at their most popular, as they seem to be hard at work themselves in a campaign of recovering the nasty side of progressive rock. But on their behalf we do suggest one thing, that perhaps musicologists would do well to take them just a bit more seriously in their recent suggestion that "early 70s ELP made Johnny Rotten look like a fucking walk in the park."[33]

Notes

1. We dedicate this article to the memory of Emily Wasserman (1976–2005), a student in our Spring 2004 graduate seminar on progressive rock at the University of Colorado, Boulder.
2. The nearly simultaneous appearance in the late-1990s of three books on progressive rock, by Macan (1997), Martin (1998), and Stump (1997), has resulted in a discourse focused on the British and, to a lesser extent, European, contribution to the movement. For the sake of argument, we have followed this trend. But we hasten to note that, as some of the authors in Holm-Hudson (2002) point out well (but others ignore), progressive music had a strong footing in North America at the same time.
3. In praise of the band The Mars Volta, Red Hot Chili Peppers guitarist John Frusciante commented on the media's misperception of the connection between progressive and punk: "What they're doing with combining the energy of punk rock and progressive rock . . . I never agreed with the media's perception that those two kinds of music were opposite or something. In L.A., it seemed like a lot of the best punk musicians were also into prog. Like, Pat Smear, for instance, is a huge fan of The Mars Volta now, and it's like he was always a big Yes fan" (Corva 2005, p. 50).
4. Numerous authors have criticized progressive rock musicians for their upward mobility. Progressive rockers of the late 1960s and early 1970s have been accused of making music "acceptable for upper-class approbation" (Rockwell 1986) and "respectable enough to please Mum and Dad" (DeRogatis 1996, p. 84), "consciously aiming at their 'betters,' the people in the suits and bowlers" (Stokes 1986, p. 405), and having "an ambition to be taken seriously in classical or avant-garde musical circles" (Tucker 1986, p. 480).
5. One well-known example of obscenity as political agitation from this time period is the "Fish Cheer" by Country Joe McDonald and the Fish at the Woodstock Festival in 1969. Along similar lines were the obscene, antagonizing songs of The Fugs in the late 1960s.
6. Although this disparaging definition of "prog" comes from the tongue-in-cheek *Rock Snob's Dictionary*, the authors' implication that progressive rock may even be unfit for rock snobbery is nevertheless an indicator of progressive rock's low status in the discourse of rock. The full entry is as follows: "Prog. Abbreviation for *progressive rock*, a term used to describe the single most deplored genre of postwar pop music, inhabited by young musicians who, entranced by the eclecticism, elaborate arrangements, and ostentatious filigrees of the Beatles' *Sgt. Pepper* era, distorted their enthusiasm into a 1970s morass of eternal song suites with multiple time signatures, ponderous space-cadet or medievalist lyrics, ridiculous capes and headpieces (especially where Yes's keyboard player, Rick Wakeman, was concerned), and an overall wretched bigness of sound, staging, and hair. But while prog's most egregious culprits (ELP, Yes, Jethro Tull, Rush) are easy objects of ridicule, the postmodernist penchant for rummaging through every single chapter of rock's past has made even these bands worthy of Snob investigation and adulation" (Kamp 2005, pp. 97–98).
7. What to Bangs "looked like a theremin" was undoubtedly Emerson's trusty modular Moog ribbon controller (interestingly, today the Moog company does distribute Theremins). Probably Bangs's mistake would have been known to anyone at the time at all familiar with Emerson's equipment. But nearly conclusive proof that Bangs had made this mistaken identification was furnished by Emerson himself in 1996, when he signed Mark Glinsky's ribbon controller with the following sentiments: "To Mark—Don't Wipe This on Your Arse! Keith Emerson." Glinsky was a "local roadie" for the same ELP 1974 tour that Bangs had reviewed; on his "Emerson, Lake and Palmer Ring" website he features a picture of himself with Emerson holding the aforementioned autographed ribbon controller, see "Emerson Lake and Palmer," http://www.markglinsky.com/msgelp.html. This incident

suggests of course that Emerson remembered well his antics on that particular tour. But there is also the strong possibility suggested here that Emerson may have remembered Bangs's evocative description about the way in which he used his equipment on stage. The context even suggests that Emerson may have even relished a bit in the fact that Bangs had perpetrated an inaccuracy in his 1974 article (and perhaps Emerson now justifiably relishes too in the fact that he came across as a rather "nasty" character in the article, despite subsequent assessments to the contrary that tend to be voiced by his critics).

8. On the "war criminals" moniker and its use see studies such as Spicer (2000, p.103n2), Sheinbaum (2002, p. 21), Hung (2003, p. 93). Sheinbaum later confessed having followed Macan in this tendency to quote Bangs out of context (Sheinbaum 2004, p. 956).
9. This version can be heard on ELP's live LP *Welcome Back My Friends to the Show That Never Ends . . . Ladies and Gentlemen, Emerson, Lake and Palmer.*
10. In his analysis of *LTA* Parts One and Two, Gregory Karl refutes the idea that King Crimson were superficially borrowing formal structures from 19th century romantic music and instead achieved a similar effect working through pop song structure "by transforming the materials of rock music from within, rather than by importing unassimilated material and procedures from a foreign realm" (Karl 2002, p.122).
11. See Spicer 2000 for a discussion of the disparate musical influences in "Supper's Ready." Although no one purports to have discovered all of Genesis's copious literary borrowings, some of the most important are discussed in Spicer (ibid.) and (Nicholls 2004 pp. 129–33). We have also drawn from Finnegan 1994.
12. In an interview with Henry Fielder, Gabriel described the story as "a type of Pilgrim's Progress" (Finnegan 1994).
13. Gabriel foreshadows the appearance of "666" with pervasive alliteration, viz., "six saintly shrouded men"; "super-sonic scientist," etc.
14. On the ballad tradition see Atkinson 2002.
15. Gabriel presents this critique subtly at first: in "Dancing with the Moonlit Knight," for example, the instrumental depiction of an aggressive dance turns with a film-like cut to a scene where, with a hint of new anger in his voice, Gabriel sings "there's a fat old lady outside the saloon;/laying out the credit cards she plays Fortune/The deck is uneven right from the start/and all of their hands are playing a part."
16. On the concept of Verdian tinta see Rosen 1997.
17. For an interpretation of "cock rock" aesthetics, see Frith and McRobbie, pp. 383–84.
18. John Covach's classic musical analysis of "Close to the Edge" (1997) has now been joined by a number of detailed analytical studies, many of which seek more fully to combine musical analysis with the consideration of other (visual, social, aesthetic, etc.) factors: see Sheinbaum 2002, Macan 1997, von der Horst 2002 and Rycenga 2002. Yes's spirituality and their "Yessonatas" are discussed at length in MosbØ 1994. Rycenga and Martin also treat Yes's mystical and religious themes. On Yes's androgynous image see Macan and von dir Holst. Although it is at times difficult to sort out the relationship between his own political views and that of his subject, Martin aptly describes Yes as a "musical force" and suggests that listening with a "radical openness" will help "further the vision" (p. 236). Martin's Marxist slant is a welcome complement to musicological and spiritualist readings of Yes and if it is perhaps unsuccessful in painting a holistic picture, his book offers many clues as to the true nature of the Yes "force," including a welcome appreciation of the formative nature of the first two albums.
19. Jon Anderson quoted in Macan 1997, p. 70.
20. See Platoff 2005 for a discussion of Lennon's politics and the divisions in the political left at this time as reflected in the reception of Lennon's music.
21. An essay from 1964 by Paul Johnson reveals the extent to which English conservatives—much to the consternation of the conservative author—courted the Beatles and began to "worship at the shrine of 'pop culture'"(2004, originally 1964).
22. Ironically, Gendron's history reveals how rock actually bolstered the cultural elite that sought out the liberating stimulus of the youth culture that the Beatles had come to represent. "Highbrow" writers claimed that the music of the Beatles was a welcome stimulant for a bored avant-garde in the late 1960s. Critics as esteemed as Susan Sontag, Richard Poirier and Joan Peyser invoked the sensuality and beat of the Beatles music to question the absence of pleasure in an overly intellectualized discourse of high art music (Gendron 2002, pp. 202–203 and Roka 2004, pp. 23–24). Ned Rorem compared the Beatles to Schumann and proclaimed the revival of the art song to an avant-garde dominated by seri-

alism (Gendron 2002, p. 200; Stump 1997, p. 86). According to Rorem: "the artful tradition of great song has been transferred from elite domains to The Beatles and their offshoots who represent—as any non-specialised intellectual will tell you—the finest communicable music of our time" (Rorem 2004: 103, originally 1968).

23. Frank Zappa reminds us of the more base motivations behind playing rock music in his "anthropology" of the rock and roll band in which he crudely describes phallic displays by guitar players in their quest for easy sex with groupies (Zappa 1989, pp. 164–165)
24. Among the many conservatory-trained musician who cast themselves as rebels, Daryl Way, violinist of the band Curved Air and Royal College of Music graduate, stated that classical music was a "dead art . . . as dead as the Dodo" (Way quoted in Carr 1971, p. 17). Robert Fripp, a self-taught guitarist from a working-class family, expressed similar criticism about the state of Western art music, describing the symphony orchestra as a "dinosaur" bound for extinction (see Tamm 1991, p. 26).
25. Macan's theory about the appropriation of classical forms by progressive rock bands such as Yes is that this was a response to challenges posed by psychedelic music. 19th century extended forms such as the multi-movement suite allowed for lengthy music that could suspend time without relying on excessive improvisation (Macan 1997, pp. 40–46).
26. Sheila Whitely argues that participation in the counterculture was not limited to the middle classes (Whitely 1992, pp. 4–5). Andy Bennett demonstrates Whiteley's point by showing how working class youth were involved in progressive rock in his study of a working class English band that specializes in pub performances of Pink Floyd covers (Bennett 2000, pp. 172–173).
27. For examples of this see Stokes (1986), Chambers (1983), Frith (1981, pp. 212–213) and Cutler (1993).
28. This dark ages trope has also been useful for descriptions of earlier periods in rock history, such as the early 1960s period of shallow teenage pop perceived of as a brief lull before the reinvigoration of authentic rock and roll by the Beatles (see Ward 1986).
29. Although Gendron is misguided in thinking that rock musicians in the late 1960s depended on critics for cultural accreditation, he does acknowledge that rock critics were equally dependent on rock music for their own cultural accreditation (Gendron 2002, p. 190).
30. Christgau quoted in Gendron 2002, p. 210.
31. This attitude toward the early days of progressive rock is evident in the interviews of most of the members of Genesis in the video, *The Genesis Songbook*, 2001.
32. Keith Emerson goes even further in recounting progressive rock's nasty side in his recent autobiography (Emerson 2004).
33. In the notes of this CD package each member individually boasts of the aggressiveness of the band, from Carl Palmer's proud acknowledgement of the group's pomposity as a "saber-rattling band" to Keith Emerson's and Greg Lake's descriptions of pre-punk behavior (McCulley 1996).

References

Atkinson, David. 2002. *The English Traditional Ballad: Theory, method and practice*. Aldershot, UK: Ashgate.

Atton, Chris. 2001. "'Living in the Past'?: value discourses in progressive rock fanzines." *Popular Music* 20(1), pp. 29–46.

Bangs, Lester. 2002. "The Blood Feast of Reddy Kilowatt! Emerson, Lake and Palmer Without Insulation!" In *Mainlines, Blood Feasts, and Bad Tastes: A Lester Bangs Reader*, edited by John Morthland, pp. 47–55. New York: Anchor Books.

Bennett, Andy. 2000. *Popular Music and Youth Culture: Music, Identity and Place*. New York: St. Martin's Press.

Bennett, Graham. 2005. *Soft Machine: Out-Bloody-Rageous*. London: SAF Publishing.

Bowman, Durrell S. 2002. "Let Them All Make Their Own Music: Individualism, Rush and the Progressive/Hard Rock Alloy, 1976–77." In *Progressive Rock Reconsidered,* edited by Kevin Holm-Hudson, pp. 183–218, New York: Routledge.

Carr, Roy. 1971. "'Music Still Has to Stand On Its Own Merits'—says Darryl Way of Curved Air," *New Musical Express,* Jan. 2, 1971, p. 17.

Chambers, Iain. 1983. Urban Rhythms: Pop Music and Popular Culture. New York: St. Martin's Press.

Corva, Francis The. 2005. "The Mars Volta Tell It Like It Is," *Chord.* Feb. March 2005, pp. 48–50.

Covach, John. 1997. "Progressive Rock, 'Close to the Edge,' and The Boundaries of Style." In *Understanding Rock: Essays in Musical Analysis,* edited by John Covach and Graeme M. Boone, pp. 3–31, New York: Oxford.

Cutler, Chris. 1993. *File Under Popular: Theoretical and Critical Writings on Music.* Brooklyn, NY: Autonomedia.

DeRogatis, Jim. 1996. *Kaleidoscope Eyes: Psychedelic Music From The 1960s To The 1990s.* London: Fourth Estate.

Eisen, Jonathan, ed. 1969. *The Age of Rock.* New York: Vintage Press.

Eliot, T.S. 1922. *The Wasteland.* New York: Boni and Liveright.

Emerson, Keith. 2004. *Pictures of an Exhibitionist.* London: John Blake Publishing.

Finnegan, Jason, Scott McMahan et al.1994. *The Annotated Lamb Lies Down on Broadway.* http://www.rawbw.com/~marka/music/lamb.html (accessed October 18, 2005).

Kumar, Krishan. 1990. "Utopian thought and communal practice: Robert Owen and the Owen communities. " *Theory and Society* 19, pp. 1–35.

Frith, Simon. 1981. *Sound Effects: Youth, Leisure, and the Politics of Rock 'n' Roll.* New York: Pantheon Books.

Frith, Simon and Angela McRobbie. 1990. "Rock and Sexuality." In *On Record: Rock, Pop, and The Written Word,* edited by Simon Frith and Andrew Goodwin, pp. 371–389, New York: Pantheon Books.

Gendron, Bernard. 2002. *Between Montmartre and The Mudd Club: Popular Music and the Avant-Garde.* Chicago: University of Chicago.

Gentle Giant. 1971. *Acquiring the Taste* (record album notes).

Gracyk, Theodore. 1996. *Rhythm and Noise: An Aesthetics of Rock.* Durham, NC: Duke University Press. Hatch, David and Stephen Millward. 1987. From Blues to Rock: An Analytical History of Pop Music. Manchester, UK; Wolfeboro, NH, USA: Manchester University Press.

Holm-Hudson, Kevin, ed. 2002. *Progressive Rock Reconsidered.* New York: Routledge.

Hung, Eric Hing-Tao. 2003. "Defining Art Music in Great Britain, 1955–1975." Ph.D. diss., Stanford University.

Inglis, Ian. 2000. "Men of Ideas? Popular Music, Anti-Intellectualism and the Beatles." In *The Beatles, Popular Music and Society,* edited by Ian Inglis, pp. 1–22, New York: St. Martin's Press.

Johnson, Paul. 2004 (originally 1964). "The Menace of Beatlism." In The Lennon Companion, edited by Elizabeth Thomson and David Gutman, pp. 39–42. Cambridge, MA: Da Capo.

Kamp, David and Steven Daly. 2005. *The Rock Snob's Dictionary: An Essential Lexicon of Rockological Knowledge.* New York: Broadway Books.

Karl, Gregory. 2002. "King Crimson's *Larks' Tongues in Aspic*: A Case of Convergent Evolution." In *Progressive Rock Reconsidered*, edited by Kevin Holm-Hudson, pp. 121–142, New York: Routledge.

Macan, Edward. 1997. *Rocking The Classics: English Progressive Rock and The Counterculture.* New York: Oxford.

Martin, Bill. 1998. *Listening to the Future: The Time of Progressive Rock, 1968–1978.* Chicago and La Salle, IL: Open Court.

Martin, Bill. 1996. *Music Of Yes: Structure and Vision in Progressive Rock.* Chicago: Open Court.

McCulley, Jerry. 1996. Emerson, Lake and Palmer—*Brain Salad Surgery* (notes to CD reissue). Santa Monica, CA: Rhino Records.

MosbØ, Thomas J. 1994. *Yes: But What Does It Mean? Exploring the Music of Yes.* Milton, WI: Wyndstar.

Nicholls, David. 2004. "Virtual Opera, or Opera between the Ears." *Journal of Royal Music Association*, 129(1): 100–142.

Oxford English Dictionary. 1989.

Palmer, John R. 2001. "Yes, 'Awaken', and the progressive rock style," *Popular Music* 20 (2), pp. 243–261.

Platoff, John. 2005. "John Lennon, 'Revolution,' and the Politics of Musical Reception." *The Journal of Musicology* 22(2): 241–267.

Rockwell, John. 1986. "The Emergence of Art Rock." In *The Rolling Stone Illustrated History of Rock & Roll.* Edited by Anthony De Curtis and James Henke, pp. 492–499. New York: Random House.

Roka, Les. 2004. "A Day in the Life of American Music Criticism: The 'Sgt. Pepper' Debate of 1967–1969." *Journalism History* 30:1 (Spring 2004), pp. 20–30.

Rorem, Ned. 2004 (originally 1968). "The Music of The Beatles." In *The Lennon Companion*, edited by Elizabeth Thomson and David Gutman, pp. 99–109. Cambridge, MA: Da Capo.

Rosen, David. 1997. "Meter, character and tinta in Verdi's operas." In *Verdi's middle period, 1849–1859: Source studies, analysis, and performance practice.* Chicago: University of Chicago Press.

Rycenga, Jennifer. 2002. "Tales of Change within the Sound: Form, Lyrics and Philosophy in the Music of Yes." In *Progressive Rock Reconsidered*, edited by Kevin Holm-Hudson, pp. 143–166, New York: Routledge.

Sheinbaum, John J. 2002. "Progressive Rock and the Inversion of Musical Values." In *Progressive Rock Reconsidered*, edited by Kevin Holm-Hudson, pp. 21–42, New York: Routledge.

————. 2004 "Mainlines, Blood Feasts, and Bad Taste: A Lester Bangs Reader (review)," *Notes* 60 (4).

Smith, Bradley. 1997. The Billboard Guide to Progressive Music. New York: Billboard Books.

Smith, Sid. 2001. *In the Court of King Crimson.* London: Helter Skelter Publishing.

Spicer, Mark S. 2000 "Large-scale strategy and compositional design in the early music of Genesis." In *Expression in pop-rock music: a collection of critical and analytical essays,* Walter Everett, ed., pp. 77–111, New York: Garland.

Stokes, Geoffrey. 1986. "The Sixties." In *Rock of Ages: The Rolling Stone History of Rock and Roll.* Edited by Ed Ward, Geoffrey Stokes and Ken Tucker, pp. 249–463, New York: Rolling Stone Press/Summit Books.

Stump, Paul. 1997. *The Music's All That Matters: A History of Progressive Rock.* London: Quartet Books.

Tamm, Eric. 1991. *Robert Fripp: From King Crimson to Guitar Craft.* London: Faber and Faber.

Thompson, Dave. 2005. *Turn It On Again: Peter Gabriel, Phil Collins and Genesis.* San Francisco: Backbeat Books.

Tucker, Ken. 1986. "The Seventies and Beyond" In *Rock of Ages: The Rolling Stone History of Rock and Roll.* Edited by Ed Ward, Geoffrey Stokes and Ken Tucker, pp. 467–621, New York: Rolling Stone Press/Summit Books.

von der Horst, Dirk. 2002. "Precarious Pleasures: Situating 'Close to the Edge' in Conflicting Male Desires." In *Progressive Rock Reconsidered,* edited by Kevin Holm-Hudson, pp. 167–182, New York: Routledge.

Ward, Ed. 1986. "The Fifties and Before" In *Rock of Ages: The Rolling Stone History of Rock and Roll.* Edited by Ed Ward, Geoffrey Stokes and Ken Tucker, pp. 17–246, New York: Rolling Stone Press/Summit Books.

Weinstein, Deena. 2002. "Progressive Rock As Text: The Lyrics Of Roger Waters." In *Progressive Rock Reconsidered,* edited by Kevin Holm-Hudson, pp. 91–109, New York: Routledge.

Whiteley, Sheila. 1992. *The Space Between The Notes: Rock and the Counter-Culture.* London: Routledge.

Willis, Paul. 1978. *Profane Culture.* London: Routledge and Kegan Paul.

Zappa, Frank, with Peter Occhiogrosso. 1989. *The Real Frank Zappa Book.* New York: Poseidon Press.

Recordings Cited

The Beatles. *Sgt. Pepper's Lonely Hearts Club Band.* EMI. 1967.

Emerson, Lake and Palmer. *Tarkus.* Atlantic. 1971.

Emerson, Lake and Palmer. *Welcome Back My Friends To The Show That Never Ends . . . Ladies and Gentlemen, Emerson, Lake and Palmer.* Manticore. 1974.

Genesis. *Foxtrot.* Charisma. 1972.

Genesis. *Selling England By The Pound.* Charisma. 1973.

Genesis. *The Lamb Lies Down on Broadway.* Charisma. 1974.

Gentle Giant. *Acquiring the Taste.* Vertigo PHCR-4202. 1971.

Jethro Tull. *Thick As A Brick*. Chrysalis. 1972.

King Crimson. *In the Court of the Crimson King*. Atlantic. 1969.

King Crimson. *Larks' Tongues in Aspic*. Atlantic. 1973.

The Nice. *The Best of the Nice featuring Keith Emerson*. Jimco JICK 89391. 1994.

Yes. *Time And A Word*. Atlantic. 1970.

Yes. *The Yes Album*. Atlantic. 1971.

Yes. *Tales From Topographic Oceans*. Atlantic. 1973.

Videos Cited

The Genesis Songbook. Eagle Vision USA. 2001.

Beyond Soul 18

Key Terms

- Soft soul (romantic soul)
- Philadelphia International Records (PIR)
- Disco
- Funk
- Slap-bass technique
- Blaxploitation film
- Reggae
- Riddim
- Rastafarianism
- Burru
- Mento
- Ska
- Rock steady
- Toasting
- Dub
- Island Records
- Rap
- Hip-hop
- Crew/posse
- Break
- Scratching/back spinning
- Old school rap
- Gangsta rap

Key Figures

- Dr. Martin Luther King, Jr.
- Kenny Gamble
- Leon Huff
- Thom Bell
- Giorgio Moroder
- Steve Dahl
- George Clinton
- Parliament/Funkadelic
- Sly and the Family Stone
- Sly Stone
- Larry Graham
- Stevie Wonder
- Earth, Wind and Fire
- Chris Blackwell
- Bob Marley
- The Wailers
- Run-D.M.C.
- Beastie Boys
- Public Enemy
- 2 Live Crew
- M.C. Hammer
- Ice-T
- NWA
- Snoop Doggy Dog
- Tupac Shakur (2pac)
- Notorious B.I.G.

Courtesy of Photofest

"My music actually speaks closer to me than anything I could ever do. If you listen to the songs I've written, or to the songs of others I record, you will hear how I feel. I guess it's the deepest me."

—STEVIE WONDER

Soft Soul

The Changing Soul Landscape

As we have seen the late 1960s and early 1970s saw a number of new music styles emerge as the rock industry began to expand and fragment. In case the reader hadn't noticed, these styles (folk rock, heavy metal, singer/songwriters, etc.), were largely performed by white artists for audiences. But what about black pop in the 1970s? How was soul music, the dominant black pop style of the 1960s, holding up at decade's end? As it turns out, black popular music was undergoing a similar fragmentation process for several reasons. For one, the two biggest soul powerhouses, Motown and Stax, were starting to show the early signs that they were going into decline. Motown's problems started in 1967 when the Holland/Dozier/Holland production team left the company in a dispute over money. It was a harbinger of things to come—Berry Gordy's stingy contracts and royalty agreements were also becoming sticking points for his artists. Although Stevie Wonder and Marvin Gaye renegotiated their contracts and stayed with the company, many would soon leave, including Mary Wells, the Temptations, Four Tops, Jackson 5, Ashford and Simpson and Martha and the Vandellas. Gordy himself seemed to be losing interest in the constraints of the music business; in 1971 he shut down the company's Detroit operations and moved to Los Angeles to be closer to the Hollywood film industry. In 1982 he signed a distribution agreement with media giant MCA, and in 1988 sold the company outright for $61 million. Ever the shrewd businessman, Gordy held onto Jobete Music, the hugely profitable publishing firm that holds the copyrights for virtually all the hits from the Motown catalogue.

Unfortunately for the owners of Stax, things did not turn out nearly so well. When **Dr. Martin Luther King, Jr.** was assassinated at the Lorraine Motel on April 4, 1968 just a few blocks from the Stax studios, tensions increased between black and white employees. Sadly, the casual atmosphere of racial harmony that the company had enjoyed since its inception began to unravel. Around the same time, owners Jim Stewart and Estelle Axton became aware of the fact that in the fine print of their distribution contract with Atlantic Records, they had inadvertently sold the rights to the master tapes of records that Atlantic distributed. Realizing that they had been tricked into essentially giving away the store, Stewart and Axton promptly ended their association with Atlantic's wily Jerry Wexler and eventually sold the company to Gulf and Western for just under $3 million, far less than what it was worth. Under it's new owners, Stax floundered; questionable business and accounting practices led to a 1973 IRS investigation and its eventual bankruptcy in January 1976.

The Rebirth of Stax

After Stax closed, federal marshals seized the theatre at 926 East McLemore Ave and Union Planters Bank (ironically where Stax former co-owner Estelle Axton used to work), and sold the building to a church for $10 in 1980. Eight years later it was torn down. However, like a phoenix rising up from a deserted vacant lot, the Stax Foundation, spearheaded by former employee Deanie Parker has built an exact replica of the theatre (including the famous marquee) at its former location as a museum and civic landmark. It is called the Stax Museum of American Soul Music.

King's assassination was in many ways the Altamont of the civil rights movement. In spite of the many gains that had been made, the turbulence of assassinations and race riots did not sit well with what was becoming a generally quieter mood of the country. Soul music had always been inescapably linked with the movement, and they both seemed to be running out of steam by the early 1970s. On the other hand, with radio networks and record companies adapting to the growing and changing pop market, it was only inevitable that soul music would change as well. Radio programmers were reluctant to play music that was confrontational, or even reminiscent of the conflicts of the 1960s, and were only too glad to play anything new that wasn't. Some record labels responded by shifting their attention away from black artists to white acts. Exhibit A on this point was Atlantic, which despite its well-earned reputation as one of the finest jazz, R&B and soul labels in the 1950s and early 1960s began to focus more of their attention on signing white acts such as Led Zeppelin, Cream, and Crosby, Stills, Nash and Young by the 1970s.

Black pop was nonetheless expanding and fragmenting into nearly as many styles in the 1970s as white pop, and this chapter will take a closer look at those styles.

The Sound of Philadelphia

One of the most popular new black pop styles became known as **soft soul**, or **romantic soul**. It is, as its name suggests, a smoother, more sophisticated style than 1960s soul, designed to be danceable and listener friendly, with non-confrontational romantic lyrics. Soft soul records were often orchestrated with lush strings and horns, extra percussion, and rich vocal harmonies. The style was the logical extension of the Motown sound, as and the predecessor to disco, it represented a move toward a more important role of the producer. Because the most important soft soul producers lived in Philadelphia, soft soul records are sometimes referred to as reflecting a "Philadelphia Sound." It was a fitting return to prominence in pop music for the City of Brotherly Love, the birthplace of *American Bandstand* and so many dance and novelty records in the early 1960s.

SOFT SOUL OR ROMANTIC SOUL
A highly produced and polished soul style from the early 1970s that emphasized lush string and horn arrangements and smooth vocal harmonies.

Soft Soul

Characteristics of Soft Soul

1. Highly produced and orchestrated; smooth vocals
2. Medium tempo dance tunes; slow, torchy romantic ballads
3. Predecessor to disco and more recent romantic soul styles
4. Center of development: Philadelphia
5. Great commercial and crossover appeal

Key Soft Soul Recordings

- "If You Don't Know Me By Now"—Harold Melvin and the Blue Notes, 1972
- "Then Came You"—the Spinners ,1974
- "For the Love of Money"—the O'Jays, 1974

The architects of soft soul were the songwriting/producing team of **Kenny Gamble** and **Leon Huff**, and independent producer **Thom Bell**. Gamble had apprenticed with Leiber and Stoller in New York before returning to his hometown where he teamed up with Huff. The two began working as independent pro-

Music Cut "Love Train" (Kenny Gamble/Leon Huff—the O'Jays

Personnel: Walter Williams, William Powell, Eddie Levert: vocals; Bunny Sigler: guitar, keyboards; Norman Harris: guitar; Ron Baker: bass; Vincent Montana Jr.: percussion; Earl Young: drums; other musicians unidentified. Recorded at Sigma Sound Studios, Philadelphia, PA; produced by Kenny Gamble and Leon Huff. Released 1973 on Philadelphia International; 13 weeks on the charts, peaking at #1.

As one of the most popular soft soul groups, the O'Jays racked up nine Top 40 hits in the 1970s, six of which hit the Top 10. "Love Train" was their biggest hit, peaking at #1 in March 1973 for one week. The group formed in Canton, Ohio in 1958, and although they never had a Top 40 hit after 1980, they continue to perform to this day, albeit with different personnel than their glory days. The group's producers, Kenny Gamble and Leon Huff, met in 1964 when both worked in Philadelphia's Schubert Building, the city's version of New York's Brill Building. Often producing records at Sigma Sound (where "Love Train" was recorded), their success led to the eventual forming of Philadelphia International Records in 1971.

ducers, and scored a #4 hit in 1967 with their song "Expressway (to Your Heart)" by the white group Soul Survivors. In the wake of that success, they began assembling acts for their own Excel, Gamble, and Neptune labels, before forming **Philadelphia International Records (PIR)** in 1971. Over a five-year period beginning in 1968, Gamble and Huff produced 30 records that went gold. The most important artists at PIR were Harold Melvin and the Blue Notes ("If You Don't Know Me By Now," #3, 1972), the O'Jays ("Love Train," #1, 1973), MFSB (an acronym for Mother Father Sister Brother, a band consisting of the studio musicians at Philadelphia's Sigma Sound Studios where Gamble and Huff worked), and the Three Degrees ("When Will I See You Again," #2, 1974).

Bell's rise to fame paralleled Gamble and Huff's, with his first hit coming in 1968 with the Delfonic's "La La Means I Love You," which went to #4. Among his biggest acts were the Stylistics ("Betcha by Golly, Wow," #3, 1972), the Spinners ("Then Came You," #1, 1974 and six other Top 10 hits between 1972 and 1980.) Other soft soul artists who rose to fame in the wake of the success of soft soul included Al Green ("Let's Stay Together," #1, 1971), Billy Paul ("Me and Mrs. Jones," #1, 1972), Roberta Flack ("Feel Like Makin' Love," 1974, one of her three #1 hits in the 1970s), and Barry White ("Can't Get Enough of Your Love, Babe," #1, 1974).

Disco—The Underground Revolution

DISCO

Dance oriented pop that incorporates synthesizers, drum machines, and lush orchestrations that emerged in the late 1970s.

Soft soul was just a warm up for what would become the biggest trend in pop music history in terms of record sales. In fact, from 1976 to 1979, **disco** became such an enormous cultural phenomenon that it transcended music in a way that mirrored the swing era of the 1930s and 1940s. Disco's most important feature was that it was intended—like swing—to be dance music, and nothing more. Its musical ancestors included the minimalism of James Brown; lush string and horn orchestrations from Motown and Philadelphia International Records; percolating percussion from Latin music; and vocal chants and honking saxophones from rhythm and blues. It also incorporated new technology, making extensive use of synthesizers and drum machines. Disco emerged at a time when much of rock had seemingly become too artsy (art rock), too pretentious (heavy metal), or too self absorbed (singer/songwriters) to care about dancers any more. By the mid-1970s, public dancing as a popular activity was seemingly a distant memory from the early 1960s. In reconnecting pop music to dancing, disco paved the way for the dance-oriented MTV Generation of the 1980s and its superstars Michael Jackson, Madonna, and Prince. Disco also was an important influence on new wave, rap and hip-hop culture.

Disco's origins were in the European and East Coast dance clubs known as discotheques that first became popular during the early 1960s. These clubs generally employed DJ's to play records rather than hire live bands out of economic necessity. By the early 1970s, discos had fallen out of favor with rock's mainstream audience and went underground, catering primarily to the black, Hispanic and gay subcultures. Around 1973 their popularity started to rebound, a trend that was due in part to the ever-increasing skills of DJ's to seamlessly merge one song into the next, using two turntables while keeping the beat constant (disco records often had the beats per minute—bpm—marked on the label). This technique enabled dancers (who were often worked into a frenzy by ingesting cocaine and other uppers) to stay on the dance floor for extended periods of time. Discos initially did not impose dress codes, but it became fashionable for patrons to dress to the nines, enabling them to fantasize that they were the featured performers while they did their best dance moves. As a result of this environment, disco's cultural ethos was able to turn the tables on the established rock culture and let the DJ's, producers, and dancers become the stars instead of the rock singers and instrumentalists.

Disco

Characteristics of Disco

1. Pop oriented dance music whose most important characteristic is the relentless pounding emphasis on every beat
2. Produced in the studio using synthesizers, drum machines
3. Lush strings orchestrations, predominant use of percussion instruments, vocal chants

Key Disco Recordings

- "Love to Love You Baby"—Donna Summer, 1975
- *Saturday Night Fever* Soundtrack—the Bee Gees/Tramps, 1977

Disco Conquers the Airwaves

Disco records were initially ignored by radio, but around 1974 began to get extensive airplay. It was in that year that the first bona fide disco hits emerged, "Rock the Boat" by the Hues Corporation and George McCrae's "Rock Your Baby." Both entered the Top 40 on June 15th; on July 6th "Rock the Boat" hit #1 and was replaced the following week by "Rock Your Baby," which stayed there for two weeks. By the following year disco hits were popping up with regularity, with Van McCoy's "The Hustle," Elton John's "Philadelphia Freedom" and KC and the Sunshine Band's "Get Down Tonight" and "That's the Way (I Like It)" all hitting #1. Late in 1975 Donna Summer, the 'queen of disco' emerged for the first time with the hit "Love to Love You Baby" (#2). Produced by European producer **Giorgio Moroder**, who created a symphony of synthesized sounds over a drum machine beat, "Love to Love You Baby" featured Summer repeating the title over and over in fake orgasmic ecstasy. She later went on to hold the #1 spot for a cumulative 13 weeks in a one year stretch in 1978 and 1979 with four #1 hits, including "Bad Girls," which stayed at the top for five weeks in the summer of 1979. Summer later became a born-again Christian and renounced her disco heritage.

By 1976, disco ruled the airwaves, as everybody and everything in pop culture came under its influence. Among the #1 hits of the year were Walter Murphy's adaptation of Beethoven's *Fifth Symphony*, "A Fifth of Beethoven;" Johnny Taylor's "Disco Lady;" and LA DJ Rick Dees' "Disco Duck." Even Paul McCartney got into disco mode with "Silly Love Songs" (#1) with his group Wings. 1976 was also the year that the established-but-floundering English group the Bee Gees introduced their new revamped disco sound with "You Should Be Dancing," also a #1 hit. The song proved to be merely a warm-up for the group, who the following year appeared on the soundtrack LP to the disco movie ***Saturday Night Fever*** starring John Travolta, which eventually sold an estimated 30 million copies worldwide. The Bee Gees had three #1 singles from the album—"How Deep Is Your Love," "Stayin' Alive" and "Night Fever"—and had three more #1's the following year. The movie itself grossed a stunning $130 million. Throughout 1978 and 1979, disco dominated films, TV, radio, and advertising. There were all-disco radio stations; remakes of Beatles, Beach Boys and classical music set to disco beats were common; even the Rolling Stones couldn't escape disco fever, and profited handsomely with 1978's #1, "Miss You." For a brief moment at the start of 1979, the most popular band in America was the gay-novelty disco group the Village People.

The Backlash

However, it didn't take long before a disco backlash began, and "Death To Disco" and "Disco Sucks" T-shirts and buttons began popping up around the country. It all seemed harmless enough at first, but on the night of July 12, 1979, one of the most surreal events in the history of pop culture revealed just how hated the music had become. When Chicago DJ **Steve Dahl** first came up with the idea for a "Disco Demolition Night" during a nighttime double header at the White Sox' Comiskey Park, it was more of a gimmick than anything. Dahl, after all, was one of the disco haters, and he let his listeners on WLUP know it daily. But even he was shocked when 59,000 other disco haters showed up (the White Sox were averaging 16,000 fans at home games), wearing Led Zeppelin and Black Sabbath T-shirts, shouting, "*disco sucks!*" and throwing empty bottles and records around. When the first crate of disco records was dynamited between games, it ignited a riot as thousands of fans stormed the field, tearing up turf and causing so much chaos and destruction that the second game had to be cancelled. From that moment on, disco just seemed to lose its cool. Before long, Casablanca Records, the leading disco label, was in serious financial trouble and Studio 54, New York's hippest discotheque, closed. By 1980, disco was dead.

Surely the anti-disco backlash was caused in part by the music's overwhelming popularity and the inevitable pendulum swing away from it. There was also the natural dislike of the music by those fans that held the musical virtuosity of real performers in high regard, since disco was created largely in the studio using synthesizers and overdubbing technology. But there was also an uglier side to the backlash as well, fueled by homophobic and racist sentiments. Because disco was perceived by many as gay or black music, it was an easy target for the invective from many of the young white males who made up the base of the heavy metal audience. But the death of disco was a shock system for the music business, which experienced an 11 percent drop in sales in 1979 after a to the decade of unprecedented growth.

Funk

Funk Defined

FUNK
An evolution of R&B and soul characterized by a heavy rhythmic groove, use of minimalism and group vocal chants.

Even as soft soul and disco was smoothing out the grittiness of soul, a more primal form of black pos was emerging that became known as **funk**. The most important element in funk is the groove, formed by layers of syncopated patterns that form a tightly woven rhythmic fabric. Minimalism—simple one and two-bar repeating phrases that create a trance-like effect—is often used. Funk is also loosely structured, with extended jams, long improvisations, and stream of consciousness lyrics common. Funk singers employ all kinds of vocal tricks, from shrieks and screams, guttural noises and grunts, sometimes locked in rhythmically to the band, sometimes floating above it out of rhythm. Group vocal chants are also common. Funk was the most intense and powerful form of black pop music to date, and yet artists such as Sly Stone and Stevie Wonder experienced great crossover success. It was also highly influential to jazz/rock fusion, hip-hop and rap, as well as to a number of alternative rock bands in the 1980s and 1990s.

The godfather of funk is James Brown. His work in the mid-1960s codified the style, especially 1965's "Papa's Got a Brand New Bag" and 1967's "Cold Sweat." Some scholars view his 1970 recording of "Get Up (I Feel Like Being a) Sex Machine" as the single defining recording of the style. These recordings paved the way for other artists to also make innovative contributions to the genre. Besides James Brown, the two most prominent funk pioneers were George Clinton and Sly Stone.

The godfather of funk is James Brown.

Funk

Characteristics of Funk

1. Most important element: the rhythmic groove, especially between the bass and drums
2. Typical instrumentation: bass, drums, guitar, electric keyboards, horns
3. Minimalism: simple two- and four-bar repeating phrases that create a trance-like effect
4. The rawest and earthiest form of black pop to date
5. Vocalists employ shrieks, screams, grunts, etc.; group vocal chants common

Key Funk Recordings

- "Get Up (I Feel Like Being a) Sex Machine"—James Brown, 1970
- "Thank You (Falettinme Be Mice Elf Agin)"—Sly and the Family Stone, 1970
- *Shaft*—Isaac Hayes, 1971
- *Talking Book, Innervisions*—Stevie Wonder, 1973
- "Tear the Roof Off the Sucker (Give Up the Funk)"—Parliament, 1976

George Clinton

George Clinton (1940–) is one of the most eccentric and colorful musicians of all time. Leading a loose aggregation of musicians known at various times as **Parliament, Funkadelic,** the P-Funk All Stars, and the Mothership Connection, Clinton produced some of the most adventurous recordings of the 1960s and

George Clinton.

1970s. Growing up in Plainfield, New Jersey, he founded a vocal group called the Parliaments at age 15; 12 years later, Clinton was working as a staff writer at Motown when the group had their first hit with "(I Wanna) Testify" (#20). After leaving Motown, Clinton began recording a blend of funk rock and psychedelic music on the Westbound label with two different bands, Funkadelic and Parliament (dropping the 's' in 'Parliaments' after a legal dispute with Motown over the name).

Throughout the 1970s, Clinton built up a cult following through innovative concept albums and dazzling concert experiences. Performances would often include Clinton, dressed in elaborate costumes (rivaling those of David Bowie), jumping out of a coffin while other band members at various times wore diapers, smoked marijuana, and simulated sex acts. A giant flying saucer named the Mothership descended from a huge denim cap. Musically, Clinton mixed influences from psychedelia, R&B, and jazz; lyrically he created cosmic and imaginary worlds with characters such as the Cro-Nasal Sapiens, the Thumpasorus People, and Dr. Funkenstein, all of whom engaged in a sort of primeval struggle for existence. One critic described all this as either James Brown on acid or a black Frank Zappa. As you might imagine, Clinton had a limited crossover appeal to white audiences, although two Parliament albums from the 1970s, ***Mothership Connection*** and ***Funkentelechy vs. the Placebo Syndrome*** peaked at #13 and are certified platinum. Clinton's highest charting single came in 1976 with Parliament's "Tear the Roof Off the Sucker (Give Up the Funk)" (from *Mothership Connection*), which peaked at #15. His groups over the years have included such heavyweight musicians as former James Brown band members Bootsy Collins, Maceo Parker and Fred Wesley. His musical motto is "Free your mind and your ass will follow."

Sly and the Family Stone

Like George Clinton's groups, **Sly and the Family Stone** created a hybrid of soul, R&B, psychedelic rock and jazz, but were able to do it with a much greater degree of crossover success with 11 singles hitting the Top 40 between 1968 and 1974, three of which hit #1. The group was led by Sylvester Stewart (aka **Sly Stone**, 1944–), who started his career in the Bay Area as a DJ on soul station KSOL and record producer for Autumn Records. In 1966 he formed the Family Stone with his brother Freddie on guitar, sister Rose on vocals and keyboards, **Larry Graham** on bass, Gregg Errico on drums, Jerry Martini on sax and Cynthia Robinson on trumpet. The group's members created a unique multi-gender, multi-ethnic chemistry with two women and two white musicians (Errico and Martini). Their first national hit came in 1968 with the #8 "Dance to the Music." Within two years, the band had two #1's ("Everyday People" and "Thank You [Falettinme Be Mice Elf Agin]"), a #2 ("Hot Fun in the Summertime"), and had performed at the 1969 Newport Jazz Festival and Woodstock. A third #1 single came in 1971 with "Family Affair."

Sly's success was due to his ability to combine irresistible sing-along hooks, infectious dance rhythms, a unique blend of different styles (who knew that soul could be psychedelic?), and lyrics that generally preached of love, peace and understanding. Occasionally Sly engaged in harsh social commentary, as evidenced by his singles "Don't Call Me Nigger, Whitey," "Sex Machine" and "Stand," and the 1971 album *There's a Riot Going On*, the groups only #1 LP. One of the key elements to the sound of the Family Stone was the bass playing of Graham, the creator of an innovative **slap-bass technique** that has become a staple of all subsequent funk and jazz/rock fusion. Graham left the group in 1972 to start Graham Central Station. Around this time, Sly was becoming notorious for no-shows at concerts, and as rumors of drug addiction flourished, the Family Stone began to unravel. By the mid 1970s, they disbanded. Recent years have found many of the Family Stone's most memorable hits being used for high-profile national advertising campaigns.

Other Important Funk Bands

Other funk artists also achieved enormous crossover success during the 1970s. **Stevie Wonder** reinvented himself as a singer/songwriter/synthesizer conceptualist with an amazing creative streak between 1972 and 1976 in which he had four Top 5 albums (***Talking Book***, ***Innervisions***, ***Fulfillingness' First Finale***, and ***Songs in the Key of Life***), eight Top 40 singles—five of which hit #1—and won 11 Grammy Awards. Among the funk classics that Wonder penned during this period were "Superstition," "I Wish," "Higher Ground," and "Living for the City," as well as the pop-friendly "You Are the Sunshine of My Life." **Earth, Wind and Fire**, formed in 1969, used Latin rhythms, jazzy horn lines and an interest in Egyptology to achieve 14 Top 40 hits (including the #1 "Shining Star" in 1975) and eight platinum albums between 1974 and 1979. Other popular funk groups include Kool and the Gang, with 22 Top 40 hits in the 1970s and 1980s, including "Funky Stuff" and "Jungle Boogie," the Ohio Players ("Funky Worm," 1973), the Commodores ("Brick House," #5, 1977) and the Isley Brothers ("It's Your Thing," #2, 1969).

Music Cut "Superstition" (Stevie Wonder)—Stevie Wonder

Personnel: Stevie Wonder: drums, clavinet, keyboards, synthesizers, vocals; Scott Edwards: bass; Steve Madaio: trumpet; Trevor Laurence: tenor sax. Recorded 1972 in New York, NY; produced by Stevie Wonder, Malcolm Cecil, Robert Margouleff. Released November 1972 on Tamla; 16 weeks on the charts, peaking at #1.

From the LP *Talking Book*, "Superstition" was Stevie Wonder's first #1 hit since 1963's "Fingertips (Part 2)" and the first hit of an intensely creative period between 1972 and 1976 in which he had four more #1 singles. The song was written and first performed for Wonder's tour with the Rolling Stones in the summer of 1972. Wonder wrote the song at the drums and played most of the instruments on the record, but it is his funky clavinet playing that is the song's most distinctive feature. The song was originally written for guitarist Jeff Beck to record, but Wonder recorded it himself first when Beck was too busy with his own album to get to it right away. "Superstition" won two Grammy Awards in 1974, for Best Male R&B Vocal Performance and Best R&B Song.

Two other artists, Isaac Hayes and Curtis Mayfield achieved pop success scoring music for what became known as the **blaxploitation films**, movies made by black directors and actors that had inner-city themes of drug deals and ghetto shootings. Hayes, the former Stax writer who broke out onto his own with the landmark LP ***Hot Buttered Soul*** in 1969, became the first black composer to win an Academy Award for Best Score for 1971's ***Shaft*** soundtrack LP. Mayfield scored the highly successful ***SuperFly*** in 1972, emphasizing his high, falsetto vocals and a smooth, pop oriented brand of funk.

Reggae

What Is Reggae?

REGGAE
A Jamaican style that evolved from the country's indigenous folk music, American R&B, and traditional Afro-Caribbean music; it is associated with the Rastafarian movement.

Reggae is an indigenous Jamaican music that evolved in the late 1960s from native folk music, American R&B and traditional Afro-Caribbean music. Soon after its emergence on the island, Jamaican reggae recordings began to make a presence in the U.S., and in 1969 two, Desmond Dekker's "Israelites" and Jimmy Cliff's "Wonderful World, Beautiful People" hit the American Top 40. By the early 1970s, rock musicians such as Johnny Nash and Paul Simon were co-opting reggae rhythms into their own music. Nash had a #1 hit with his "I Can See Clearly Now" and a #12 hit with his cover of Bob Marley's "Stir It Up"; Simon hit #4 with "Mother and Child Reunion," recorded in the Jamaican capital city of Kingston. In 1973 the Jamaican film *The Harder They Come* was released, introducing American audiences to the music and its star, Jimmy Cliff. In Boston, a city with a large student population, the film was so popular that one theatre ran it for more than seven years without interruption. In 1974, Eric Clapton's cover of Marley's "I Shot the Sheriff" became the most popular reggae song in American pop history when it went to #1. Throughout the 1970s and 1980s, other artists and bands, including the Clash, Elvis Costello and the Police recorded reggae-inspired music. Reggae in the 1970s became the latest form of black music to become trendy in England, following the trad jazz-skiffle-R&B-blues lineage. Two Birmingham groups, the English Beat and UB40, were among the many that formed in the UK in response to the popularity of the Jamaican music.

RIDDIM
The intertwined patterns played by the bass, guitar, and drums that is a characteristic of reggae.

The primary rhythmic feature of reggae is the **riddim**, or the intertwined patterns played by the bass and drums. Each instrument in the band has a clearly defined role to play: while the guitar provides choppy, "up stroke" strumming on beats two and four, the bass and drums are locked into a syncopated beat that often de-emphasizes the downbeat of each measure. Most reggae is played slowly, allowing the resulting polyrhythms and lyrics to be clearly heard. Because reggae came from the oppressed lower class in the ghettos of the capital city of Kingston, its lyrics often convey themes of political protest, social injustices, racial equality, and the Rastafarian movement.

Reggae

Characteristics of Reggae

1. Combines influences from Jamaican folk (mento), American R&B, Afro-Caribbean music
2. Intertwined patterns played by the bass, drums, and guitar known as "riddim"
3. Lyrics often refer to social injustices, political dissent, racism
4. Identification with Rastafarian movement

Key Reggae Recordings

- "Israelites"—Desmond Dekker and the Aces, 1969
- *Burnin'*—Bob Marley and the Wailers, 1973
- "I Shot the Sheriff"—Eric Clapton, 1974

Rastafari Culture

RASTAFARIANISM
A religious movement originating in Jamaica espousing African repatriation; characterized by songs of political protest, smoking of ganja and wearing of dreadlocks.

Rastafarianism is a religious movement whose followers believe they will be repatriated to their African homeland and escape Babylon (a metaphor for their oppressors in the New World). It was inspired by the writings of Marcus Garvey, a writer and political activist who wrote of the "crowning of a black king" who will "be the redeemer." In 1916 he moved to Harlem and started a "Back to Africa" movement before eventually moving to the continent himself. When Ras Tafari Makonnen was crowned king of the African nation Ethiopia in 1930 and took the name Haile Selassie, many clergymen in Jamaica saw this as a sign that Garvey's predictions had come true. (The word "Ras" is a title that loosely translates to prince or duke.) Rastafarians reinterpreted the Bible to suit their needs, and in time developed their own cultural values that included songs of social and political protest, the smoking of ganja (marijuana) as a sacramental herb, and wearing the hair in dreadlocks. As the movement spread throughout Jamaica, Rastafarian songs were slowed down and mixed with an African influenced drumming style known as **burru**. At this point in time, roughly the mid-1960s, the Rastafarian culture began to intermingle with the popular music of Jamaica to provide the basis for reggae.

BURRU
A drumming style adopted by and associated with Rastafarian musicians.

MENTO
The indigenous folk music of rural Jamaica dating back to the 19th century; an ancestor of reggae.

Historical Background to Reggae

Reggae's roots go back to the indigenous folk music of Jamaica known as **mento**, which first appeared in rural areas in the 19th century. Mento's popularity began to fade in the 1940s, when American swing bands such as those of Benny Goodman and Count Basie rose to popularity in the urban dancehalls of Kingston. To emulate them, local musicians formed road bands that played their version of swing music at public dances. By the late 1950s Jamaican youth began copying the R&B records of Fats Domino and Louis Jordan they were hearing on radio broadcasts from New Orleans, Miami, and Memphis, and developed their own variation of the music known as **ska**. Ska (an onomatopoeic word originating from the sound of the strong, sharp offbeat accents) is an up tempo music that combines an R&B-influenced walking bass with accents on the offbeats from mento. It was extremely popular on the island in the early 1960s, and one ska record, Millie Small's "My Boy Lollipop" even hit #4 on the American charts in 1964. The most popular ska band in Jamaica at this time was the Skatalites, led by trombonist Don Drummond.

SKA
A Jamaican precedent to reggae characterized by R&B influences, walking bass and strong, sharp offbeat accents played on the guitar.

In the summer of 1966, temperatures soared on the island, making ska too fast to play or dance to, and a slower, updated version emerged known as **rock steady**. More relaxed and looser rhythmically than its predecessor, rock steady simplified the bass and drum syncopations of ska, but retained the offbeat accents. Rock steady appealed to the Jamaican lower-class youth known as the Rude Boys, urban hooligans that were generally against the system who sometimes engaged in civil disobedience. Whereas ska lyrics, like those of American R&B, concerned themselves with love and sex, the influence of the Rude Boys and Rastafarian culture into rock steady resulted in songs with themes of social and political protest.

The Dancehall Culture

Another factor that had an impact on the evolving music styles in Jamaica during the 1950s and 1960s was the dancehall culture. The many dancehalls throughout Kingston increasingly became safe houses where the lower class could gather and listen to and dance to music, often provided by portable sound systems that played records. In an attempt to liven up their shows, the DJs who operated these sound systems began to deliver spontaneous commentary on the proceedings,

TOASTING

The spontaneous commentary provided by DJs at dancehall parties in Kingston, Jamaica, that usually involved the creative use of rhyming, interesting verbal sounds, and nonsense syllables.

DUB

A process in which DJs mix interesting sections of different songs together.

usually in some creative way that involved rhyming, interesting verbal sounds, the use of different dialects, and nonsense syllables. This practice became known as **toasting**. In addition, DJs began to mix interesting sections of different songs together—a process known as **dub**—to create even more excitement, and often toasted over the top of the dub. Eventually these styles made their way into recording studios, resulting in hit songs from artists such as King Stitt and U Roy. In the 1970s, Caribbean expatriates such as Kool Herc and Grandmaster Flash took the techniques of dub music and toasting to the Bronx where they played important roles in the incubation of hip-hop culture.

By 1968 the evolution from rock steady to reggae was complete: the music had slowed down even further, while becoming more intense and driving. The word reggae comes from the local slang term "raggay," or raggedy. Central to the rise in popularity of reggae worldwide was **Chris Blackwell**, the heir to a British fortune who spent much of his youth living in Jamaica. In 1961 Blackwell founded **Island Records**, the driving force behind Millie Small's "My Boy Lollipop." In 1964, Blackwell met and signed Jamaican singer Jimmy Cliff to Island, launching his career with a series of records that became hits in Europe. Cliff eventually had an American hit ("Wonderful World, Beautiful People") and was the star of the influential film *The Harder They Come*. Blackwell also signed Desmond Dekker who released "Honour Thy Father and Mother," a #1 hit on the island in 1963. Dekker later went on to have the 1969 hit "Israelites," which went to #1 in the United Kingdom and #9 in the United States. In the late 1960s, Blackwell turned his attention to rock acts such as Traffic, Jethro Tull, and Emerson, Lake and Palmer, but in 1972 signed the reggae artist who was destined to be the music's biggest star: Bob Marley.

Bob Marley and the Wailers

Bob Marley.
Courtesy of Photofest

By the time he died of cancer at the age of 36, **Bob Marley** (1945–1981) had not only become the most famous reggae musician on earth, but a national hero to his fellow Jamaicans. After moving to the shantytown slums of Kingston from rural Jamaica at age 14, Marley began playing guitar and writing songs. At 17, he recorded several lackluster singles with the help of producer Leslie Kong; the next year he formed the Teenagers, later renamed the Wailing Rudeboys, and then simply the Wailers. The original lineup included singers Peter Tosh and Bunny Livingstone. In spite of occasional singles that were hits on the island, the Wailers endured years of financial hardship—Marley even worked in a factory in Delaware for a period. In 1969, they signed with producer Lee Perry, who beefed up the band with the addition of brothers Aston and Carlton Barrett on bass and drums. Over the next three years the Wailers became enormously popular in Jamaica, and were signed to Island in 1972. Their first Island LP, *Catch a Fire,* received favorable international acclaim; their second, *Burnin'* included two of Marley's most famous compositions, "I Shot the Sheriff" and "Get Up, Stand Up." Both songs address issues of importance to Jamaicans: "Sheriff" relates a misunderstanding and violent altercation with law enforcement, while "Get Up" addresses fundamental Rastafarian beliefs. When Eric Clapton's cover of "I Shot the Sheriff," went to #1 in both England and America, Marley was poised for worldwide stardom. Around this time both Tosh and Livingstone quit the group to pursue solo careers, but Marley brought in the I-Threes vocal group (which included his wife Rita) for their successful international tour in 1974, their first outside of Jamaica.

Music Cut "Get Up, Stand Up" (Bob Marley/Peter Tosh)—the Wailers

Personnel: Bob Marley: guitar, vocals; Aston "Family Man" Barrett: bass, guitar; Carlton "Carlie" Barrett: drums; Earl Lindo: keyboards; Bunny Livingston: percussion, vocals; Peter Tosh: guitar, vocals, keyboards. Recorded April 1973 at Harry J. Studios, Kinston, Jamaica; produced by Chris Blackwell. Released April 19, 1973 on Island; did not chart.

As the opening track from the Wailers' 1973 LP *Burnin'*, "Get Up, Stand Up" sets the album's tone. Although some believe the song to be a political anthem to take action against oppression. It is also interpreted as reaffirming a basic tenant of Rastafarianism: that Haile Selassie is the living God. The liner notes to the Wailers' compilation album *Legend* says this about "Get Up, Stand Up": "This is the cutting call-to-arms that kicked off the *Burnin'* album. Seldom has the Rasta ethos been spelled out with greater sagacity, yet the theme transcends all religious and political boundaries."

Leading the wave of reggae's international popularity, the Wailers went on to record six gold albums for Island, including *Rastaman Vibration* in 1976, which went to #8 on the U.S. charts.

Marley used his growing fame to expound upon his political viewpoints, which included social activism, rebellion against the system, and his belief in Rastafarianism. His reverential stature in his native country climbed to levels normally reserved for popular religious leaders or heads of state, and as a result, was wounded in an assassination attempt in December 1976 that forced him into exile for more than a year. In 1980, after collapsing while jogging in New York's Central Park, Marley discovered that he had cancer in his brain, liver, and lungs. His final album *Uprising* was released shortly before he died on May 11, 1981. In his short time in the spotlight, Bob Marley defined the music and politics of reggae for the worldwide rock community.

Other Reggae Artists

Other influential Jamaican ska, rock steady, and reggae artists to emerge in the 1960s and 1970s were Toots Hibbert, leader of Toots and the Maytals, Peter MacIntosh, going by the name Peter Tosh, Prince Buster, Judge Dread, and the abovementioned Desmond Dekker and Jimmy Cliff.

Rap

The Origins of Hip-Hop

Rap music is one part (along with break-dancing and graffiti art) of a cultural form known as **hip-hop** that emerged in the South Bronx neighborhoods of New York City in the late 1970s. It is the latest extension of the blues-jazz-R&B-soul lineage of musical expressions that have emerged from the black cultural experience in America. Its most obvious musical connection to previous rock styles are funk (especially James Brown's) and disco; however, rap is an entirely different animal altogether that continues to evolve and assimilate other musical influences. Because of the violent and graphic nature of the lyrics in much of contemporary rap, the genre and its purveyors have been at the center of an enormous amount of controversy, perhaps more than any other style in pop music history. But a closer look at the origins of rap and its motivations reveals that perhaps not all of the anger and outrage directed toward it is warranted.

RAP
A style characterized by the use of spoken word (rather than singing) with funk oriented rhythm accompaniment, often using sampled sounds and minimalism; one element of hip hop culture.

HIP HOP
A cultural form of expression consisting of rap music, graffiti art, and break-dancing that emerged in the South Bronx and other inner city neighborhoods in the late 1970s.

Hip-hop has been described as the most sweeping American cultural movement of the late 20th Century, and it is through rap music that its message has been transmitted to the American mainstream audience. In the years leading up to the emergence of rap, black youth culture was nearly invisible to the rest of the country, the exceptions consisting primarily of athletes and crime reports. However, black athletes in the 1960s for the most part lived in a conservative sports climate, without a true cultural identity of their own, and often did not connect with the black youth of the streets. Hip hop and rap has changed all of that. As Bakari Kitwana states in his authoritative book *The Hip Hop Generation:* "Because of rap, the voices, images, style, attitude, and language of young Blacks have become central in American culture, transcending geographical, social, and economic boundaries." Today, because of rap, hip-hop is omnipresent in national TV ads, fashion, movies and movie stars, and professional sports, particularly basketball. Rap lyrics have also articulated the issues that confront many young blacks, such as police brutality, unemployment, drugs, and gangs. Of course civil rights leaders from previous generations had also addressed these issues, but not in such a confrontational manner.

Hip-hop emerged as a form of self-expression for the largely black and Hispanic communities of the South Bronx in New York City.

Hip-hop emerged in the mid to late 1970s as a form of self-expression for the largely black and Hispanic communities of the South Bronx in New York City, in an attempt to negotiate with their oppressive and dismal living conditions. Facing an economic crisis, New York City narrowly avoided bankruptcy in 1975, the same year that President Gerald Ford announced that he would veto any congressional bill that included a bailout for the city (resulting in the famous *New York Daily News* headline "Ford to City: Drop Dead"). During this period the Bronx had been devastated by the ravages of reduced federal funding, shifting and disappearing job opportunities, and the diminished availability of affordable housing. To further complicate matters, the borough had been literally cut in half in the 1960s by the construction of the Cross Bronx Expressway, which destroyed more than 60,000 homes in stable neighborhoods and effectively isolated the southern half of the borough. The resulting infestation of slumlords and toxic waste dumps, increase of violent crime, and the loss of city services created an urban crisis that left the South Bronx in squalor. When a two-day citywide power outage occurred on July 13 and 14, 1977, hundreds of stores in the area were looted and vandalized, resulting in hundreds of millions of dollars in damage. After President Jimmy Carter made a highly publicized tour of the destruction, the South Bronx was characterized as a war zone in the media and through sensationalized films like *Fort Apache, The Bronx.*

The Beginnings of Rap

CREW/POSSE

An informal inner city neighborhood group formed as a means of providing identity and support for its members.

In response to these sordid living conditions and the destruction of traditional institutions such as neighborhood associations and community centers, residents of the area began to fashion their own cultural values and identities. By the late 1970s, informal neighborhood groups called **crews** or **posses** began forming as a means of providing identity and support for their members. (This kind of group identity remains deeply rooted in hip-hop culture, and references to crews or posses are frequent in rap recordings.) At parties and other social gatherings, it became fashionable for crews to display graffiti art, break-dancing moves and play records as a way to gain notoriety and celebrity. In the earliest stages of rap's development (around 1977), DJs such as Bronx native Afrika Bambaataa (Kevin

Donovan) and two Caribbean expatriates, Kool Herc (Clive Campbell) and Grandmaster Flash (Joseph Saddler), would spin records in innovative ways to create excitement. Kool Herc in particular was instrumental in developing the art of mixing smooth transitions between two turntables to feature the **break**, or the most danceable, instrumental sections of records. Kool Herc also began to recite rhymes to accompany his mixing, a technique he inherited from his native Jamaica, where it was called toasting. Grandmaster Flash is given credit for perfecting the practice of **scratching** or **back spinning**, or playing a record back and forth quickly to create a scratching sound. Eventually MCs (master of ceremonies) were added to take over most of the rhyming and vocal interactions, and began to attract the most attention from audiences. These were the earliest rappers.

BREAK
The most danceable, instrumental section of a record.

SCRATCHING/BACK SPINNING
To play a record back and forth quickly to create a scratching sound.

Throughout this stage of development, rap was still pretty much contained to the Bronx, Harlem, and a few other neighborhoods in New York City. In September 1979, the outside world got its first glimpse of the new style when "Rapper's Delight" by the Sugar Hill Gang of Sugar Hill Records hit #36 on the pop chart and eventually sold over a million copies. Sugar Hill Records was owned by Sylvia Robinson, a former R&B singer ("Pillow Talk," #3, 1973) who had noticed how street MC's that added lyrics and chants to funk and disco records were becoming popular in New York City. To capitalize on the fad, in September 1979 she put together three New Jersey teens who recorded a rap over a rhythm track derived from Chic's early summer #1 hit "Good Times." Not only did the song popularize the word *rap,* but "Rapper's Delight" also alerted MCs and DJs to the commercial potential of the new style. Within the next few years, more rap singles—all on small, independent labels such as Sugar Hill—became big sellers, including "The Breaks" by Kurtis Blow, and Afrika Bambaataa and the Soul Sonic Force's "Planet Rock." This first generation of rappers performed what has become known as **old school rap**, most of which had themes of fun and partying. However, one record from this era that signaled a significant change of direction was Grandmaster Flash and the Furious Five's "The Message" from 1982. A graphic (and controversial) description of the harsh realities of ghetto life in the South Bronx, "The Message" was the first rap record to address social issues, and laid the groundwork for an essential part of rap's future development.

OLD SCHOOL RAP
The first generation of rap, characterized by party themes and the use of turntables to achieve scratching and back spinning effects.

"The Message" was the first rap record to address social issues, and laid the groundwork for an essential part of rap's future development.

Rap

Characteristics of Rap

1. Rhythmic and rhyming spoken lyrics with rhythmic accompaniment heavily influenced by funk and disco
2. Use of sampled sounds and pieces of existing songs that are repeated to create a minimalist, hypnotic effect
3. Early rap (old school) included the use of scratching and back spinning of turntables to create percussive effects
4. Often has a shuffle or swing beat, with heavy accent on the backbeat (beats two and four)

Key Rap Recordings

- "Rapper's Delight"—the Sugar Hill Gang, 1979
- "The Message"—Grandmaster Flash and the Furious Five, 1982
- *Raising Hell*—Run-D.M.C., 1986
- *As Nasty as They Wanna Be*—2 Live Crew, 1989

Music Cut "Walk This Way" (Steven Tyler/Joe Perry)—Run-D.M.C.

Personnel: Joseph "DJ Run": vocals; Darryl "D.M.C." McDaniels: vocals; Jason "Jam Master Jay" Mizell: turntable; Steve Tyler: vocals; Joe Perry: guitar. Recorded 1986; produced by Rick Rubin and Russell Simmons. Released July 1986 on Profile; 16 weeks on the charts, peaking at #4.

Run D.M.C.'s innovative reinterpretation of Aerosmith's "Walk This Way" was a milestone in the development of rap. Not only did it appeal to fans of both metal and rap music, it was instrumental in showing that the two music styles were not incompatible and paved the way for other rock and pop artists to begin incorporating rap and hip-hop elements into their own music. In addition, the music video of the song, which shows Run D.M.C. and Aerosmith's Steve Tyler and Joe Perry dueling on opposite ends of a revolving stage, was itself an innovation and the first hybrid rap video played in heavy rotation on MTV. This recording of the song was included on Run D.M.C.'s 1986 LP *Raising Hell*, which went platinum the day it was released.

East Coast Rap

Throughout the early 1980s, rap expanded further into the pop charts, and its influence began to extend outside of the Bronx and into other urban areas such as Roxbury in Boston, the Fifth Ward in Houston, Overtown in Miami, and Watts and Compton in Los Angeles. In 1986 rap albums by two New York groups reached multi-platinum status, ***Raising Hell*** (#3) by **Run-D.M.C.** and ***Licensed to Ill*** (#1) by the **Beastie Boys**, signaling a new level of commercial appeal of the music. Both albums went platinum almost immediately. Run-D.M.C., consisting of three middle-class and college-educated rappers (Run, aka Joseph Simmons; D.M.C., aka Darryl McDaniels; and Jam Master Jay, aka Jason Mizell) had already achieved the first gold rap album with 1984's ***Run-D.M.C.*** *Raising Hell* was propelled by an ingenious piece of marketing, a rap remake of Aerosmith's 1976 hit "Walk This Way," recorded with that band's Steve Tyler and Joe Perry. "Walk This Way" hit #4 and sold over a million records to fans of both rap and metal, and its innovative video was the first of the genre to receive airplay on MTV. Run-D.M.C. had a harder edge than earlier rap groups, and featured an innovative vocal technique: Simmons and McDaniels would often finish each other's lines instead of trading verses. The Beastie Boys, the first important white rap group, had a #7 hit with "You've Got to Fight for Your Right to Party" from *Licensed to Ill.*

Run-D.M.C.

Run, aka Joseph Simmons
D.M.C., aka Darryl McDaniels
Jam Master Jay, aka Jason Mizell

Other East Coast rappers also emerged during this time, including Public Enemy, L.L. Cool J. (Ladies Love Cool James), the female trio Salt-n-Pepa, Queen Latifa, and Miami's 2 Live Crew. By this time rap was becoming more militant, aggressive, contentious, and controversial. One of the pioneers of what would eventually become known as gangsta rap was Philadelphia's Schoolly D (Jesse Weaver), whose 1986 narrative about a Philadelphia gang, "PSK—What Does It Mean?" is widely credited with inventing the style. In 1987, the Bronx's Boogie Down Productions (KRS-One and DJ Scott LaRock) released the classic *Criminal Minded,* an album that was also influential in gangsta rap's development.

East Coast Rappers

- Run-D.M.C.
- Beastie Boys
- Public Enemy
- L.L. Cool J.
- Salt-n-Pepa
- Queen Latifa
- 2 Live Crew

LaRock was shot to death later in the year in an eerie foreshadowing of rap's future violence.

CNN for Black Culture

In 1988, **Public Enemy**, led by rapper Chuck D, his sidekick Flavor Flav and the Bomb Squad production team, released the controversial LP ***It Takes a Nation to Hold Us Back***, which stepped up the rhetoric of black anger to levels above and beyond Schoolly D and BDP. Calling themselves the "prophets of rage," PE combined the politically charged rhymes of Chuck D with the Bomb Squad's heavily layered avant-garde rhythm tracks. Chuck D was also critical of the white-controlled media (as related in 1988's "Don't Believe the Hype"), and called rap "CNN for black culture." PE has encountered more than its share of controversy, from 1988's volatile "Bring the Noise," to the statement by Professor Griff, the group's "minister of information," that Jews are responsible for "the majority of wickedness that goes on across the globe."

The 1989 LP ***As Nasty as They Wanna Be*** by **2 Live Crew** became the first recording ever to be declared obscene by an American court, even though the group included a warning label on the cover and simultaneously released an edited version called ***As Clean as They Wanna Be***. Led by founder Luther Campbell, the group's #26 hit "Me So Horny" created a moral outrage that prompted evangelical Christian attorney Jack Thompson of Miami to file suit against Campbell. In 1990 a Broward County judge declared the album to be legally obscene, making it illegal to sell, and in short order record retailers in Ft. Lauderdale and Huntsville, Alabama, were arrested for selling it (both were prosecuted but acquitted). The band was also arrested for performing the songs in a Hollywood, Florida, nightclub. Eventually *Nasty* sold more than two million copies (eight times as many as the clean version), a jury cleared 2 Live Crew after 13 minutes of deliberation, and in 1992 the 11th U.S. Circuit Court of Appeals reversed the obscenity ruling. However, by that time 2 Live Crew had disbanded.

West Coast and Gangsta Rap

Meanwhile, California was becoming a hotbed of rap development. Oakland's **M.C. Hammer** (Stanley Burrell) released the pop-accessible LP ***Please Hammer Don't Hurt 'Em*** in 1990 (containing the #8 hit "U Can't Touch This" and two other Top 10 singles), which stayed at #1 for 21 weeks and sold ten million copies, making it one of the bestselling rap albums of all time. But other West Coast rappers, particularly those from the ghettos of Los Angeles, were turning up the threatening and menacing tone of gangsta rap to the boiling point. The

West Coast Rappers

- M.C. Hammer
- Ice-T
- NWA
- Ice Cube
- Dr. Dre
- Snoop Doggy Dog

The West Coast gangsta rap that emerged in the 1990s is among the most controversial music ever produced.

West Coast gangsta rap that emerged in the 1990s is among the most controversial music ever produced. The main point of contention was the use of the first-person accounting of vivid descriptions of violence, rage, and sexist degradation rather than the more passive third person used in previous rap narratives such as "The Message." One of the first instances of the style on the West Coast came from **Ice-T** (Tracy Morrow), who assumed the persona of a hardened Los Angeles criminal in his 1986 record "6 'n the Mornin'." This and subsequent other Ice-T recordings were criticized as glorifying violence, when in reality the songs usually sent a not-so-subtle message that crime and violence doesn't pay. His newly formed group Body Count received national notoriety with the release of its self-titled debut album in 1992, which contained the track "Cop Killer." The song was denounced by police departments all over the country, as well as President George H. W. Bush, Vice President Dan Quayle, and the Parents Music Resource Center, and was ultimately dropped from the album by Time Warner, owner of Sire Records. In response, Ice-T left the label.

The controversy over gangsta rap escalated further with 1989's double platinum ***Straight Outta Compton*** by **NWA** (Niggaz with Attitude), a Los Angeles-based group led by Ice Cube (O'Shea Jackson) and Dr. Dre (Andre Young). Although the album went multi-platinum, it incensed rap's detractors with its narratives of gang violence, drive-by shootings, and drug dealings in songs like "Gangsta Gangsta" and the title cut. The most offensive song, "Fuck tha Police," caused the FBI to send a warning letter to the group's label, Priority. Unlike Ice-T's earlier recordings, the songs on *Straight Outta Compton* offer no social commentaries, but instead are vicious tirades directed toward women, the police, and the group's adversaries. Although NWA began to unravel in the early 1990s, they had another smash hit with 1991's ***Efil4zaggin*** (*Niggaz 4 Life* spelled backwards), which hit #1 two weeks after its release and went platinum.

Music Cut "6 'n the Morning" (Tracy Marrow)—Ice-T

Personnel: Tracy Marrow (Ice-T): vocals; The Unknown DJ: production. Recorded 1986; produced by The Unknown DJ. Released 1986 as the B-side to "Dog 'N the Wax (Ya Don't Quit-Part II)" on Techno Hop; did not chart.

Even though "6 'n the Morning" was released as merely the B-side of one of Ice-T's lesser-known singles, it is today recognized as one of the formative tracks in gangsta rap. The song starts with a wake up call: "6 'n the morning' police at my door," and proceeds to make references to bitches and ho's, staying one step ahead of the LAPD, and how "livin' in the city is a serious task." Surprisingly, considering its importance and influence, it was Ice-T's first rap record.

Gangsta Rap

Characteristics of Gangsta Rap

1. Lyrics use first-person accounting of gang-related themes that include violence, rage, and sexual degradation
2. Hard-hitting, angry vocal delivery
3. Guns, sirens, and other urban sound effects often used

Key Gangsta Rap Recordings

- *Straight Outta Compton*—NWA, 1989
- "Cop Killer"—Body Count, 1992
- *The Chronic*—Dr. Dre, 1993
- "Hit 'Em Up"—Tupac Shakur, 1996

In 1992 Dr. Dre, along with producer Marion "Suge" Knight started the independent label Death Row, which released Dre's landmark debut LP ***The Chronic*** in 1993. The album went triple platinum, hit #3 on the charts, spawned two Top 10 singles, and introduced Dre's understudy, **Snoop Doggy Dog** (Calvin Broadus). Reviews of Snoop and his lazy drawl style of rapping were enthusiastic, which fueled excitement about his own forthcoming debut LP. However, while recording the album in August, Snoop and his bodyguard were arrested for the murder of a man they claimed was a stalker. When ***Doggystyle*** was finally released in November, the pent-up anticipation resulted in it becoming the first debut album in history to enter the *Billboard* pop chart at #1 (it eventually went quadruple platinum). After a lengthy trial in late 1995 and early 1996, Snoop was cleared of all charges. His second album, ***The Doggfather***, was released later that year. Snoop has since become a celebrity beyond the scope of rap, with his numerous movie and TV roles.

The East Coast-West Coast Rivalry

In the mid-1990s, an ugly East Coast-West Coast rivalry developed from an ongoing feud between **Tupac Shakur (2pac)** (1971–1996) and the **Notorious B.I.G.** (Christopher Wallace, aka Biggie Smalls) (1972–1997) that ended with the brutal murders of both artists. The feud started after 2pac was shot and robbed outside a New York recording studio in November 1994. 2pac implicated B.I.G. for the attack, and after some back and forth bickering between the two camps released the single "Hit 'Em Up," a malicious attack that boasted of sleeping with B.I.G.'s estranged wife, Faith Evans. Shakur was murdered in a drive-by shooting on September 7, 1996; B.I.G. was also subsequently murdered in a similar shooting on March 9, 1997. Although conspiracy theorists believed that B.I.G.'s death was retribution for 2pac's and amid reports of LAPD corruption, neither case has been solved. The Notorious B.I.G.'s final album ***Life After Death*** was released within days of his murder, and sold 700,000 copies in the first week and went diamond in less than two years. It also spawned two #1 singles that were both certified platinum, making B.I.G. the first entertainer in history to have two posthumous #1 hits. Like B.I.G., 2pac has achieved a degree of immortality: his death has prompted somewhere in the vicinity of 15 compilations and reissues. In 2002, filmmaker Nick Broomfield made a documentary of the tragic story of these two artists entitled *Biggie and Tupac*.

By the mid-1990s, an ugly East Coast-West Coast rivalry began to develop that consumed the attention of the entire rap community and in the end turned violent and tragically lethal.

The Notorious B.I.G. was the first entertainer in history to have two posthumous #1 hits.

With so much common talent and perspective to share, the murders of Tupac and the Notorious B.I.G. were tragic and unnecessary. While their music was difficult for many middle Americans to listen to, it is important to remember that the stories that Tupac, B.I.G., NWA, and others related were not fictional ones. These artists did not invent the miserable conditions in the ghetto, or the gang-related warfare, or drive-by shootings. Like the first blues singers from the Mississippi Delta who came nearly 100 years before them, rappers are their generation's voice of the downtrodden and oppressed, of people who otherwise aren't being heard. When miserable living conditions exist for some Americans, like they did in the South Bronx in the 1970s and still do in many urban areas, the results can have far-reaching effects. As rock critic Mikal Gilmore states: "The America that we are making for others is ultimately the America we will make for ourselves. It will not be on the other side of town. It will be right outside our front door."

Name ______________________ Date ____________

STUDY QUESTIONS

1. What were some important differences between soft soul and funk?

2. Name three reasons why there was a backlash against disco.

3. In what ways did James Brown influence funk?

4. Name three differences between the music, bands and careers of George Clinton and Sly Stone.

5. How did American music and Jamaican reggae cross influence each other?

6. Why was reggae used for social protest, and describe its relationship to the Rastafarian movement.

7. Explain how rap emerged from the South Bronx in the late 1970s.

8. What is the importance of Run-D.M.C.'s "Walk This Way"?

9. How specifically did gangsta rap differ from previous rap styles?

10. In what ways did the East Coast-West Coast rivalry escalate?

19 The Nineties and Beyond

Key Terms

- Grunge
- Emo
- Boy bands
- Rapcore
- Napster
- Mp3
- File sharing
- Audio Home Recording Act
- iTunes Music Store
- DRM
- Music streaming

Key Figures

- Nirvana
- Pearl Jam
- Phish
- Radiohead
- The Dave Matthews Band
- Beck
- Weezer
- New Kids on the Block
- Boyz II Men
- Backstreet Boys
- 'NSync
- Mariah Carey
- Britney Spears
- Eminem
- Shawn Fanning

Courtesy of CBS/Photofest

"I think one of the reasons I pushed myself so hard and worked so hard is because I never felt special. Like, the one thing that made me feel special was my music."

—MARIAH CAREY

The Triumph of Alternative Nation

Nirvana

On January 11, 1992, Michael Jackson's multi-platinum album *Dangerous* was knocked out of the #1 spot on the *Billboard* charts by an album released by a relatively unknown band from Seattle. There seemed to be some sort of cosmic significance to the moment: the King of Pop, his sequined glove and highly produced post-disco dance music was dethroned by a group wearing torn jeans and T-shirts who were uncomfortable with stardom, and played music that eschewed glitz and glamour and embraced the do-it-yourself attitude of post-punk alternative rock. Although Nirvana's *Nevermind* would end up spending only two weeks at #1, it effectively sent a clear message to the music industry: the 1980s were over. Alternative Nation was alive and growing in the 1980s, it just wasn't very visible to the major labels. With the success of *Nevermind*, the gulf between "what people said was hip to listen to" and "the kind of stuff which we all really listened to" had finally been bridged, according to Nirvana guitarist Kurt Cobain. In many ways it was the perfect album to come along at the perfect time to wipe the slate clean once and for all of the dominance of Michael, Madonna, and Prince and let Alternative Nation finally emerge.

Nirvana's beginnings go back to 1987 and the tiny town of Aberdeen, Washington, 100 miles southwest of Seattle, where guitarist/vocalist/songwriter Kurt Cobain (1967–1994) grew up. Cobain's early years could easily be described as miserable. At age eight, his parents divorced, forcing him to move back and forth from one set of relatives to another. Growing older, he grew increasingly sullen, resentful and withdrawn. As an artistic youth who did not fit in with most people in the redneck logging town, Cobain was often beat up by other kids just because he was "different", including once for befriending an openly gay fellow student. But he found solace in music: first the Beatles, then metal, and finally punk. In 1987, around the time he turned 20, Cobain and fellow Aberdonian Krist Novoselic (bass) formed what would eventually become Nirvana, moving to nearby Olympia to work the Olympia-Tacoma-Seattle bar circuit. While working its way through a series of drummers, the band signed with local independent label Sub Pop and in spring 1989 recorded its debut LP ***Bleach*** at a cost of $606.17. Containing 12 Cobain original songs, *Bleach* received favorable reviews from the underground rock press, and sold an impressive 35,000 copies. Along with a number of other Seattle bands that included Mudhoney and Soundgarden, Nirvana was defining a style that journalists were beginning to identify with the city's music scene and call grunge. Shortly after recording *Bleach*, Nirvana finalized their lineup with the addition of drummer Dave Grohl.

During the summer of 1989, Nirvana recorded several song demos with producer Butch Vig, with the intention of shopping them around to major labels. After eventually signing with Geffen imprint DGC for $287,000, they recorded ***Nevermind*** in the summer of 1991 and released it in September. Propelled by Cobain's brilliant, generational songwriting and the powerful, dynamic playing of Grohl and Novoselic, *Nevermind* quickly sold out its initial printing of 50,000 copies and hit the charts in early November, where it stayed for the next 50 weeks. Propelling the album was the Gen X anthem "Smells Like Teen Spirit," which peaked on the charts at #6 on its way to a platinum certification. In the heady months that followed the album's release, the band toured heavily, released three more singles, and appeared on *Saturday Night Live*, giving the program its highest ratings in months.

In February 1992, Cobain married singer Courtney Love, with whom he fathered a daughter. The relationship was turbulent, and with persistent rumors of heavy drug usage, became the focus of a relentless paparazzi harassment that put the couple in constant media spotlight. Cobain had at this point become the de facto spokesman for Alternative Nation, a role he loathed and was ill prepared to assume, and this pressure no doubt contributed to his early death. In the last year of his life, there were no less than five incidents that were either suicide attempts or could be perceived as such, including three drug overdoses. The last of these occurred on March 4, 1994 while the band was on tour in Europe; after a short hospitalization, Cobain returned to the U.S. and checked into the Exodus Recovery Clinic in Los Angeles. On April 1, after telling security he was going out for some cigarettes, Cobain escaped from the clinic and disappeared. After several days of frantic searching by family and police, his body was discovered in a small room above the garage of his Seattle home. The cause of death was a self-inflicted gunshot wound to the head, estimated to have occurred on April 5. Although a suicide note was found, speculation that he was murdered has persisted to this day. As the primary composer for a group that has now sold more than 50 million records worldwide, Kurt Cobain has become one of the most commercially successful songwriters in pop music history. His death was mourned by millions of fans, and he was eulogized by numerous tributes on radio and MTV in the weeks and months that followed.

Nirvana was defining a style that journalists were beginning to identify with Seattles music scene and call grunge.

Kurt Cobain has become one of the most commercially successful songwriters in pop music history.

Music Cut "Smells Like Teen Spirit" (Kurt Cobain/David Grohl/Krist Novoselic)—Nirvana

Personnel: Kurt Cobain: vocals, guitar; David Grohl: drums, vocals; Krist Novoselic: bass, vocals. Recorded May 1991 at Sound City Studio, Van Nuys, CA; produced by Butch Vig. Released September 10, 1991 on DGC; 20 weeks on the charts, peaking at #6.

The opening track and biggest hit from Nirvana's monster LP *Nevermind.* Kurt Cobain wrote the basic four-chord riff, but the song didn't come together until the group jammed on it for nearly an hour, tinkering with dynamics and the arrangement. Cobain's main influence was the Boston-based alternative band the Pixies, who often used stop-start dynamics in their songs. "This really sounds like the Pixies," bassist Krist Novoselic commented after hearing the playback in the studio. "People are really going to nail us for it." "I was trying to write the ultimate pop song," Cobain later told *Rolling Stone.* "I was basically trying to rip off the Pixies. I have to admit it. When I heard the Pixies for the first time, I connected with that band so heavily that I should have been in that band—or at least a Pixies cover band. We used their sense of dynamics, being soft and quiet and then loud and hard." Much has also been made of the song's lyrics, which are indecipherable enough as to cause rock journalist Dave Marsh to call it "the 'Louie Louie' of the nineties." What is plainly heard is the repeating plaintive cry, "Here we are, now entertain us," which are widely interpreted to be a call for Generation X revolution, a "My Generation" for the nineties. It certainly became an anthem for many X-ers, as it very quickly sold a million copies and helped propel Nirvana to superstardom.

Grunge and the Seattle Scene

In spite of Cobain's personal traumas, Nirvana had managed to finish their fourth album, ***In Utero*** in the summer of 1993, and posthumously released ***MTV Unplugged in New York***, recorded from the TV special taped the previous year. Both LPs hit #1 and went multi-platinum, and *Unplugged* won the 1995 Alterna-

Grunge

Characteristics of Grunge

1. Punk influences, both in music and in attitude
2. Slow, plodding tempos
3. Simple chord progressions
4. Avoidance of virtuosity, pretension or posturing
5. Start-stop dynamics
6. Lyrics are often of dark and murky themes, sung in a plaintive, lamenting manner
7. Accompanying fashion included plaid flannel shirts, ripped jeans, stocking caps and mountain boots.

Key Grunge Recordings

- *Deep Six*—C/Z Records, 1986
- *Nevermind*—Nirvana, 1991
- *Ten*—Pearl Jam, 1991

GRUNGE
A style associated with Seattle in the 1990s that incorporates elements of punk and heavy metal; also associated with a fashion statement of flannel shirts and ripped jeans, etc.

tive Music Grammy Award. By this time Nirvana had succeeded in almost single-handedly returning the rock mainstream to a punk esthetic with an updated style that became known as **grunge**. Grunge eschewed the virtuosic artistry and pretentiousness of metal; songs were often slow and plodding, and usually contain very little in the way of chord progressions. Choruses often are set apart from verses simply by start-stop dynamic contrasts. The style had evolved in the mid- to late-1980s in Seattle's thriving underground rock scene, with support from local radio stations, a prospering underground rock press and the indie label Sub Pop. Other Seattle bands signed to Sub Pop included Soundgarden, Mud Honey, Screaming Trees and Alice in Chains. Pearl Jam, another Seattle band formed in 1990, was able to benefit from the growing interest in the city's music scene and sign with major label Epic. Their debut LP ***Ten*** sold seven million copies and stayed on the charts for 100 weeks.

Other Nineties Alternative Rock

The success of the Seattle bands gave a huge boost to the already existing alternative rock scene that had flown mostly under the radar during the 1980s. Among the more creative and inspired alternative artists from the 1990s are Phish, Radiohead, the Dave Matthews Band, and Beck. **Phish** could be described as a Grateful Dead redux, with it's eclectic mix of bluegrass, country, folk, and rock and roll, all tied together with a whimsical sensibility and improvisational spirit. The group formed in late 1983 while its four members, guitarists Trey Anastasio and Jeff Holdsworth, bassist Mike Gordon and drummer Jon Fishman, were students at the University of Vermont. Early on, keyboardist Page McConnell joined the band and Holdsworth left, giving the group its permanent lineup. Over the next several years, Phish toured extensively, and cultivated a devoted fan base by interacting with them during performances and becoming one of the first rock bands to create an Internet Usenet newsgroup in 1991. In the late 1980s the group released three self-produced albums, including ***The Man Who Stepped into Yesterday***, which was based on Anastasio's senior thesis. In 1991 they signed with Elektra Records, and have since been one of the most prolific recording bands ever, releasing 14 studio albums, seven conventional live albums, and CDs of 27 live concerts; they have also released six videos on DVD. The group also has a website,

Key Nineties Alternative Recordings

- *Under the Table and Dreaming*—Dave Matthews Band, 1994
- *Pinkerton*—Weezer, 1996
- *Odelay*—Beck, 1996
- *OK Computer*—Radiohead, 1997

livephish.com that allows fans to download many of their recent concerts in mp3 or FLAC format. However, like the Grateful Dead, Phish has always put their primary focus on their live shows, and have developed a fan-based community similar to the Dead's "Deadheads" that often follow the band faithfully from one show to the next.

Radiohead.

The band that eventually became **Radiohead** first came together at prep school in Oxford, England, calling themselves On a Friday because it was the only day of the week they could all practice. From the beginning the members have been Thom Yorke on guitar and vocals, Ed O'Brien on guitar, Jonny Greenwood on lead guitar and his brother Colin Greenwood on bass, and Phil Selway on drums. In 1989 the group broke up while each member went off to college but reunited in 1991. Later that year a self-produced demo caught the attention of EMI, who signed the band. Around this time they also changed their name to Radiohead, a name that was inspired by a song on a Talking Heads album. After the release of the EP *Drill*, the group released their album debut ***Pablo Honey***, which yielded their only American hit single, the #34 "Creep." Heavy touring hampered the bands efforts to return to the studio, but in 1995 they released ***The Bends***, which together with a European tour warming up for R.E.M. brought Radiohead more acclaim. The breakthrough came in 1997 with the release of their third album, the multi-platinum ***OK Computer***. The album won praise for its unconventional tendencies in combining the best values of alternative rock (angst-ridden lyrics, post-punk attitudes, etc.) with an ear toward creat-

Music Cut "Paranoid Android" (Thom Yorke/Jonny Greenwood/Ed O'Brien/Colin Greenwood/Phil Selway)—Radiohead

Personnel: Thom Yorke: vocals; Jonny Greenwood: guitar; Ed O'Brien: guitar; Colin Greenwood: bass; Phil Selway: drums. Recorded September 1996 at St. Catherine's Court, Bath, England; produced by Nigel Godrich. Released May 26, 1997 on Capitol; peaked at #3 (UK), did not chart in U.S.

"Paranoid Android" is the most ambitious song on Radiohead's profound and disturbing 1997 LP *OK Computer.* Its basic construction was inspired by John Lennon's "Happiness Is a Warm Gun," which moves from tenderness to primal scream to doo-wop parody and somehow works. Said vocalist Thom Yorke: "Walked into the rehearsal room one day, 'Well, you know "Happiness Is a Warm Gun," you know how that's like three songs put together? Let's do that.' And I didn't obviously think it was going to work, until we put it together finally, which was a fucking shock." "Paranoid's" construction with three basic parts gives it somewhat of an art rock quality. The Fender Rhodes electric piano is also used in the song, a tribute to one of jazz trumpeter Miles Davis' seminal works. "We're just obsessed by *Bitches Brew*," remarked Yorke, "or anything even vaguely like it. That's a record for the end of the world." "Paranoid Android" was recorded in actress Jane Seymour's 15th-century manor house near Bath, England, which Yorke believes is haunted.

The Dave Matthews Band.
Courtesy of Photofest.

ing unusual and experimental electronic textures. Influences to the album include jazz trumpeter Miles Davis' *Bitches Brew* LP, the works of film composer Ennio Morricone, and 20th century avant-garde classical composer Krzysztof Penderecki. Since releasing *OK Computer*, Radiohead has released four more highly regarded albums. They have also won three Grammy Awards, for *OK Computer*, 2001's ***Kid A***, and 2009's ***In Rainbows***.

The Dave Matthews Band, led by the transplanted South African guitarist/vocalist, has become one of rocks most popular alternative bands since their inception in the early 1990s. Like many alternative bands, their initial success came by connecting with college audiences through non-stop touring. After self-releasing ***Remember Two Things*** in 1993, the band was able to sign with RCA and release ***Under the Table and Dreaming*** the following year. Helped in part by the #9 hit single "What Would You Say" and the popular "Ants Marching," the album went quadruple platinum. In 1996, their single "So Much to Say" was awarded a Grammy for Best Rock Performance by a Duo or Group with Vocal, and since 1998 the band has released three #1 albums and no less than six live LP's. The sound of the DMB combines pop oriented world beat and loose jam-band sensibilities with touches of country and folk.

One of the most inventive and original musicians in the 1990s was Beck Hansen, who goes by the name **Beck**. He is the son of Bibbe Hansen, a part of Andy Warhol's Factory scene in the 1960s and the grandson of Al Hansen, an important figure in the New York art scene who is best known for helping launch the career of Yoko Ono. After trying his hand at acoustic blues, folk and poetry, Beck made his first recordings in 1992; by 1994 he signed a lucrative contract with Geffen and released ***Mellow Gold***, a #13 hit. Geffen also re-released the underground smash "Loser," which became a Hot 100 #10 hit. "Loser" captures the essence of Beck's ability to create his own musical universe, combining bottleneck blues guitar, a hip-hop beat, rap lyrics and an infectious sing along hook. Subsequent albums ***Odelay*** (1996) and ***Mutations*** (1998) received Alternative Music Grammy Awards.

Emo

Another interesting hardcore offshoot is **emo**, although it is one of the most misunderstood and hated terms in contemporary music. To many bands, being labeled "emo" will provoke an angry outburst even though they might not be able to define the term. Andy Greenwald, author of the one definitive book on the subject, *Nothing Feels Good: Punk Rock, Teenagers and Emo*, says this about emo: "It has been a source of pride, a target of derision, a mark of confusion, and a sign of the times. It's been the next big thing twice, the current big thing once, and so totally over millions of times. That's pretty impressive. And contentious. And ridiculous. Good thing too—because so is emo." One thing that *can* be said is that emo is short for emotional; as one fan put it in *Nothing Feels Good*, "Emo is music charged with emotions that people can relate to. Music that makes people feel they're not alone in their sadness . . . or even in their happiness." Her response illuminates one more truth about emo: more than anything it signifies a close, personal relationship between a band and its fans.

EMO
An umbrella term describing a 1990s music style that combined a hardcore punk musical esthetic, poetic and self-indulgent lyrics, and a go-for-it live performance attitude.

Emo's beginnings date back to the mid-1980s in Washington, D.C. and the band Rites of Spring, which combined a hardcore punk musical esthetic, poetic and self-indulgent lyrics, and a go-for-it live performance. In describing their show, one fan said, "They just didn't hold back at all. They were completely charismatic. There wasn't any real distinction from the role of the audience and the band. There was this insane connection; as soon as you saw it, you wanted it." Around 1985 the word emocore first came into usage to describe the synthesizing of punk and self-searching. When Rites of Spring broke up after only 15 shows, emo's development passed to two West Coast bands, Seattle's Sunny Day Real Estate and San Francisco's Jawbreaker, and eventually to the rest of the country with bands such as Jimmy Eat World, the Get Up Kids and the Promise Ring. Perhaps the most influential emo band from the mid-1990s was **Weezer**, formed in Los Angeles in 1992. Emerging in the post-Nirvana grunge world of working-class angst, Weezer was something altogether different. The band is led by lead singer/guitarist and primary songwriter Rivers Cuomo, whom Greenwald describes as: "a fully formed nerd singing about what he knew best: vintage clothes, random trivia, and trouble with girls." After signing with Geffen, the band released their debut album ***Weezer***, which won fans and yielded two popular singles, "Undone—The Sweater Song," and "Buddy Holly." When the second album, the darker and less fan-friendly ***Pinkerton*** was negatively received by critics and fans, Cuomo retreated into seclusion. When Weezer finally resumed touring in 2000, to their surprise they found a new fan base that had discovered *Pinkerton* in their absence. Initially deemed a failure, it became the defining emo album of the 1990s.

Music Cut "El Scorcho" (Rivers Cuomo)—Weezer

Personnel: Rivers Cuomo: lead guitar, lead vocals; Brian Bell: rhythm guitar; Matt Sharp: bass; Patrick Wilson: drums. Recorded January 1996 at Sound City Studio, Van Nuys, CA; produced by Weezer. Released September 1996 on DGC; 10 weeks on the charts, peaking at #19.

"El Scorcho" is the first released and highest charting single from Weezer's highly regarded *Pinkerton*. It was recorded during breaks while songwriter and lead vocalist Rivers Cuomo was a lonely Harvard student. The lyrics to "El Scorcho" reveal Cuomo to be a bumbling and shy college nerd who lacks the courage to speak to an attractive coed of Japanese descent. Exasperated after agonizing through much of the song, he finally cries out, "I wish I could get my head out of the sand. 'Cause I think we'd make a good team!" Much of *Pinkerton's* imagery comes from the Puccini opera *Madame Butterfly*, which is set in 1890s Japan. There are references to Japan and the opera throughout, and the album's name comes from one of the opera's characters, B. F. Pinkerton. Although it was a commercial flop after its 1996 release, *Pinkerton* had found a new audience by the time Weezer returned to touring in 2000, and sales for the album rebounded, making it the touchstone emo album of the 1990s. Says author Andy Greenwald, "*Pinkerton* reduced emo to its contemporary, most popular, and profitable definition: the toe-tapping sound of sensitive, self-questioning boys complaining."

Teen Pop

The Boy Bands

One of the biggest trends in recent pop history came in the form of teenage vocal groups and solo singers. Teen pop was nothing new—the industry had been pushing them since the late 1950s with the Teen Idols; early examples of teenage **boy bands** include the Monkees, the Osmonds, and the early Jackson 5. However, the

BOY BANDS

A popular 1990s and 2000s group format led by young male vocalists; examples include New Kids on the Block and Boyz II Men.

Boy Bands

- New Kids on the Block
- Boyz II Men
- 'NSync
- Backstreet Boys

teen pop of the late 1990s and early 2000s was a record sales juggernaut that dwarfed all previous eras. Consider these facts: the Backstreet Boys set an all-time record for first week album sales when 1999's *Millennium* sold 1.13 million copies. Britney Spears topped that in May 2000 when *Oops!... I Did It Again* sold 1.3 million in its first week; unfortunately she had already been outdone two months earlier when 'NSync's *No Strings Attached* sold 2.4 million copies. Three albums, three weeks, nearly five million albums of teen pop sold. The first boy band to really take off in the 1990s was **New Kids on the Block**, which formed in Boston in 1984. Their breakthrough came with their second LP ***Hangin' Tough***, which contained two #1 and one #2 singles. Their next album, 1990's ***Step by Step*** hit #1, went triple platinum and with the title cut yielded their biggest hit single. During their heydays the New Kids made $200 million in concert sales and $800 million in merchandise revenues. Quick on their heels were **Boyz II Men**, who made their breakthrough in 1991 with two Top 5 singles; their third album, 1992's ***II*** went diamond in just over a year and yielded two #1 and one #2 singles. According to their website they have sold more than 60 million albums; their singles include "One Sweet Day," a 1995 collaboration with Mariah Carey that is the biggest hit in *Billboard* history.

For a two-year run at the end of the millennium the hottest acts in the pop world were The Backstreet Boys and 'NSync. Both bands were the brainchildren of Lou Pearlman, who had the instincts to know that boy bands would sell once the grunge mania subsided, and put both groups together with Monkees-style auditions in the early 1990s. First to break were the **Backstreet Boys**, who in 1996 and 1997 released two albums, ***Backstreet Boys*** and ***Backstreet's Back*** that together sold roughly 50 million copies worldwide. 1999s ***Millennium*** sold nearly that many. All told, they have sold an estimated 200 million albums. **'NSync** was formed in Orlando in 1995, and under Pearlman's direction toured extensively overseas before breaking into the U.S. market (Pearlman earlier used the same strategy with the Backstreet Boys). Their self-titled debut album was released in the U.S. in March 1998; within two years it was certified diamond, pushed by two Top 10 hits. The group disbanded in 2002 after Justin Timberlake left to start a highly successful solo career. After becoming successful, both the Backstreet Boys and 'NSync sued Lou Pearlman for defrauding them of millions of dollars and won their cases. Pearlman is now serving time in a federal penitentiary for a host of crimes including money laundering.

The Girls Respond

Boys weren't the only ones getting in on the teen pop gravy train. TLC, the female counterpart to Boyz II Men broke big in 1994 with *CrazySexyCool* achieving diamond status, the first album by a female group to do so. They also racked up four #1 singles between 1994 and 1999. But TLC was just a warm up for **Mariah Carey**, whose amazing career has so far generated 18 #1 singles, 14 platinum or multi-platinum albums (including two that are diamond certified), five Grammy Awards and an estimated 200 million albums sold. Carey was an unknown 18-year-old in 1988 when her demo tape fell into the hands of Columbia Records president Tommy Mottola at a party. Mottola, who had a hunch that Carey was destined for greatness, immediately signed her. Over the next couple of years, Mottola spent $800,00 producing Carey's self-titled debut album, $500,000 on her first video, and another $1 million dollars in promotion. The two also became romantically involved and married in 1993 (and subsequently divorced in 1997). Carey's first five single releases went to #1, the first artist ever to accomplish the feat. Her two biggest selling albums, 1993's ***Music Box*** and 1995's ***Daydream***, both peaked at #1 and achieved diamond status. Carey left Columbia in 2001 and signed with Virgin, but was dropped from the label after an emotional breakdown. She has since signed with Island and had another multi-platinum album in 2005 with ***The Emancipation of Mimi***.

Carey's emotional problems pale in comparison to those of **Britney Spears**, who has very publicly gone from "schoolgirl to snake-wielding burlesque dancer to Kevin Federline's wife to head-shaving mom to MTV awards show bust to suicide risk," as author Steve Knopper humorously notes. She signed with Jive Records in 1997 as a 15-year-old former Mouseketeer on Disney's *The New Mickey Mouse Club*. Her first album, 1999's ***. . . Baby One More Time*** debuted at #1 and yielded the smash #1 hit of the same name. Her next three albums also debuted at #1, making her the first female artist to accomplish the feat. Spears has also included Madonna-influenced tightly choreographed dance routines into her shows that include fist jabbing, pounding feet and provocative hip movements. Although her personal life has pretty much been a disaster, she is a pop icon that as *Rolling Stone* declared "cultivated a mixture of innocence and experience that broke the bank."

Music Cut "One Sweet Day" (Mariah Carey/Walter Afanasieff/Wanya Morris/Nathan Morris/Shawn Stockman/Michael McCary)—Mariah Carey, Boyz II Men

Personnel: Mariah Carey: vocals; Boyz II Men: vocals; Walter Afanasieff: synthesizers, programming; Tristan Avakian: guitar; Babyface: keyboards; Terry Burrus: piano; Loris Holland: organ; David Morales: bass; Dan Shea, Gary Cirimelli, Satoshi Tomiie: keyboards, programming. Recorded 1994–1995; produced by Mariah Carey, Walter Afanasieff. Released November 14, 1995 on Columbia; 46 weeks on the charts, peaking at #1.

"One Sweet Day" debuted on the charts at #1 on November 26, 1995, where it stayed for 16 continuous weeks (which means it was #1 throughout the months of December, January, February and half of March!). The song is the #1 hit in *Billboard* history, and just one of Mariah Carey's incredible 18 #1 hits. The song was a collaboration between Carey and Boyz II Men, who were independently working on songs celebrating friends who had recently died. The song is included on Carey's diamond certified album *Daydream*.

Rap in the Millennium: The Controversy Continues

Eminem

At the turn of the millennium, rocks newest lightening rod for controversy was white rapper **Eminem** (Marshall Mathers III) (1973–). With lyrics that include graphic depictions of violence and bizarre sexual exploits, misogyny and ho-

Eminem has drawn some of the harshest criticism of any artist in recent history.

mophobia, Eminem has drawn some of the harshest criticism of any artist in recent history. Mathers endured an impoverished and troubled childhood, shuffling back and forth between homes in Jefferson City, Missouri and Detroit. After taking up rap at 14—initially using his initials M&M as a moniker—and working his way through a number of groups in Detroit, he made his first record in 1995 as a member of Soul Intent. His debut as a soloist, ***Infinite*** followed in 1996, which received lukewarm revues. Around this time, Mathers created an alter ego named Slim Shady, through whom he began to comment on his own troubled personal life. He bitterly spoke of his girlfriend, who left him and barred him from seeing their child. He also related scathing stories of his mother, who was accused of physically and mentally abusing his younger brother (she later filed a lawsuit against her son, claiming that his comments caused emotional distress and damage to her reputation). While his own personal life was beginning to disintegrate into drug and alcohol abuse (and a suicide attempt), Mathers released ***The Slim Shady EP***, a breakthrough that drew his first positive reaction from the rap community.

After taking second place in the freestyle category at the 1997 Rap Olympics MC Battle in Los Angeles, a Mathers demo tape caught the attention of producer Dr. Dre. Within minutes of their first meeting (in which Dre was reportedly shocked to learn that Eminem was white), the two began recording "My Name Is," which led to Eminem's signing with Interscope in 1998. The song was later released as a single and included on 1999's ***The Slim Shady LP***, which went triple platinum. By the time his third album was released in the summer of 2000, Eminem had become a phenom: *The* ***Marshall Mathers LP*** became the fastest selling rap album in history, selling nearly two million copies in its first week alone. With this album, Eminem drew his largest criticism to date, with its homophobic overtones in "Kill You," and a graphic description of killing his wife in "Kim" (which caused her to attempt suicide and later divorce him). In the context of this controversy, Eminem surprised everyone by appearing at the 2000 Grammy Awards ceremony in a duet with the openly gay Elton John. In 2002 he appeared with generally good reviews in the film *8 Mile*, loosely based on his life, and continued to spark controversy by attacking Moby and Limp Bizkit in the song "Without Me." His latest releases, including 2002's ***The Eminem Show*** have caused little uproar, suggesting that like many controversial rock personalities before him, Eminem's shock value has perhaps worn off somewhat.

Music Cut — "Stan" (Marshall Mathers, Dido Armstrong, Paul Herman)—Eminem

Personnel: Eminem: vocals; Dido: vocals; John Bigham: guitar; Mike Elizondo: bass. Recorded 1999–2000 at The Record Plant; produced by Eminem and The 45 King. Released May 23, 2000 on Aftermath/Interscope; 15 weeks on the charts, peaking at #51.

"Stan," from Eminem's *The Marshall Mathers LP*, is the scary tale of an obsessed fan that writes a series of letters to Eminem that get increasingly frustrated, angry, and finally rage-filled over the star's lack of response. By the third verse, Stan is speeding down the freeway, speaking into a tape recorder while "on a thousand downers" with his pregnant girlfriend screaming and locked in the trunk. In the final verse, Eminem finally responds, only to realize that it is too late. "He's crazy for real, and he thinks I'm crazy, but I try to help him at the end of the song," said Eminem about the fictional Stan. "It kinda shows the real side of me." "Stan" also cleverly mixes in a hook from Dido's song "Thank You," which is heard at the beginning of the song and between each verse.

New Rap Derivatives

When rap first appeared in the late 1970s, many critics cheerfully announced that it was a fad and would quickly go away, which of course it didn't. While mainstream rap has continued to sell millions of records and produce superstars such as 50 Cent, Lil Wayne and Jay-Z, some creative artists have incorporated rap elements into other seemingly disparate music styles. The first instance of this was arguably the rap/metal Run-D.M.C./Aerosmith collaboration "Walk This Way" in 1986. Since then groups such as Limp Bizkit, Linkin Park and Rage Against the Machine have further explored what is alternately called **rapcore** or metal rap. Erik Shrody, aka Everlast has found a niche with what might be called acoustic blues rap, while other artists such as Kid Rock have experimented with crossing rap and Southern rock. Other rap fusions include country rap (Bubba Sparxxx, the Moonshine Bandits), jazz rap (Jazzkantine, Us3), Christian rap (Lecrae, Trip Lee) and even comedy rap (Rehab).

RAPCORE
An umbrella term describing bands that combine elements of rap with hardcore, metal or punk.

The Music Industry in the Eighties and Nineties: Living Large in L.A.

The Majors Rule

The music industry—and in particular the major labels—had experienced tremendous growth in the 1970s, only to suffer a debilitating post-disco crash that sent sales figures plummeting. As painful as that medicine was, to say the record business rebounded nicely would be a gross understatement. The 1980s and 1990s were the best of times for the major labels, a time when new sales records were constantly being set, new technologies emerging, and new stars were being made, sometimes overnight. Consider this: of the Top 100 Albums compiled by the RIAA, 65 were released in the 1980s or 1990s. A grand total of five have come from the 2000s, the highest ranked being *No Strings Attached* by 'NSync, which sits at #54. For the major labels, the 1980s and 1990s was a time for getting fat and living large.

And the men behind the scenes at the majors did just that. Some made staggering amounts of money, sometimes for no other reason than an executive shake up, as in the case of longtime industry insider Charles Koppelman, who when ousted as president of EMI-Capitol in 1997 was given a going away present of a $50 million contract buyout. Sometimes just surviving in the business paid huge rewards; venerable A&M president Gil Friesen bought a home in the upscale Brentwood section of Los Angeles in 1985 for $1.45 million—and added on a second floor in the 1990s for $4.9 million. Sound impressive? These guys were just upper middle management. The big guys did much better. Chris Blackwell of Island Records sold his company for $300 million in 1989; David Geffen sold Geffen Records for stock to MCA in 1990 and made an estimated $800 million when MCA was in turn sold to Matsushita the next year. Richard Branson sold Virgin Records in 1992 for $950 million. And Clive Calder, owner of Zomba Records, the signatory label for the Backstreet Boys, 'NSync and Britney Spears, sold out to German conglomerate BMG in 2002 for $2.74 billion. That's *billion*—with a B.

The 1980s and 1990s were the best of times for the major labels.

Industry wide, sales figures for records, tapes and CDs jumped from $3.5 billion to nearly $13.5 billion between 1982 and 2000. Growth like that naturally caught the attention of Wall Street investors, who jumped in with a series of mergers and corporate takeovers that ultimately put the industry into the hands of a small number of large multi-national conglomerates. Although consolidation of the music industry had been going on since the beginning of the rock era, by the late 1970s six super-major labels had emerged that controlled the lion's share of record sales and distribution. Four of those six, CBS, Warner, RCA and MCA were American owned; of the other two, PolyGram was owned by German and Dutch interests while Capitol-EMI was British. Further consolidation in the 1980s and 1990s reduced the number of majors to five when the German owned BMG bought RCA, Sony bought CBS, and PolyGram and MCA were bought by the Canadian owned Seagram Company and renamed Universal Music Group. To even refer to these companies as labels is somewhat of a misnomer, as they are actually umbrella corporations that own the many smaller—and familiar—labels that have been gobbled up over the years. For instance, Universal now owns A&M and Motown; Sony owns Columbia, Arista and Epic; Warner owns Atlantic and Elektra; EMI owns Capitol, Blue Note and Virgin.[1]

What did consolidation mean for artists and consumers? Fredric Dannen, author of the 1990 industry exposé *Hit Men* described the majors at that time as the "sovereign states" of pop music. "Today, there is virtually no American pop singer or rock band of national stature that a major does not, in one way or another, have a piece of. The days are gone in which a pint-sized company can launch [a national act] with independent distribution." By the mid-1990s, artists had fewer places to go to get a contract signed, the independent labels that still existed were essentially shut out of distribution networks, and consumers were left with fewer choices as to what to buy. After years of battling with independent labels and fickle consumers, it seemed as if the major labels had finally achieved permanent market dominance.

But Wait . . .

But we must not underestimate the power of hubris, in this case the pop music industry's collective ability to screw up a good thing. Let's start with the drug-induced decadence that came with the times, because many executives seemed hell bent on outdoing their artists in living the rock and roll lifestyle. Exhibit A was Casablanca Records president Neil Bogart. Bogart had the company offices palatially designed to match Rick's Café in the movie *Casablanca* (get it: Humphrey *Bogart—Casablanca*?), had music blare from giant speakers, and made drugs—and lots of them—available at all times. Danny Davis, an industry veteran who had worked for everyone from Phil Spector to Berry Gordy, was not shy about describing the lunacy of his short stay at Casablanca to Dannen in *Hit Men*. Some gems: "At three o'clock in the afternoon an adorable little girl would come up and take your *order* for the following day's *drug supply*." Or even better: "I would go into a meeting, and there on the desk would be maybe a gram and a half of controlled substance (cocaine). We would sit there till maybe about seven-thirty, eight o'clock, when the gram and a half was gone. We've been in this meeting since five o'clock, not a fucking thing has been done, and now . . . they would go into their desk and pull out the ludes (Quaaludes). Anyway, they got beer and the ludes.

[1]In 2008 Sony acquired BMG, reducing the number of majors to just the "Big Four": Universal Music Group, Sony Music Entertainment, Warner Music Group, and EMI. All of the big four labels are themselves wholly owned subsidiaries of huge multi-national conglomerates.

And they would pass out the ludes as if they were feeding elephants at a circus." Casablanca, which was heavily invested in disco artists, crashed in the early 1980s and Bogart died of cancer soon after.

The industry also made a number of strategic mistakes that seemed like good ideas at the time but in fact weren't. One was the mid-1990s decision to stop selling singles. During the 1980s and 1990s labels were making huge profit margins off CDs, and singles, by then also released on CD, became increasingly viewed as nothing more than loss leaders that were cannibalizing album sales. Once the single was killed off in 1998, consumers had no choice but to buy a $17 CD if they wanted to buy their favorite song. Initially this was great for business, but eventually buyers felt ripped off. "If you only sold hand lotion in five-gallon bottles, pretty soon people would be tired of it," says producer Albhy Galuten. "You can't go around forcing people to buy something that they don't want." No wonder that so many consumers felt no shame in obtaining single songs for free illegally once they found out about Napster.

Another major blunder the industry made was to allow the killing off of the mom and pop record store. Brick and mortar record stores had traditionally fostered a sense of community as a hangout for music lovers, musicians, and other hipsters; in addition, they were the only place where records could be purchased. However, that all changed in the 1990s when big box stores like Walmart and Best Buy began selling records at deeply discounted prices that the small stores could not match. Consumers flocked to the boxes, which before long accounted for 65 percent of CDs sold. The first casualties of the box store bargains were the small locally owned record stores, but eventually even the large chains like Tower and Musicland (Sam Goody) went out of business. With their newfound clout the big boxes began to dictate the terms of what they would and wouldn't sell, which meant that labels sometimes had to airbrush over risqué album covers or produce clean versions of CDs with explicit lyrics. Once Walmart and Best Buy decided to reduce the shelf space in their record sections, consumers were left with soullessly sterile purchasing environments with a limited selection of only the biggest selling pop CDs.

The Majors Meet Their Match

Napster

The cumulative effect of the drugs, decadence, arrogance, corporate consolidation and bad business decisions left the music industry in a very vulnerable condition by the end of the 1990s. Of course, the record labels themselves did not know this at the time, nor could they have known, but a 19-year-old college student was about to wreak havoc on their industry with a simple little computer program. **Shawn Fanning** was a Metallica-loving student at Northeastern University in Boston in the fall semester of 1998 when he came up with the idea for **Napster**. Like many teenager hackers of the day, he was completely sucked in by the Internet and its possibilities, especially for gaming and networking. Early on he had learned about **mp3** files, and built up his own digital music collection, but was frustrated with the difficulties in trading them via the search engines of the day. Shawn's idea for Napster (named after his online nickname) was to establish a central server where users could log on and see a display of the mp3 titles on the hard drives of everyone else who was currently logged on. Then, using the pro-

NAPSTER
A digital file-sharing website introduced in 1999 by Shawn Fanning.

MP3
A digital file format that compresses sound files to approximately 1/10 normal size with little apparent loss of fidelity.

FILE SHARING
The transferring of digital files, usually from one computer to the other via the Internet.

gram's search engine, they could easily find a specific piece of music by artist or title, and download it to their own computer. Napster's trick was that it only contained *lists* of user's songs—the actual mp3 transfer, called **file sharing**, took place only between the individual users, and did not involve Napster's central server.

Napster and file sharing technology would not have been possible without the development of the mp3 file format. It was created after German psychoacoustic researchers figured out a way to compress CD quality audio files into a size approximately 1/10 as big without a noticeable loss of sonic quality, making them ideal for storage on computer hard drives and easy to transfer. Once the protocol was perfected, it was registered with the Moving Picture Experts Group (MPEG) division of the Geneva, Switzerland-based International Organization for Standards (known as ISO) for certification in 1991. They named the technology ISO-MPEG-1 Audio Layer 3, or mp3. Because the Internet was so new and not widely used at the time, the significance of the mp3 standard was not readily apparent. However, once Netscape introduced the first web browser application in 1994, the Internet boom was off and running, and it didn't take computer savvy music fans long to figure out they could share their music with their friends, and that there was a whole world of other people's music out there for the taking—and it was *free!* Things accelerated in 1997 when MP3.com went online offering 3,000 songs for free download from their website. Within a year it became the most popular site on the World Wide Web, getting three million hits per month. "Mp3" replaced "sex" as the most searched for term on the search engines of the day.

It was starting to become clear by this time that the ramifications of this new way of obtaining music could possibly be enormous; it was nothing less than a new business model that might remake the entire music industry as it currently existed. There was only one problem: making copyrighted songs available for unlimited sharing online was illegal. A few astute entrepreneurs realized that working out licensing agreements with the majors to make their music legally available could potentially be profitable, but they didn't get very far with label executives. "Some of them were more interested in experimenting than others," related Gerry Kearby, founder of Liquid Audio, a digital rights management firm. "But they were, in effect, buggy-whip manufacturers, trying to keep the auto at bay as long as they could." Adding to the problem was the fact that most major label executives were not computer savvy or were too caught up in their fast times/fast money lifestyles to even know that things were changing so radically so fast. That is, until Napster came along.

The RIAA Lawsuits

As Napster gained in popularity and started acquiring investors and employees, Shawn Fanning moved to Silicon Valley and set up an office in San Mateo. It was around this time that his fledgling company first caught the attention of the Recording Industry Association of America, who viewed what they were doing as out and out piracy. Although conversations between Napster and the RIAA were cordial at first, they quickly turned ugly. Napster really had no business plan as of yet (they were considering whether to sell subscriptions or merchandise online, among other things), but the RIAA was resolute: nothing short of the removal of all their signed artists from the sight was acceptable. Negotiations stalled; meanwhile Napster was growing so fast its servers were having a hard time keeping up with demand. By October 1999 there were 150,000 registered users sharing 3.5

million files, and it was still expanding at an astonishing rate. Then, on December 6, the RIAA filed suit, claiming that Napster was guilty of "contributory and vicarious copyright infringement." No one at Napster was surprised by the lawsuit, which they were confident of winning. Their defense was based on the protection granted under the 1992 **Audio Home Recording Act**, which allowed consumers to make personal copies of copyrighted material. Napster also claimed that its service was not unlike copying machines or VCRs, whose manufacturers are not held responsible for the potential illegal use by the owners of their products. Nonetheless, at the one-day trial held on July 26, 2000, Judge Marilyn Hall Patel of the Federal Court in San Francisco ruled that Napster was in fact violating copyright laws. Although appeals would drag the case on for another year, in the end Napster was shut down. In the meantime, Shawn Fanning became a generational folk hero as the kid who single-handedly stuck it to the man. As Steve Knopper writes in *Appetite for Self-Destruction*, Fanning became "a symbol, a rebellious David-vs.-Goliath type who invented the coolest slingshot ever."

Although the RIAA ultimately won the Napster case, the publicity surrounding it brought the whole file sharing issue to the national spotlight, which only served to increase its popularity. Downloading music was fun, it was free, and for thousands of college students and other music fans it was a way to get back at the major labels, who had for years been forcing them to shell out $17 for an entire CD that often only contained two or three good tracks. By the time of the trial, Napster was getting five million connections a month, and other file sharing sites had already begun to go online. Gnutella began operating in May 2000 using a decentralized form of the peer-to-peer protocol Napster had used, which seemingly made the company safe from legal suit. Not long after its launch, the company publicly released the software's source code on the web, and within weeks several other file-sharing sites, including Kazaa, Limewire, Morpheus and Grokster popped up. Meanwhile, new statistics showed that sales of CDs, LPs and tapes in 2000 fell by nearly 10 percent from the previous year, the first downturn since 1982. At the same time, blank CDs outsold prerecorded ones for the first time ever. It seemed pretty clear to music executives that instead of buying CDs, consumers were downloading music illegally and burning their own custom CDs. It was also clear that shutting down Napster had not solved the digital piracy problem. Meanwhile, record labels began laying off hundreds of employees and severing the contracts of many artists to cut costs.

The RIAA explored their options and decided to return to the courtroom. Going after sites like Grokster (which the Supreme Court effectively shut down along with Morpheus and Kazaa in 2005 with a unanimous ruling that were violating copyright law) was a no-brainer, but they didn't stop there. Citing the terms laid out by the 1998 Digital Millennium Copyright Act (DMCA) which required Internet service providers (ISP's) to turn over the names of their users, the RIAA in 2003 began serving subpoenas to hundreds of suspected copyright violators, with the threat of fines of up to $150,000 per illegally copied song on their computers. To actually bring lawsuits against the very consumers they were trying to turn into customers was an extreme step to take, but one the RIAA felt they had no choice in doing. "We didn't want to be suing, but there weren't a lot of alternatives," said one industry source. "It's one thing when you're looking from the outside and saying how stupid this is, but it's another thing when you're seeing half your company laid off." It was indeed a public relations mess, especially when the press chose to run stories on the straight-A college students or unsuspecting parents who got sued. But the lawsuits continued on until late 2008, by which time more than 35,000 had been filed, with an average settlement of $3,500.

The iTunes Music Store

The fact that the RIAA started suing customers in 2003 was only partly due to the fact that the industry struggled to come to grips with online piracy and to figure out a plan of attack. But the bottom line was that until Apple Computer launched the **iTunes Music Store**, consumers had no convenient, inexpensive and legal option to buy music online. The iTunes Music Store was part of Apple CEO Steve Jobs's "Digital Hub Strategy" that aspired to make the company's Macintosh computer the "center of your lifestyle." Apple first introduced the iTunes software, which at the time only played mp3s and burned CDs, in early 2001; their next step was to design a portable player that would interface smoothly with the software, thereby freeing consumers from their computers. On October 23, 2001 the iPod was introduced, and although it wasn't the first portable mp3 player on the market, it was the first really *cool* one, and quickly became a have-to-have consumer electronics gadget. (As of this writing, Apple has sold more than 200 million iPods.) But Apple's Jobs still needed to obtain licenses from the major labels before he could legally provide iPod purchasers music to buy online. Jobs not only had to overcome the still persistent bias against digital music sales by the big five major labels, but work out complicated licensing agreements with them, the artists, and publishers as well. In the end, everyone agreed on fees of 99¢ per song (of which Apple kept 22¢), and typically $9.90 per album. All music would also be encoded with Apple's FairPlay digital rights management (**DRM**) technology to limit the number of copies that can be made. (The FairPlay encryptions have since been removed.) When the iTunes Music Store opened on April 28, 2003, 200,000 songs were available from nearly every major artist (major exceptions included Led Zeppelin, which has since come on board, and the Beatles), and it was an instant smash hit. Today there are more than 10 million songs available and more than six billion songs have been sold, accounting for 70 percent of all online legal digital music sales worldwide.

But the popularity of the iTunes Music Store did not stop the illegal downloading. Although it is difficult to gauge how much piracy goes on, the research group BigChampagne estimated that in 2006 there were approximately one billion tracks downloaded illegally—*every month*. In the meantime, the industry was reeling. Album sales have dropped seven out of the eight years since 2000 (the exception being 2004, the first year that legal digital downloads were figured in), and the drop off rate has reached epic proportions. 2008's total album sales of 428 million units were a 14 percent drop from 2007, which dropped 15 percent from 2006. In all, album sales have plummeted 45 percent since 2000's mark of 785 million units. Although legal digital downloads have been an area of tremendous growth, their growth is starting to wane. Digital album sales rose 53 percent in 2007, but only 32 percent to 65 million units in 2008; likewise, digital single-track sales rose 45 percent in 2007, but only 27 percent to 1.07 billion units in 2008. Only three albums in 2008 sold more than two million copies (although the three—Lil' Wayne's *Tha Carter III*, Coldplay's *Viva la Vida*, and Taylor Swift's *Fearless*—show a remarkable diversity in consumer taste), a dramatic change from the days when the benchmark for a big seller was ten million. (Which begs the question: will there ever be another diamond certified album?) Meanwhile, since

2000 more than 5,000 record company employees have been laid off and approximately 3,000 record stores have closed.

The Future

The End of the World as We Know It?

So, did Napster and the iTunes Music Store kill the music business? Is it really the end of the line for the major labels? Well, the short answer is we don't know yet. We do know that digital album sales will probably never make up for the loss of CD sales, and that consumers clearly have shown a preference for singles rather than albums.[2] One could also make the assumption that sales in the 1990s—when consumers *had* to buy $17 albums—were artificially high and were bound to fall eventually. As we know, a similar downturn occurred in the early 1980s, but the industry had the trifecta of *Thriller*, MTV and the introduction of the CD to pull it out of that slump. The coming of the digital age revealed a music industry that was woefully inefficient and ill prepared to respond to the changes afoot, and was extremely slow to respond to those changes. When the industry finally did get around to addressing online piracy, it was astonishingly off target. "They left billions and billions of dollars on the table by suing Napster—that was the moment the labels killed themselves," says Jeff Kwatinetz, CEO of The Firm, a management company. "The record business had an unbelievable opportunity there. They [consumers] were all using the same service [Napster]. It was as if everybody was listening to the same radio station. Then Napster shut down, and all those 30 or 40 million people went to other [file sharing services]." However, one industry insider says there were pressures from other sources as well. "A lot of people say, 'the labels were dinosaurs and idiots, and what was the matter with them?' " says Hilary Rosen, who was CEO of the RIAA at the time. "But they had retailers telling them, 'You better not sell anything online cheaper than in a store,' and they had artists saying, 'Don't screw up my Walmart sales.' "

And yet, in spite of all the recent turmoil, the music industry is still thriving. The major labels are still showing a profit—they just don't have the oligopolistic control over the marketplace they once had. Sure, sales are down and companies are tightening their belts, but the same thing is happening to many other industries in the Internet era, including newspapers and radio. And to be fair, consumers have many more options for spending entertainment dollars these days, including video games, cell phones, DVDs and big screen TVs. More than $11 billion has been spent on home video products since 2000; it's plausible that some of that money might have gone to CDs in the pre-DVD days. And really, the case could be made that the role music is playing in people's lives is simply changing from what it once was. Although there is still a great demand, it might be that "music is not as important now as it once was," says producer and A&R executive George Drakoulias. "Instant gratification has removed some of the allure. Music feels like it has become more disposable and cheap, with less staying power." For sure, pop music is being compartmentalized in today's world into other formats

---

[2] Isn't it interesting that we still use the terms "album" and "label" even though they hearken back to the 1950s and when 12" vinyl records were the standard media format?

like ringtones and games such as Guitar Hero and Rock Band. TV programs like *American Idol* and *Hannah Montana* are creating pop singing sensations before they even have a record contract.

Tremendous changes are taking place in the entertainment world even as we speak, and the author freely acknowledges that it is entirely possible that by the time this edition is published, much of this discussion will be outdated. However, one trend that seems to be emerging at the moment is a movement away from consumers actually "owning" music to simply "accessing" it. A March 2009 study by the NPD Group, an industry market research organization, found that teenagers acquired 19 percent less music in 2008 than in 2007. CD sales among this group were down 26 percent and digital purchases were down 13 percent in the same period. On the other hand, a similar poll of British teens found that **music streaming**—free and legal music available on demand over the Internet—is rapidly gaining in popularity. Legal services such as MySpace Music, Rhapsody, imeem and Spotify allow users to play any song, anytime, and on any device. Sites such as MySpace Music are free and supported by advertising, while others like Rhapsody and Spotify charge a nominal monthly subscription fee. Record labels and artists are paid with royalties for each time a track is played as well as a share of the advertising or subscription revenues. Labels have also become much more aggressive in merchandising other products such as T-shirts, posters and DVDs for their clients as an additional revenue stream. There are also more legal iTunes-like stores today such as eMusic, the Amazon Music Store, Yahoo Music, and even Napster, which has re-emerged from bankruptcy as a music store, streaming audio site, and online radio station.

Dylan Gets the Final Say

But enough about the labels and the business; what about the music itself? What lies ahead for rock and pop music? There's a lot of complaining going on today about the quality of pop music, so perhaps the case could be made that it is the music itself, and not the industry, that is in trouble. Some say there is nothing good anymore; others say that it's all derivative of something from the past; while still others complain that there is no new movement or style, no rap, punk or grunge to unite the field and lead the way. In reality, all these things are true to one extent or another, but a larger truth is that the term pop music itself may be oxymoronic in today's world. With the gatekeepers (the major labels) out of the way, consumers are free to control exactly what they want to be entertained with, how to search for it, and how to be kept abreast of any new developments in it. And they can move on to something else whenever they want. "Pop music is the music that the most people are listening to most of the time," writes Helium.com contributor Gordon Ashley. "But the sheer volume of content that can be sifted from the mind-boggling expanse of the Internet will make that idea obsolete. And without the money-makers tightly holding the strings and manipulating what the most people are digging on most often, the idea of a definable pop culture will disappear."

And with the Internet and the technology available today, more people than ever are making music. Digital Audio Workstations (DAW) such as Apple Logic Pro, Digital Performer and Cubase are becoming less expensive, more comprehensive and easier to use; getting your music "out there" is also simpler than ever with sites such as MySpace and YouTube. And when it is out there, who knows who is going to hear it and what they're going to do with it. "Music now has the possibility of having a much larger gene pool," says Robert Thompson, professor of pop culture at Syracuse University. "There are more mutations out there than before simply because there are more opportunities for something to actually get into the distribution system." And as we have seen, that new distribution system—the Internet—is radically different than the old one of just a few years ago when CDs were sold in record stores. Today it is possible for an artist to "easily bypass the traditional infrastructure—going into the studio, sending singles to radio stations—and make songs available for download almost as soon as they're written," according to Dan Brown of CBC News Online.

Whether all of this is a good thing or just going to lead to the creation of a clutter of crappy music is yet to be seen. A similar revolution has already taken place in the video world, where inexpensive, easy to use technology has allowed almost anyone to make and edit movies. (You only have to look as far as YouTube to see whether or not that has produced anything interesting.) However, as Chris Anderson writes in *The Long Tail: Why the Future of Business Is Selling Less of More*, "Talent is not universal, but it's widely spread: give enough people the capacity to create, and inevitably gems will emerge." Perhaps the future of music is best summed up by Peter Rojas, founder of Engadget and co-founder of RCRD LBL, a free, online-only music label launched by Downtown Records. "I don't pretend to know what the industry will look like in ten years, but the funny thing about all of this is that music itself is healthier than ever. The Internet, combined with low-cost (or even no-cost) digital tools, has led to an explosion of creativity, with millions of amateurs making music for every conceivable genre, sub-genre, and microgenre, and then sharing their creations online. We have an infinite number of choices available to us, and when content is infinitely abundant, the only scarce commodities are convenience, taste, and trust. The music companies that are successfully shaping the Internet era are recognizing that the real value is in making it easier to buy music than to steal it, helping consumers find other people who share their music tastes, and serving as a trusted source for discovering new music."

As one wise and prescient man first said back in 1963, "The times they are a-changin'." Indeed they are.

Name ______________________________ Date ______________

STUDY QUESTIONS

1. Why was Nirvana's album *Nevermind* hitting #1 in 1992 so significant?

2. What are some of the reasons that Seattle was important to grunge?

3. Which album proved to be the commercial breakthrough for Radiohead, and what were some of the influences on its music?

4. Describe emo and how it came about.

5. Describe how Mariah Carey was discovered and some of her successes and failures.

6. What are some of the controversies that Eminem has embroiled himself in?

7. Describe the culture of the music business in the 1980s and 1990s.

8. Describe exactly what MPEG Audio Layer III is and its role in changing the record business in the late 1990s and early 2000s.

9. Who is Shawn Fanning and why did he play such an important role in the evolution of the record business?

10. Describe some of the ways that the music industry is changing. Give your thoughts on what the future holds.

Index

A

B

C

F

G

H

I

J

K

L

M

N

O

S

T